AL-QA'IDA'S MYSTIQUE EXPOSED
Usama bin Laden's Private Communications

YONAH ALEXANDER
MICHAEL S. SWETNAM

Copyright © 2015, Potomac Institute Press
Yonah Alexander and Michael S. Swetnam
All rights reserved.

No part of this book may be reproduced in any form by any electronic or mechanical means (including photocopying, recording, or information storage and retrieval) without permission in writing from the copyright holders.

Book Cover: Alex Taliesen
Background on cover: Untranslated: Undated Statement- re American Conversions to Islam. http://www.dni.gov/files/documents/ubl/english/Undated%20statement%20re%20American%20conversions%20to%20Islam.pdf.

Disclaimer: The Publisher, Institute and Authors cannot be held responsible for errors or any consequences arising from the use of information contained in this publication; the view and opinions expressed do not necessarily reflect those of the Publisher, Institute and Authors.

Pursuant to 17 U.S.C. § 105, government-produced materials are not copyright protected. As such, Potomac Institute Press and the authors do not hold the copyright to works of the United States government appearing in this publication.

Usama bin Laden correspondences courtesy the Office of the Director of National Intelligence bin Laden Bookshelf: http://www.dni.gov/index.php/resources/bin-laden-bookshelf.

ISBN: 978-0-9963960-0-4 Paperback

Published, 2015 by the Potomac Institute Press
Potomac Institute for Policy Studies

Potomac Institute for Policy Studies
901 N. Stuart St, Suite 1200
Arlington, VA, 22203
www.potomacinstitute.org
Telephone: 703.525.0770; Fax: 703.525.0299
Email: webmaster@potomacinstitute.org

AL-QA'IDA'S MYSTIQUE EXPOSED
Usama bin Laden's Private Communications

This book is dedicated to the victims of terrorism and in honor of those who serve in combating terrorism nationally, regionally, and globally.

Table of Contents

Introduction xi
  1. 9/11 and its Aftermath xiii
  2. Usama bin Laden's Life xv
  3. The Hunt for Usama bin Laden and the May 2, 2011 Raid xx
  4. Propaganda and Psychological Warfare xxv
  5. Methodological Note xxxix
  6. Acknowledgements xl
  7. Endnotes xli

Part One: Letters Likely Written by Usama bin Laden 45
  1. Call for Guidance and Reform, 13 April 1994 45
  2. Letter to Brother Ilyas 52
  3. Letter to Shaykh Mahmud, 26 September 2010 54
  4. Letter to Shaykh Mahmud and Shaykh Abu Yahya 62
  5. Letter from UBL to Atiyah 65
  6. Letter to Shaykh Abu Yahya 2 68
  7. Letter to Uthman 69
  8. Undated Letter 3 81
  9. Zamrai (UBL) Letter to Unis 85

Part Two: Letters Likely Written to Usama bin Laden 90
  1. Letter to Abu 'Abdallah al-Hajj 90
  2. Letter to Shaykh Abu Abdallah, 2 September 2009 94
  3. Letter to Shaykh Abu Abdallah, 17 July 2010 96
  4. Letter dtd 13 October 2010 110
  5. Letter dtd 24 November 2010 118
  6. Letter to Abdallah 128
  7. Letter to UBL from daughter Khadijah 130
  8. Verbally Released Document for Naseer Trial 132
  9. Letter addressed to Shaykh 136
  10. Letter to Shaykh from Abu Abdallah (UBL) 138

Part Three: Letters to/from Members and Leaders 141
  1. Letter from Al-Zawahiri dtd August 2003 141
  2. Letter dtd 21 May 2007 147
  3. Letter to Shaykh Azmaray, 4 February 2008 151
  4. Letter dtd March 2008 155
  5. Letter to 'Abd Al-Latif 166
  6. Letter dtd 18 July 2010 168

7. Letter dtd 09 August 2010 170
8. Letter to Shaykh Abu Yahya 176
9. Letter dtd 5 April 2011 178
10. Letter to Brother Hamzah 187
11. Letter to Um 'Abd-al-Rahman, 26 April 2011 189
12. Letter to Shaykh Mahmud 193
13. Letter from Hafiz 201
14. Letter Addressed to Atiyah 203
15. Letter to My Beloved Brother 208

PART FOUR: AL-QA'IDA'S INTERNAL ISSUES AND CONCERNS ... 210
1. Letter to Muhammad Aslam, 22 April 2011 210
2. Terror Franchise 212
3. Spreadsheet 227
4. Letter Regarding Abu al-Hasan 232
5. Letter to Shaykh Abu-al-Layth, Abu-Yahya,
   Shaykh 'Abdullah Sa'id 234

PART FIVE: SELECTED COMMUNICATION WITH
EXTERNAL BODIES 236
1. Letter to Ansar Al-Sunnah Group 236
2. Letter to Mujahidin in Somalia dtd 28 December 2006 238
3. Letter to Special Committee of al-Jihad's Qa'ida of the
   Mujahidin Affairs in Iraq and to the
   Ansar al-Sunnah Army 245
4. Letter to Hakimullah Mahsud, Leader of
   Taliban Movement 249
5. A Letter to the Sunnah People in Syria 251
6. Ideas as Discussion with the Sons of the Peninsula 270

PART SIX: SELECTED SPECIFIC TOPICS 272

   A. Islamic Emirate
   1. Lessons Learned Following the Fall of the
      Islamic Emirate 272
   2. Letter to Islamic Emirate of Afghanistan 275

   B. Islamic Nation
   1. Message for General Islamic Nation 278
   2. Message for all Muslims Following
      US State of Union Address 284

   C. Afghanistan
   1. Summary on Situation in Afghanistan and Pakistan 291
   2. Undated letter re Afghanistan 298
   3. Afghani Opportunity 301

D. Arab Spring
 1. Undated Message re Egypt Demonstrations 318

E. Revolution
 1. Suggestion to End the Yemen Revolution 323
 2. Letter about Revolutions 326
 3. Message for Islamic Ummah in General 328
 4. Undated Statement 333
 5. Undated Statement 2 336

F. United States
 1. Letter to the American People 338
 2. Despotism of Big Money 341

G. Europe
 1. German Economy 342
 2. Report on External Operations 345

H. Africa
 1. Letter dtd 07 August 2010 350
 2. Study Paper about the Kampala Raid in Uganda 363

PART SEVEN: SELECTED RELIGIOUS TOPICS 372

A. Jihad
 1. Jihad and Reform Front, 22 May 2007 372

B. Fatwas
 1. Letter re Fatwas of the Permanent Committee 376

C. General
 1. Undated Statement re American Conversions to Islam 379
 2. Message to Muslim Brothers in Iraq and to the Islamic Nation 381

PART EIGHT: SELECTED MISCELLANEOUS TOPICS 404
 1. 06 Ramadan 404
 2. Letter to Badr Khan, 3 December 2002 406
 3. Gist of Conversation Oct 11 408
 4. Request for Documents from CTC 416
 5. Instructions to Applicants 417
 6. Letter Implications of Climate Change 421
 7. Message from Abu Hammam al-Ghurayb 428
 8. Undated Letter 430
 9. Undated Letter 2 432

PART NINE: LETTERS TO FAMILY AND FRIENDS 434
   To or From UBL
     1. Letter from Zamray, 07 August 2010 434
     2. Letter to Sons 'Uthman, Muhammad, Hamzah,
        Wife Um Hamzah 436
     3. Letter From Abu Abdallah to his Mother 438
     4. Letter to Brother from Abu Abdallah 440
   Private Letters to Selected Individuals
     1. Letter to Abu Sulayman 442
     2. Letter dtd 16 December 2007 444
     3. Letter from Khalid to 'Abd-al-Latif 447
     4. Letter to Wife 449
     5. Letter from Hamzah to Father dtd July 2009 453
     6. Letter to Aunt Umm-Khalid 459
     7. Letter to Sister Um-'Abd-al-Rahman 462
     8. Letter from Qari, early April 464
     9. Undated Letter from Khalid Habib 466
     10. Letter from Khalid to Abdullah and Abu al-Harish 467
     11. Letter from Khalid to his Son 468
     12. Letter to Um Abid Al-Rahman 471
     13. Letter to Aunt 473
     14. Letter to Brother Fatimah 475
     15. Letter to daughter Umm-Mu'adh 477
     16. Letter to Hamza 479
     17. Letter to Um Sa'ad from Aunt Um Khalid 480
     18. Letter to Umm Khalid from Sarah 482
     19. Letter to 'Abd-al-Rahman 483

SELECTED BIBLIOGRAPHY 485
   Books 485
   Articles 491
   Government Documents 499
   Databases/Websites 503

INDEX 507

ABOUT THE AUTHORS 518

INTRODUCTION

An ancient Asian maxim observes that "the truth is one; sages call it by different names." At a time when the United States marked the 14th anniversary of 9/11, the most devastating terrorist attack on the homeland during peacetime, four well-grounded realities with immense strategic implications emerged.

First, learning from past historical experiences provides better analytical tools to assess future potential threats to national and global security concerns as well as to craft improved "best practices" responses to combat conventional and unconventional challenges.

Second, tragically, the history of mankind is filled with ideologically and theologically- based communications that have heavily contributed to distortions, suspicions, hatred, violence, and warfare in the struggle for power within and among societies.

Third, individuals, groups, and states indoctrinated by endless extremist political intentions based on self-righteousness and sacred missions "in the name of God," have continuously resorted to exercising barbaric capabilities against perceived enemies, both weak and strong.

And fourth, if contemporary civilization—embracing ethnic, religious, racial, tribal, and national communities and peoples—is to survive expanded dangers to its very existence by the potential utilization of "doomsday" weapons of mass destruction such as cyber, biological, chemical, radiological, and nuclear capabilities, it is critical for the United States and their friends and allies to fully understand the "mindsets" of the "evil-doers" and their evolving modus operandi, tactics consisting of "propaganda by the deed," and the "deed by propaganda."

It is in view of these permanent fixtures of international life that the current study was undertaken. The purpose of *Al-Qa'ida's Mystique Exposed: Usama bin Laden's Private Communications* is to provide

INTRODUCTION

a rare window into the covert life of the founding leader of one of the most dangerous terrorist movements in modern times.

The rationale for this effort seems rather obvious. After all, removing secretive veils of any terrorist group, large and small, is most challenging in light of the very nature of such "underground" movements which are conducting "warfare in the shadow." It is not surprising therefore that ordinary observers and even major national and international intelligence agencies are confronted by formidable firewalls of complicated puzzles related to reliable information on leadership, membership, recruitment, funding, training, supply of weapons, affiliated groups, and operational plans.

Fortunately for the U.S. government and subsequently for the international community at large, untangling a substantial part of al-Qa'ida's enigmatic nature became easily possible following the raid on bin Laden's compound in Pakistan on May 2, 2011. Selected declassified correspondence of the infamous leader that is contained in this book is provided courtesy of the U.S. Office of the Director of National Intelligence.

This accessible material that consists of 100 original letters has been divided into nine segments: letters likely written by Usama bin Laden; letters likely written to Usama bin Laden; letters to and from members and leaders; selected communications with external bodies; selected specific topics; selected religious topics; selected miscellaneous topics; and letters to family and friends. Each of the original documents contains an abstract for purposes of clarity. A selected bibliography, an index, and "About the Authors" are also incorporated.

To be sure, the overt "public face" of bin Laden as well as that of his successor Ayman al-Zawahiri are revealed by vast existing governmental and academic literature published during the past two decades. It is suffice to mention two earlier studies co-authored by both Yonah Alexander and Michael S. Swetnam that contributed to this intellectual effort.

More specifically, some six months before 9/11 they first published *Usama bin Laden's al-Qa'ida: Profile of a Terrorist Network*

(Ardsley, New York: Transnational Publishers, Inc., 2001.) The second published volume is *Al-Qa'ida: Ten Years After 9/11 and Beyond* (Arlington, VA: Potomac Books Press, 2012) with an Introduction by Charles E. Allen (former Under Secretary for Intelligence and Analysis, U.S. Department of Homeland Security, and Assistant Director of Central Intelligence and Collection, Central Intelligence Agency). These studies commended extensive international attention and were translated into numerous foreign languages such as Dutch, Greek, Korean, Polish, and Turkish.

These two volumes provided surveys, analysis, and insights into the origins of al-Qa'ida; its leadership and membership; the evolution of the organizational structures; the establishment of key affiliated networks; the conduct of major operations nationally, regionally, and globally and their human psychological, political, economic, and strategic implications. The working of governmental, intergovernmental, and non-governmental responses to the manifold challenges to the security interests of the international system.

Although much of the foregoing information is familiar to researchers, students, and the general public, many more works are forgotten or perhaps even unknown. It is for this reason that the co-authors of this latest study decided to provide a context, focusing on the 9/11 attack, the life and death of Usama bin Laden, and the propaganda and psychological warfare record of the movement. It is hoped that this background drawn from earlier and current updated research undertakings will enable readers to better comprehend and appreciate the private communications assembled in this new study.

1. 9/11 and its Aftermath[*]

The people of America were traumatized by extraordinary personal and national insecurity when 19 suicide terrorists mounted simultaneous and massive attacks on September 11th, 2001.

---

[*] The following section is adapted from Y. Alexander and M.S. Swetnam. *Al-Qa'ida: Ten Years After 9/11 and Beyond*, Potomac Institute Press, 2012.

Introduction

The perpetrators, members of the radical Islamist international network al-Qa'ida ("the base"), hijacked four United States (U.S.) commercial airlines and crashed them into the Twin Towers of the World Trade Center in New York City, New York and the Pentagon in Arlington, Virginia, and a third unintended target, a field in Shanksville, Pennsylvania. This brutal assault that killed nearly 3,000 Americans and nationals from over 90 different countries, represented the deadliest non-state terrorist operation in world history.[1]

The catastrophe of 9/11, like the "day of infamy" over 60 years earlier, has dramatically defined America's vulnerability to external attacks by both sub-state and state actors. But unlike the December 7, 1941 attack on Pearl Harbor by Japan, the one unprecedented strike by al-Qa'ida has resulted in more devastating human, political, social, economic, and strategic costs to the United States than World War II.[2]

The "long war" against "militant Islam" as declared by President George W. Bush on September 20, 2001.[3] Subsequently, on October 6, 2001, America, leading an international coalition of allied countries, launched a massive military operation against al-Qa'ida's sanctuary and its Taliban protectors in Afghanistan. This effort, labeled "Operation Enduring Freedom," was intended to keep the homeland safe.[4] Similarly, U.S. President, Barack Obama, has regarded the battle in Afghanistan (also adversely affected by al-Qa'ida members and Taliban insurgents from "no-man's land" in Pakistan) as a "war of necessity."[5] By 2015, the American troops are withdrawing from Afghanistan but terrorism and other forms of violence are continuing.

Moreover, another long and costly war was undertaken by the Bush presidency in March 2003 against Iraq. The rationale for this new military action was based on the assessment that the Baghdad regime led by Saddam Hussein had links with al-Qa'ida and was engaged in a campaign to develop weapons of mass destruction (WMD).

Although the United States and its coalition partners defeated Iraq's military, and executed Saddam after his capture and trial, the United States has continued to endure mounting terrorist and insurgent attacks with high costs in human lives, economic damage, and dire political consequences.[6]

President Obama declared on October 21, 2011, that the American military engagement in Iraq would end on December 31, 2011, when the last U.S. soldiers would exit the country.[7] This full withdrawal strategy raised concerns regarding Iraq's security capabilities such as to confront continuing threats of sectarian violence and Iran's growing influence in the region.[8]

What actually happened in Iraq was even worse. An unprecedented strategic development is the emergence of in June 2014 of the "Islamic State of Iraq and al Sham" (also known as ISIS and subsequently the "Islamic State" or Da'esh). This newly formed Jihadist movement has launched its offensive drive in Iraq and Syria with fanatical levels of violence. By Spring 2015, the Islamic State, under the leadership of Abu Bakr al-Baghdadi (who proclaimed himself the head of the Caliphate), was successful in establishing links with affiliate terror organizations in the Middle East (e.g. Egypt), Asia (e.g. Pakistan), and Africa (e.g. Nigeria).

Clearly, the Islamic State, which evolved out of a predecessor of the former al-Qa'ida in Iraq, is based on radical ideologies of Salafism with global ambitions. In seeking the leadership of the Muslim world, it constitutes a challenge to the al-Qa'ida mission under current leadership of bin Laden's successor Ayman al-Zawahiri.[9] For instance, according to some media reports in 2015, the Islamic State members released a video clip threatening to execute a 9/11 style attack against the United States.[10]

2. Usama bin Laden's Life[*]

Usama bin Laden was born in 1957 in Saudi Arabia as the 17th son of 51 children of Muhammad bin Laden. His father was of Yemeni descent from the village of al-Ribat; his mother was a Saudi. Muhammad bin Laden left al-Ribat in 1931 and founded the construction company

---

[*] The following section is adapted from Y. Alexander and M.S. Swetnam. *Al-Qa'ida: Ten Years After 9/11 and Beyond*, Potomac Institute Press, 2012.

INTRODUCTION

the Bin Laden Group with his brothers. The company became heavily involved in Saudi government contracts building everything from the holy mosques in Mecca and Medina to highways and palaces. The bin Laden family business proved to be incredibly lucrative and the family amassed a fortune estimated at billions of dollars.

From an early age, Usama bin Laden was raised as a strict Islamist. Due to his close relationship with Mecca's mosques and the Saudi royal family, his father welcomed many pilgrims during the Hajj season. Even after his father died, visitors continued to pour into the home of the then thirteen-year-old Usama bin Laden.

Usama bin Laden is believed to have received a civil engineering or public management degree around 1980 from King Abdulaziz University in Jeddah, Saudi Arabia, though some contend that he fell short of obtaining a diploma. During his education he had two very distinguished teachers: Abdullah Azzam, who later collaborated with him in Afghanistan; and Mohammed Qutb, the famous Islamic philosopher. While bin Laden was attending university one of the most formative experiences of his adolescence occurred: the Soviet invasion of Afghanistan.

During the early stages of the mujahideen resistance, bin Laden traveled to Afghanistan and Pakistan to meet with scholars and leaders who had been guests at his family's house. He began lobbying for the mujahideen and successfully raised large amounts of money for their cause.

After university, bin Laden left Saudi Arabia for Afghanistan to join the mujahideen. He not only brought fresh recruits but also large amounts of cash and badly needed construction machinery. In 1984, he built a "guesthouse" in Peshawar, Pakistan, which would be the first station for new recruits for the mujahideen. The Maktab al-Khadamat (MAK) was established by Abdullah Azzam at bin Laden's guesthouse and was active in supporting the resistance. MAK was successful in funneling money into the war zone; building tunnels and hospitals; generating media and publications; and drawing support for the mujahideen around the world, especially in Afghanistan, but also in places like Yemen. The MAK was known to have a recruiting office in Brooklyn, New York, at the Alkifah Refugee Center.

Around 1986, bin Laden decided to chart a separate course from MAK. He built his own camps and trained his own fighters. Within two years he had six camps such as al-Masadah- the Lion's Den. He ran several successful assaults, with help from ex-military advisers from Egypt and Syria who brought much-needed experience, and participated in several battles, including the battle of Jalalabad.

Two years later, bin Laden realized that it was necessary to keep documentation of the people who traveled through his guesthouse, camps, and Afghanistan. He wanted to be able to track his friends and fellow mujahideen fighters as well as to be able to give answers to families with missing loved ones and friends who were out of touch. This network became known as "al-Qa'ida" (or the base). Following the Soviet withdrawal from Afghanistan in 1989 he went back to Saudi Arabia, while al-Qa'ida remained headquartered in Peshawar, Pakistan.

The Afghan war, however, did not end with the Soviet retreat. The rebels' hostilities continued initially against the Moscow-backed government and then between opposing factions (the Taliban and the Northern Alliance). During the same period in Saudi Arabia, bin Laden gave several public speeches relating to the Afghan victory, the failures of the Saudi government, and other Middle East security challenges. The Saudi government became concerned with his activities and placed a travel ban on him.

In August 1990, American troops arrived in Saudi Arabia at the invitation of the Saudi government to protect the Kingdom from a potential Iraqi attack. Bin Laden was furious that the Saudi government had sought and received a Western government's help and that non-Muslim forces were based in the same country as the Muslim holy sites of Mecca and Medina. Consequently, bin Laden met with several religious leaders to begin rounding up recruits. The Saudi government then attempted to stop his activities, and by 1991 bin Laden had been expelled from Saudi Arabia.

INTRODUCTION

Bin Laden used his connections to leave the country for Pakistan and later travel back into Afghanistan. There, he tried to work out a settlement between the warring factions battling for power while gathering support for a new jihad. In late 1991, after his efforts at mediation in the Afghan civil war had failed and several attempts were made on his life, bin Laden left for the Sudan.

Bin Laden was attracted to the Sudan for several reasons. The strict Islamist ideology of the new regime under the National Islamic Front appealed to him, and the regime sought his help. There were also several business opportunities for construction projects, including major highways, ports, and airports. Bin Laden set up several new companies in Sudan which would use these projects to provide income and support al-Qa'ida's activities while serving as a front to transport weapons and men. He also found employment and homes for several hundred "Arab-Afghans," who could not or would not return home after the jihad in Afghanistan.

While in Sudan, bin Laden set up al-Qa'ida's headquarters in the Riyadh section of Khartoum. It is reported that bin Laden funded and had remote, if not direct, involvement in several terrorist operations that took place in the early-to-mid 1990s in Yemen, Saudi Arabia, Somalia, Egypt, as well as the 1993 World Trade Center bombing in New York. Bin Laden and other members of al-Qa'ida worked to put aside their differences with Shi'a terrorist organizations and tried to unify them under al-Qa'ida against their perceived common enemies. Bin Laden and al-Qa'ida held several talks with elements within the Iranian government and the terrorist organization Hezbollah; it is believed that bin Laden sent members of his group to Hezbollah camps in Lebanon to receive training.

While bin Laden was living in Sudan, Saudi intelligence conducted several assassination attempts against bin Laden. The Saudi government froze his assets in the early 90s and publicly withdrew his Saudi citizenship in 1994. Usama was also denounced by members of his family. Following his public denunciation, bin Laden formed the Advice and Reform Council (ARC) as the political arm of al-Qa'ida. Through the ARC, bin Laden and his associates published several statements condemning the Saudi and Western governments.

By 1996, Sudan was under extreme international pressure to deport bin Laden and his followers. The Sudanese government, seeking relief from an embargo against its country, asked bin Laden to leave whereupon he relocated to Afghanistan.

Upon his return to Afghanistan, bin Laden began to issue several public statements and fatwas calling for all Muslims "to kill Americans and their allies, civilian and military, [as] an individual duty." The first notable fatwa issued by bin Laden, "Message from Usama bin Laden to his Muslim Brothers in the Whole World and Especially in the Arabian Peninsula: Declaration of Jihad Against the Americans Occupying the Land of the Two Holy Mosques; Expel the Heretics from the Arabian Peninsula," came in 1996. During this time he increased his media exposure, giving his first interview to CNN, in 1997, as well as declaring additional fatwas.[11]

Bin Laden set up several training camps for his new jihad against the United States. From these camps, bin Laden financed and helped plan several terrorist operations, such as the Khobar Towers bombing in 1996 in Saudi Arabia, the 1998 bombings of the American embassies in East Africa, and the 2000 attack on the USS *Cole* in Yemen. While the United States retaliated for the 1998 embassy bombings with cruise missile strikes on al-Qa'ida training camps in Afghanistan and thwarted several other plots linked to bin Laden, such as the 2000 millennium plot, bin Laden's vast network of resources and his devoted following enabled him to continue his jihad. The umbrella framework of the International Islamic Front for Jihad against Jews and Crusaders which bin Laden and associates set up in Afghanistan in February 1998 served as a "clearing house" and coordinating body for many groups worldwide.[12] From Afghanistan, al-Qa'ida was able to launch its most unprecedented assault: the September 11, 2001, attacks on the World Trade Center and the Pentagon.

Early in the 2001 invasion of Afghanistan, U.S. forces were believed to have been close to locating bin Laden in the mountain region of Tora Bora. However, he managed to elude the United States and remained at large for the next decade despite the $25 million bounty offered for his capture. It remains unclear how much influence bin Laden

Introduction

had on the planning of operations or how much contact al-Qa'ida central had with its affiliates during his time in hiding. Bin Laden remained active in the public sphere, releasing occasional audio and video messages aimed at followers worldwide and remaining the international face of al-Qa'ida.

Though he was believed to be hiding somewhere in the Afghanistan-Pakistan border region, bin Laden had been living in a compound in Abbottabad, Pakistan, near the Pakistani capital of Islamabad since 2005. U.S. officials first became alerted to the possibility of bin Laden's presence in the area in the summer of 2010. Several months of intelligence work confirmed bin Laden's location in the compound. Early in the morning on Monday, May 2, 2011, Pakistani time, a U.S. Navy SEAL team raided the compound, killing bin Laden.

3. The Hunt for Usama bin Laden and the May 2, 2011 Raid[*]

U.S. intelligence services had been searching for Usama bin Laden since before the 9/11 attacks. U.S. forces had been close to locating bin Laden during the attack on Tora Bora in late 2001, although bin Laden managed to elude capture and avoid U.S. and Coalition forces then and for most of the past decade. While it was widely speculated that bin Laden was living in the mountainous area of the Afghanistan-Pakistan border, he was eventually found and killed in a walled compound in Abbotabad, Pakistan, a short distance from the Pakistani capital of Islamabad.

Intelligence on the likely whereabouts of bin Laden since Tora Bora began to emerge in the summer of 2010 while the U.S. monitored one of bin Laden's couriers. The courier, Abu Ahmed al-Kuwaiti, first came to the attention of U.S. officials when his name was mentioned during the interrogations of several al-Qa'ida associates in U.S. custody, many of them at CIA-operated secret prison sites in Eastern Europe.[13] Officials came to suspect that the courier was a significant member of al-Qa'ida during the subsequent interrogation of Khalid Sheikh Mohammed, who attempted to obfuscate the courier's

---

[*] The following section is adapted from Y. Alexander and M.S. Swetnam. *Al-Qa'ida: Ten Years After 9/11 and Beyond*, Potomac Institute Press, 2012.

identity and importance in the organization in contrast with known information.[14]

The lead on the existence of a courier, al-Kuwaiti, close to bin Laden at first consisted only of his nom de guerre. This led to an intensive investigation by U.S. intelligence agencies that eventually led them to bin Laden in Abbotabad. In 2005 the courier's family name was discovered, and his phone calls and emails were intercepted. This surveillance revealed his full name, Sheikh Abu Ahmed, a Pakistani who was born in Kuwait.[15] U.S. intelligence's investigation of al-Kuwaiti coincided with a reorganization of intelligence assets and a refocusing of priorities and resources in South and Central Asia. Dubbed Operation Cannonball, the end result was, by 2005, an increase of CIA agents and assets in Pakistan who were able to follow up on the al-Kuwaiti lead.[16]

Officials monitoring al-Kuwaiti identified his car in Peshawar and were able to trace it to the Abbotabad compound.[17] With the compound now under scrutiny, the CIA began monitoring it from a nearby safe house.[18] U.S. intelligence officials grew increasingly suspicious of the compound due to its high security walls, tinted windows, burned trash and other unusual measures used to maintain the privacy and anonymity of the occupants. Officials concluded that the compound was used to house a relatively senior official in the al-Qa'ida network, although it did not yet have a clear indication that it was bin Laden. After continuing its surveillance into 2011, it was able to advise the National Security Council, (NSC) which began planning military options against the compound, that they were "between 50% and 80%" certain that the house was occupied by bin Laden and several associates.[19]

Once it had been confirmed that bin Laden was likely to be residing in Abbotabad, the NSC began deliberating on the proper course of action, with President Obama chairing several meetings prior to the May 2nd raid.[20] The President's advisers were unable to reach a unanimous decision. The commander of the U.S. military's Joint Special Operations Command, Vice Admiral William McRaven, was asked in February 2011 to plan a strike against the compound. He came up with three options: "a high-altitude bombing raid by B-2 bombers, a 'direct shot' with cruise missiles, or a helicopter assault using a team of U.S. commandos."[21]

The first two suggestions were ruled out due to unacceptable levels of collateral damage, including annihilating the compound and any bodies, and leaving no verification that bin Laden had been killed.[22] A ground operation by American special forces would reduce the risk of civilian casualties and confirm bin Laden's presence at the compound, but carried several risks of its own. The raid would be deep in Pakistani territory, and would be considered a violation of Pakistani sovereignty, and a failure of the raid would likely precipitate a foreign policy crisis for the United States. After much deliberation by the NSC, a raid by U.S. Navy SEALs, who had been preparing for this operation for several months using a full replica of the compound, was given a green light.

Most importantly, and perhaps most controversially, the Pakistani government was not informed of the raid before being carried out. While the United States and Pakistan had cooperated on previous intelligence and counter-terror efforts, the United States had, in recent years, begun to suspect the reliability of the Pakistani government and the ISI-P. There was a general feeling among top U.S. officials, including Secretary of State Hillary Clinton and Chairman of the Joint Chiefs Adm. Mike Mullen, that segments of the ISI-P had been cooperating with the Taliban, and may have even been aware of bin Laden's whereabouts.[23]

As a result of the mistrust of Pakistan, the military had to plan the raid around keeping the Pakistanis uninformed until as late in the operation as possible. It also had to plan for the potential failure of the raid and the Pakistani reaction. The helicopters that ferried the SEALs over the Pakistani border from Afghanistan flew low to the ground and were equipped with radar-deflecting and noise-reducing technology. The United States had previously not acknowledged that such helicopters existed in order to avoid detection by Pakistani air defenses.[24] The SEALs had also built into their plan the possibility that they would have to engage the Pakistani military if discovered.

In preparation for such a scenario they deployed two helicopters full of SEALs as a reserve force.[25]

In the early morning of Monday, May 2, Pakistani time, the SEAL team crossed into Pakistan; the team that was chosen for this mission was SEAL Team 6, which had been hunting for bin Laden in Afghanistan since 2001. There were 23 SEALs on two Black Hawk helicopters, along with an interpreter and a tracking dog. In addition, there were two dozen more SEALs in reserve. Originally, the two Black Hawks were to drop the SEALs off and leave within several minutes. One would hover above the compound, allowing the SEALs to descend into the courtyard. The other helicopter would hover above the roof to allow the team to fast rope down onto the building, and then put more SEALs outside to ensure a surprise attack. As a result of the intense heat, the helicopter pilot who was attempting to hover over the compound could not keep the aircraft steady and was forced to attempt to land. During the landing, the tail and rotor became caught on the compound's high walls rendering the aircraft unusable for the operation. After this misstep the second Black Hawk chose to land on the ground rather than attempt to hover. Before finishing the mission, the commandos blew up the damaged helicopter so that the technology inside would not be compromised.[26]

As the SEALs entered the compound, a firefight ensued as al-Kuwaiti fired on them from the guesthouse. He was killed, and his wife was killed in the crossfire. As the team reached the main building, the commandos blew open the front door and shot and killed the courier's brother, whom they believed had been preparing to fire on them. Bin Laden's son Khalid was also killed as the team made its way up the stairs. Bin Laden was found on the third floor with an AK-47 rifle and a Makarov pistol within arm's reach. A SEAL shot him in the left eye and the chest, killing him. Bin Laden's wife was wounded while trying to attack one of the SEALs.[27]

The codeword "Geronimo" was announced following the operation to inform the President that the SEAL team had killed or captured

INTRODUCTION

Usama bin Laden. In order to verify that the remains were bin Laden's, a commander on the ground made a visual identification. Then a digital image was sent to the CIA, where it was processed through a facial recognition system. One of bin Laden's widows also identified the remains. When the remains reached Afghanistan, a DNA test was done and initial results showed a high correlation with the DNA on file that had been obtained by the Saudi government from members of the bin Laden family. Further DNA testing was done that provided "100 percent certainty" that the remains were bin Laden's.[28]

Overall, the operation took 38 minutes, eight minutes longer than had been planned; the discrepancy in time was the result of the mechanical failure of one of the helicopters. In addition to bin Laden, his son, the owner of the compound, and several others were killed in the raid. The SEALs left the compound with several computer drives and other hardware, which would subsequently be searched for intelligence, as well as with bin Laden's body. He was buried at sea within twelve hours of his death, in accordance with Islamic tradition, depriving al-Qa'ida supporters of a potential burial shrine.[29]

Pakistan claimed the death of bin Laden "illustrates the resolve of the international community, including Pakistan, to fight and eliminate terrorism," though the incident exacerbated feelings of distrust and wariness between both nations.[30] The Pakistani government has stated since that "… the US had made 'an unauthorized unilateral action' that would not be tolerated in the future."[31] The Pakistani Foreign Office further stated "… such an event shall not serve as a future precedent for any state, including the US."[32]

Relations between the two nations' intelligence agencies have deteriorated considerably. According to former CIA officials, this distrust exists in part due to the relationship the ISI-P has with the Taliban.[33] There is also the question of how Pakistani intelligence could not have known that bin Laden had been living in Abbottabad given that the compound is a very short distance away from a Pakistani Military base and the Pakistan Military Academy. Some individuals within the United States believe that the Pakistani government sheltered bin Laden and was fully aware of his location. This lack of faith has in turn aroused suspicion by the Pakistanis.

Senior Pakistani officials have said that the secrecy of the bin Laden raid illustrated a "deep distrust."[34]

4. Propaganda and Psychological Warfare[*]

There is ample historical evidence that terrorist groups from ancient to contemporary times have followed the guidance provided by Sun Tzu in *The Art of War* that "the acme of skill is not winning hundred battles, but to subdue the armies of the enemy without fighting." The purpose of propaganda and psychological warfare is therefore to demoralize the "enemy" by breaking down its will to resist and fight and simultaneously strengthen the resolve of one's own combatants and their allies to continue the battle until victory.

Thus, al-Qa'ida has continuously followed this approach to warfare. Its public face is reflected in the propaganda and psychological warfare as conducted by Usama bin Laden himself and his associates. That is, the movement relies on the media to spread its jihadist propaganda and to recruit new members.[35] Increasingly, al-Qa'ida has utilized new avenues to spread its message, including the Internet (jihadist websites, YouTube, social networking sites, etc.) and magazines.[36] By taking advantage of different modes of communication, al-Qa'ida has been able to spread its message to a broad audience. Al-Qa'ida's message resonates with some sympathizers who will heed the call to violence and others who will echo the word of violent jihad throughout the virtual community.[37]

In many ways, al-Qa'ida has changed its approach to warfare. Rather than focusing on conventional methods, it strives to inflict both immediate harm and long-lasting fear in its victims and the wider global audience.[38] Terrorist attacks can scar a nation's populace long after the actual incident has occurred. Through the instillation of fear, al-Qa'ida is able to disrupt a nation's normal way of life. An attack can cause people to change their daily routines and to constantly fear for their safety, thereby undermining important pillars of a society

---

[*] The following section is adapted from Y. Alexander and M.S. Swetnam. *Al-Qa'ida: Ten Years After 9/11 and Beyond*, Potomac Institute Press, 2012.

such as business, culture, and trust.[39] This psychological targeting of an enemy's audience is achieved through a continuous threat of violence and can be used to encourage changes in behavior among the enemy.[40]

Since 9/11, Usama bin Laden was extensively engaged in electronic political communication to spread his propaganda and psychological warfare messages. The following are selected examples of these efforts:

1. **Source: NBC Nightly News (video on YouTube)/PBS News Hour**
   - Date Published: 7 October 2001
   - *Available at: http://www.youtube.com/watch?v−Q-St8s9RKEU; http://www.pbs.org/newshour/terrorism/international/binladen_10-7.html*
   - Statement Title: Unknown
   - Document Title: Bin Laden Statement
   - Speaker: Usama bin Laden
   - Summary: Shortly before the first wave of American attacks against the capital of Afghanistan, bin Laden issued a statement declaring, "I want to tell the US and its people, I swear by God, by Allah, he who has praised the sky, that the US will not have peace." He goes on to say the Muslims have been blessed with destroying America, "Every Muslim after this event [should fight for his religion…"

2. **Source: PBS News Hour & The NEFA Foundation**
   - Date Published: 9 November 2001 (Released 13 December 2001)
   - *Available at: http://www.pbs.org/newshour/bb/terrorism/july-dec01/video_12-13a.html*
   - Statement Title: Unknown
   - Document Title: "Usama Bin Laden Claims Responsibility for the 9/11 Attacks"
   - Speaker: Usama bin Laden
   - Summary: In this 60 minute video, bin Laden, speaking to a room of supporters, talks about the success of September 11th, making it clear he was the mastermind behind the attacks.

With very specific detail, he talks about how calculated the attacks were, such as the number of floors that would be directly impacted. He also mentions where he and his fellow men were at the exact time of the attack, saying they had known the attacks would take place on September 11th a week in advance. At one point he says, "This is all that we hoped for." Aside from discussion about the attack, the video depicts bin Laden at a site where a U.S. helicopter crashed in southern Afghanistan.

3. Source: CNN
- Date Published: 27 December 2001
- *Available at: http://edition.cnn.com/2001/WORLD/asiapcf/ central/12/26/ret.bin.laden.statement/index.html*
- Statement Title: Unknown
- Document Title: "Bin Laden Calls Sept. 11 Attacks 'Blessed Terror'"
- Speaker: Usama bin Laden
- Summary: In this 34 minute video, bin Laden calls the September 11th attacks, "blessed terror" and accuses the West of hating the Islamic faith, "It's very clear that the West in general, and America in particular, have an unspeakable hatred for Islam." Bin Laden also touches upon the bombing of an al-Qa'ida base and mosque in Khost, chastising the American troops for affecting the lives of civilians, "Those who claim to be humane and free, we have seen their real crimes."

4. Source: BBC News
- Date Published: 12 November 2002
- *Available at: http://news.bbc.co.uk/2/hi/middle_ east/2455845.stm*
- Statement Title: Unknown
- Document Title: "Bin Laden's Message"
- Speaker: Usama bin Laden
- Summary: In this statement, bin Laden accuses the American government of being gangsters and butchers, who are killing women, children, and elderly people. He says George Bush is the "pharaoh of this age" and he urges people to put as much distance between themselves and the White House as

possible. He also justifies al-Qa'ida's attacks by saying, "You will be killed just as you kill, and will be bombed just as you bomb." In bin Laden's eyes it is unfair that the people of Iraq are being treated unjustly, while those in the West are enjoying stability and happiness.

5. Source: BBC News
- Date Published: 12 February 2003
- *Available at: http://news.bbc.co.uk/2/hi/2751019.stm*
- Statement Title: Unknown
- Document Title: Bin Laden tape: Text
- Speaker: Usama bin Laden
- Summary: In this audio message, bin Laden talks about a number of important values, including showing good intentions, continuously preparing for jihad, and being mindful of the psychological warfare the Americans are using. He also questions the capability of the United States and its allies in defeating the Muslim world, while trying to instill morale among the Muslim community, saying "…honest Muslims…should move, incite, and mobilize the [Islamic] nation…"

6. Source: BBC News
- Date Published: 16 February 2003
- *Available at: http://news.bbc.co.uk/2/hi/not_in_website/ syndication/monitoring/media_reports/2768873.stm*
- Statement Title: "Sermon for the Feast of the Sacrifice"
- Document Title: Bin Laden Tape Urges Jihad
- Speaker: Usama bin Laden
- Summary: In this 53 minute message, bin Laden blames both President Bush and British Prime Minister Tony Blair for attacking the Muslim world, accusing them both of using the war on terrorism as a cover-up for their true goal of destroying the Islamic religion. According to bin Laden, the true objective of both countries is to establish a "Jewish superstate", claiming the current events in Pakistan are foreshadowing what is to come throughout the rest of the region.

7. **Source: *Guardian* (UK)**
    - Date Published: 8 April 2003
    - *Available at: http://www.guardian.co.uk/world/2003/apr/08/afghanistan.alqaida*
    - Statement Title: Unknown
    - Document Title: Latest Bin Laden Tape Urges Suicide Attacks
    - Speaker: Usama bin Laden
    - Summary: In this video, bin Laden urges Muslims to carry out suicide missions in Pakistan, Afghanistan, Bahrain, Kuwait, and Saudi Arabia. He states, "…jihad against them is your duty." He also explains that those who cannot physically take up the fight must do so financially, as should women by providing fighters with food.

8. **Source: NEFA Foundation & CNN World**
    - Date Published: 4 January 2004
    - *Available at: http://articles.cnn.com/2004-01-05/world/binladen.tape_1_bin-laden-tape-audiotape-voice-of-osama-bin?_s=PM:WORLD*
    - Statement Title: Unknown
    - Document Title: Usama Bin Laden Audiotape
    - Speaker: Usama bin Laden
    - Summary: In this audiotape, bin Laden talks about the importance of waging jihad and overthrowing regimes in the Middle East that are collaborating with the United States. During his message he declared:
    - *There can be no dialogue with occupiers except through arms…Islamic countries in the past century were not liberated from the Crusaders' military occupation except through jihad in the cause of God. Under the pretext of fighting terrorism, the West today is doing its utmost to tarnish jihad and kill anyone seeking jihad…Jihad is the path, so seek it.*

9. **Source: CNN & MSNBC**
    - Date Published: 15 April 2004
    - *Available at: http://edition.cnn.com/2004/WORLD/asiapcf/04/15/binladen.tape/index.html*

Introduction

- Statement Title: Unknown
- Document Title: "Europe: No Deal with Bin Laden"
- Speaker: Usama bin Laden
- Summary: In an audiotape delivered to Al Jazeera and Al-Arabiya, bin Laden offered European countries the opportunity to enter into a truce with al-Qa'ida, if they pulled their troops from the Islamic countries they were currently residing in. Caveats to this truce include the offer being on the table for only three months, and the exclusion of the United States from any chance at a peace offering. Aside from this offer, bin Laden also threatened to take revenge on the United States for the killing of Sheikh Ahmed Yassin, the founder of Hamas.

10. **Source:** *The New York Times*
    - Date Published: 29 October 2004
    - *Available at: http://www.nytimes.com/2004/10/30/ international/middleeast/30qaeda.html?scp=1&sq=In%20 Video%20Message,%20Bin%20Laden%20Issues%20 Warning%20to%20US&st=cse*
    - Statement Title: Unknown
    - Document Title: "In Video Message, Bin Laden Issues Warning to US"
    - Speaker: Usama bin Laden
    - Summary: In his first video appearance in over a year, bin Laden again threatened the American people by warning that if they wanted to avoid another attack like September 11th, they needed to discontinue their attacks on the Muslim world. He stated, "Your security is not in the hands of Kerry or Bush or Al Qaeda; your security is in your own hands." While no direct threats were made, the surfacing of this video only four days before the Presidential election suggested the fate of America and the next President could be related to one another.

11. **Source:** *Guardian* **(UK)**
    - Date Published: 16 December 2004
    - *Available at: http://www.guardian.co.uk/world/2004/dec/16/ alqaida.saudiarabia1*

AL-QA'IDA'S MYSTIQUE EXPOSED

- Statement Title: Unknown
- Document Title: "New Bin Laden Tape Posted on Website"
- Speaker: Usama bin Laden
- Summary: In this audiotape, bin Laden expresses his happiness over the attack on the U.S. Consulate in Saudi Arabia. He also criticizes the Saudi Arabian royal family, saying they and not "holy warriors" are the ones who are at fault for the current state of the country. He states, "The sins the regime committed are great…it practised injustices against the people, violating their rights, humiliating their pride…" He demands change because in his opinion the country's elite has done nothing to rectify their wrongdoings.

12. Source: *Guardian* (UK)
- Date Published: 20 February 2006
- *Available at: http://www.guardian.co.uk/world/2006/feb/20/alqaida.terrorism*
- Statement Title: "I Will Never Be Taken Alive"
- Document Title: "Bin Laden: 'I Will Never Be Taken Alive'"
- Speaker: Usama bin Laden
- Summary: In this audiotape, bin Laden declares he will never be taken alive, but will instead live free. Throughout his speech he makes a comparison between Saddam Hussein and the U.S. military in Iraq, calling the fight both barbaric and repressive. He is positive the jihad is growing in strength and mocks President Bush's belief that the conflict in Iraq ended in 2003. Finally, he criticizes the incorrect figures released by the Pentagon in regards to the number of American troops killed and injured during battle, as well as increases in suicide rates and a decrease in morale.

13. Source: *The Washington Post*
- Date Published: 8 September 2007
- *Available at: http://www.washingtonpost.com/wp-dyn/content/article/2007/09/07/AR2007090700279.html*
- Statement Title: "The Solution"
- Document Title: "Bin Laden Predicts US Failure in Iraq"
- Speaker: Usama bin Laden

- Summary: This 25 minute video addressed the ongoing war in Iraq and the consequences that would ensue if the American people continued to oppress the Muslim world. He stated, "The blood of the Muslims will not be spilled with impunity." Husain Haqqani, an expert on Islamic terrorist groups, believed the purpose of this video was to increase morale within al-Qa'ida while simultaneously denouncing the United States and its Western views.

14. Source: Global Terror Alert/NEFA Foundation
- Date Published: 20 September 2007
- *Available at: http://www.globalterroralert.com/al-qaida-leaders/30-usama-bin-laden-qcome-to-jihad-a-speech-to-the-people-of-pakistanq.html.*
- Statement Title: "Come to Jihad: A Speech to the People of Pakistan"
- Document Title: Unknown
- Speaker: Usama bin Laden
- Summary: Again, the people of Pakistan were urged to take up the fight against President Pervez of Pakistan, this time by bin Laden himself. In this video, bin Laden claimed it was the duty of the Pakistani people to overthrow their President because his continued alliance with the United States was against Islam, making violence against him justifiable.

15. Source: *The Long War Journal*/NEFA Foundation
- Date Published: 23 October 2007
- *Available at: http://nefafoundation.org/index.cfm?pageID=44; http://www.longwarjournal.org/archives/2007/10/osama_bin_laden_on_t.php*
- Statement Title: "A Message to the People of Iraq"
- Document Title: "Osama bin Laden on the State of Iraq"
- Speaker: Usama bin Laden

- Summary: In this video, bin Laden criticizes the failures of al-Qa'ida throughout Iraq, including the dividing of ranks, violation of al-Qa'ida laws, and ignorance towards God being the sole authority. He says those who have violated the law need to be punished, because while everybody makes mistakes only the best admit to them. Bin Laden's comments on al-Qa'ida provide insight into the problems the organization is facing within the borders of Iraq.

16. Source: *The Guardian* (UK)
- Date Published: 30 November 2007
- *Available at: http://www.guardian.co.uk/world/2007/nov/29/usa.afghanistan*
- Statement Title: "Message to the Peoples of Europe"
- Document Title: "Bin Laden: Europe Must Quit Afghanistan"
- Speaker: Usama bin Laden
- Summary: In this video, bin Laden calls upon European governments to end their cooperation with the United States in Afghanistan, saying, "the American tide is ebbing," and "It is better for you to restrain your politicians who are thronging the steps of the White House." He reiterates his role in al-Qa'ida rather than the Taliban and criticizes both the United States and European countries for their continuing attacks on Afghanistan. Shortly after this video was released, the Afghan government issued a statement denouncing bin Laden's comments and saying their people were not killed by NATO troops but by Islamic extremists.

17. Source: The NEFA Foundation
- Date Published: 3 January 2008
- *Available at: http://nefafoundation.org/index.cfm?pageID=44*
- Statement Title: "The Way to Frustrate the Conspiracies"

INTRODUCTION

- Document Title: "Usama Bin Laden: 'The Way to Frustrate the Conspiracies'"
- Speaker: Usama bin Laden
- Summary: In this audiotape, bin Laden's main focus is on calling upon insurgents in the Islamic State of Iraq to join the al-Qa'ida organization. He also makes a statement directed towards Palestine in which he says, "we will widen the scope of our jihad and we will not recognize Sykes-Picot borders… Blood for blood, destruction for destruction."

18. **Source: The NEFA Foundation**
    - Date Published: 19 March 2008
    - *Available at: http://nefafoundation.org/index.cfm?pageID=44*
    - Statement Title: "May Our Mothers Be Bereaved of Us If We Fail to Help Our Prophet"
    - Document Title: "Usama Bin Laden 'May Our Mothers Be Bereaved of Us If We Fail to Help Our Prophet'"
    - Speaker: Usama bin Laden
    - Summary: In this audio recording, bin Laden denounces the cartoons, criticizing Islam, which were published in Denmark. He refuses to acknowledge their attempts at asserting free speech by saying, "If there is no check on the freedom of your words, then let your hearts be open to the freedom of our actions…"

19. **Source: The NEFA Foundation**
    - Date Published: 21 March 2008
    - *Available at: http://nefafoundation.org/index.cfm?pageID=44*
    - Statement Title: "The Way for the Salvation of Palestine"
    - Document Title: "Usama Bin Laden 'The Way for the Salvation of Palestine'"
    - Speaker: Usama bin Laden
    - Summary: In this audiotape, bin Laden talks about reclaiming control of Palestine. He also urges al-Qa'ida members and supporters to welcome "brothers" from Palestine and allow them a place among the mujahideen in Iraq, saying "The mujahideen coming from outside shall encounter their brothers within…and the Muslims shall delight in their clear victory."

20. Source: The NEFA Foundation
- Date Published: 22 May 2008
- *Available at: http://nefafoundation.org/index.cfm?pageID=44*
- Statement Title: "A Message to the People of the West from the Shaykh Usama Bin Laden: The Reasons for the Conflict on the Sixtieth Anniversary of the Israeli Conquest"
- Document Title: "Usama Bin Laden 'A Message to the People of the West'"
- Speaker: Usama bin Laden
- Summary: In this new audio recording, bin Laden reiterates that the Palestinian issue is al-Qa'ida's main focus. He goes further by saying the Palestinian issue has been a motivating factor for his viewpoints since he was a young child. Then, in an attempt to justify al-Qa'ida's acts of terrorism, bin Laden claims "The real terrorism and the armed assaults are being carried out by a leader who is the most terrible instrument of war humanity has ever seen..." Finally, he states the Israelis are the real terrorists because they have killed many civilians including women and children.

21. Source: The NEFA Foundation
- Date Published: 29 May 2008
- *Available at: http://nefafoundation.org/index.cfm?pageID=44*
- Statement Title: "A Message to the Islamic Nation"
- Document Title: "Usama bin Laden 'A Message to the Islamic Nation'"
- Speaker: Usama bin Laden
- Summary: In this audio recording, bin Laden targets Muslim youths and asks them to take up arms and defend their brothers in Palestine who are facing a great battle in the Gaza Strip. He firmly believes the only way to reach Palestine is to continue to wage jihad on the governments, including Egypt, surrounding the land of the Jews.

22. Source: NEFA Foundation
- Date Published: 15 January 2009
- *Available At: http://nefafoundation.org//index.cfm?pageID=44*

Introduction

- Statement Title: "A Call for Jihad to Stop the Gaza Assault"
- Document Title: "Usama Bin Laden, ' A Call for Jihad to Stop the Gaza Assault'"
- Speaker: Usama bin Laden
- Summary: This audio recording by bin Laden calls on youth to take up arms and join the jihad against the Zionist-Crusader alliance. He also blames the Gaza raid on a declining U.S. economy. Lastly, bin Laden requests donations from faithful Muslims.

23. **Source: NEFA Foundation**
    - Date Published: 14 March 2009
    - *Available At: http://nefafoundation.org//index.cfm?pageID=44*
    - Statement Title: "Practical Steps to Liberate Palestine"
    - Document Title: "New Bin Laden Audio, 'Practical Steps to Liberate Palestine'"
    - Speaker: Usama bin Laden
    - Summary: In this audio recording, bin Laden asks "how long must our family in Palestine live in fear, while we enjoy security--albeit a false, temporary security?" He is speaking about why the situation in Gaza, or "the holocaust," as he refers to it, is further reason why Muslims need to detach themselves from the "hypocrites."

24. **Source: NEFA Foundation**
    - Date Published: 19 March 2009
    - *Available At: http://nefafoundation.org//index.cfm?pageID=44*
    - Statement Title: "Fight On, Champions of Somalia"
    - Document Title: "New Bin Laden Audio 'Fight On, Champions of Somalia'"
    - Speaker: Usama bin Laden
    - Summary: This audio recording by the al-Qa'ida leader condemns "the decision of former Somali Islamic Courts Union (ICU) president Shaykh Shareef to join in a peace initiative with the interim Somali government." It is bin Laden's opinion that he is abandoning his religion.

25. Source: NEFA Foundation
- Date Published: 16 June 2009
- *Available At: http://nefafoundation.org//index.cfm?pageID=44*
- Statement Title: "Speech to the Pakistani Nation"
- Document Title: "Usama Bin Laden 'Speech to the Pakistani Nation'"
- Speaker: Usama bin Laden
- Summary: In this audio recording, bin Laden states that President Obama "ha[s] instilled new seeds to increase the hatred and revenge towards America" and that U.S. citizens should prepare themselves for the future.

26. Source: NEFA Foundation
- Date Published: 14 September 2009
- *Available At: http://nefafoundation.org//index.cfm?pageID=44*
- Statement Title: not available
- Document Title: "Usama Bin Laden's 9/11 Message to the American People"
- Speaker: Usama bin Laden
- Summary: In this audio recording, bin Laden urges the Untied States to stop supporting Israel and, in exchange, "offered to respond to this decision in accordance with sound and just principles; otherwise, it is inevitable that we will continue our war of extermination against you on all possible fronts."

27. Source: NEFA Foundation
- Date Published: 25 September 2009
- *Available At: http://nefafoundation.org//index.cfm?pageID=44*
- Statement Title: "A Message from Shaykh Usama bin Laden to the People of Europe"
- Document Title: "Usama Bin Laden 'Message to the People of Europe'"
- Speaker: Usama bin Laden
- Summary: This audio recording asks Europe to cease its NATO partnership with the United States or face the consequences.

INTRODUCTION

28. Source: MEMRI Jihad & Terrorism Threat Monitor Project
- Date Published: 2 October 2010
- Statement Title: "Save Your Brothers in Pakistan"
- Document Title: not available
- Speaker: Usama bin Laden
- Summary: This audio message by the leader of al-Qa'ida discusses the flooding in Pakistan and urges the relief effort to be increased. In his eyes, not enough has been done by the Pakistani government to help those in need.

29. Source: NEFA Foundation
- Date Published: 9 November 2010
- *Available At: http://nefafoundation.org//index.cfm?pageID=44*
- Statement Title: "To the French People"
- Document Title: "A Message from Usama Bin Laden to the French People"
- Speaker: Usama bin Laden
- Summary: This audiotape explains to the French why its citizens are being kidnapped. It is because France will not allow women to wear a jihab; therefore, capturing its citizens is retaliation.

30. Source: NEFA Foundation
- Date Published: 18 May 2011
- *Available At: http://nefafoundation.org//index.cfm?pageID=44*
- Statement Title: not available
- Document Title: "Usama Bin Laden Final Audio Message: 'To the Muslim Ummah'"
- Speaker: Usama bin Laden
- Summary: This is the final audio message given by bin Laden and it was released after his death. It encourages and supports the revolutions in Tunisia, Egypt, and Libya. Bin Laden warns youth that they should not be hasty with their actions, but should rather seek the advice of those with expertise and experience before carrying out anything.

5. Methodological Note

It is against the foregoing detailed context of Usama bin Laden's life and death that his surrealist portrait is beginning to be painted. Various insights related to al-Qa'ida's evolution, ideology, objectives, modus operandi, and strategic impact nationally, regionally, and globally are also revealed with sober clarity.

And yet, this panorama of the reign of terror mounted by bin Laden and his malevolent movement only partially sketches the landscape on canvas.

As indicated previously, an additional opportunity for untangling of al-Qa'ida's mystique has fortunately been afforded by the public availability of Usama bin Laden's private correspondence captured during the SEALs' operation on May 2, 2011. The Office of the Director of National Intelligence (ODNI) provided a complete reproduction of over 100 declassified letters and other miscellaneous documents found in the compound. The communications originally written in Arabic were translated into English by the United States Government.

A major ebook is *2015 Osama bin Laden's Bookshelf: Complete Declassified Documents and Letters by the Terrorist Leader on Wide Range of Topics, plus Letters from Abbottabad (Usama bin Ladin and al Qaeda)*. This undertaking was sponsored in addition to the United States government and the Office of the Director of National Intelligence by the Department of Defense, Combating Terrorism Center at West Point, U.S. Military Academy, and Congressional Research Service.

The purpose of *Al-Qa'ida Mystique Exposed: Usama bin Laden's Private Communications* is not to duplicate the foregoing scholarly efforts but to provide an updated follow-up to the two earlier studies by Yonah Alexander and Michael S. Swetnam: *Usama bin Laden's al-Qa'ida: Profile of a Terrorist Network* (Ardsley, New York: Transnational Publisher, February 2001) and *Al-Qa'ida: Ten Years After 9/11 and Beyond* (Arlington, VA: Potomac Institute Press, 2012).

Introduction

The co-authors of the current work have incorporated verbatim the 100 Abbottabad declassified documents to make them more accessible to readers within the context of their previous publications. Although short abstracts are also provided for each letter, no analytical effort has been made to identify with certainty the author of each document or the intended receivers. It also should be noted that there are spelling mistakes of some translated material as well as other grammatical inconsistencies.

Despite these and other shortcomings, it is hoped that this volume will be useful to experts and general readers as well as stimulating future study of Usama bin Laden, al-Qa'ida, and its network.

6. Acknowledgements

This book, like many dozens of earlier volumes published in the past 20 years, benefits from the continuing support of our core three academic institutions: the Inter-University Center for Terrorism Studies (a consortium of universities and think tanks in more than 40 countries); the International Center for Terrorism Studies at Potomac Institute for Policy Studies; and the Inter-University Center for Legal Studies at the International Law Institute. Special gratitude is due to the leadership of Potomac Institute for Policy Studies, including General Alfred Gray, USMC (Ret.), Chairman of the Board of Regents; Thomas O'Leary, Executive Vice President, Strategy and Planning; and Gail Clifford, Vice President for Financial Management and Chief Financial Officer. Kathryn Schiller Wurster, Chief of Staff in the Office of the CEO, provided encouragement and guidance on this project and staff member Alex Taliesen designed the cover. Sherry Loveless, Managing and Production Editor at the Potomac Institute Press, deserves appreciation for her professionalism in producing the volume under a tight-time-publishing schedule.

Sharon Layani (Research Associate and Coordinator at the International Center for Terrorism Studies) also provided extraordinary support in preparing the manuscript for production.

She also ably administered the research contributions of several interns, particularly Julia Johnson (Johns Hopkins University) and Julie Byrne (The Catholic University of America) for organizing the documents for production; Veeravaroon Mavichak (American University) for preparing the bibliography; and Caitlin Davis (Duquesne University), Daniel Marfurt- Levy (George Mason University), and Tyler J. Townes (Central Michigan University) for developing the Index.

Finally, as always, a disclaimer is in order. The co-authors, the participating academic institutions and their staff, and the Potomac Institute Press, cannot be held responsible for errors or any consequences arising from the use of information contained in this publication. Moreover, the views and opinions expressed in this volume do not necessarily reflect those of the Publisher and the institutions involved in the study.

7. Endnotes

1. The literature on al-Qa'ida before 9/11 was rather limited. See, for example, Yonah Alexander and Michael S. Swetnam, *Usama bin Laden's al-Qa'ida: Preface of a Terrorist Network*, (Ardsley, NY: Transnational Publishers, Inc., 2001). The best account of 9/11 is Kean, Thomas, and Lee Hamilton. 9/11 Commission, "9/11 Commission Report." Last modified July 22, 2004. *http://www.911commission.gov/report/911Report.pdf*. In the post September 11 period a proliferation of studies were published. One of the major books is Peter Bergen, *The Longest War: America and Al-Qaeda Since 911*, (New York, NY: The Free Press, 2011). For more recent books, consult selected bibliography.
2. For a media report on Pearl Harbor, selected at random, see Kluckhohn, Frank. "Japan Wars on U.S. and Britain; Makes Sudden Attack On Hawaii; Heavy Fighting At Sea Reported." 1941. *http://www.nytimes.com/learning/general/onthisday/big/1207.html*.
3. See, Bush, George. "War on Terror". Joint Session of Congress. U.S. Congress. Washington, DC September 20, 2001.

INTRODUCTION

4. See, Richard Stewart, *US Army in Afghanistan: Operation Enduring Freedom*, (Washington, DC: Defense Department, Army, Center of Military History, 2004).
5. See, Williamson, Elizabeth and Peter Spiegel. *Wall Street Journal*, "Obama says Afghan War 'of Necessity.'" Last modified August 17, 2009. *http://online.wsj.com/article/ SB125054391631638123.html*. This "War of Necessity" has already cost the U.S. according to Defense Department reports, 1,727 Service members killed. A latest source for this statistic is *The New York Times*, "U.S. Military Deaths in Afghanistan." Modified August 17, 2011. *http://www.nytimes.com/2011/08/18/ us/18list.html*. For more recent article on Afghanistan, see *The Washington Post*, September 7, 2015.
6. *The New York Times*, "Iraq News- Breaking World Iraq News." Modified November 11, 2011. *http://topics.nytimes.com/top/ news/international/countriesandterritories/iraq/index.html*.
7. *Ibid*. 6.
8. Martinez, Michael. CNN, "U.S. pullout in Iraq raises concerns about Iran." Modified October, 2, 2011. *http:// articles.cnn.com/2011-10-21/middleeast/world_meast_iraq-iran-influence_1_iran-and-iraqiran-iraq-war-iraqi-militias?_s=PM:MIDDLEEAST*. For a report on Iraq's outlook see: Cigar, Norman. *Al-Qaida, The Tribes, and the Government: Lessons and Prospects for Iraq's Unstable Triangle*, Quantico, VA: Marine Corps University Press, 2011.
9. Yonah Alexander and Dean Alexander. *The Islamic State: Combating the Caliphate Without Borders*, (Lanham, MD: Lexington Books, 2015).
10. Perez, Chris. "ISIS threatens another 9/11-style attack on social media." *New York Post*, April 13, 2015. Accessed September 4, 2015. http://nypost.com/2015/04/13/isis-threatens-another-911-style-attack-on-social-media/
11. CNN, "Timeline: Osama bin Laden, Over the Years." May 2, 2011. *http://articles.cnn.com/2011-05-02/world/bin.laden. timeline_1_bin-laden-group-usama-bin-king-abdul-aziz-university?_s=PM:WORLD*.
12. *Ibid*. 11.
13. Mazzetti, Mark, Helene Cooper, and Peter Baker. *The New York Times*, "Clues Gradually Led to the Location of Osama bin

Laden." May 2, 2011. *http://www.nytimes.com/2011/05/03/world/ asia/03intel.html?_r=1&scp=54&sq=bin%20laden&st=cse.*
14. *Ibid.* 13.
15. BBC, "Timeline: The Intelligence Hunt Leading to Bin Laden." May 6, 2011. *http://www.bbc.co.uk/news/mobile/world-south-asia-13279283.*
16. *Ibid.* 13.
17. *Ibid.* 13.
18. Miller, Greg. *The Washington Post*, "CIA Spied on Bin Laden from Safe House." May 5, 2011. *http://www.washingtonpost. com/world/cia-spied-on-bin-laden-from-safe-house/2011/05/05/ AFXbG31F_story.html.*
19. Von Drehle, David. "Killing bin Laden: How the U.S. Finally Got its Man." *TIME Magazine*, May 20, 2011. *http://www.time. com/time/nation/article/0,8599,2069455,00.html.*
20. *Ibid.* 13.
21. *Ibid.* 15.
22. *Ibid.* 15.
23. *Ibid.* 15.
24. Drew, Christopher. *The New York Times*, "Attack on Bin Laden Used Stealthy Helicopter that had been a Secret." May 5, 2011. *http://www.nytimes.com/2011/05/06/world/asia/06helicopter. html?_r=1&scp=24&sq=bin%20laden&st=cse.*
25. Scherer, Michael. *TIME Magazine*, "Obama Pushed for 'Fight Your Way Out' Option in bin Laden Raid." May 3, 2011. *http:// swampland.time.com/2011/05/03/obama-pushed-for-fight-your-way-out-option-in-bin-laden-raid/.*
26. Dozier, Kimberly. Siasat.pk, "Abbotabad Mission Details Revealed by USA: Osama bin Laden's Guns Found 'only after' US Navy SEALs Killed him." May 18, 2011. *http://www.siasat. pk/forum/showthread.php?66234-Abbotabad-Mission-details-revealed-by-USA-Usama-bin-Laden-s-guns-found-only-after-US-Navy-Seals-killed-him.*
27. Harnden, Toby. *The Telegraph*, "Osama bin Laden Dead: Wife was Shot in the Leg not Killed." May 3, 2011. *http://www. telegraph.co.uk/news/worldnews/al-qaeda/8490814/Osama-bin-Laden-dead-wife-was-shot-in-the-leg-not-killed.html.*
28. MSNBC, "How the US Tracked Couriers to Elaborate bin Laden Compound." May 3, 2011. *http://www.msnbc.msn.com/*

id/42853221/ns/world_news-death_of_bin_laden/t/how-us-tracked-couriers-elaborate-bin-laden-compound/.
29. *Ibid.* 27.
30. Dwyer, Devin. ABC News, "Osama Bin Laden Killing: Pakistan Reacts Cautiously to U.S. Raid on its Soil." May 2, 2011. *http://abcnews.go.com/Politics/usama-bin-laden-killed-pakistan-reacts-cautiously-us/story?id=13507918#.TtekX7JFuso.*
31. Perlez, Jane and David Rhode. *The New York Times*, "Pakistan Pushes Back Against U.S. Criticism on Bin Laden." May 3, 2011. *http://www.nytimes.com/2011/05/04/world/asia/04pakistan.html?pagewanted=1&_r=1.*
32. *Ibid.* 31.
33. *Ibid.* 31.
34. *Ibid.* 31.
35. Seib, Philip, J.D. *Military Review*, "The Al-Qaeda Media Machine.".
36. Anti-Defamation League, "Jihad Online: Islamic Terrorists and the Internet." 2002. *http://www.adl.org/internet/jihad_online.pdf.*
37. Fattah, Hassan. *The New York Times*, "Al Qaeda Increasingly Reliant on Media." September 30, 2006. *http://www.nytimes.com/2006/09/30/world/30jordan.html?pagewanted=1.*
38. Hanser, Robert D. "Psychological Warfare and Terrorism." *https://kucampus.kaplan.edu/documentstore/docs09/pdf/picj/vol2/issue1/Psychological_Warfare_and_Terrorism.pdf.*
39. EJournal USA, Countering the Terrorist Mentality. Foreign Policy Agenda: U.S. State Department/Bureau of International Information Programs. May 2007 *http://www.au.af.mil/au/awc/awcgate/state/counter_terr_mentality_may07.pdf.*
40. *Ibid.* 38.

Part One: Letters Likely Written by Usama bin Laden

> **1. Call for Guidance and Reform, 13 April 1994**
>
> Bin Laden addresses his concerns about the actions of the King of Saudi Arabia, particularly his disregard for Saudi scholars and unjust treatment of the Saudi people. Bin Laden claims that the Kingdom is plagued by corruption, restriction of freedoms, and a disregard for the "true" Muslim people. This letter presents Bin Laden's call for internal reforms by the King including but not limited to an end to the unjust treatment of the citizens and scholars.
>
> From: Usama bin Laden
>
> http://www.dni.gov/files/documents/ubl/english/CALL%20FOR%20GUIDANCE%20AND%20REFORM%2013%20April%201994.pdf

Full Translation

Page 1

Guidance and Reform Council

Release number 2

SUBJECT: OUR CALL FOR GUIDANCE AND REFORM

We pay tribute to God, ask for His help, forgiveness, guidance, and may He protect us from our own sins and bad deeds. Whoever God guides none will mislead, there is none to guide the misleader, and I bear witness that there is no God but the one God and there is none who share his power, and I bear witness the Muhammad is the servant of God and his messenger.

We bless God Who in his book said, "You (true believers) are the best of people ever raised up for mankind, you enjoin all of what God ordained and forbid what is wrong, and you believe in God" (Qur'an 3:110).

Blessings and peace be upon God's messenger Muhammad who said, "The people who don't punish the tyrant, God may have him punish all of them" (Hadith as stated by Abu Dawud, Tarmadhi, and al- Nisa'i).

I extend my greetings and pray for the blessings of God to the king of Saudi 'Arabia Fahd Ibn 'Abd-al-'Aziz al-Sa'ud and to all the Muslim people of the Arabian Peninsula.

I address you, the king, and say that you have frequently addressed me and often insisted and repeatedly asked me to come back to Saudi Arabia, and you have tried your best and exerted all means and efforts for that to take place.

God is aware how much I want to be in my country, which is the only one I seek to be in, because in it the revelation took place and God's message was given, and it is the country where I was born and spent my childhood.

That said, the past events and the ensuing evidence convinced me to stay outside the country for the time being, and underlined the fact that there is something hidden behind your efforts.

I am not stating these words as a result of doubts and assuming the worst to take place, however what took place in the past, in forbidding me to give advice and to travel, which was followed two years ago by freezing my money, and by having me slandered in your media outlets inside and outside the country, and your trying to sever my relationship to the country and its people by confiscating and revoking my citizenship and ID documents, and by doing that without any misdeed or a crime that I committed. I declare that I rely on God, and that I left as a result of your efforts to deter me from carrying out my duty to give advice and state the facts, and all of this supports what I am trying to say.

I really don't give much attention to these facts because they are minor personal matters, and because our disagreement is not based on trivial personal matters and minor faults, but is based on the most important issues of the nation. Previously, in my first release, I promised to come back to this subject; to fulfill my promise I am issuing this release to reveal the truth and to fairly treat the people, "So that those who were to be destroyed (for their rejecting the faith) might be destroyed in the presence of clear evidence, and those who were to live (believers) might live in the presence of clear evidence" (Qur'an 8:42).

I will sum up what I am going to say without giving details. I will be short in my address until such time as I can give the details in presentations to follow, God willing. It will suffice in this address to hint at things without saying them, and I will do that to preserve the written words, (TN: avoid) the slip of the tongue, and I will limit my presentation to the following:

First: For a long time, our respected scholars and preachers have been advising and reminding you to adhere to kindness, leniency, wisdom, and they gave you good advice that calls for reform and repentance from committing grave sins and evil deeds, which include trespassing on the citizens' legitimate rights and from the precise religious guidelines.

I am sorry to say that all of what you did wasn't limited to renouncing them (scholars) and turning them away, but you made fun of them, ridiculed and discredited them, you followed the aforementioned transgressions with more severe and powerful forbidden actions which you enforced in the country of religion and monotheism. Keeping silent is no longer agreeable, and overlooking things is not acceptable.

PAGE 2

As a result of your transgression, overstepping the grave sins limits and revoking clear Islamic rules, a group of scholars who were fed up with what is taking place, and who suffered your acts of deception that deafened their ears. These acts of yours clouded their eyes, their smell of corruption inflicted their noses, clouded their eyesight, and they vowed to God to reject your actions. These people called for reform to correct and change the situation, and they were joined by hundreds of educated people, merchants and ex-officials who sent you petitions and memos requesting reform. When the Gulf war took place in the year 1411h (circa July 1990 to June 1991), about 400 of these people sent you a petition calling for reform and putting an end to your unjust dealing with the people. You have neglected their advice, made fun of the advisers, and the situation is getting worse.

The people who extended their advise continued, sending you new petitions and memos, most important of which is their memo sent in Muharram 1413h (circa July 1992) in which they diagnosed the ailment and prescribed the medicine, basing themselves on the Shari'ah. They also submitted a scholarly presentation covering the wide gap in the regime philosophy and the main defects in the governing structure, which covered the marginalization and neutralization that the Scholars and preachers suffer from, and are hunted for.

The memo also covered the rules and regulations that are enforced in the country and that legalize and forbid matters without basing such decisions on God's Shari'ah. It also touched on the country's media situation where it is becoming the means to canonize people and influential persons, falsify the truth, slander the true people, and shed crocodile tears to mislead the people without carrying any serious action. It also covered the squandered and confiscated legitimate rights of the people, and the failure and corruption of the country's administration.

The memo covered the financial and economic situation of the country, the horrible destiny that will be the outcome of the high interests that broke the back of the country, and squandering money to satisfy personal whims!!! As well as the taxes, fees, and excise duties imposed on the people!!! The memo also covered the lousy general services in the country that are becoming worse after sending the memo, and that include water services, which is one of the most important daily needs. All of these are forcing our brothers to live in a state of austerity, renounce worldly pleasures, and restrict their spending in fear of what is going to take place; May God help them.

The memo revealed the hopeless situation and covered what was prevalent during the Gulf crises; i.e. the small count (TN: of the fighting force), its lack of readiness, the failure of its General Command; all of which took place despite the astronomical amounts of money spent on it. As to justice and its courts, the memo revealed that man-made laws replaced Shari'ah laws. The memo also revealed that the country's foreign policy neglects the Muslims' issues, supports the enemies against the Muslims, an example of which is what recently took place in Gaza, Jericho, Algeria, etc. Everyone is aware that enforcing man-made laws, supporting the atheist over the Muslim is considered to be a part of the ten items that contradict Islam, as was deemed by the religion scholars to include Shaykh Muhammad Ibn 'Abd-al-Wahhab; may he rest in peace.

Despite the fact that the memo's composition was supple and kind, refers to the words of God, was amiable, contained true facts, and despite the fact that Islam gives importance to sharing advice with and extending advice to the rulers, and despite the position and the number of the memo's signees and supporters, it still didn't have the approval of its recipients who refused it, opposed it, and badmouthed and punished the people who signed and supported it.

PAGE 3

Despite all of what took place, the banner and the flags (TN: of Islam) didn't drop down, and will never drop down as long as there is an eye that blinks and a heart that beats. Instead, a new group of scholars and advisers formed a Human Rights Committee to support the truth and the oppressed. This committee was received in the same way and had the same fate as the other committees, and that took place with the blessings of the ruler's official organizations that were tasked by the regime to defend it instead of defending the religion. The committee's members were badmouthed, blamed for things they didn't do, and the true scholars who didn't accept to be blackmailed and exploited were ousted; and we don't recommend any to God.

Through an open conspiracy with other scholars, panels were formed to issue renouncing and rebuttal replies whose composition are similar to that of the security and media declarations, and aren't based on the mandated true Shari'ah words. As expected, these panels lost their status and duty after they were stripped of their independence and were annexed to the Royal Bureau that gives them their orders which they have to execute. The creation of these panels gave the people the justification to refrain from trusting them; instead they trust the scholars and preachers whose crises and problems that they passed through proved that they are worthy of the people's trust and support.

Second: What is taking place in the country, to include corruption, restricting the freedom of the people, waging a war on the true people and hunting them within and outside the country, we from our position outside the country, to fulfill our declaration and extend advice, declare that we will continue with the work of our scholars in the interior to extend advice, and enjoin what is right and forbid evil. We will do that because we are an indivisible part of the call for Islam, and are united with it in our aim and fate. On this occasion we declare that we are holding fast to the demands mentioned in the advice memo, we support the legitimate Human Rights Committee, and all other legitimate demands.

Due to the difficulty that we face in carrying out our work in the interior as a result of the existing state of intimidation and subjugation, we from our current position (TN: in the exterior), in consultation with some of our brothers in the Arabian Peninsula, have formed a committee to extend advise and to support the truth, which we named, "The Advice and Reform Committee".

In conclusion, we beseech God to have this nation follow the right path, to honor those who obey Him, degrade those who disobey Him, enjoin what is right and forbid what is wrong, have our best people rule us, dismiss our evil persons, and have us join forces in our devotion and devoutness, "Verily never will God change the condition of a people until they change it themselves" (Qur'an 13:11).

Our last words are, "Praise is to God the Lord of all".

Date: 2/11/1414h corresponding to 13 April 1994

Written on behalf of them (NFI) by,

Usama Bin Muhammad Bin Ladin

(End of translation)

PART ONE: LETTERS LIKELY WRITTEN BY USAMA BIN LADEN

> ## 2. Letter to Brother Ilyas
>
> This letter is contains a response to a previous correspondence indicating that the sender should refer the matter at hand to Shaykh Mahmud. It is indicated that the matters discusses relate to the media. The sender then requests to be kept informed of the receiver's actions taken and wishes him well in his task.
>
> Date: 7 August 2010
>
> From: Zamrai (UBL)
>
> http://www.dni.gov/files/documents/ubl/english2/Letter%20to%20Brother%20Ilyas%20al-.pdf

1 page translated where necessary from Arabic

Translation begins here:

In the name of God, Most Gracious, Most Merciful

Praise is God the Lord of all, and blessings and peace be upon His Messenger, His people, and His companions.

To brother Ilyas al-((Kashmiri))

I pray that peace and the blessings of God be yours,

I hope that you, your family, and all the brothers are well and enjoying good health when you receive my letter.

I received and read your letter, and re the advice requested on the media issues, I kindly ask you to refer this matter to Shaykh Mahmud. Also I note that we have important work that Shaykh Mahmud will inform you with its details, I hope that you will carry this work in the best way you can, and I will pray to God to grant you success.

I Hope that we will maintain our correspondence and that you will keep me informed with the steps that you have taken in executing the work given to you.

I end up with praying to God to grant you success, to safeguard you, to help you cooperate with you brothers in support of the religion, and praise is to God the Lord of all, and May peace and God's blessings be upon His messenger Muhammad, his people, and companions.

Best regards,

Your brother ((Zamrai))

Friday, 26 Sh'aban 1431-h (circa 7 August 2010)

(End of translation)

3. Letter to Shaykh Mahmud, 26 September 2010

Communications to the French people, tribes, and brothers in the Maghreb are discussed. Here, Zamray requests to negotiate with the French to release prisoners, and he inquires about Taliban prisoners. The anniversary of 9/11 is mentioned and there is a discussion on methods of secure communication. Zamray requests that no brothers hold interviews and that wills of the recently fallen brothers be brought to light. He requests funds, books, and family updates.

From: Zamray (UBL)

Letter to Shaykh Mahmud 26 September 2010

Page 1

In the name of Allah the most gracious and the most merciful.

Thanks be to God, the Lord of the Worlds, and peace and prayers be upon our prophet Muhammad, on his family and all of his companions

To the generous brother, Shaykh Mahmud, May God protect him.

Peace, mercy and the blessings of Allah be upon you

I hope this letter finds you, your family and all of the brothers' well and in good health

I received your generous letter and here are some of the responses to its content

-With respect to the letter of Brother Abi Mus'ab 'Abd Al- ((Wudud)), we were able with the grace of Allah to open it and read its content. I shall attach a letter next time, God willing. I also urge you to inform me as to whether the research was done on establishing a truce with the apostates to send it to the brothers in Algeria, or not. If that was established, please send me a copy of it. Otherwise, send me the section that was written

-I recommend instructing the brothers in Al-Sahab to focus on the translation of the jihadist literature into French and other languages of our brothers in Africa. This issue is extremely important, as Shaykh Bashir Al-((Madani)) had indicated in his report concerning the Islamic Maghreb which is attached. I recommend that you send a copy of it to Shaykh Abi Muhammad and a copy to the brothers in Al-Sahab after reviewing it. You will also send it to our brothers in the Islamic Maghreb to increase their focus in translating the jihadist literature into French and into local languages.

Page 2

Please send the names of the tribes that Shaykh Bashir Al-Madani had mentioned in his report and, in general, the tribes of the area (Islamic Maghreb); so long as the writing would be varied and clearly identifies the vowels from others.

-Attached is a statement for the French people – please provide it to al-Jazeera al-Arabiyah channel and the International al-Jazeera channel. Also attached is another copy of the statement in a special chip to the brothers in the media, as well as a taped section as an experiment to America's statement for your review and provision of your comments. Destroy it afterwards.

-Please send a letter to the brothers in the Islamic Maghreb urgently that includes an indication for them to negotiate with the French to release their prisoners in exchange of money. Otherwise, the negotiation with the French would be based on lifting their injustice from the nation, just like their interference in the Islamic Maghreb affairs. Amongst the most important demands would be their withdrawal from Afghanistan, although the beginning of the negotiation prior to signing the agreement would not make them commit to anything.

Part One: Letters Likely written by Usama bin Laden

I urge you to issue a circular to the brothers indicating that the negotiations with the Europeans would first include their withdrawal from Afghanistan and with the Americans to first relinquish the support to the Jews. The Jews' issue would not be added to the negotiations with the Europeans because it is a given. When the Americans are forced to relinquish the Jews, the Europeans would abandon them as well.

-With respect to the French journalists in the custody of the Taliban, it is necessary to confirm if they are spies. The idea is to tie their release with the egress of the French from Afghanistan. Should they not provide a timeline for their withdrawal, they would then be killed. If there is suspicion, negotiations would be established for a ransom.

-With respect to the work in America, Brother ((Tufan)) is not appropriate. However, with respect to our Brother ((Al-Basha)), my assessment is that the mission is above his capacity.

Page 3

-With respect to the book 'Pivotal Points' and what you had mentioned about its author, I would recommend that you propose to me a method to benefit from it without getting into recommending the author. In my letter to Brother Bashir, I had made reference to the writer and it would be best to delete this indication prior to sending the letter to Bashir – this is if the letter was not sent yet.

-With respect to Yemen, I shall provide you the opinions I had mentioned, in the next letter, God willing. **With respect to what Brother Tufan had written, I shall provide that to you as well.**

-A few days following the last commemoration of September eleventh's blessed attacks, a speech by Shaykh Abi Muhammad was issued. His dealing with al-Jazeera attracted attention and, other channels also broadcasted the news before it did. However, it broadcasted it during a news report where most of the Muslims worldwide were sleeping and made it the last section of the news. Then they placed the news in the news tape and it to remain for 24-hours. However, they deleted it from the news tape a few hours later without justification for the lack of interest to the speech. Please provide us with your expectations and your analysis of this issue. It would be best if you could query Ahmad ((Zaydan)) about it.

-Amongst the previously attached material you had provided me, there was an article attributed to our Brother Sayf Al-(('Adl)) entitled "Biography of the Slaughterer Leader Abi Mus'ab Al- Zarqawi". May God have mercy on him. After reviewing it, it became clear to me it was falsely attributed to our Brother Sayf Al-'Adl as it included an offense to our Brother Abi Mus'ab Al- Zarqawi, May God have mercy on him. Also, to our Brother Sayf and to the organization, in general. It included a strong motivation to the brothers in Iraq to erect a state which components for success had not been completed. It indicated that the author - not Sayf Al-'Adl mentioned in the article, that he had taken an authorization from me and from Shaykh Abi Muhammad to deal with the case of Abi Mus'ab, May God have mercy on him while at that time, the unity was not achieved between us and the Jama'at Al-Jihad. Therefore, any individual living with us at that time would say that he had taken authorization from me and from Shaykh Abi Hafs, May God have mercy on him, while the writer had not mentioned anything about Shaykh Abi Hafs, May God have mercy on him.

Page 4

Although there was no problem mentioned, and we did not give the authorization to anyone to resolve it. It also included a narration of unfounded stories, hence the need to analyze the critical points contained in that article and clarifies what the author had wanted to interpolate. I also urge you to deny its attribution to Sayf and remind them he is in jail, which prevents him from reviewing it and acquitting himself from it. Also, that there are individuals, as well as services belonging to countries in the area whose mission is to defame the Mujahidin and disfigure their picture. The denial would be that Sayf al-'Adl is innocent from what was said, without adding in the description of our brother.

In your previous letter, you had mentioned Sayf Al-'Adl with Shaykh ((Abi Al-Khayr)), and Shayk Abi Muhammad Al-((Zayat)) which led to the mention of this information. It is special and obvious because Shaykh Abu Al-Khayr and Shaykh Abu Muhammad are above our brother Abi Khalid Sayf al-'Adl; although I believe that he has efforts that would benefit the jihad and the Mujahidin. However, in the military work, that is without taking over the general command or the representation whether he is the first deputy or the second. I ask Allah the Almighty to release all of them.

-With respect to the communication over the internet, we have no objection in communication of general messages. However, even with what the brothers had mentioned regarding al-Asrar al- Mujahidin program, the secrecy of the external work does not allow its use. I recommend confirming with the interested brothers that the external work would only be through the trusted messengers.

-Attached is a letter to Sahib al-((Tib)) (Var: al-Tayib) – please review it and sent it. Also review his letter to us, to include a copy of his letter and my letter to Shaykh Abi Muhammad. You shall receive a letter to Shaykh Abi Muhammad in my next letter.

-Attached is a letter to Brother Bashir Al-Madani – please deliver it to him. If he traveled, then the delivery should be through the regular route and through a credible messenger.

Page 5

- Please task the necessary resources to gather information on the two journalists from Denmark working with the newspaper that insulted the Prophet and who were expelled from Pakistan, but were later returned under foreign pressure.

- Please provide me with the information that I asked for on the brothers in Iraq. Did you send them the general policy? What happened with the responses of the brothers that you sent to them?

-Ask the brothers in the regions to not hold any interviews with jihadi media for the reasons that I mentioned before, including the lack of professional standards that people in this profession have established, and not having enough credibility, and the brother who conducts the interview does not have the qualifications to run it and choose the appropriate questions. You must have noticed that the latest tapes by Abu-Dajanah al-Khurasani (may God rest his soul and accept him among His martyrs) show the difference between the statement that he made on his own and in the interview. The questions that were presented to him were not appropriate for a man who wanted to sacrifice his life within days or hours.

-Please send me the living wills of the 19 brothers that are with the media.

-Regarding storing the wheat, I suggest that you dedicate two brothers from those areas who are qualified, have business sense, and have experience in trade. You should ask them to add wheat, sugar, and grain to the things that they deal with. They should have a good warehouse that water cannot get into and should be above the flood line. You should have them store the amount that you need. Keep in mind that a reserved amount should be sufficient for at least a year. They should sell it and replace it and this way it stays fresh.

Page 6

You should agree with them that they will stop selling the stored amount as soon as a crisis hits. They will benefit from this deal and we do not expect them to allow us to use their warehouses without benefits to them.

The warehouse should be located in an area that would be accessible to the brothers when necessary.

The other method that I mentioned, but is difficult to utilize if you are moving a lot, is to buy clean barrels that were used for food and drinks, not for chemicals, and they should be sealable. You should wash them and dry them in the sun for a day. These barrels have a rubber top to make it airtight and make it possible to store fresh grain for seven years without allowing bugs to get to it.

Part One: Letters Likely written by Usama bin Laden

-Regarding the intermediary brother, you can contact him directly on issues related to letters and money. Also, I sent his money to him.

-Please update me on the program that will be done by Ahmad Zidan on the tenth anniversary.

-Regarding the escort, I prefer to have a Pashtun, but our security situation does not allow us to use an immigrant.

As for his isolation from his area, I prefer that he isolates himself from his area. We should arrange for a business cover for him. It would be best if he is married and does not have kids or infants.

Page 7

-We sent a letter to the brothers at the front, but I did not receive a confirmation from you that they received it. The same applies to the letter for brother Abu-Anas al-Subay'i and the letter for the children of Shaykh Sa'id (may God rest his soul).

-Also, I did not receive a confirmation from you on receiving the statement on the flood. Please give me the reasons that prevented it from being broadcast through the media. After a while, please delete it and replace it with the second statement. If you cannot publish it within the next two weeks, then do not publish it, because it needs to be updated. Please let me know what is causing the delay and the reason that the intermediary is late and did not make it on the date that we agreed upon, the 27th of August. Also, please make sure that you confirm with the intermediary to receive a letter from us of 15 October. This letter will include a message to the American people before the midterm congressional election at the beginning of November. In the previous letter, I told you the 20th, but I am afraid of delay as was the case last time. Please make sure that the intermediary is on time this time.

-Please send us any books available to you on strategies. Keep in mind that there are many of them on the internet.

-Regarding my wife who is coming from Iran, keep her in a safe location until we conduct further communications and consultation on the issue of sending Hamzah to Qatar or keeping him there. We should also make sure of the security situation before his mother comes to us.

-Regarding sending the money to me, please send me a complete statement on my fund. Also, please send me 30,000 euro from my personal fund. If there is not enough money in my personal fund, please take money, as a loan, from the general account. Please keep some money in my personal fund for my wife and children to use once they arrive from Iran.

Page 8

Please delete the older letters to them, and attached are new letters for them. Also, ask brother 'Abd-al-Latif to bring us letters from them.

-Attached is a letter from my son Khalid to the media.

Finally: I pray to God almighty to protect you and grant you success in all that pleases Him. Praise be to God, and prayers and peace be upon prophet Muhammad, his family and companions.

God's peace, mercy and blessings be upon you

Your brother, Zamray
Al-Sabbat, 17 Shawal 1431
(TN: Saturday, 26 September 2010)

PART ONE: LETTERS LIKELY WRITTEN BY USAMA BIN LADEN

> ### 4. Letter to Shaykh Mahmud and Shaykh Abu Yahya
>
> Zamrai writes about a current disagreement between members and calls for it to be settled in a friendly and calm manner. Issues with brothers in the Islamic Maghreb are being resolved as well.
>
> Date: 4 December 2010
>
> From: Zamrai (UBL)
>
> http://www.dni.gov/files/documents/ubl/english/Letter%20to%20Shaykh%20Mahmud%20and%20Shaykh%20Abu%20Yahya.pdf

In the name of Allah, the most gracious, the most merciful

All thanks to Allah, the lord of both worlds, and may prayers and peace be upon our prophet, Muhammad and, upon his companions, Furthermore...

To both of my dear brothers/ Shaykh Mahmud and Shaykh ((Abu Yahya)), may Allah bless them.

May Allah's peace, mercy, and blessing be upon you.

I hope you receive my message while both of you, your families and children, and all the brothers are in good health, furthermore...

I received the letter for the brothers in the Islamic Maghreb by Shaykh Abu Yahya, dated 28 Rabi' al-Awwal 1431 (TN: 14 March 2010), and I read it. The letter contains great benefit, but I have one remark about one statement, and this does not mean that preaching and harshness should be applied when it comes to answers, guidance, and recollection. I had hoped you would have completed this statement,

"Take notice that the more common of the harsh terms that we received from our virtuous forefathers (may Allah bless them) took place during an era when the nation was taking off and the Muslims were strong."

I also consider that whoever wrote this letter and since this is his jurisprudence and way of thinking, after more research and reflection, he will find that what was stated in the second letter, dated 28 Shawwal 1431 (TN: 07 October 2010), when talking about the method of making decisions with regard to jurisprudence issues and reference to certain situations that opinion taking will take place via the majority and will realize that what was stated in the first letter was accurate. This is just like stating what the scholar Ibn Abu Al 'Izz Al-Hanafi (May Allah bless him): [Scripts and texts of the book and Sunnah and the ancestors of the nation agreed that a ruler, an Imam of prayers, an emir of war, and a person who performs charity is obligated to be obeyed when it come to jurisprudence issues. He (TN: the ruler) does not have to obey his followers' sources. Indeed, they have to obey him when it comes to these matters and abandon their own opinion for his opinion. The interest of a group and harmony and the corruptions and disagreement within a unity is considered greater than these partial issues. Therefore, it is not allowed for rulers to undermine the rule of other rulers. And what is considered correct is praying behind each other. Abu Yusuf narrated that when he went for the pilgrimage with Harun Al Rashid. When the ruler was undermined, when Malik told him (Abu Yusuf) that the ruler did not perform ablution and people prayed behind him, Abu Yusuf was asked, "Did you pray behind the Khalifah?" He (Yusuf) said, "Praise Allah, he is the emir of believers. Insinuating that not performing prayers behind people who are in charge is an invented heresy."]

This is an important and dangerous matter, and this is a substantial matter. If disagreement is not resolved via friendly and calm reflection, it will be just like what happened with our brothers in the Islamic Maghreb. If you perform a close examination of a few statements in both letters and others, it will become clear, Allah willing.

Therefore, I ask you to perform more research on the matter, and due to shortness in time, I will give a decision in the upcoming letter, which will be sent with a facilitator who is going to bring Hamza and his mother.

Finally, I ask Allah the mighty to grant us success...and all thanks to Allah, Lord of both worlds...and may peace and prayers be upon his prophet, Muhammad, and his companions...

And may Allah peace, mercy, and blessing be upon you... Your brother,

Zamrai

Friday, 27 Dhu I-Hijja 1431 (TN: 04 December 2010)

5. Letter from UBL to Atiyah

Bin Laden elaborates on the revolutions taking place in Egypt, Yemen, Libya, and Oman, as well as the responses of America and other Middle Eastern countries. Bin Laden calls for the Mujahidin to support the revolutions, after which the Caliphate has the potential to be restored.

Date: Unknown

From: Usama bin Laden

http://www.dni.gov/files/documents/ubl/english/Letter%20from%20UBL%20to%20Atiyah.pdf

UBL to Atiyah identified in a folder titled "to send"

4 pages translated where necessary (extended summary) from Arabic

During and Post Arab Revolutions Actions
Translation begins here:

Pages 1 and 2

To Shaykh ((Mahmud)),

I am sure that you are following up on the news media on the events taking place; the downfall of the Tunisian tyrant, the revolutions taking place in Egypt, Yemen, Libya, Oman, and the protest marches in Algeria, Morocco, Jordan, and Lebanon.

These are gigantic events that will eventually engulf most of the Muslim world, will free the Muslim land from American hegemony, and is troubling America whose Secretary of State declared that they are worried about the armed Muslims controlling the Muslim region. We also note that Egypt is the most important country, and the fall of its regime will lead into the fall of the rest of the region's tyrants, and the existing international situation doesn't allow the West to support

((Mubarak)) and the West's position towards the Libyan revolution is a weak one. All of this indicates that the Western countries are weak and their international role is regressing.

What is taking place today is critical to our nation, whose religion for centuries has been attacked. Circa two decades ago, the events to correct the situation in Syria, Algeria, Egypt and Yemen failed; and we have to exert all efforts to safeguard the Muslim's actions in the bigger revolutions that are taking place today, and have the countries abide by the Shari'a laws. Up till the moment, there isn't anyone who is performing the important duty of guiding the nation to adhere to the Shari'a laws, and in previous speeches I have suggested that the true Muslims form a Shura (TN: Consultation) Council to follow up on the nation's issues and to extend their advice to them. Time is passing, nothing was done, and it is for the Mujahidin to carry this duty to liberate the nation and restore the glory of its religion.

Though the Mujahidin have several duties to perform, their main duty now is to support the revolutions taking place. Although carrying Jihad in Afghanistan until we impose the laws of God in that country is an important duty that we are carrying out and are able to bleed the main infidel (TN: America), yet our main duty now is to liberate the billion and a half people and have them get hold of their holy places. Our Jihad in Afghanistan encouraged the nation to rise to get rid of the pressure imposed by the agents of America; the country that believes it is the great power that can wipe out or elevate whomever it wants. The nation members acted and carried their popular uprisings, and most of these uprisings love Islam. We in Afghanistan aren't encountering a popular uprising but are encountering the widespread strong actions of a Jihadist Movement.

Pages 3 and 4

History taught us that the people in revolt will change the existing situation, and we at the moment should exert our efforts to guide them and to prevent their being represented by the half-solution people such as (TN: the Muslim) Brotherhood, and we hope that the next stage will be the reinstating of the rule of the Caliphate. As to the Muslim Brotherhood, we note that the young generation's adhering to true Islam is a matter of time, as can be noticed by the Internet reply of

Shaykh ((Abu Muhammad)) who is a Brotherhood member, in which he said that within the Muslim Brotherhood there are factions who now adhere to true Islam, and there is also a powerful Salafist faction within the Brotherhood.

Based on the above, it isn't a good thing for us to remain fully occupied with the Afghanistan front, and we should work first on liberating the nation. We got what we wanted from the Afghanistan front by shattering the prestige of the world's main infidel, and though we will continue our Jihad there, yet we should give our main attention to the Muslim nation's revolution that should be illuminated with the monotheism dogma in order to reinstate the rule of the Caliphate.

We should increase our directed media efforts that call for a specific plan that we consult, agree upon and adhere to. I belief that our actions for the forthcoming stage of events should be:
1: Support the people and encourage their rebellion against the rulers.

2: The post-rulers' eviction stage is to be an education stage and the correction-of-notions stage.

We should guide the nation by mobilizing our literate writers, poets, and technicians to advise and guide the nation's men, and we should leave the work in Afghanistan to the administrative and field men.

Upon your receipt of my letter, your administrative work in Waziristan will end, and you are to appoint the person (NFI) to succeed you. You will quickly make arrangements for your safe travel from your area to Peshawar and its suburbs till such time we arrange for you a quiet house in the area that we are in, in which you can contemplate, produce, carry out the above- mentioned task, follow up on the media work, and communicate with us to exchange and revise our ideas to be addressed to the nation, and to verbally discuss the monumental event that is taking place.

Before I end, I note that my words on this matter might be different from my words on other subject covered in our previous correspondence, because we have to really mobilize now due the great event taking place.

(End of translation)

PART ONE: LETTERS LIKELY WRITTEN BY USAMA BIN LADEN

> ## 6. Letter to Shaykh Abu Yahya 2
>
> The short letter mentions those who were recently martyred.
>
> Date: Unknown
>
> From: Zimray (UBL)
>
> http://www.dni.gov/files/documents/ubl/english2/Letter%20to%20Shaykh%20Abu%20Yahya%202.pdf

In the name of Good the most merciful

Praise be to God and prayers and peace be upon Prophet Muhammad, his family and companions

To the honorable brother, Shaykh Abu-Yahya, May God protect him,

I hope that you receive this letter while you and all the brothers are well, in good health, and closer to God.

I received your letter and I read it and I was very pleased with the advice in it. May God reward you for it.

I comfort myself and comfort you for our brothers who were killed on this great path. May God consider them martyrs as we do. These brothers are Shaykh Abu-al-Layth, Shaykh Ibn-al- Shaykh, Shaykh 'Abdallah Sa'id, Shaykh Abu-Mansur al-Shami, Shaykh Abu-Salih al-Sumali and whoever was with them. I pray to God to accept them, let them reside in His paradise, comfort us for our loss, and reward us.

Regarding what was mentioned in your letter, I promise to send you a letter that contains the speech that you mentioned, God willing.

I pray to God to grant us success in what pleases Him, steadfastness on this path until we meet him, and victory over the infidels. Praise be to God.

Your Brother,
Zimray

7. Letter to Uthman

> The author focuses on al Qa'ida's main objective in the war against America: to stop America from achieving its objectives, spreading evil, and preventing Muslims from creating an Islamic state. The necessity of fighting Americans is underlined as a religious duty. The author, who remains unnamed, believes that this mission can be achieved by pressuring American policymakers through operations that target American oil interests abroad as well as by leading a media campaign that suggests these operations are the result of a lack of security in the Middle East, Afghanistan and Somalia.
>
> Date: Unknown
>
> From: Unknown (possibly UBL)
>
> http://www.dni.gov/files/documents/ubl/english/Letter%20to%20Uthman.pdf

(Fully translated)

Page 1 of 10

In the name of God, The Most Merciful, The Most Compassionate.

Thanks be to God, and peace and prayers on our Prophet Muhammad, his kinsmen, and followers.

To my dear brother 'Uthman, may God protect you.

I hope my letter finds you, your family, and all the brothers in good health and may you be more pious and closer to God.

I start my letter by stressing that it is imperative that our main objective in our war with America has to be clear.

What do we want?

Our objective is: What was summarized in the chapter after the 11th [September].

America has to stop its evil, such as its support to the Jews, and leave the Muslims alone so they (the Muslims) can establish an Islamic state where Islam will prevail. You all know that fighting for Muslims has many goals. The greatest one is to ensure that God's faith prevails. God Almighty says, "And fight them until there is no more tumult or oppression, and there prevails justice and faith in Allah altogether and everywhere; But if they cease, verily Allah Doth see all that they do." (Surat al-Anfal, Verse 39) One of the goals is for the infidels to stop their aggression against Islam and its adherents. God Almighty says, "Fight ye the chiefs of unfaith for their oaths are nothing to them: That thus they may be restrained." (Surat al-Tawbah, Verse 12)

We want to fight to force the enemy to stop its aggression against us, which can happen, God willing, by fighting the United States, the leader of infidels. It is a known fact that the American people, who are represented by the Congress and the White House, are the holders of the supreme power in the US and they are the ultimate decision makers. Thus, we have to focus on killing and fighting the American people.

Page 2 of 10

Fighting Americans and their allies in Afghanistan is an obligation and a compulsory religious duty to defeat them and eject them, God willing. This will require a great deal of time and effort. It is within our right to stop this war [against us] from its main source, which is the American people, who are the power that can stop it as soon as possible. Therefore, we have to put the administration of the White House and the Congress - where the command post for the operations against us is located - under direct pressure by using the equation of fear. That can only happen by directly affecting the American people through conducting operations inside America and affecting the American economy by targeting oil abroad, particularly in the countries that export oil to the US. Consequently, the American citizen will certainly feel the impact in his oil bill.

This needs to be accompanied by a large media campaign, part of which we could air in the US media, if possible, indicating that these operations are the result of the lack of security in our land, particularly in Palestine, Iraq, Afghanistan, Pakistan, and Somalia, and that is what was summarized in the chapter after the September 11 attacks. America will not dream of security until security becomes a reality in Palestine.

You are all aware of one of the most important matters when there is a conflict between two sides: Each side needs to be informed about its enemy's culture, history, his way of thinking, his strengths, and his weakest points. This will help in making the best decisions, with God's help.

By following the development of the struggle between us and the statements made by the American politicians, as well as studying the reality of the war between us and examining [the Americans'] previous wars, it became clear to us that attacking the US from within is of extreme importance. It is the number one objective and the main way to lead us to what we want. The impact of attacking the US - from the inside - against the Americans cannot be compared with attacking the US from the outside, besides attacking [the Americans'] allies and agents.

If we reflect on the history of the US, it has fought about 60 wars. The common denominator of most of those wars was that they did not end with the use of the military from outside but ended when public dissatisfaction increased and because of internal opposition. For example, in their Vietnam War, 57,000 soldiers were killed. The war did not end because of losing this large number of soldiers but because they were forced to withdraw when their President Nixon made a mistake by ordering a military draft to continue fighting the war, which impacted every American person. As a result, the people revolted in large anti- war protests, and they withdrew. As you are aware, their current policy to deal with their shortage of soldiers is [by offering] large monetary incentives so as to avoid the mistake made by Nixon.

Page 3 of 10

In summary, our war with the US will not end by fighting its allies. Even fighting the Americans themselves outside America may or may not end it. It all depends on their financial ability to bear the costs of the war.

The population of the US is 300 million. One thousand soldiers were killed in Afghanistan and 4000 in Iraq. This means that only a small number of them were impacted, which is not enough to make [the American people] revolt and force the politicians to stop the war.

Statistics show that the percentage of thieves and criminals in American prisons is seven per thousand. This is the highest percentage in the world, a fact that [the American] people are living with, even though it is putting lots of pressure on its security nerves.

You all know that the number of people who die in the US as a result of civilian behaviors is very high. For example, the number of people who die from smoking is 400,000, which is a large number compared with the number of people killed in the war in Iraq and Afghanistan. However, [the American people] did not come out in large demonstrations calling for shutting down the tobacco companies.

Using a very simple calculation, if we divide the number of the Americans killed in Afghanistan, which is about 1000, by 300 million, assuming that each soldier has a set of two parents still alive and a sister or a brother, the percentage of the American people killed in their war in Afghanistan is 3.3 per million. However, to reach the proportion of Americans killed in Vietnam, we need more than a 100 times that in Afghanistan. Yet, the war did not end because of the large number [of casualties]. The population of the US then was 150 million.

Page 4 of 10

It is becoming more obvious that the small percentages of the nations' disasters, which are numerous, do not usually impact peoples' causes, their anger, and their revolt. They usually learn to deal with them. If we are relying on the number of enemy deaths, then the road ahead of us to win the battle in Afghanistan is very long.

The number of unemployed in the US has increased since September 11 and after the wars in Iraq and Afghanistan and reached ten percent of the work force. This is a very large number when compared with the number of people killed in Afghanistan, which is one percent of 1000. These unemployed people know that the reason for their unemployment has to do, in part, with the large spending to support the two wars in Iraq and Afghanistan, and in part, to do with greed and financial and administrative corruption in New York and Washington. This large number of people has not been able to stop the source of the damage afflicted on them, but rather they contributed with others to topple the Republican administration that caused them this damage, and they voted for the Democrats in Congress and the presidency, which did not change much.

If the ten million unemployed were not able to end what caused the damage afflicted upon them in a radical way, 3000 Americans who are the fathers, mothers, and brothers of the 1000 people killed in Afghanistan will not be able to end the war.

Consequently, this highlights the importance of external work, particularly inside America, to put pressure on 300 million Americans, so that all the American people react to stop the unjust war that has put pressure on Muslims, particularly in Palestine, Iraq, Afghanistan, and Pakistan. To support my point, the impact of the fear that hit them after Omar Farouk (Var.: 'Umar al-Faruq [sic], may God grant him release, even if the airplane did not explode, made them incur direct and indirect expenses, about 40 billion dollars, which is double what the [US] administration has spent on the war each year for the last eight years.

Nations and people can deal with disasters in the percentage of three per thousand, and just imagine how much more 3.3 per one million is. Of course, they will deal with it for long decades.

Page 5 of 10

There is another factor that is part of the equation in their war in Iraq and Afghanistan, which is of greater dimension for the people: Their economic conditions are bad. If this were not the case, they would continue their war for decades without the American people feeling the impact of these grueling wars that are taking place away from its land.

I have previously mentioned that there are 10 million unemployed people as a result of the deterioration of economic conditions; however, their attempts were not sufficient to end the issues (TN: meaning the war against Muslims).

If we find out our enemy's weakest point, as long as we want to achieve our main objective, we have to conduct our operations inside the US. Dealing with this enemy requires that you attack its security, and particularly, its economy.

One large operation inside the US will affect the security and the nerves of 300 million Americans, while killing 1000 Americans in eight years has very little impact on their nerves. Thus, our main war should be directed to put pressure on the American people inside the US by attacking oil from outside the US, which will be followed by gathering the best capabilities for this great work.

If we have sufficient human and financial capabilities to carry out the previous plan, and we have some left, there is no harm in attacking the Americans from outside.

It is known that the Organization will have a large number of mujahidin to work against the US at the open fronts.[This is] due to the very particular qualifications required for those working in the external operations division. Those whose security conditions do not allow them to travel through airports are qualified to work in the external operations division, and they can be in charge of planning or training the brothers who will work in this division (the external operations division).

(TN: Begin bold font) **As previously mentioned, it seems to me that the operations inside the US are the most important works of the [al-Qa'ida] Organization, as long as they are possible, because they impact the security and the economy of the American people as a whole.** (TN: End bold font)

The fight of the Islamic world against the US is like a big dam. In front of the dam are several clay villages on both sides of the river. Some of the tyrants went to the dam and opened some of its gates that should not have been opened and the dam's water flooded the villages. As a result, people were hurt and terrified, and some of the brave men hurried to save the elderly, women, and children, working hard and putting their lives in danger to save them.

Page 6 of 10

But what they needed was a crucial and important idea that requires less effort than what they exerted to take away their significant suffering and save their energy. They needed to send some of their knights to those who opened the dam and caused all kinds of suffering, to punish them, and to drive them away from the dam, and then to close the gates to put an end to the great suffering of the people.

This is our situation. Our first priorities should be to conduct operations that will impact the largest number of the American people. It is the people's anger against the decision makers in the White House, the Congress, and the Pentagon that will shut the doors of the dam, God willing.

As a result, we will have saved the time and the effort of the 'Ummah (TN: Muslim community) so that we achieve the objective, which is to stop the US from supporting Israel, and it will withdraw its army from the Muslim land and leave the Muslims alone to deal with their enemies.

-- Security should be provided to the brother in charge of external operations, and that should be done in two phases:

First: Select an appropriate and safe place in Pakistan for him. He needs to give a training course to prepare the leaders and the trainers for external operations. I think that the number of the trainees in the first class should not exceed ten brothers.

Second: Carefully select the trainees for this round. They have to be qualified to become leaders in external operations and trainers for the rest of the members. The most important qualifications they should have:

-- A person has to be pious and patient. During training in training camps, any person we notice who displays boredom, does not finish the tasks assigned to him, and gets mad quickly, we have to remove from the external work, which requires precision and patience. In Kenya, the brothers stayed f inside the house or nine months. In such an abnormal environment, arguments between the group of people sent to the land of the enemy to carry out the mission may have detrimental results. One of the brothers may lose his composure and disobey the emir. This is from experience and not just a possibility.

Page 7 of 10

-- They need to apply proficiency at all times, as the Prophet says, "Allah loves when one of you engages in any work, he should carry it out with proficiency." There are many sad events and stories caused mainly by negligence and lack of proficiency.

-- They need to have a strong conviction about the importance of external work, and that it is the main avenue to weaken the US so that it will relinquish Israel and stop its wars against Muslims and leave them alone, God willing.

-- Intelligence, astuteness, acuteness, and possession of knowledge.

-- The capability of taking the training for the length of the period that is agreed upon. The training will be taken in the house that will be arranged for them to stay in, and , for everyone's safety, they will not leave it until they complete the training. To guarantee this, they need to make a pledge before entering the house and registering for the training.

I think Shaykh Mahmud should be with them in this training to enrich the lectures with discussions and educated conversation. After completing the external operations course, Shaykh Mahmud can give the qualified brothers the leadership training. I think of Shaykh Younis (Var.: Yunis) as a very distinguished person who we need to pay attention to and provide him with the opportunity to work with Shaykh Mahmud in the training to prepare leaders.

Suggestions:

After completing the two training sessions, I see Shaykh Younis moving with some brothers out of Afghanistan and Pakistan, and they can start their work from there, on the condition that Shaykh Mahmud is in charge of facilitating the external work before you.

Important remark: You are aware of the importance of secrecy in [our] work. I tried so hard to comply with secrecy to the point that I avoided learning about the plans of the external work. But when the external work was delayed, I found myself forced to contribute to the matter. The secrecy of the [external work] needs to be protected, and only those in the external operations division with the need to know should know about it. Work is directed from me to Shaykh Mahmud to Shaykh Younis, who is charge of the external operations in Africa, except from the Islamic Maghreb from Libya to Mauritania, since it is under the emirate of brother Abu Mus'ab 'Abd-al-Wudud, and the horn of Africa is under the emirate of the al-Shabaab al-Mujahidin Movement.

Page 8 of 10

-- It is necessary that we have a development and planning department.

This is even if the prevalent idea in our nation is that development happens as life goes on. Mistakes are made and we learn from them and evolve. This often takes long years. However, establishing a development center will save us decades. A person may think at first that he does not have the ability to develop, but work will develop with time in the manner I previously mentioned.

Even though it will be cost us an enormous amount of money to exclusively dedicate ourselves capabilities to think of ways to develop any specific field, God willing, instead of continuing in our traditional ways, it is one of the most important matters as it is the first step in this field. The researchers in the development center, God willing, will present us with research and studies that will contain very crucial ideas that will save us lots of effort, time, energy, and money. The development center will have to develop itself using whatever is available, particularly to increase reading and studying in general, and studying the fields we need in particular. I think the person in charge of this [development] center should be one of the brothers who likes this kind of work and has the ability to do it, particularly a passion for reading and deducing the benefits.

Attention needs to be paid to our Western brothers in this [development] center and in the external operation center. Our brother Abu Talha al-Almani (TN: Abu Talha, the German) should be in this [development] center as an instructor and trainer. He will be useful providing you with ideas on working inside the US. We should also take advantage of our brother 'Azzam al- Amriki (TN: 'Azzam, the American) who can look for research on the Internet that was published by Western centers, Americans in particular, and translate what the brothers would find of use in this field. He ('Azzam) can also write his views on working inside the US, and it will be beneficial if he provides a training class to teach English to the members of the center.

The supervisors in the center can refer back to Shaykh Mahmud, with a caveat that all the members of the center have to be in a safe place, away from the battlefield.

-- What will be useful is to determine the specialties that we need, prioritize them, and then assign some young people to exclusively study and become proficient in those sciences and specialties, such as computer engineering and chemistry, of which manufacturing explosives is one topic and which is something we have a dire need for.

Page 9 of 10

We will send some of the brothers who are bright - and it is not known that they have joined the ranks of the mujahidin - to study t universities and task them to take classes in the fields that we need to develop. The situation of the brothers, security-wise, will be comfortable, and they can access any Websites as they wish and buy books and products without raising any questions.

One of the specialties we need that we should not overlook is the science of administration. It is an independent science and a very important one where there is an abundance of expertise. Also, we should not overlook strategic politics [TN: political science]. We need a brother or two in these specialties. This is inexpensive and we will benefit greatly from it in many fields, as it will provide us with a sound opinion during the events that our 'Ummah will be going through.

(TN: Begin underline) What you have in your hands is a living experience that bore fruit and which is the realization of the brothers, during the time of Shaykh 'Abdallah 'Azzam, may he rest in peace, that the mujahidin needed to have scholars with them. So we made several attempts to have shaykhs [TN: Islamic scholars] and scholars with us at the fronts so they can educate the youth, but nobody came to stay with us permanently ... sending some young people to study Shari'a and then they return to us. (TN: End underline)

-- We have to prepare ourselves that after sending some of the brothers, we may only get 40 percent back due to factors such as the family burden (TN: starting a family and having children) and the psychological factors that follow.

We should not forget the geographic and time differences. They are two dangerous factors for the individual since we do not see him (TN: the operative) and we are not in contact with him, which may cause him to forget some of the things we agreed upon, start to lose interest, and gradually change the path he is on.

-- Attached are Basir and Abu Hurayra's letters, which I previously requested from you.

-- Attached is a letter to Shaykh Abu Muhammad. Please send it to him when you can. If you haven't already sent him the previous letter, please do not send it and send him this one instead.

Page 10 of 10

-- Please advise whether my son Khalid's letter to Khamenei was published or not. Also please send me the reactions to the letter if it was published.

(TN: Begin green highlight) That was corroborated by the number of NATO troops, under the leadership of the US to fight al-Qa'ida in Afghanistan, which exceeds 100,000. Obama decided to add 30,000 troops after the Americans spied on al-Qa'ida in Pakistan and Afghanistan and mentioned that al-Qa'ida's permanent members are about 100. Many people found it strange to send more than 100,000 soldiers to fight 100 people. What they do not know is that the 100 people that the US is fighting are determined to attack the US in its homeland, which is where the danger they face hides. Bush stated during his presidency that we will fight them over there so that we don't fight them over here. So we have to pay attention to that.

A few days ago, the US Secretary of State made a statement indicating that the biggest danger that America faces is not Iran or Korea, it is al-Qa'ida. The secret does not lie in al-Qa'ida threatening US interests abroad, as Iran does, for example, by expanding in the region particularly in Iraq and Lebanon and competing against the American dominance, but it lies in al-Qa'ida's determination to attack the US in its homeland. (TN: End green highlight)

8. Undated Letter 3

Family updates, security details/movement, document compilations, and health issues are discussed. There seems to be a preparation for a move, and as well as the 10th anniversary of 9/11.

Date: Unknown

From: Unknown (possibly UBL)

http://www.dni.gov/files/documents/ubl/english/Undated%20Letter%203.pdf

Page 1

In the name of God, The Most Merciful, The Most Compassionate.

Thanks be to God, The Lord of the universe, and peace and prayers be upon our Prophet Muhammad, his family and all his followers.

Peace and God's blessings be upon you.

First, it comforts me to hear your news, which I have waited for so long and longed for in years passed, especially after I received the great news of your departure from Iran, thanks be to God. I hope that my letter finds you well and in good health, God willing.

I also would like you to inform me of the news of the dear son Hamza and his brothers who are in Iran and Syria, as well as the news of Wafa' and Sa'd's children, may God have mercy on his soul and may He accept him among the martyrs and elevate his stature and may He have him in the company of the prophets, the lovers of truth, the martyrs and the righteous people. We also pray that God reward us for his loss and grant us a successor.

As far as I am concerned, God Almighty has been very generous to me, thank God. However, I have been living for years in the company of some of the brothers from the area and they are getting exhausted — security wise — from me staying with them and what results from that. Consequently, it is hard for them to do some of the things I ask them to. One of the hardest things is to ask them to bring one of my family members. However, because of the importance of your coming, how long I have waited for your departure from Iran, and the years that you spent there patiently (may God add them to your good deeds), I have used all my energy and I have tried so hard, as God is my witness, to convince them to agree. But sadly, I came to realize that they have reached a level of exhaustion that they are shutting down, and they asked to leave us all. They mentioned that our number is large and beyond what they can handle, so we started telling them that you will come alone and they will not feel any new burden. They did not care - that's how much they are in a state of shut down. So I suggested having Khalid leave and having you come instead, so that our number remains the same, and they refused. Then we suggested having you come for a visit for a limited time and then having you return to Hamza while we work on your permanent return, and they refused that also and stated that they can't and that it is beyond their ability. As a result of what I mentioned above, I think that I have to leave them, but it will take few months to arrange another place where you,

Page 2

Hamza, and his wife can join us. I ask for your forgiveness and I hope you will understand the situation and pray that God makes it easy to reunite, God willing. Trust me; I am determined to take advantage of any opportunity, God willing.

I also would like to share with you some of my positions. We are awaiting the tenth anniversary of the blessed attacks on New York and Washington which will be in nine months. You are well aware of its importance and the importance of taking advantage of the anniversary in the media to embody the victories of Muslims and communicate what we want to communicate to people. I have been in correspondence with the brothers to provide Al-Jazeera with several statements when the channel starts covering the attacks on the first of September. So I sent you all the statements and ideas I have on my computer to contribute to putting together the statements for this important anniversary, while waiting for God Almighty to facilitate your return and fill our hearts with joy, and to assist me in my path and in my messages. I have sent the brother from your side what is needed to purchase a computer for you and everything that is needed for it and flash drives which you will be using to send me your letters, writings, and ideas that you would like me to include in the statements. I have sent you a video statement about two months ago but it has not been broadcast in the media yet. I plan to redo it before broadcasting it.

PS: I was informed that you visited an official dentist in Iran complaining about a filling she put in for you. If she put in the filling for you more than a year before your departure from Iran, then do not worry about it. Otherwise, you need to go the doctor and complain about the filling in your molar and ask to have the filling replaced.

Comment: Our security situation here does not allow us to go to doctors, so please take care of all your medical needs, particularly your teeth, and keep the prescriptions from every doctor you go to, so we can get you the medication when you come to us, God willing, whenever you need it. I wish you good health and stability.

It is also of extreme importance, security wise, to learn Urdu and your presence with families from the region will be of help to you. I hope you work hard at it. Please ask Hamza to teach Urdu to his son. His younger brothers have been learning Urdu for a while.

In closing, I pray to God Almighty to protect you, may He grant you success in what pleases Him, and may He facilitate your return. He is Most Capable. I would like you to inform me of the reasons they told you before your release justifying why you were the first in my family to be released, and also what they

Page 3

mentioned to you about the children, Fatima, and her husband, and the rest of our brothers in Iran. Everybody here sends their regards. Peace and God's blessings be upon you.

Abu 'Abdallah

[TN: The following are duplicate paragraphs copied from the letter and pasted at the bottom.]

I also would like to share with you some of my positions. We are awaiting the tenth anniversary of the blessed attacks on New York and Washington which will be in nine months. You are well aware of its importance and the importance of taking advantage of the anniversary in the media to embody the victories of Muslims and communicate what we want to communicate to people. I have been in correspondence with the brothers to provide Al-Jazeera with several statements when the channel starts covering the attacks on the first of September.

I will ask the brother from your side to buy you a computer and all that is needed for it. I will attach all the statements and ideas I have on my computer for your review hoping you will provide me with your observations and ideas. I will also ask the brother to purchase flash drives you will be using to send me your letters, ideas, and suggestions.

9. Zamrai (UBL) Letter to Unis

> Usama bin Laden addresses those who were previously held prisoner and those who hope to seek liberation. He also discusses the need to expose children to the world of martyrdom and battle. Additionally, he mentions different revolutions and demonstrations, and the need to view them as lessons.
>
> Date: Unknown
>
> From: Zamrai (UBL)
>
> Zamrai (UBL) letter to Unis
>
> http://www.dni.gov/files/documents/ubl/english/Zamrai%20UBL%20letter%20to%20Unis.pdf

(TN: Religious introduction)

To the Islamic Ummah in general, Peace be upon you with the mercy and blessings of Allah…

[To] my Muslim Ummah:… The people of the world, who were previously held prisoner, have succeeded in escaping from the slavery of their tyrant rulers. In recent history, the people of Eastern Europe, which lived a long contract under the slavery of the global communist regime, [have done so]. When the Soviet Union was established, they staggered under the Hindu Kush, appearing weak to the rest of the world. This was until the European people began to feel this weakness and seized their historic opportunity, starting in a single country, the revolution against the corrupt communist factions. This was duplicated by the brothers in neighboring countries, where revolution spread until it reached Eastern Europe and the slavery in which they were living under the global communist wave. Today, we are living a reality similar to this. Our nations have been living for centuries under unsatisfactory religious, social, cultural, and economic conditions. This was, of course, due to Western dominance. For centuries the awareness and development of the Ummah's people went mute. It has come to a point in which, by God, Western [military] bases, commanded by America, have advanced throughout Afghanistan itself. Just as [those oppressed] under the Hindu Kush began to stagger [out of the slavery] which had been perceived as a weakness to the world, where they lost their prestige, [we too] have the rare historic opportunity to escape from this accumulation of tyrannical rule, where [we] are held prisoner. [We have] to take charge of the reins and free ourselves from the Western dominance. This opportunity was illuminated with the revolution in Tunisia, where the Ummah had been forgotten. The Muslim sentiment was ignited as well in Egypt, where the Ahl al-Kinanah (TN: Egyptians) took the coal [that had been ignited] from their neighbors to spread the revolution to oust those not working [for the Ummah] in their homeland. With the Muslim revolution in Egypt, this shall ignite the sentiments felt by [the rest of] the Islamic Arab World.

[To] my Muslim Ummah: The success in the Tunisian revolution in toppling the tyranny put an end to the thought that there could not be a change in the ruling party, aside from one of two means: Either a military coup or by the presence of <u>foreign</u> forces. The Ummah assured that, once the people entered the equation with such a force, [the revolution] grew and [began to] creep into the shuddering hearts [of the people], where they stood witness to those that viewed it as their legitimate duty to <u>oust those not working [for the Ummah]</u> and to restore what was stolen from them of their Brothers' rights... in the land of Egypt... Thus, it is upon the Muslim population within Egypt and elsewhere to join together and stand shoulder to shoulder in protection of this revolution and the fruits thereof. Each Muslim must exert him/herself to their full extent.

Among the primary reasons for the success of the revolutions is learning from previous experiences, particularly the history of revolutions. I stress this, not directly specific to studying the reasons for the success of these revolutions, but rather, to show the reasons for success, or the effect of reviewing [the past] and not wasting <u>this</u> rare historic opportunity. Among those <u>revolutions</u> which must be reviewed is a study of the escaped [opportunity] for a revolution when the Muslims in Egypt expelled the military [commander related to the] 'Abd-al-Mun'im Riyad square [incident]. This was a great opportunity to expel the regime which existed until today. However, the Shaykh 'Abd- al-Qadir 'Awdah, Allah have mercy on him, disgraced the blood of the Muslims and believed the lying military [commander] and persuaded the people to return and obey [the government's] orders. If the people were to have remained, rather than disperse… [if they were to have] betrayed the Shaykh, [they could have realized their revolution]. However, [the Shaykh] did them in and the thousands of innocent followers. We ask that Allah have mercy on all of them.

Among them: The Muslims' revolution in Algeria main… (TN: The author appears to leave space to edit in future drafts.) for the efforts of the revolution were lost due to the corrupt godliness.

Among them: The million-strong demonstration in Sanaa, for this opportunity was lost as well with the dialogue between the President and the head of the opposition, Shaykh 'Abdallah Bin Husayn al-Ahmar (TN: Deceased leader of the Yemeni Islah Party) and Shaykh 'Abd-al-Majid al-Zindani (TN: Former Head of the Yemeni Islah Party's Shura Council), for, at the expense of the people, they believed him. Then, it wasn't long before they realized that he went back on his previous pledges [for change] on many of the issues in which they agreed upon.

Among them: The French revolution, which continued until the ruling party was uprooted.

Among them: The Iranian revolution, whose leaders insisted on freeing the country of the regime completely. Even after they expelled the Shah, leaving matters to the Shahbur, where the people were calling for the return of the Shah, they did not stop the revolution. When this continued, despite shedding the regime of their blood supply, [they were insistent] on removing the entire regime.

The main areas of concern for those preparing to achieve liberation are as follows:

First: The psychology of the King, his nature. It must be understood that the greatest evil is that in which a man can kill from within his family. The man kills his father or his brother in viewing the severity in nature of the King. This is what explains their regard for the blood of their people's children, which their King is threatening.

Likewise, the betrayal characteristics that the majority of them (TN: ruling parties) display, which unsettles those whom they govern. [This betrayal is in the form of the ruling party's inability in] being balanced in their rule (TN: abnormal spacing). The greatest concern of theirs being revenge on those who threaten their rule. They view this as an insult above all other insults. Likewise, many eras ago, when Ibn al-'As (TN: literally, 'the disobedient people) expelled 'Abd-al-Malik... 'Abd-al-Malik did not welcome [the change] and was not satisfied until he returned three days later and killed him. This is during the time of successors and this was the first betrayal in Islam.

Second: The importance of a steadfast position in the leadership and its boldness and seriousness in fearing blood[shed]. If, for instance, in this citizen there lies corrupt godliness, for it is as the poet al-Nil stated: "They support the war of peace, as long as blood is shed in [what they perceive as] the time for bloodshed."

The Arabs say that killing prevents death. For in Egypt, one dies due to [his] corruption [within] the regime, as seventy thousand die annually due to the oppression [of the regime]. Based on statistics of illnesses, [citizens die] due to pollution of the water [supplies] as a result of the factories of the large businessmen aligned with the authorities, from which, hundreds die of daily. [Likewise}, tens of thousands [die annually] due to pollution of the environment.

Thus, from the palace, the regime destroys the souls of the people, just as though an unarmed man is killed by gunfire. He does as he wishes with the blood of the Muslims in Egypt. One must be cautious of the corrupt godliness and understand that freedom will not be achieved without great sacrifice. Bleeding out [the enemy] does not separate [the link of] their vital [organs]. I understand completely that exposing the <u>Children of the Ummah</u> to battle/death is extremely difficult, however, there is no other means to rescue them. There is no other way to rescue them. The Almighty [Allah] stated [...kill them...] For there is no one that may go into battle without being exposed to death.

PART TWO: LETTERS LIKELY WRITTEN TO USAMA BIN LADEN

> **1. Letter to Abu 'Abdallah al-Hajj**
>
> Abu 'Abdallah is ordered to manage brothers and delegate duties of Shaykh Mahmud and others. A member is requested to support the Mujahidin in "hotspots" like Palestine, Iraq, Afghanistan, Somalia, and the Maghreb. The letter mentions finances, visiting delegates, and the fight between Sunni and Shia.
>
> Date: 17 December 2007
>
> From: Unknown
>
> http://www.dni.gov/files/documents/ubl/english/Letter%20to%20Abu%20Abdallah%20al-Hajj.pdf

To the Generous Brother Abu 'Abdallah al-Hajj 'Uthman (may God bless you)

Peace be upon you, with God's mercy and blessings

I hope you, the brothers, families and children are doing well, and you are closer and closer to God…

So,

1. Your message that you sent to us with Shaykh Abu Muhammad and brother 'Abd-al-Latif has arrived. However, we could not open it and we think there was an error from your side at the time of sending it. Thus, we need for you to please to resend a copy of it, but first make sure it will open.

2. In regard to your previous suggestion to assign Shaykh Mahmud to do the suggested duties, this is good. However, his assignment should include the highest responsibility of messages that are coming from Shaykh Abu Muhammad for a year (Hijri year). Also add one more task to Shaykh Mahmud's duties. He needs to be one of the spokesmen for the organization. He also needs to be in charge of the preaching, provoking Jihad and supporting the Mujahidin in hotspots such as Palestine, Iraq, Afghanistan, Somalia and the Islamic Maghreb. Also he should support the Islamic State of Iraq and defend it from any disproval and rumors. He also needs to respond to the front of betrayals, frustrations and inconsistencies led by Salman al- 'Awdah and anyone who is similar to him. His answers should be tranquil not instigating, educated and objective according to the Shari'ah principles. His responses should address only the people that he selects, because many government spokesmen are unstable and he needs to ignore them. It is better if he comments on what Saudi 'Arabia channels have been circulating, incorrect news that stated al-Qa'ida has links to Iran. He also needs to take the first opportunity and talk about both magnificent Shaykhs Abu 'Ubaydah al-Banshiri and Abu Hafs al- Masri (may God have mercy on them), and their rules in Jihad and their rank among the Mujahidin. He should respond to any unfair nonsense criticism against them, this disapproval that has been repeating over and over by 'Abdallah Anas and his son-in-law.

3. In regard to your advice to assign Sa'dun to do some accounting duties, this is good.

4. In regard to assign Shaykh Abu Layth based on Shaykh Abu Muhammad's recommendation, this is good too.

5. In regard to Yasir's bail, you (nfi) did not sponsor him, which is fine.

6. In regard to the messages that are directed to the Emirs of al-Qa'ida in countries and regions, these messages need to be signed by me or Shaykh Abu Muhammad. I informed you, and God is my witness.

7. In regard to the delegate that visited you and delivered to you a message, they claimed that message was from our friend, then you received something of suspicious accuracy. I am saying to you, it is very important to find out the truth of that delegate and deal with them based on your finding. I am not going to hide it from you, the majority of the delegates are following same path of that man (nfi) who surrendered our brother Sharif (may God send him free). You need to mention this when you start dealing with them, because it is vital, and these people have no shame in allowing the apostate state intelligence to lead them. The point is, these people are satisfied performing this religion based on what the idol allows them to do. They abandoned this religion; this religion as a whole belongs to God Almighty. Because of them, there is a real threat against the establishment of the Islamic Emirate, and their desire to withdraw from it, and you need to be careful of them. Therefore, every demand will delay and weaken the appointed Jihad. You have to reject it and excuse yourself from it, and they must keep in mind that they have no right to give any promises for the state that involve war against Muslims on their behalf. Otherwise, it will be a succession run by the intelligence, and do not disclose your secrets to them. When you sit with them, I need you to mention to them that God sets Sahib Sharif free. America will target us everywhere in this life and our position is to defend ourselves and religion. We are with anyone who is interested in Jihad or making peace according to Shari'ah principles.

- In regard to the message suggesting that the fight between Sunni and Shia should stop, we should explain the matter to our friend, because it is based on deception and sophisms. They are the ones who ignited this war and insist to keep it going. It is in their hands; they could make it calm, but their goal is to control the Islamic world, from Iraq to the Arabian Peninsula.

8. I need you please to take the amount of 10,000 dollars out from my account and put it in the Mujahidin's balance.

9. I have recently received the amount of 12,000 euro designated for the Mujahidin. Please take this amount from my account that is in your side and put in the Mujahidin's balance. I need you to inform me of this in your next message, so this amount will be accounted for by the designated people. Also I need you please to take out amount of fifteen thousand Kaldars (TN: rupees) from my account for the Mujahidin to purchase three sheep, unless you need the money for something more important.

10. 35,000 euro has arrived from your side, with the message that we could not open, may God reward you with good deed, and please send the rest.

11. I attached a message to brother Bakr, it is important, and I need you please to work together with brother 'Abd-al-Latif to deliver the message to him.

In the end, may God be with you and peace be upon you, with God's mercy and blessings

17 December 2007

2. Letter to Shaykh Abu Abdallah, 2 September 2009

> Miqdad reports that three books detailing a mission have been translated into Urdu and Pashtu. The books discuss topics such as approaching foreigners, the purity of the Muslim approach, and the rulings covering martyrdom attacks. Finally, Miqdad discusses plans for a new book in which "Zionist Crusaders" will be addressed in length.
>
> From: Abu Miqdad
>
> http://www.dni.gov/files/documents/ubl/english2/Letter%20to%20Shaykh%20Abu%20Abdallah%20dtd%202%20September%202009.pdf

(Page 1 of 1)

In the name of Allah, and may prayers and peace be upon his messenger and his companions

The honorable Shaykh Abu 'Abdallah…may Allah bless him

May Allah's mercy and peace and blessings be upon you…and happy 'Eid…and we ask Allah to bring back to Muslims al-'Eid holiday and the month of Ramadan and to grant us and our nation in Yemen victory and blessing…

I ask Allah the almighty that you and the ones you love and the honorable family are in good health…furthermore,

Attached with this letter is a gift for the month of Ramadan. It consists of a report clarifying the condition of the struggle with Allah's enemies, in addition to good news about victory, which was visible on the horizon. Furthermore, books that we were able to compose that reflect our mission were translated into Urdu and Pashtu, and the three books are:

1- "Manhaj Al-Ghuraba' Fi Muwajahat Al Jahiliyah" (TN: The Approach of the Strangers/Foreigners in Confronting the Pre-Islamic Epoch, i.e. state of ignorance)

2- "Aham Min Tabri'at Al Ashkhas…Safa' Al Manhaj" (TN: The purity of the methodology (Muslim approach) is more important than absolving (the guilt) of the people)

3- "Ahkam Al-Gharat Al-Fida'iyah Wa Al-Tatarrus" (TN: The Rulings Covering Martyrdom Attacks and on Taking Humans as Shields)

And shortly, Allah willing, we are going to compose a book titled "Al Sira' Al Islami Al-Sahyu Sahlibi…Haqiqiya Wa Jathurah Wa Iba'dah" (TN: Islamic Zionist Crusaders…the Truth about Them and Their Distant Roots), which falls under a series we called "Salsala Bina' Al-Shakhsiya al-Muslima" (Series on the Building of the Muslim Personality). And we ask Allah the almighty to guide us to success while composing this series.

I wrote this letter in order to keep in contact with you, and I hope that you receive my letter and respond to it, to make sure that our letter arrived, since the last letter was lost on the way. Everyone over here sends their regards, especially my children Asadullah Al-Miqdad and Sayfullah Khalid.

And, until we meet, we ask Allah not to waste our trust…

Your brother, 'Abd-al Majid 'Abd-al-Majd, "Abu Miqdad"

12 Ramadan 1430 (TN: 2 September 2009)

PART TWO: LETTERS LIKELY WRITTEN TO USAMA BIN LADEN

3. Letter to Shaykh Abu Abdallah, 17 July 2010

This lengthy letter addresses many different topics. It covers the following subjects and more: the situation in Yemen, war with the American government, family, brothers, an operation against polytheist Barelvis, Pakistan, the Taliban, imprisonment, a documentary, and al Qa'ida's media presence.

From: Mahmud

http://www.dni.gov/files/documents/ubl/english2/Letter%20to%20Shaykh%20Abu%20Abdallah%20dtd%2017%20July%202010.pdf

(Fully translated)

Page 1

In the name of God, the Merciful, the Compassionate

To: Our Dear Shaykh, ((Abu 'Abdallah)), may God keep him and look after him and gird him and guide him and instill wisdom in his words and his deeds, that it may fill his heart, amen.

Peace be upon you, and God's mercy and His blessings,

Praise be to God that you are well. We have received your latest messages on Thursday, 3 Sha'ban (TN: year unspecified), and we had previously prepared that which you are reading now.

These are some of the points that we can write about at present, based on your last message; there are others that will wait for another opportunity, may God assist us.

1. Regarding Yemen, dear Shaykh, what you have said is good and deep, and we ask God to increase your understanding, wisdom, and

guidance. I bring you good news that has made us joyful, and we consider it a result of what God has given you and us of His wisdom, accuracy, justice, and prudence, as well as strength of aim and fire. But I would ask that you focus on the current reality in its details, which is that the war has become a reality. And what is war other than that which you have known and experienced? War in its beginning

Page 2

is youth. But now we are faced with the reality of how to proceed wisely while including our youth and our men. I'm not saying that we should be weak in front of our popular base or make concessions for them. In fact, we should lead them and take them by their hands toward maturity, God willing. But this is a fluid operation of the utmost difficulty, so let us focus on the operational mechanisms by which we can apply what you mentioned- and thank you for that. So the issue is: Do we strike the Americans or the apostates? We have expressed to you our opinion on the matter, and you know better than we do. As well, the issue of exiting the battlefield entirely is a dangerous and risky thing. Saying that we should not escalate, as it seems to me, is ambiguous and will not be practical. The young men want "the line" and "the operations." Every day, there are recommendations to the leadership for operations, opportunities, and observation (surveillance and reconnaissance). Thus, there need to be clear and definitive orders. The issue of leaving the southerners, for example (the movement) (TN: the Southern Secessionist Movement), or others to take over governing, given what you have mentioned, causes me to hesitate. Perhaps

Page 3

there is another option, which is: Instability and chaos. This is better than the control of apostate infidels.

At any rate, I will begin by writing to ((Abu Basir)) to pave the way for this strategy in general terms, God willing. I ask that God guides me to that which is right and good and sound. Perhaps ((Abu Muhammad))'s letters to you include discussion of this issue, which can help inform your opinion.

In summary: Are brothers are now engaged in an actual war with the government, and of course with the Americans? They have even begun striking the security headquarters, as you have heard, even a few days ago in Abyan. Is it appropriate for us to say, "Stop the escalation. We don't want a war in Yemen!"? I do not support such a position, and all my brothers here, as they have told you of their opinions, do not support it. We believe it to be a fundamental mistake. So do we push in the direction of a ceasefire? How, and what would the conditions of that be? (We should enter into the details of such an idea and grant it permission. We then explain to them our strategy and relay to them all of what you said when you wrote, etc.) We should

Page 4

respond to the questions: Would the Americans and Saudis be satisfied with a ceasefire in the first place? And what will become of our brothers who are committed to the ceasefire? Anyway, I have attached the most recent letters from Abu Basir, but there were one or two messages before these. He promised - and I wrote to him asking him to be quick about it - to send detailed messages about their status.

2. Dear Shaykh, the brothers in Somalia are waiting for a message from you and for orders, and they also await consultation and settlement in the matters that they brought up. It would be nice if you could do something especially for them that we could convey to them to make them happy.

3. I want to give you the good news that Shaykh Abu Muhammad is well and in good health. His family is with him, as is one of the Arab brothers. We ask God to keep them concealed, to keep them well, and to bless them. I have attached his letters, which have been waiting for a while. He issued a statement on the passing of Shaykh Sa'id, and before that he had sent us a statement about Turkey. We held these up because disseminating them wasn't appropriate at the time we received them due to their coinciding with the saga of the Freedom Flotilla

Page 5

and its tragic end, in addition to the sympathy of the Turkish people to the matter and the position of the Turkish government, etc. After consulting with Abu Muhammad, we cancelled publication of the statements altogether. This is something I had wanted to mention to you.

4. With regard to what happened with al-Hafiz, I had written to you about it, God rest his soul. As for his children, they are fine and doing well, and I was to reassure you that we are looking after them and guiding them and their families. I have given them money and other assistance, and I have pledged to help his other, Sudanese family. God willing, we are still expanding our assistance to them, giving them gifts, and standing beside them. They have asked me for nothing that I have not answered with "yes," even their father's weapon (which was a non-specific weapon from the general use stock, a Krinkov). (('Abd-al-Rahman)) told me that he wanted it to remain with him, so I left it there for four months, and then we will see. Maybe I will allow them to keep it. The Shaykh had written in his will that his weapon was to return to the general use stock, and he stipulated this in his will. They know this, but they wanted to keep it with them. I renewed the vehicle for 'Abd-al-Rahman, and they are all still doing the work that he left for them. In fact, I have increased 'Abdallah's stature and his tasks, may God assist in that. 'Abdallah (with us, we use the name Muhammad ((Khan)), but he is also known as ((Muslim))) has become one of our military leadership figures, and Lord have mercy, he is a lion. 'Abd-al-Rahman is following in his footsteps (he works in

Page 6

Special Tasks and belongs to the security committee). Usamah is still young, and he is about to go to Pakistan with his sister, Umm ((Hafsah)), for her treatment. We ask God to heal her and treat her heart.

5. Shaykh ((Yunis)) (Var.: ((Younis))) is still present. As you see, we wrote to you and we are waiting for clear and final permission. Once we get that, we will tell him to move, when he is ready, with God's help. I will record his complete CV, God willing, and tell him about the message.

6. Shaykh ((Ilyas)): God willing, I'll inform him of what you mentioned myself and explain it to him. He has sent you the attached messages, as you can see. I met him recently, and he is doing well. You should write him a letter.

7. With regard to the operation in Lahore against the polytheist Barelvis, we have alerted our brothers, and I personally alerted Hekmatullah ((Mahsud)) that he must declare that they "had no connection to it," and that our method with these errant sects is "to proselytize with wisdom, sound preaching, and explanation." I was insistent upon this particular wording, praise be to God.

8. With regard to the negotiation, Esteemed Shaykh, I would briefly say, with God's help, that the Pakistani enemy has begun to correspond with us and with the (TN: Pakistani) Taliban (((Hakimullah))), ever since al-Hafiz, God rest his soul. We were consulting back and forth, and then we shared some consultation with Abu Muhammad recently when we resumed correspondence with him. Our stance was essentially: We are ready to quit the fight with you, as our battle is primarily with the Americans; however, you entered into it with them. If you leave us alone, then we will leave you alone. But otherwise, we are men, and you will see something that will astonish you, and God is with us.

We leaked information (via Siraj ((Haqqani)), and with the help of the Mahsud brothers and others, via their communications) that al-Qa'ida and the Pakistani Taliban were preparing large-scale, destructive operations in Pakistan, but that the groups' leadership had halted the operations in an attempt to calm the situation and absorb the pressure from the Americans. But if Pakistan were to direct its evils against the Mujahidin in Waziristan, then the operations would move forward, including very large operations that were ready and would occur in the heart of Pakistan (this is the gist of the information we leaked via a number of avenues, and it certainly reached them).

As a result of this, they began sending people to us from the intelligence. They sent messages to us via some of the Pakistani Jihadist groups that they are comfortable with, including the Harakat al-Mujahidin, led by Fadl-al-Rahman ((Khalil)). One of their messengers came to us conveying a message for us from the intelligence leadership, including Shuja' ((Shah)) and others, saying that they wanted to talk to us as al-Qa'ida. So we gave them the same message, nothing more. After a while (about three

Page 7

weeks ago), they sent the same man once more. What was noteworthy this time was that they also inserted Hamid ((Gul)) into the meeting, and Fadl-al-Rahman Khalil attended as an advisor. They sent a message saying, "Give us some time, a month and a half or two. We are trying to convince the Americans and pressure them to negotiate with al-Qa'ida, and to convince them as well that negotiating with the Taliban without al-Qa'ida is of no use. Just wait a little bit. If we are able to convince the Americans, then we (meaning the Pakistanis themselves) have no objection to negotiating with you and sitting down with you." So the brothers said to them, "We will inform our command of your message." And only the messenger went.

As for the Taliban movement, Hakimullah and his companion, Qari ((Husayn)), informed me that the Punjabi government (Shah Baz ((Sharif))) had sent them word that they wanted to negotiate with them and that they were ready to agree to an arrangement with them that they would not carry out any acts inside Punjab (in the sphere of control of the government, which does not include Islamabad or Pindi), as well as that they were ready to pay any price, etc. The negotiations were ongoing, according to them. We stressed to them that they should consult with us in all matters, and they promised to do so. In my last meeting with Hakimullah, I asked him, and he said to me, "There is nothing new, and if anything new comes up, we will tell you." I told him what was going on with us, and that we were being very wary of them. Hakim thinks that we should not show ourselves or sit down with them, and I was supportive of this position in principle. I told him, "At any rate, we don't agree to anything without consulting our leadership, or in reaching an understanding with you."

This is basically a summary of what took place. As you know, this is just talk!

So are the Pakistanis serious, or are they just playing with us? We must be cautious and ready and aware. We must maintain our focus and determination. Of course, they are in a difficult position, as well, and they see their lords and masters, the Americans, in an extremely difficult position, too. This is a government mired in hypocrisy, but there is refuge in God.

So I ask you, what is your opinion? Our opinion, Shaykh, is as I said: We will take advantage of any genuine opportunity for a truce with the Pakistanis so that we can focus wholly on the Americans. This is clear. Yes, there may be difficulty in it for many of our Pakistani brothers; don't forget the brothers in Swat. The Mahsud brothers are our allies and very close comrades,

Page 8

as are others, and even the groups that are with us. But with God's help, it is possible to make them understand, and to explain to them the importance of the matter and how good it could be.

9. Our brother, 'Azzam al-((Amriki)) (TN: "the American"), is fine and doing well, praise be to God. The rumor spread by the Pakistanis was false, but we didn't know exactly what was true. Was it a mistake they made, or a suspicion? Or was there a specific ruse behind it?

10. The brothers imprisoned in Iran and their families are fine, God willing. But no one has come so far since Anas al- ((Subay'i)), and as I told you, he was the last of the brothers to come. He came alone after his family traveled to Libya via Turkey, via a communiqué to the al-Qadhafi Foundation. God willing, if we're able, we will arrange for the family to come. But Shaykh, perhaps the matter is more difficult than you imagine, in terms of the route and searches between us and Peshawar. For this reason, I think we would prefer to keep them for the time being in a place far from us, where they are safe.

Then we can take our time making arrangements for them, God willing.

11. As for your recommendation regarding your son, ((Hamzah)), I don't know Hamzah. He was young, but he has grown up. Maybe I can ask Brother Nu'man al-((Masri)), who was close to him for a time when they were in prison, I think. If you trust in his steadfastness and his emotional strength, then this is a good recommendation. Maybe God will facilitate his safe exit, and the exit of all the other brothers. How do you think he should get to Qatar? If they get him out, they will send him to us using the well-known smuggling routes, and he will make it here. But how should he go after that? Is it appropriate for him to coordinate with the Qatari embassy in Pakistan, for example? But the Americans will definitely take him! So the matter requires that we study it in detail and be careful and take precautions. Otherwise, if we are able to tell the Iranians to let him go to Qatar, we will try to do that.

12. Searching for an aide-de-camp: I was previously aware of the discussion about the aide-de-camp with al-Hafiz. By the way, I read all your messages to al-Hafiz, God rest his soul, as they came, and we would read them and consult one another about them. Now, I share your messages only with ((Abu Yahya)), and no one else. As for the other brothers, depending on the specific focus or the area in which it is possible to get advice, I will take a portion of the message - perhaps paragraphs - and show it to 'Abd-al-Rahman al-((Maghrebi)) if it pertains to media policy, as an example. If it pertains to external activity, I might show the relevant paragraphs to other brothers. As

for the aide-de-camp, I would say that God willing, we will make every effort to search.

Page 9

13. We will do what you said regarding the brother in the couriers: We will question him and check his background and his qualifications, may God keep you all. I previously wrote to you my opinion that we should reduce our correspondence. I have another recommendation, which is that we should encrypt our correspondence. Is it possible for the people on your end to learn the Mujahidin Secrets program? I will attach it, along with an explanation of it. Perhaps your assistants can learn it and use it in their correspondence.

14. I will try to search for the book al-Tatarrus (TN: The Barricade), by Shaykh Abu Yahya, and attach a copy to you, along with a few other theories. If I'm unable to find it now, I'll do it another time, with God's help.

15. I want to inform you that Brother Hamzah al-Jawfi, God rest his soul, was killed during an airstrike by spy aircraft in South Waziristan (Wana). Others were killed with him, but we still haven't confirmed exactly who. It's possible that ((Abu- al-Husayn)) al-Masri was among them.

16. God willing, we will request information about ((Abu Bakr)) al-Baghdadi and his deputy, and about the great partisan ((Abu Sulayman)). We will try to ask the partisan brothers and others and get a clearer picture, with God's assistance. God willing, we will continue our efforts toward unity, as we have indeed done. We have written to them in messages of condolence for the two martyred emirs that perhaps this is an opportunity to renew efforts of unity and to find a new structure that combines everything, etc.

17. The idea about a documentary about you, in coordination with Al Jazeera and Al Sahhab, is something we will work at. I will consult with Munir, and we will send the idea to Zaydan and ask for his questions. But I think that your answers should be recorded in audio at a minimum. I had previously asked you, Shaykh, for tapes that

we could keep about your history, life, and everything, and about how the idea of Jihad developed with you, etc. Many things. Our brother Munir sent you questions and what not, but you did not respond, so we left the matter for the time being. But I am insisting on this matter, and I think it's something we need to do. Also, Dear Shaykh, some recorded audio of shorts speeches to the brothers here especially, where you could let them hear you without anyone taking a copy of it. We could keep them in our archive or destroy them, per your order. But we should do this for the people, to put them at ease regarding appointments of personnel and other issues, and so you can urge them to listen and obey, to be patient and steadfast, and to raise their awareness and concern. Al-Jawfi, God rest his soul, said, "I am with Usama Bin Laden, but I'm not with Hafiz ((Sultan)), or Khalid al-((Habib)), or ((Mahmud)). Likewise, we have

Page 10

others who nearly make statements, and those who are not like that. We ask God to help us in that which for us and for you is good.

18. With regard to a media presence, thank you so much for the recommendation. I consulted with the brothers, and we think that at this time, and for the indefinite future, we should not be present in the media, owing to our remaining hidden and to security, and to avoid the monitoring by spies. We are suffering in this war of espionage and absorbing the pressures of the United States and Pakistan. We had the thought of moving outside Waziristan in the near future. Perhaps some of us will go to Nuristan, and others will remain. A section goes and a section stays. As we told you before, we have a good battalion there led by "Faruq al-((Qatari))." He is an esteemed brother from the proven cadre. He recently sent us word that he made things ready there to receive us, and that the locations are good and there are partisans, and everything else. We ask for God's assistance.

19. You had asked that I suggest the names of some prepared brothers so that one might become a deputy of mine. First, I ask God's help in that with which I have been tasked. Shaykh, this is a great responsibility, and I am not equal to it. I fear that I squander, go too far, or lose things. I had asked Shaykh Sa'id in secret to excuse

me, in shame, because I was also saying to myself, "Who is for the brothers, the work, and for Jihad, that would have need of me?" We have lost cadre and leaders, as we know, and I fear this may be from the fleeing and the slow progress, etc. At any rate, may God help me as he helps you. I ask God to relieve me and quickly prepare someone better than I to take charge. I would say that I do not think anyone is completely ready to take charge right now, except Shaykh Abu Yahya. And by the way, during the final days of al-Hafiz, Abu Yahya was the second deputy, based on the directive that came from you to designate a second deputy. He is now my deputy, and I think he is the most prepared of the brothers.

However, I am not sold on this, and I hope that I will find another person. The reason is this: I think he should be assigned full time to academics, jurisprudence, fatwas, and climbing the academic ladder. If we busy him with management, I suspect we will lose his knowledge and qualifications. It was asked of our master, 'Umar, "Why not assign one of the senior companions of the Prophet?" His answer was, "I would hate to sully them with work."

Page 11

The sullying would be in two senses: First, that they would be subjected to unrest in their minds, which would in turn corrupt their faith. Second, it would harm their dignity in the hearts of the people. Someone in charge is faced with bickering, recriminations, and arguments and such.

Thus, I have always felt that Abu Yahya should be far removed from this. But I haven't found anyone more suited or better than he. In fact, he is better and more deserving than I am.

Of the remaining, Shaykh Yunis still needs to grow up, and needs to become more mature and get more experience. He has a smart and clever mind, God bless him, but one of the biggest problems people like him have is that they are considered new, and people won't be satisfied with him. Anyway, he's already tasked with work that he has begun, may God assist him in it.

A possibility is our brother, 'Abd-al-Rahman al-Maghrebi. He has a very sound mindset and a sturdy faith, in our assessment. He has ethics beyond reproach and is secretive and patient. He is sound in his thinking and is very aware. He is suitable for command, God willing, and may God look after him. His only problem will be with the senior people; those who have been around longer than he will hardly accept him (I mean the older shaykhs; you know who I'm talking about). But this could be solved by a clear appointment from you, not in writing, but in an audio recording at the very least. There is no choice other than this in a case such as 'Abd-al-Rahman's, if I had to appoint him. Of course, he is now in charge of Al Sahhab, but he could be removed from that and promoted. Maybe I'm perceiving the matter to be more sensitive than it is. I await your counsel.

In the new generation, there are good brothers and the cadre and leadership of the future, may God strengthen them. We are working to prepare the cadre and ready the leadership. I will bring you good news that will make you happy, with the help of God. But our circumstances are difficult, Shaykh, and we are trying, but this war of espionage has really worn us down.

From the senior Egyptian brothers who remain with us, we have ((Sa'duf)), Amir al-((Fatah)), ((Abu al-Miqdad)), and ((Abu Sulayman)) (who was living in Khowst with al-Jawfi in the days of the Emirate, driving a taxi). These men are all with us in our work, but most of them are not suited to this matter. Except Abu al-Miqdad, who might be the best of them, and is certainly the best in terms of his ideology and point of view. But there is difficulty when it comes to his ethics.

As far as the Algerian brothers, we have ((Abu 'Uthman)), but he isn't suited for this matter. We have someone better than he, a brother named (('Abd-al-Jalil)), who came to us during the last days of the Emirate. He was put in prison in Kabul by Sayyaf's men, but they released him (there were three of them: Sayf Bin 'Umar 'Abd-al-Rahman al-((Masri)) and 'Azzam al-((Zahrani)), God rest his soul). This brother is

Page 12

good and might be qualified in the near future. We might try him out as a deputy now. I will look into the matter and study it, and then I'll respond to you in another letter. Perhaps you remember, he's the one that al-Hafiz recommended to you previously to be a spokesman for al-Qa'ida.

I ask God to release our brothers who are in prison. They come to help and to carry the burden, and they are good men. Abu Muhammad al-((Zayyat)), ((Abu al-Khayr)), and ((Sayf al-'Adl)), and others. But to be safe, if God ordains their release, they should spend six months (or even a year) getting familiar again with how things work, and so they can renew their contacts, activities, and livelihoods. At present, they are relatively close, and they consult incrementally in matters. After this, they could take on affairs. We ask God to free them and with them, may He bring success for Islam and the Muslims, and may He make them and us suitable servants.

20. Speaking of some problem, though I don't want to occupy you with problems, but perhaps this is something that you should be aware of. I've attached a paragraph that I wrote in a message to brother Abu Basir al-((Wuhayshi)) (he had asked me for a summary of the situation with us).

21. God willing, I will reread the letter slowly and respond to you in the next missive regarding the important paragraphs that I didn't get to here, such as the idea about you issuing a statement in which you say that we are correcting some things that have come hastily from us. This should be very precise and balanced and studied. We might need to undertake some measured steps before this. Let me assure you, Dear Shaykh, that we are making every effort to refine our course, assess our officials in every location, and communicate with worthy and learned people and religious students and other. We are working hard at this despite all the difficulties (we are in contact with a group of religious students, and I will choose two or three of them, along with one to three educated men, for that which I had indicated, including critiques, scrutiny, and advise for us, and I will tell them that we want to be corrected, etc., as you had

mentioned). God willing, this is everything. We will begin this and pave the way for you. We are continually making corrections, even before this, during, and after this, with the help of God, in matters of ideology, excessiveness, extremist, etc. In matters of ethics, taste, and moderation, and in matters of general thought, analysis, research, and Jurisprudence, may God assist us.

Page 13

22. There are other attachments: The advise and the sympathy; a long but good article by Abu Yahya entitled "Jihad and the Battle of Uncertainties" (I'm unable to find it, unfortunately); the latest in a series of my articles in the magazine "Vanguards of Khorasan"; media directives; Abu Yahya's message to members of the media.

This is what I am able to respond with. God is great, and makes all things happen for us. He will bring victory soon. Regards.

Mahmud

Saturday, 5 Sha'ban 1431 (TN: 17 July 2010)

PART TWO: LETTERS LIKELY WRITTEN TO USAMA BIN LADEN

> **4. Letter dtd 13 October 2010**
>
> Likely addressed to bin Laden, this letter provides a summary on the imprisonment in Iran, the movement of Arab Mujahidin into Iran, the security between Pakistan and Afghanistan, and the division of al Qa'ida into different groups. A comprehensive summary is included as part of the document itself.
>
> From: Abu-'Abd al-Rahman Anas al-Subay'i
>
> http://www.dni.gov/files/documents/ubl/english/Letter%20dtd%2013%20Oct%202010.pdf

Summary: This is a letter dated 13 OCT 2010 from Abu-'Abd- al-Rahman Anas al-Subay'i to unidentified shaykh (TN: Possibly UBL), giving him a summary per the shaykh's request for the previous period, which was the imprisonment in Iran. Al-Subay'i mentioned that after the fall of the Islamic Emirate of Afghanistan, many of the Arab Mujahidin left for Iran. The first group was arrested after they entered, but they were deported, after their pictures and fingerprints were taken, to countries of their choosing. Most of them chose to go back to the same countries where they came from, such as Morocco, Yemen, Great Britain, and Saudi Arabia. Due to the instruction by Mullah Muhammad 'Umar for the Arabs to leave Afghanistan, the tightening of the border with Pakistan, and the arrest of the mujahidin in Pakistan, the Arab mujahidin started fleeing to Iran again. The Iranians were watching the mujahidin through their Iranian supporters and started arresting them in groups, where they were detained in a secured place. The writer described how the Iranians divided the Arab mujahidin into four groups. The first group contained the leadership of al-Qa'idam to include Shaykh Sulayman Abu- Ghayth, Shaykh Muhammad al-Islambuli, the shaykh's sons, Abu-Muhammad al-Masri, Sayf al-'Adl, Jihad son of Abu- Jihad, and the Persian individual responsible for the group, which means most of the group in Shiraz (TN: More groups and names mentioned in the source document). After four years in this concentration camp, they were moved to another place in Karaj area, which is a guarded residential place that was an attachment for a training airport, but many refused to be transferred to this residential area.

(Full translation)

Page 1

In the name of God, the Most Gracious, the Most Merciful

Dear Brother and Honorable Shaykh, may God protect him and keep him safe

Peace and God's mercy and blessings be upon you,

Praise be to God whom we call on for help and who suffices everything for us. I hope that this message finds you and your kind friends. I also hope that God fights his enemies for He is the only one who has the strength to do that. I am going to take this rare opportunity to ask God Almighty to bless you during the Fitr Holiday (TN: Festival of the breaking of the Fast). May He make it a good beginning for us and for the entire Muslim community. I am also going to pray to God that He accepts our [fasting] during the month of Ramadan and to save us all from hellfire. He is compassionate and generous.

Dear brother,

In the beginning, I want to criticize you the same way a younger brother would criticize his older brother for not letting us know how you are doing. God only knows how much I want to see you, to know how you are doing, and how your health is. (TN: our concerns about) Your health preoccupied us while incarcerated in that land of the oppressive people. We were especially concerned because of delay in your news and audio speeches. I hope you know how much you mean to us. I ask God to reunite us with the Prophet, peace and prayers be upon him, along with the martyrs, the pious ones, and righteous. I ask God to reward us with martyrdom for His sake in a way, time, and place that would please Him. May God comfort our hearts by allowing us to strike His enemy and the enemy of the believers. Amen, Amen, Amen

PART TWO: LETTERS LIKELY WRITTEN TO USAMA BIN LADEN

Dear brother,

If you asked about our circumstances during this past period, it is no secret how out of place this religion is among these people whose mannerisms resemble those of the Jews and the hypocrites from everything we have seen of them. Praise be to God, He saved us from them. He has instilled fear in their weak hearts so that they get what they deserve in this life before the afterlife. This was a time for self-reflection and to take advantage of everything that God made available to us during that period. Praise be to Him.

I have received your kind request to summarize the events of this past period, and I will do my best to do so.

Dear brother,

After the fall of the Islamic Emirate in Afghanistan, many of those who left Afghanistan moved to the rejectionist Persian country. The first group was betrayed upon their arrival to Iran and was detained. By the grace of God, they were deported to countries of their choice. This was only after many of them were photographed and their fingerprints were taken. May God seek revenge on them (TN: the Iranian authorities). Some of the countries the brothers chose were countries from which they had come.

Page 2

Some of the countries were Morocco, Yemen, Saudi Arabia, and Britain, along with other countries. Whether intentionally or unintentionally, other countries, like Malaysia, China, Indonesia, Singapore, and others, overlooked the arrival of the brothers. Of course, the families of those brothers were detained in hotels and then they were taken to a school in Arak area (TN: City in Iran).

After the case of the first group of brothers was closed, many families, along with the Arab brothers, left Afghanistan based on advice from Mullah Muhammad 'Umar, God bless him and us, to evacuate the border area between Afghanistan and Pakistan so as to ease the pressure on the mujahidin and the Muslims in the area who do not have many resources. After Pakistan started closing in on us, and detentions were taking place in main cities like Karachi, Lahore and smaller cities, a second group started to move toward Iran and tried to spread out within cities like Zahedan, Shiraz, Mashhad, Tehran, Karaj and others. This was approximately after the 'Id al-Adha in 1422 (TN: February 2002). At the end of Ramadan 1423 (TN: November 2002), approximately one year after the fall of the Islamic Emirate of Afghanistan, the second campaign against the Arab mujahidin in Iran started. There was an effort to locate them and to monitor their Iranian supporters who were aiding and abetting them. They were renting out homes for them and buying them mobile phones because it is difficult to do so, for Iran requires official documentation for such matters whether one is Iranian or foreign. Of course, the detentions did not stop throughout this year, but only some were detained and not all. Homes were being monitored, with the exception of a few homes of those who did not deal with these supporters either because it was not necessary or because of security considerations. After the monitoring was discovered, some changes were made to the security protocol. In fear that they would lose sight of the brothers once again, the Iranian intelligence and authorities went in and arrested the brothers. Without doubt, the brothers, without their families, were imprisoned. The families were all rounded up and later met up with the brothers in tightly secured and fortified detention centers. The detention centers were run by three security systems: The intelligence, the Revolutionary Guard, and the judicial authority in the prison system. There was also [security] from the offices of their evil leader Khameini. May God humiliate him in this life before the afterlife for what he has done to the mujahidin, their families, and their children. They (TN: the Iranian authorities) were united in their wiliness, which they have inherited from their fathers, and came up with the idea of gathering the [mujahidin] in one place (This is what they tried to deceive to make it look like, but it was really the detention of families along with women and children). They achieved what they wanted to do in the beginning, and the brothers were split into four groups.

The first group included al-Qa'ida leaders Shaykh Sulayman Abu-Ghayth; Shaykh Muhammad al-Islambuli; and your sons Sa'ad, 'Uthman, Muhammad, and Ahmad Hasan. It also included Abu-Muhammad al-Masri, Sayf al-'Adl, Jihad Ibn Abu Jihad, and the Iranian brother who took care of them (this is almost all the members in the Shiraz area).

The second group included brothers from the Islamic Fighting Group. They are Shaykh Abu al-Mundhir, Shaykh Salih, Shaykh Musa, Abu-Hazim, Abu-Malik, Shakir-Allah, and Siraj (the al-jazeera cameraman). Also there are Abu al- Ward, 'Abd-al-Ghaffar, Hatib, and 'Abdallah. A few months later, Shaykh 'Abdallah Sa'id and al-Zubayr al-Maghribi, who were living in Tehran, were arrested along with the Iranian brother who took care of them.

Page 3

The third group included Shaykh Abu Hafs al-Muritani, who was arrested first. He was followed by Abu-al-Samh, Abu- Dujanah, Abu-al-Miqdad 'Abd-al-'Aziz al Masriyyin, Abu- 'Abdallah al-Jaza'iri, Abu Suhayb al-'Iraqi, Abu al-Harith al-'Iraqi, Harun al-Kurdi and others (Basically the brothers who are living in the Karaj area) and the Iranian brother who took care of them.

The fourth group included Abu Ziyad al-Mawsili , Abu 'Amr and Salim, Abu Hammam al-Sa'idi, 'Abd-al-Muhaymin, Bassam, Abu Islam al-Busnah, Abu Hafs al-'Arab, Khubab, and Salah al-Yamani (who lived in Mashhad).

As for those who were not in those groups, they are:

The single men: Qassam and al-Dahhak (he was arrested then joined with the group that was imprisoned in Tehran (I was in that group)). After the others were reunited with their families and before sending us off to Karaj, about four years later, he was separated from us in a deceitful way. They charged him with cursing KhameinI, God's greatest evil.

Among the single men were Suhayb and Hanzala the Jordanians, 'Abd-al-Rahman al-Kurdi, 'Abd-al-Ghaffar al- Libi, Salah al-Libi, another brother who came from Libya, and the son of another brother who had come from Britain. I think that I heard the brothers say that the son of Abu Jihad and the son of Shaykh al-Islambuli (TN: were among the single men).

Those who are married and families: Abu Tarik al-Masri and his family, Shaykh Abu al-Walid al-Masri (Tehran), the widows and the wives of the imprisoned brothers who were in Mashhad like the families of Shaykh Abu Khabbab, Shakir al- Masri, Abu al-Hasan al-Masri and his married daughters. From Shiraz, I think that it was the family of Shaykh Abu- Hafs al-Kumandan (TN: the commander).

Dear Shaykh,

In the end, as far as I know, the situation settled as follows:

The first group, whose location was referred to as Sisast, or 300 in Farsi, was divided within the first detention center in Tehran and was located in a military area. This area was basically a training ground for the groups that were sympathized with by the rejectionist regime in Iran. This is based on evidence I saw that would point to that. There was evidence such as prohibited items, traces of bullets, mortars, and other things. (This was after we were reunited with families, about a year after detention.)

Group A: This includes your family (including the families of your children), the family of Shaykh Abu Hafs the commander, the family of Abu Muhammad al-Masri, the families of Sayf al-'Adl, the family of Shaykh Sulayman, and the families of Shaykh al-Islambuli and his son, and Jihad (the son of Abu Jihad), I think.

Group B: In the same detention center were Shaykh Abu Hafs al-Muritani; Shaykh Abu al-Samh; Shaykh Abu Salih; Abu 'Amr; Abu Hafs; the Egyptians Abu Dujanah, Abu Humam al- Sa'idi, and Abu Ziyad al-Musali; the Libyans 'Abdallah and Abu Malik; along with the single men Qassam and al-Dahhak.

Page 4

Group C: They were sent to the same detention center a few months later. It included Abu 'Abdallah al-Muhajir, Abu al- Ward al-Libi, and Abu Tariq al-Masri. This group was reunited with Group B after Group B broke some of the hidden cameras and some doors to protest how Group C was being treated. This was especially after they discovered that the hidden cameras in the ceilings of their rooms were wired and powered on. The rejectionists and enemies of God denied that these cameras worked. This is just another example of their hypocrisy. May God fight them and embarrass them.

Dear Shaykh,

After four years of facing off with the enemies of God in charge of this infamous detention center, and after their promises to provide some sort of basic resources for us or education for our children, we were moved to another compound in Karaj. This was in the Kihan Mahr area and it consisted of a living compound that was part of an airport training facility that may have been used for private landings. Anyway, they prepared 12 housing units by fortifying them with six- or seven-meter high fences that were finished off with barbed wiring and cameras, and large metal gates. There were also two outer fences that were slightly shorter, in addition to the airport security and the towers within it. More importantly, the housing units had been renovated and offered a better living standard. I am not going to lie to you; this is not what a mujahid who cares about his religion and his morals wants. It is no secret that some of us did not even want to move there. Personally, I asked to be transferred anywhere else, even to Israel. I told them that it was probably more worthy than they were. There was also a need for those whose children were getting to an age where this place could not provide them with the resources they needed. Of course, Abu Dujanah was moved to a fortified house in Tehran where the treatment was better. Abu Hafs was also moved and was joined with Group A.

Dear brother,

Before I came here, specifically on 05 March 2010, after a huge act of disturbance in the new compound, Special Forces wearing black clothes and masks stormed the detention center and assaulted the men, children, and some houses. The men were detained for 101 days. Praise be to God, we returned to our families. It seemed to be that this operation was a plan to break our bones and by the grace of God, they were unable to break us and God defeated them. Afterward, they started to release prisoners from our detention center and, praise be to God, they started with me and my family. I arrived safe and sound to the rest of my family, thank God. I ask God to humiliate them and aid us in seeking revenge against them. By the grace of God, I have rejoined the jihad effort, and I ask God to grant us and the mujahidin the great honor of martyrdom for He is capable of everything.

Our dear shaykh, I am sorry that this is so long. I tried to summarize toward the end as much as possible. I hope that my summarizing did not leave anything out. Again, I express my apology for the length of this.

Page 5

In closing, I ask God to reunite us with you soon under the banner of Islam, the Islamic State, and the banner of jihad, which will continue with the promise of God to His worshippers to aid them. I send the regards of my family to yours and my regards to your son Khalid. I ask God to accept from you what you and your honorable family have given as sacrifice for the religion of God. My God elevate your status and grant us faithfulness in our words and our deeds. Also, I remind you to pray for us and our children to be good and useful for His faith. I think that this is something you will not forget. I ask God to reunite us while we are doing well with faith and life. I ask God to protect you so that you continue to be a thorn in the throats of His enemies and a joy to those who are patient and on the path of jihad and the religion.

The last of our prayers is praise be to God, the lord of the universe.

Always,
Your brother, Abu-'Abd-al-Rahman Anas al-Subay'i
13 October 2010

PART TWO: LETTERS LIKELY WRITTEN TO USAMA BIN LADEN

> ## 5. Letter dtd 24 November 2010
>
> This letter to Abu 'Abdallah (likely UBL) addresses 11 different points/issues ranging from the United States midterm election to family transportation and organized attacks. Mahmud talks about Pakistan, brothers, and weapons.
>
> From: Mahmud, likely 'Atiyatallah
>
> http://www.dni.gov/files/documents/ubl/english/Letter%20dtd%20November%2024%202010.pdf

Sender is someone with signed name of Mahmud (var. Mahmoud) (tn: more likely 'Atiyatallah). Letter is addressed to "our venerable sheikh Abu 'Abdallah (tn: more likely UBL).

Aside from the traditional greetings, the "Adha" holiday wishes, and compliments writer dates this letter on Tuesday November 24 2010 (17 Dhu al-Hijjah 1431 H). Writer addresses 11 points/issues which are translated below:

Page 1 of 4

1. (tn: Gisted paragraph) Writer refers to the United States election of November (TN; more likely the mid-term election of November 2010); he watched the election on the BBC. Through the writer's analysis with the "brothers' especially Abu Yahya and Munir (var. Mounir) who decided to delay publishing any comments until possibly "our sheikh" (the writer puts it) has the chance to review, add, and/or modify final output with English translation to it. Writer states he is including a copy for the "sheikh" (meaning UBL) to give his last word. Writer indicates saying "…and our Nour al-Din (('Azzam)) added his comments too and all is ready for you to review the file."

2. (tn: verbatim) I would like to draw to your attention that we are using the name of ((Munir)) (var. Mounir) for "brother" 'Abd al-Rahman al-((Mughrabi)) (var. Abdel Rahman al-((Moughraby))).

3. (tn: comprehensive Gisted paragraph) With regard to our overall situation, there are fears about rumors that possibly the military will carry out an attack again in North Waziristan because of the American pressures. However, these pressures have lessened since Obama's visit to India and did not visit Pakistan. Pakistanis sent for recruitment here in the North are telling each other: if communications do not stop from Miran Shah and Mir 'Ali and thereabouts. And on this (level) the attack remains possible. There were indications about American pressures on them due to these communications. On this subject, Pakistanis say: "we are now going to stop all communications except those with special permits; we will permit some families and the likes. But the problem is not because of us [al-tanzim –(meaning al-Qa'ida)] or those adherents; it is those "loiterers" in the streets of Miran Shah and Mir 'Ali who do not listen to anyone and are undisciplined, (tn: they are those) like the Arabs, the Turks, the Azerbaijanis, and even the Germans and other mix of people. We advise those who are wise and intelligent from among these groups; we ask them to minimize problems and help them understand the general public interests. We are trying to form a council to coordinate with all those with Turkish dialects (the brothers from Turkey, Turkistan, Azerbaijan, possibly people from Bulgaria) – may God help.

And about these fears, we put out a plan to have some families enter Pakistan, just for contingency. We began with the first phase which is starting with a group of weak families (tn: possibly meaning poor/obedient): widows, and others. However, when we informed them, some of them refused going to Pakistan. You know well how the "brothers" and families behave! Some of them moved in fact, and some are in process of moving now.

On the military level, we purchased a quantity of ammunition and drew some simple strategies; our situation is difficult due to sharp decrease in recruits, capabilities, and the increase of spies to the point that the entire atmosphere is polluted (tn: meaning spies are everywhere) – and God is the Savior. However, we shall not be rendered disable with God power and our confidence in the Almighty.

We have decided to focus on "Mas'ud" (tn: name in quote in original text – NFI, possibly a location or a person) because the defeat of the wicked military in Mas'ud (var. Masoud) would stop it from moving forward in carry out any big operation in the North (tn: possibly a location named Shimali). Like what Abu Muhammad told us (God protect him), in his counseling that Mas'ud is the first line of defense from the North (Shimali). But you would be pleased that sheikh Abu Muhammad continues to be with us by monitoring with such an exact manner, specially with all his advices and counsels – God bless him.

I received during this month some of the new tragic events, as God willed it. Of these (tragic events):

Page 2 of 4

-- -- The death of Muhammad Khan (Muslim) aka 'Abdullah, the son of Shaykh Sa'id Mustafa Abu al-Yazid, God rest his soul, and with him was a Balushi/Arab from our recruits; his name is Mu'awiyah. He was married to one of the girls of our "brother" Abu Khalil al-((Faltawi)) (he was married to her for about two years and has one son). Now there are no more sons to sheikh Sa'id except the youngest one – 'Usamah (var. Osama) and his beautiful daughter 'Um Hafsah, who is injured – may God envelopes them by HIS care. The family is now in Pakistan; I do not know if they received the news; the "brothers" said that they would tell them about that after the holiday.

-- the death of twenty "brothers" in one or two shelling in one place almost on the holiday. They are mujahidin fighters from our "brothers" in one of our brigades, which is Abu Bakr al-Siddiq (tn: brigade) (God accept him).

And the reason was their gathering (tn: together) for the holiday. This was done despite our enforcement and reassurances to the "brothers" to avoid any gatherings. In fact, a little while before the holiday I stressed to them not to exceed their agreed upon number of five (people) in one center. But they interpret (tn: things wrong) sometime and exert themselves. Among those twenty there were some Turkish "brothers," two Kurds from Iran, three Libyan "brothers, and two or three from the Peninsula (tn: mean the Arabian Peninsula countries) and one Syrian.

Thank God, we are to HIM and return to HIM, May He (God) support us to go through this tragedy and to enable us in inheriting His Goodness.

4. Now about the subject of Hamzah and his mother: with regard 'Um Hamzah, she is ready to go to your side. However, we are waiting to verify the matter with you; also we shall take advantage of convenient "cloudy" days for their move according to your direction. With regard to directives for them to leave things in place, I have already told them not to take in anything they have from Iran with them (tn: Um Hamzah going to 'Abu 'Abdallah); they already know this and 'Abd al- Latif informed them too. They are even overdoing this (tn: making sure not to take anything) just in case. I even asked them about her teeth (tn: Um Hamzah) which she had filled in Iran; I even helped her with some of the visible mix (tn: teeth filled). By what I understood from Hamzah and I already told them that, God willing, there will be no harm from that (tn: not taking anything with them in their move). However the problem is that they said they had this done (tn: the teeth filling) in Iran under the supervision of a doctor who is associated with "those people" (NFI) where she was there and officially. I doubt – with God help – that there would be anything. Nevertheless, I preferred to mention this to you in order for you to be aware and we can consult when need be.

Consequently, if you wish that we send Um Hamzah – may God protect – let us know this time of: a) either to schedule a fix time or; b) or give us the green light to decide because we can let our agent take the convenient time after we prepare for them a convenient "cloudy" day.

With regard to Hamzah, he is very sweet and good. I see in him wisdom and politeness – God Bless him. However, our beloved sheikh, he is a young man who lived years in prison; sadly enough, he is now put in nearly another look like prison on our side; and this is why he is wary from this; he comes back to me asking me that he should be trained and participate in giving. He does not want to be treated with favoritism because he is the son of "someone" and as such God Bless him. I calm him down as we pray together and find him to be an easy going and warm – thank God; I reminded him with what had happened to Sa'd, because Sa'd died – PBUH – as he was impatient and more persistent than he is (tn: Hamzah); and (tn: reminded him) to thank God that he is in a safe place and that with patience all will happen and be fine. I promised him to plan some safe training for him: firing arms and with various weapons; however, I am somewhat behind (tn: in this promise) than what I like. Perhaps I will get to do this in the coming days – God willing.

Also I promised him (tn: Hamzah) with useful books and files; also he has a computer; thank God he is patient and intelligent. If you like to write him, please write him something proper (tn: encouraging).

Furthermore, I wish you would write on your own to Um Hamzah for any clear explanations, recommendations, and reminders; I will give them to read it (tn: what you write) on their own. May God have His blessings on you.

Now with regard the guard we have tried (tn: working) in this; the "brother" whom I tasked this job informed me that he has the following: ((but the special subject matter, the "brother" who is with me, is a "brother" who is a mujahid and received his training with us; he returned after he spent here almost four months. He is about thirty five (35) years old (I will verify this with him more); he is married; has small children (but I will send you their number, the age of each one next time – God willing), and he used to have a shop or some shops in Lahore; he is a savvy person, mature, confident, and understands the subject matter of renting, selling, and purchasing homes, including all necessary procedures to lead a civil life; he knows how to behave in cities with God help. However, he is not a Pashtu; he is a Punjabi; what is your opinion? As far as I am concerned, I will send you all the information about him the next time around – God help me)).

And just like you see, my friend continues to verify the character and qualifications of this man; but anyway (tn: remember) he is an Urdu/Punjabi.

May be I will find this time our "brother" Elyas Kashmiri; he may have a qualified person.

Page 3 of 4

And like you may have noticed from what I said, Hamzah is now with us in the province. Some projects came to a stop because 'Abd al-Latif is away now. The problems increased with the death of Muhammad Khan and brother Mu'awiyah al-Balushi; they were overseeing road planning and expansion deep into Baluchistan by visiting safe places. May God reward them because they went and explored places and planned things; but a little bit after they returned to the area, they were martyred in a shelling, Thanks be to God.

5. I would like to tell you about our "brothers" who – Thank God – completed the deal well of the Afghan Ambassador and we freed him. May be you were able to watch the news. We received all or most of the money (it is possible that some money is kept with the warrant agent, but "they" may have receive the sum by now); the warrant agents are from Al Haqqani (tn: Capital "AL" means family or tribe) from whom comes al-Hajji Ibrahim, the brother of Jalal al-Din, another man. The accomplishment of this sum is (equivalent to three million dollar) which we received in local currency.

6. With regard to the pledge, we made the pledge (during the last three years and one half after the "brothers" came from Iran) to sheikh Sa'id only; but I am his deputy at some circumstances, especially when sheikh Sa'id was away and the matter was urgent (for example: one "brother" was traveling to work overseas and we need to have him pledge; and when sheikh Sa'id is the South and I am in the North, etc.). Now I am in charge of overseeing and accepting pledges. Also I said to Abu Yahya to do the same in some circumstances, like what I did when sheikh Sa'id (tn: was in charge). One time the "brothers' of sheikh Yunis were traveling and I was away; it was difficult for me to meet them before they left. At that time, I sent them an audio recording and blessed the pledge by asking sheikh 'Umar Khalil (var. Omar Khaleel) in a letter asking him (tn: Khalil) to accept the pledge from these "brothers" in my behalf, which he did.

On our part, we take them (tn: pledges) in behalf of sheikh 'Usamah Bin Ladin as we say a statement in such format: "I pledge to you in behalf of sheikh 'Usamah Ben Ladin and to whomever from the emirs is tasked over me to carry out the jihad mission for the sake of God's kingdom and the nation of Islam which governs in God's laws; and to protect the secret of the "jama'ah" (group) and to be wherever ordered to be.

7. With regard the "brothers" who are prepared and ready for the responsibility in the future, like I mentioned to you before: brother (('Abd al-Jalil)); there is brother Qari Sufyan al-((Magribi)) (var. Sufian al-((Mughrabi))); brother Anas al-((Subay'i)) who is good for some responsibilities – with God help – even though he is a bit difficult to an extent; but he possesses energy with good intuition and determination; you know him (tn: well). There is brother Abu Khalil who supports and helps in responsibilities; but he cannot do large things; there is a Pakistani brother named Ahmad Faruq (in charge of al-Sahab in Urdu); he is a respectable man; he knows Arabic in a good way; he possesses administrative skills, good mind, education, and dynamism; maybe we can incorporate him with in

the shurah this time – God willing. There is a brother named Abu Dujanah al- ((Masir)), AKA ((al-Basha)) – may God protect. And now we are in the process of testing/trying him to work in Pakistan; of course, Abu 'Umar al-((Masri)) (var. Abu 'Amru al-Masri); also ((Abu Salih)), Abu Ziyad al-(('Iraqi)) all are good for some of the works. There is also brother Abu Hafs al-((Shihri)) (var. Abou Hafs al-((Shahri))) who is the first cousin to Abu 'Uthman – (PBUH); He is now running the work and overseeing it in place of Abu 'Uthman; I believe he is better than Abu 'Uthman. And these are from the old "guards."

When it comes to the new generation, we have: brohter Abu 'Abd al-Rahman al-((Sharqi)) from Bahrain; a respectable young man; he is now in the foreign operations committee; a Kuwaiti brother named Abu al- Hasan al-((Wa'ili)) who works with me in communications; he participates in media; I consider him to be is a devout young man; another brother from the Peninsula (al-Jazirah) (tn: not clear if he worked for al-Jazira TV/Radio or to mean from the Arabian Peninsula). He is a fighter; we consider him to be a good man, intelligent, and honorable; his name is Abu Hamzah al-((Khalidi)) (he is the first cousin to sheikh al-((Khalidi)), who is in prison with sheikh al-((Fahd)) and sheikh al-((Khudayr)) in Saudi Arabia; he is now an emir of one brigade with us. These three have been with on the ground about three years; they continue to advance and we see blessings and success in them and from – Thank God. There are more from the new generation – and may God protect them all.

8. We are sending with this letter the sum of sixteen "lak" rupees; we sent you earlier eight and one half "lak." Based on the above, there is a balance of ten "lak" which we will send you next time – God willing. This is excellent as it is equivalent to thirty thousand Euro which you asked for and based on the currency exchange here it is 115 (the exchange rate went down and then went up). And God is with us.

With regard assigning someone who would qualify to oversee your treasury, I have a brother who can do this – God willing. I have not talked with him yet, but I shall try soon – God help me – and we shall send – God willing – a full audit.

Page 4 of 4

9. On the subject of finance and situations, let us tell you that – thank God – four months ago (around the month of this past ramadan) we completed an agreement with our "brother" sheikh Abu Yahya to merge in full with al-"tanzim" (tn: al-Qa'idah) and he agreed – may God bless him – on one condition (his condition is that he and all his brothers who were martyred: Abu al-Layth, Abu Sahl, and 'Abdallah Sa'id) is that when they joined al-"tanzim" they want to have the financial autonomy and to keep their revenues and investments. Thank God, this is over and unity is completed in a full manner in everything. Abu Yahya gave all his resources and every income he receives he transfers to the general budget; now he has for him – from the financial committee in al-"tanzim" – a special budget appropriate for his monthly needs which he can spend anyway he likes (friends, gifts, guest, network circle, etc) – Thank God.

The good news is we are in one heart, loving, confident, and cooperating; we pray God to bless us this group which got together for HIS Glory. Also I had informed Abu Muhammad (tn: possibly al-Zawahiri) about the above (tn: agreement with Abu Yahya) as well as Abu Yahya wrote him too. He is very happy; he wrote me back asking me to tell you about it. Thank God.

10. I would like to inform you that sheikh Yunis left us. However he continues to be in the frontiers area on the Baluchistan side because "they" are planning to enter – God help them – Iran. Al his friends are with him and I believe they count to be six. We pray God to cover for them and protect them.

And with regard the difficulty in communication about the killing of the "brothers," I did not send him your last letter yet; God willing, we shall send when time permits.

11. With regard the family file/folder which you sent last time to 'Abd al-Latif, it is still with me; should I delete it or would like anything from it?

And this is what God enabled me – All Glory to HIM…and there no other God but HIM.

Peace to you and may HIS mercy and blessing with you you

Mahmud

Tuesday, November 24 2010 (17 Dhu al-Hijja 1431 H)

End of letter

----

6. Letter to Abdallah

This is a letter reinforcing communication, discussing marriage, and coordinating a meeting in Peshawar.

Date: 26 April 2011

From: Khalid

http://www.dni.gov/files/documents/ubl/english/Letter%20to%20Abdallah.pdf

Arabic

In the Name of God the Most Merciful

Thanks be to God and peace be upon his prophet and his companions

To dear brother 'Abdallah

Peace and God's mercy and blessings be upon you

I pray that you receive this letter while in good health

My dear brother,
I had sent you a previous message through Shaykh Mahmud, asking for your phone number so that I can arrange the affairs of my marriage to the daughter of Shaykh Abu 'Abd-al-Rahman (God's mercy be upon him) and I hope that we will receive the number very soon God willing.

My dear brother,
I would like to recommend to you that we arrange for a meeting. If you have any suggestions, please write me and let me know.

1. We are calling you from Peshawar, and the brother who is with me will conduct the phone call with you and we agree to a place to meet at in Peshawar.

And lastly,
My father sends you his greetings. May God keep you. Peace and God's mercy and blessings be upon you.

Your brother,

Khalid
April 26, 2011

7. Letter to UBL from daughter Khadijah

> Family updates are given, as are wishes for further communication and visits.
>
> Date: Unknown
>
> From: Khadijah
>
> http://www.dni.gov/files/documents/ubl/english/Letter%20to%20UBL%20from%20daughter%20Khadijah.pdf

In the name of God the merciful, the compassionate:

To my dear dad, may God protect him from all evil. Greetings, and may God's mercy and blessing be upon you.

How are you? What is new? I hope my message reaches you and that you are well, as we are, praise God.

Dear father, I learned from Abbi-'Abdallah that we were blessed with younger brothers, Asiya and Ibrahim. May God bless you with them and make them righteous. I got your message approximately nine months ago and took great delight in it, especially your advice, which is indispensible to us. I wrote you a message and sent it but it later became clear that it did not reach you. I hope all is well. We constantly yearn for you and delight in hearing your voice messages, and 'Abdallah and 'A'ishah (TN: LNU, NFI) also. Especially 'Abdallah, he often sends you greetings and says that he hopes to see you. He says he will work hard and learn to read and write so he can send you a letter that he wrote himself.

The birth message reached us. I learn from it that we would have met, if not for the road conditions. God preordained, and what he wanted was done. Abu-'Abdallah wrote you about the travel preparations to get your opinion. When your response came with the choice that there was danger, we are staying, we understood that this is your response to our message. It became clear from my mother's message that she (TN: or possibly "it;" not clear) did not reach you. Praise God, in any case.

My father, I have a request from you. Please do not let it be any burden upon you, nor any harm to your safety, that is the most important thing. My request is that if there is any opportunity to visit you, do not let it pass us by. Ramadan is approaching. We ask God to let us obtain his fast and resurrection. We are constantly ready, God willing.

In closing, I send my greetings to Umm-Ibrahim and Safiyah. We hope you remember us in your prayers.

Greetings, and may God's mercy and blessing be upon you.

Your daughter Khadijah, 24 Rajab (TN: year unknown)

PART TWO: LETTERS LIKELY WRITTEN TO USAMA BIN LADEN

> ## 8. Verbally Released Document for Naseer Trial
>
> A personal note to Bin Laden, this letter expresses devotion to Bin Laden and his guidance. The authors convey that they are witnessing the faltering of the U.S. and its allies and they express their continued commitment to the Mujahidin.
>
> Date: Unknown
>
> From: Brothers (Abu-Bashir al-Najdi, Sultan al-'Abdali "Qattal" al-Jawadi, 'Abdallah Bin-'Umar al-Qurashi Abu-Dumdum al-Qurashi)
>
> http://www.dni.gov/files/documents/ubl/english/Verbally%20Released%20doc%20for%20Naseer%20trial.pdf

"In the name of Allah, Most Gracious, Most Merciful"

Praise be to Allah, the Cherisher and Sustainer of the Worlds; God's blessings and peace be upon the noblest of prophets and messengers, our Prophet Muhammad, and upon his good relatives and companions.

To our meritorious shaikh,

Shaikh 'Usamah, may God protect him and watch over him,

Peace be upon you, God's mercy and blessings:

I ask God, the Great and Almighty, that you will be closer to God, more devoted and in good health when my message reaches you.

Oh our meritorious shaikh, how much we miss you, miss sitting with you and looking at your enlightened face and your radiant smile.

Oh our shaikh, even though it is taking a long time, yet we are judged favorably by God the Almighty. Few more days and this ordeal will disappear, we will be awarded, we will rejoice with you and the Muslims will rejoice likewise.

Oh our shaikh:

I advise you to be devoted to God the Great and Almighty, to persevere on this path and to be patient at it.

As far as my friends and me, we bring you the good news that we will continue with our pledge. We will not yield, we will not submit; and, with God's support, we are [UI] steadfast.

We know, our shaikh, the pleasure we bring to your heart is dearer to us than the world and what's in it.

We ask God the Exalted to expedite this matter, sooner rather than later.

Oh our shaikh, I send you my best regards. Likewise, my brothers Jalbib al-Ruqi, Saif al-Najdi, Abu-al-Harith al-'Amiri, 'Isma'il al-Qusaimi, Qattal al-Najdi and Abu-Dumdum al-Ta'ifi.

Your brother in God,

Abu-Bashir al-Najdi

Saturday, Rabi' al-Thani 7, 1430

"In the name of Allah, Most Gracious, Most Merciful"

To our precious and beloved shaikh whom we loved in God, and to our wise father whom we accepted as our Emir, the mujahid shaikh, the father:

PART TWO: LETTERS LIKELY WRITTEN TO USAMA BIN LADEN

Osama bin Mohammed bin Awad bin Laden

May God protect him, look after him, make paradise his final resting place, and end his life with martyrdom in His cause, Amen.

Oh our precious shaikh, what are we to tell you as we are at the doorsteps of the sword blades and the rumbling of death. What are we to say as the doorsteps of summer and fighting the crusaders is upon us. By God, we only say that we shall continue with our pledge and that we shall remain our God's mujahidin. Move us forward, Abu-'Abdallah, as paradise is the promise. By God, we shall not forsake you and we will not replace you.

Here we are today, praise be to God, watching the faltering of the US and its allies. By God, we shall not stop, God willing, except at the doorsteps of the White House, and to raise the banner of monotheism on their so-called Statue of Liberty.

God knows, oh our shaikh, that the eyes, the hearts and all the organs yearn for sitting with you and feel at ease with your conversation. We ask God to pave the way for this and to foreordain us to meet you at the doorsteps of Mecca al-Mukarramah after conquering it and liberating it from the hands of the immoral apostates.

God be our witness, we fight in Afghanistan and Waziristan with our eyes on the Arab Peninsula. May God bring back the glory of our shaikhs al-'Aybari and al-Muqrin. We ascertain, rather we swear on the Book of God that the bloods of those heroes will not go in vain. We only await your signal. Tomorrow is near for the one who waits. Revenge, revenge, oh our shaikh, from Al Salul, and we seek support from God.

Finally, my compassionate and precious father, I advise you to be devoted to God and to persevere. Persevere as your sons the mujahidin are following your example and course. We seek God's support and in Him we trust. Our last prayer is Praise be to Allah, the Cherisher and Sustainer of the Worlds.

Your son who loves you in God

Sultan al-'Abdali "Qattal" al-Jadawi

Rabi' al-Thani 7, 1430

By God, oh our shaikh, we continue with our pledge and forward on the road we move. We shall not quit and we shall not give up. Throw us wherever you wish and you will find but men who were patient at war and were truthful at martyrdom.

By God, oh our shaikh, your patience and your perseverance are the best of what keeps us on the road. The brothers who were killed will be rewarded by God as this is the way. Do not grieve; rejoice, as victory is near.

Finally, God knows we love you in Him. My mother, my father and my relatives pray for you privately and openly; and, they send their regards. The good news is that one of my brothers martyred in Waziristan. When my father heard the news, he prostrated in thanks to God the Great and Almighty.

All those around me send you their regards.

One of your soldiers from Al-Faruq Battalion in the country of Khurasan.

'Abdallah Bin-'Umar al-Qurashi
Abu-Dumdum al-Qurashi

Saturday, Rabi' al-Thani 7, 1430

Salutaion.

9. Letter addressed to Shaykh

Abu-'Abdallah al-Halabi mentions martyrdom, and reiterates his dedication to the Shaykh. Additionally, secret letter exchanges are coordinated.

Date: 15 November or December (year unknown)

From: Abu-'Abdallah al-Halabi

http://www.dni.gov/files/documents/ubl/english/Letter%20addressed%20to%20Shaykh.pdf

Page 1

In the name of God the compassionate and the merciful

Praise be to Allah and prayers be upon his messengers and companions,

To my precious father, my beloved Shaykh, and my dear Emir, may God protect you and take care of you.

May God's Peace, his grace and blessings be upon you.

I pray to God that my letter will find you well and in good health.

God knows how ecstatic and exultant I was to receive the letters of my mother and Abu Sulayman and to see the pictures of the children who had made it to you. The letters arrived during a sad time that witnessed the martyrdom of one of God's brave warriors, Shaykh Abu 'Ubaydah al-Masri, whom I felt was a guiding father to the brothers; so many learned from that man. We pray to God to reward him for his deeds and bestow on our wounded Ummah (TN: the nation) someone with even better qualities.

My dear father, God knows I don't want to waste any of your valuable time but I really need your clarification on whether I have done anything inappropriate, written something that made you mad or antagonized you. God knows how much I love you. You are my most cherished person. I have so much respect and appreciation for you. God knows how sad I am for all the years that passed by with me unable to provide you with any support. When you asked for my help, I was incapable of assisting you and being by your side when you needed me in the past. That was the first time I wished I was an Afghani or a Pakistani. My dear Emir, God knows how much affection, love, respect, and appreciation I have for you.

Page 2

My dear Shaykh, I am waiting on one of the brothers whom I have solicited. He will be leaving to celebrate a religious holiday and I need to know from him how he arranges for the delivery of a letter to Hejaz [TC: a region in Saudi Arabia]. I will tell him who will take delivery of the letter over there and take it to uncle Bakr.

My Shaykh, please include me in your prayer and ask God to grant me patience and steadiness. May God reunite us with you.

Peace be upon you.

Your son, the neglectful, Abu-'Abdallah al-Halabi

Monday 15 Dhu l-Hijja [TC: Hijri Calendar. Year unknown – either November or December]

(TN: END OF TRANSLATION)

PART TWO: LETTERS LIKELY WRITTEN TO USAMA BIN LADEN

> ## 10. Letter to Shaykh from Abu Abdallah (UBL)
>
> Abu 'Abdallah al-Halabi expresses his happiness and gratitude about hearing from his family. He questions if he has done anything to anger the Shaykh; although he wasn't able to help him in a time of need in the past, al-Halabi is ready to serve now.
>
> Date: Unknown
>
> From: Abu 'Abdallah al-Halabi
>
> http://www.dni.gov/files/documents/ubl/english/Letter%20to%20Shaykh%20from%20Abu%20Abdallah.pdf

(Fully Translated)

In the Name of Allah, the Merciful, the Beneficent.

Praise be to Allah, the Lord of all worlds. Prayers and peace be upon His Messenger.

To the Father, the [paternal] Uncle, and the beloved Shaykh, may Allah protect and watch over all of you.

May Allah be pleased with us and with all of you. May each year find you well and in good health. May Allah have mercy on the deceased Muslims. I ask the Almighty Allah that this letter finds all of you well and in good health and soon to be relieved.

Praise Allah, I received the letter from you and I wrote back as soon as I read it. I ask that all of you coordinate with Shaykh 'Uthman [to] send the children. My beloved father, by God, immediately after reading the letter, I told him [and] he will send all of them. He said that 'Abdallah was still in the school and Suham still has a year of breast feeding. So I told him, "All of them." God willing, my dear father and emir, I want to adhere to what you wrote, listening and abiding by everything from your (TN: plural) end. For I am the negligent son to you, and they are your grandchildren. God knows that I understand that all of you miss them dearly.

My beloved shaykh, as all of you know, roughly three days after the death of [my dear wife], may Allah have mercy on her, I was wishing to propose to any widow so I that could gather my children and they wouldn't have to live without a mother and a father. I was wishing for guidance, and I told myself that I would await your (TN: plural) correspondence, but this was before, and the years passed. Most of the time, I remained in the house and it was very difficult for me and for them; however, with God's grace, [we] made it through. During the time of the holiday, 'A'ishah (Var.: 'Ayisha or 'Aisha) was very sad up into the afternoon, and no one could make her feel better.

She was there wearing her holiday dress. So, in the early morning [the next day], I took them to our old house and bathed all of them and dressed them in their holiday clothes, and praise Allah, she was much more happy. A photograph of them is attached to the letter. After this, I decided to begin searching for any widow so that I wouldn't be living in sin for the sake of my children. I proposed to the daughter of Shaykh 'Abd-al- Rahman pm (TN: sic; "pm" as given in Latin characters in the original), may Allah have mercy on him, from the family of Abu Bakr, may Allah have mercy on him. By the grace of Allah, [I proposed to her] three days before receiving the letter from all of you.

My dear father, by God, I proposed without your knowledge, and the reason for this was a lack of correspondence with all of you. If [had been communication], I wouldn't have dared to do so; however, with Allah's grace, I did so. This is difficult to go back on; however, if Allah wills it and this is not agreed upon, then I will await until Allah relieves it.

My shaykh and my emir, do not forget me in your prayers, with patience and in being steadfast. Pray that Allah rewards me with martyrdom upon His path, advancing forward and not in retreat. I am ready for any order you may give me. My father, may Allah reward all of you for the amount (TN: of money) that you sent, it was a great amount. I put/deposited it such that Allah may heal the hearts of the believers. May Allah accept this from us and from all of you. May Allah be patient with us and with all of you. Peace be upon you, with the mercy and blessings of Allah.

Your [delinquent] son, Abu 'Abdallah al-Halabi.

Dated: 20 Shawwal (TN: year not given)

My beloved Shaykh, praise be to Allah, then praise be to Allah, then praise be to Allah. The reply came with the rejection of the family of Abu Bakr al-Suri, may Allah have mercy on him. Praise be to Allah that the children be with all of you. This was the matter that made me feel compelled to propose. Praise Allah, I will wait, and this is best, so that both we and all of you may be relieved of these matters.

PART THREE: LETTERS TO/ FROM MEMBERS AND LEADERS

> ### 1. Letter from Al-Zawahiri dtd August 2003
>
> Religious histories and stories are mentioned in this letter, which is largely a theoretical message. It is mentioned that Al-Zawahiri did not intend to add to the Qur'an, but rather to clarify religious points of movement and motivations of al Qa'ida.
>
> From: Al-Zawahiri
>
> http://www.dni.gov/files/documents/ubl/english/Letter%20from%20Al-Zawahiri%20dtd%20August%202003.pdf

(Page 1 of 4)

In the name of God, the Compassionate, the Merciful

Introduction

Why this letter?

The issue of submitting to the God of all worshipers, glory and praise be to him, in providing legislation to His worshipers – despite the passing of the times and ages – is one of the most important issues of all times and ages, if it is not the number one issue. Therefore, it is one of the most serious issues of our time and age. This meaning is very important to highlight to the righteous people of this time, for their hearts to be reassured that they are engaging in the same battles that were conducted by God's messengers and their followers of the faithful people for all time.

This is for them to realize from current examples that the battle of right against wrong is one intertwined single battle – since God created the creations – the Glorified and Exalted – until Allah Almighty inherits the earth and who is on it in one battle in its objectives, its battlefields of struggle, and its distinguished sides even if the images and surface changed.

The Almighty says: (TC: Qur'anic verse). For we assuredly sent amongst every people an apostle, (with the Command), "Serve God, and eschew Evil." Of the People were some whom God guided, and some on whom error became inevitably established. So travel through the earth, and see what was the end of those who denied (the Truth). (TN: Surah 16 verse 36)

Thus have we made for every prophet an enemy among the sinners: but enough is thy Lord to guide and to help. (TN: Surah 25 verse 31)

Also praise be to him says: The same religion has He established for you as that which He enjoined on Noah - that which we have sent by inspiration to thee - and that which we enjoined on Abraham, Moses, and Jesus: Namely, that ye should remain steadfast in religion, and make no divisions. Therein: to those who worship things other than God, hard is the (way) to which thou callest them. God chooses for Himself those whom He pleases, and guides to Himself those who turn (to Him). (TN: Surah 42 verse 13)

The Almighty has also said, "All that we relate to thee of the stories of the apostles,- with it we make firm thy heart: in them there cometh to thee the Truth, as well as an exhortation and a message of remembrance to those who believe. (TN: Surah 11 verse 120)

They said: "O Shu'ayb! Does thy (religion of) prayer command thee that we leave off the worship which our fathers practiced, or that we leave off doing what we like with our property? Truly, thou art the one that forbeareth with faults and is right- minded!" (TN: Surah 11 verse 87)

Introduction – 2

(Page 2 of 4)

The Holy Qur'an in its wide, clear, and decisive handling of this focal matter has been keen to show the sides of this historic battle at the time of the Prophet and link them with their counterparts and look-alikes through time and ages. The Almighty said, praise be to Him: we sent not an apostle, but to be obeyed, in accordance with the will of God. If they had only, when they were unjust to themselves, come unto thee and asked God's forgiveness, and the Apostle had asked forgiveness for them, they would have found God indeed Oft-returning, Most Merciful.

But no, by the Lord, they can have no (real) Faith, until they make thee judge in all disputes between them, and find in their souls no resistance against Thy decisions, but accept them with the fullest conviction. (TN: Surah 4 verses 64 and 65)

The Almighty says, praise be to him: It was we who revealed the law (to Moses): therein was guidance and light. By its standard have been judged the Jews, by the prophets who bowed to God's will, by the rabbis and the doctors of law: for to them was entrusted the protection of God's book, and they were witnesses thereto: therefore fear not men, but fear me, and sell not my signs for a miserable price. If any do fail to judge by (the light of) what God hath revealed, they are (no better than) Unbelievers. We ordained therein for them: "Life for life, eye for eye, nose or nose, ear for ear, tooth for tooth, and wounds equal for equal." But if anyone remits the retaliation by way of charity, it is an act of atonement for himself. And if any fail to judge by (the light of) what God hath revealed, they are (No better than) wrong-doers. And in their footsteps we sent Jesus the son of Mary, confirming the Law that had come before him: we sent him the Gospel: therein was guidance and light, and confirmation of the Law that had come before him: a guidance and an admonition to those who fear God. Let the people of the Gospel judge by what God hath revealed therein. If any do fail to judge by (the light of) what God hath revealed, they are (no better than) those who rebel. To thee we sent the Scripture in Truth, confirming the scripture that came before it, and guarding it in safety: so judge between them by what God hath revealed, and follow not their vain desires, diverging from the Truth that hath come to thee. To each among you have we prescribed a law and an open way. If God had so willed, He would have made you a single people, but (His plan is) to test you in what He hath given you: so strive as in a race in all virtues. The goal of you all is to God. it is He that will show you the Truth of the matters in which ye dispute; (TN: Surah 5 verses 44-48)

One might ask, why are we writing this new message about "The Governance?" And what might it add to preceding publications, old and new, independent in its subjects or included with others – written by respected scholars and callers from our advanced Imams or the respected that are lagging in this issue?

It is an important question to the reader and the writer of this message, because the answer would expose the purpose behind the writing of this letter on these subjects, specifically at this moment.

The purpose of the author of this letter was not to repeat what had been written before by respected scholars concerning this serious issue, that has not lost its seriousness even with the passage of ages – since it is considered the most important and main ideological issue for which books and messengers were sent by God, and animosity happened and Jihad was launched between the people of virtue and the people of falsehood.

Introduction – 3

(Page 3 of 4)

The author does not greedily intend to add to his predecessor's works, but rather seeks to clarify several points:

First: that the battle of the Zionist Crusaders against our nation – which is a battle that is old and new – it is not only waged against the military and economic levels, but and even before all of this, together and after it is waged against the intellectual and behavioral and social levels. The battle is against the ideology of the nation –especially in the case of who would rule– and consequently, the battle against the Shari'ah of the (TC: Islamic) nation is the most important battle due to, severe consequences on the (TC: Islamic) nation, it will change the nation from the concluding nation that carries the message of monotheism that will be a witness to all people, from a nation that orders what is good forbidding what is hated, to a gathering that follows, is corrupt, exhausted, immoral, and fights among itself.

Second: That our adversaries in this battle form an alliance that is not limited only to the invading armies, creditor banks, and the corrupt companies, but also spread inside our nation and societies in a shape of tyrant leaders, bribed writers, deviant thinkers, unjust judges, and finally, the most dangerous, is in the picture of scholars who work for rulers and the modern procrastinators.

For this, we hope that this message would enlighten the connection between the internal and external enemies in their goals and in their soldiers. Also, the goal of this message – during the identification of the parties to the battle in this modern series of conflict that extended through time, regarding the Lord's right to legislate for his creation with no equivalent – to expose the veil and take off the mask of the enemies of Islam that were hiding behind it and were diluting the issue of governing, to serve the interest of the enemies of Islam from the new Crusaders and the Jews and their puppets, the Muslim country leaders. God said, praise be to him: When thou lookest at them, their exteriors please thee; and when they speak, thou listenest to their words. They are as (worthless as hollow) pieces of timber propped up, (unable to stand on their own). They think that every cry is against them. They are the enemies; so beware of them. The curse of God be on them! How are they deluded (away from the Truth)! (TN: Surah 63 verse 4)

Part Three: Letters to/from Members and Leaders

This is what this letter aims for, only pleasing God, praise be to him, and to direct the people of virtue to the landmarks of their locations versus the locations of their enemy in the immortal battlefield between infidelity and the faith, about submitting to the creator of people for his right to rule and legislate, and to warn them from the eyes of their enemies that spy on them internally and whose goal is to shake their ranks until it is overcome by the mass of the new Crusaders and their Jewish allies, for crumbs that will end in a despicable life.

Introduction – 4

(Page 4 of 4)

Whatever is in this letter of good and enlightenment, it is a success from God only, who is the gracious one and who has no partner and to whom we owe gratitude. Anything other than that is from the writer himself and the Devil (I only want to correct what I can, my success when it comes is from God, I have depended on him and he is whom I refer to). And the last of our supplications is to God, the God of our creation, and God's praise be on our Prophet Muhammad and upon his family and his companions, may peace be upon them.

Ayman al-Zawahiri
Jumada al-Akhira 1424 Hijri, AUG 2003

Introduction - 5

(End of Translation)

> ## 2. Letter dtd 21 May 2007
>
> This letter reestablishes communication and reviews a meeting that took place at the Qandahar compound. Although this is a vague note, it mentions past movements in Egypt, and a wish to communicate with the recipient even though security conditions make this difficult. The recipient is providing aid to brothers in Egypt.
>
> From: Abu Hazim and Abu 'Umar
>
> http://www.dni.gov/files/documents/ubl/english/Letter%20dtd%2021%20May%202007.pdf

Translation begins here

Page 1

In the name of Allah, the most Merciful, the most Compassionate

Thanks be to God, peace and prayers be upon our prophet

The respected brother, Dr. Abu Muhammad (May God protect him)

Blessed and good greetings from God, and invocations to God (TN: that this letter) finds you, your family, the brothers and beloved all in good health that would satisfy Allah, the Almighty

Peace, mercy, and the blessings of Allah be upon you.

Our generous brother: We ask God that you all are successful in obeying Allah, working for aiding His faith and seeking his pardon and mercy because He is the protector and has power

Our generous brother: We had a good opportunity to communicate with you after a long separation between us for long years and so much water had flown into the river (TN: meaning so many things have happened since)

Our generous brother: God had estimated for us to return to Egypt to live a phase of activating the group's initiative and reap its fruit with the grace of Allah the greatest, to Him we give thanks and praise

Our generous brother: We reminisce about the long meeting we had privately at the Qandahar compound and its impact and consequences. I remember your esteemed words concerning the importance of the group seeking to resolve the problems of all detainees and not just the detainees of the Jama'ah Al-Islamiyah (TN: the Islamic Group). By God – this is the same as what is happening now. Our brothers in the Jama'ah Al-Jihad (TN: the jihad group) headed by Dr. Fadl began these operational and positive steps to achieve what the Islamic group had achieved – such as the course correction and attempt to liquidate all the suspended problems as a result of the clashes during the nineties of this past century. The most important being the release of prisoners and not keeping any one of them in jail; also opening positive environments in relations with the security that would allow a future political and da'awa (TN: call) horizon, God willing.

Our generous brother: What we had lived and touched during our presence in Egypt was a historical transfer with complete criteria at the level of understanding the actual situation from all entities on the Egyptian land (al-Jama'ah and the regime); everyone realized that it was not in the interest of any entity not to mention the supreme interest of Islam and continuing the armed conflict in the previous fashion. We all have to quickly seek to build a joint platform of supreme interest that would serve the supreme Islamic interest, Egypt, and the Islamic groups.

God is my witness O Doctor, there are elements in all entities with very high levels of responsibility, awareness, and realizations that this great mission is, in fact, in need of strong individuals and sincere to Allah of all seen and unseen. We ask Allah to count us and you amongst them to receive the honor of serving this great faith at all times and everywhere.

Our generous brother: Everyone here is eager to talk to you and communicate with you (Al-Jama'ah - Al-Jihad). However, no doubt we realize your security conditions are extremely difficult. We ask Allah to grant you health and perhaps God had provided us this opportunity to be a bridge between you and our brothers in Egypt.

Page 2

Seek Allah's help, our generous brothers, and be a key to bounty and a lock for evil, as we ask Allah to grant us a bountiful ending for you and us and good conclusion

Our generous brother: All we ask from your Excellency during this phase is diligence on our part, as we want, in the face of Allah, praise be to him, to react positively with our brothers' initiative in the Jama'ah al-Jihad. Many of the youths are waiting for your positive reaction, driving this project forward to reach its achievement and its completion, God willing. If your highness' circumstances do not allow you to have a positive reaction with this initiative, we would wish for you to remain quiet about the matter until Allah would order having a reaction.

We assess this would have a substantial interest, God willing, that would release thousands of brothers' youths in the Jama'ah al-Jihad as Allah had released more than 12 thousand brothers in the Jama'ah Al-Islamiyah thus far. It entails opening new environments at the social and economic level for these brothers. We ask Allah to soon facilitate the opportunity to open da'awa and political horizons to achieve these initiatives with promising goals, God willing.

Our generous brother: We ask Allah to place all of your good deeds in the balance of your righteous actions until Judgment Day.

We ask Allah to grant you success for a positive step to support your brothers in Egypt in this initiative, not to mention to be in the balance of lifting the worry off your brothers in Egypt – also to open doors of bounty everywhere, God willing.

Our generous brother: We stand ready to listen to your complete point of view through the mediator between us – May God please us – most importantly is to have a dialogue and communication between us before taking any step on your end. We shall also attempt to provide you with all the details that might be useful to you in assessing the real situation, God willing.

We ask God to help one another in righteousness and piety, but help ye not one another in sin and rancor. Until we meet, I commend you to God whose entrustment shall not be lost; and do not forget us in your invocations, as we pray always for you.

Peace, mercy and the blessings of Allah be upon you

Your brothers

((Abu Hazim)) (Mustafa)
((Abu 'Umar)) (Asad)
Turrah Farm Annex

Monday, 4 Jamadi Al-Awal 1428H – corresponding to 21 May 2007

> ## 3. Letter to Shaykh Azmaray, 4 February 2008
>
> An issue in the Afghani courts is mentioned as well as a thesis on the Jihadi work in Egypt. This thesis provoked a response from a brother that is outlined in a document titled, "The Declaration on Innocence."
>
> From: Unknown
>
> http://www.dni.gov/files/documents/ubl/english/Letter%20to%20Shaykh%20Azmaray%20dtd%204%20February%202008.pdf

Page: 1

In the name of God the most merciful

Praise be to God who kept His promises and forgave us our sins and prayers and peace be upon Prophet Muhammad, his family and companions.

To the honorable Shaykh Azmaray, may God protect him,

God's peace, mercy, and blessing be upon you. I hope that you and all those who are with you are in good health enjoying God's blessings. May God grant you success in everything that would please Him and May He gather us in this life or the life to come.

1- I received your letter dated 17 December 2007.

2- May God reward you for the death of the Libyan brothers, al-Shaykh Abu al-Layth and Shaykh Abu Suhayl and other brothers who were with them. Perhaps the brothers can give you the details.

3- The (TN: unclear word) and the letter

A- In the previous letter, I talked to you about the issue of Mullah Mansur. The issue has developed. The Mullah asked him in an audio tape to hand the two that he has over to Baytallah Mas'ud (var: Baitullah) to be questioned about what Mansur accused them of. Baytallah promised to present them to some trustworthy Afghani judges. Mansur agreed and asked for more time, but then killed them. Baytallah became very angry with him and asked him to leave the area. Also, the Mullah got mad at him and fired him.

B- A while before the aforementioned incident, al-Hafiz and I agreed to not send any letters to the Mullah and to destroy my letter that is with al-Hafiz, until things become clearer, especially because al-Tayyib did not find al-Hafiz. Also, Yasir advised us in these circumstances to restrict our letters to regular niceties and only emphasize our commitment to listen and obey, because we are not sure how letters get delivered, who receives them, or who copies them. What do you think of this decision? May God help us.

4- The latest news on al-Zayyat:

A representative from the people of the country contacted one of the brothers there and asked to meet with him to talk about al-Zayyat and his partners. Al-Hafiz has the details. I do not know if what was mentioned in your last speech and in the speech of Abu Muhammad (footnote 1) about them has any relation with this move.

(TN: below is the footnote)

1) I attach for you the fourth dialogue of al-Sahab with Abu Muhammad, titled (Opinion on Events).

Page: 2

We pray to God to facilitate things. I do not have anything else to mention, except for what Mahmud told me in his tapes which I will send to you with this letter (footnote 1). I will follow up with al-Hafiz, God willing.

5- Fadil's retraction, and the declaration of innocence:

Dr. Fadil published a thesis that he titled 'The Document for Channeling the Jihadi Work in Egypt and the World.' It is a document of surrender that includes cursing and insults to Shaykh Usama and Abu Muhammad. It was also followed by a long interview with al-Hayat newspaper, in which he doubled the insults.

Abu Muhammad wrote a response to him, in a letter titled 'The Declaration of Innocence.' He sent several copies of it to a number of brothers in order for them to express their opinion on it from a scholarly and stylistic point of view, in order to be sure not to fall to the level of Fadil's document. He received responses from Shaykh Mahmud and al-Hafiz, and a revision of the letter is being conducted at this time based on those notes. I personally think that the letter is good and the brothers can add to it in other responses.

Abu Mahmud benefited from the comments of the two brothers and then decided to publish the letter in its amended form, because communication with the brothers is taking a long time and because he thought that delaying the response would not be a good thing and not let others think that there was no response because the Mujahidin are weak (footnote 2).

As you will see, Mahmud focused on chapter seven which is related to the visa and the oath. Abu Muhammad rewrote that chapter and included the feedback that was provided by Mahmud, in addition to the fatwa of Shaykh Nasir al-Fahd on the visa and the events of 9/11 and some other additions. I believe that with these changes, chapter seven is strong. We hope that it will be released soon and that it will be instrumental in showing the truth. May God help us.

6- I will send Mahmud what you asked me to send as soon as possible.

Finally, I leave you in the hands of God and I pray to Him to protect you and guard you from the enemy. May He also expedite our victory. Please convey my greetings to everyone that I know on your side. Peace be upon you.

Your loving brother,

4 February 2008

(TN: below are footnotes)

1) Mahmud's letters came in as responses to questions that I asked him after he returned safely. They can be found in a folder named (Mahmud's Tapes).
2) Attached is the original declaration of innocence under the name (Declaration of Innocence 1). You will see that some additions were added to it when compared to the copy that was sent to the brothers. I also attached to you the copy that was sent to Mahmud with his comments under the name (Declaration of Innocence – with Mahmud's Comments) and the copy that was sent to Hafiz Sultan with his comments under the name Declaration of Innocence – with Hafiz Sultan's Comments). Also, attached is the final copy of the (Declaration of Innocence) after some of the comments by Mahmud Sultan were added to it under the name (Declaration of Innocence 2).

4. Letter dtd March 2008

In this diplomatic letter, Mahmud requests that future correspondences and comments be more compatible and kind. Examples of appropriate writing and responses are given. Discussions on different cases of law, faith, and operational technicalities are adjusted.

From: Mahmud

Pages: 9

http://www.dni.gov/files/documents/ubl/english/Letter%20dtd%20March%202008.pdf

Page 1

In the name of God the most merciful

Praise be to the lord of the universe and prayers and peace be upon our prophet Muhammad, his family and companions

God's peace, mercy, and blessings be upon you.

I pray to God for you to be well and in good health, and to grant you success and blessings.

I read the comments by the two brothers and honorable shaykhs Abu-al-Hasan and Abu-Yahya on the Faith message. I was comforted and greatly pleased with their beneficial comments that are indicative, through the generosity of God, of love, honesty, and sincerity. They are great brothers and great soldiers of Islam. I pray to God to bless them and bless their leaders who have every right to be proud of them and be assured that they have real men standing by them. Praise be to God. Based on his words, it seems that Shaykh Abu-al-Hasan did not know who the writer of the letter is, but in spite of that, he was generous with his comments, details, advice, and feedback. May God reward him.

I noticed great sensitivity, especially on Shaykh Abu-Yahya's part, with the issue of some strong words in the language of the Shaykh that can be misunderstood, especially on things related to the tendency to accuse individuals and groups of being non- believers. This is the same feeling that I have and this is attributed to all that we see in terms of youth in and outside the Islamic Jihadi arena. By God, the issue of Takfir and the rapid utilization of it is one of the greatest problems and troubles. There is a rush to conflict, disagreement, and judgment. You are also aware of some of the rough terminology that in some cases and circumstances allowed others, who speak in gentler tones, to step ahead of them (TN: rough speakers), May God help us.

Therefore, I would like to urge brother Abu-Yahya and all other brothers to ensure that they emphasize this in their directions, instructions, writings, and advice.

God is the giver of success, and He guides us to the best path. We pray for His generosity and blessings.

I pray to God to support you and make us imams on the right path and an instrument for guidance. Amen.

Examples of the compatibility in the comments:

Page 2

'Atiyah:

There are many actions with specific rulings on them in the Shari'a that the rulers kept away from the ears of people. You might deny their existence (some of you or some people) because they are not used to hearing them. For example: if a ruler supports an infidel country (and aids it) against Islam and its people, and the scholar later claims that he is in charge (and legitimate and should be listened to and obeyed and should not be disobeyed), then I would call things in their Shari'a names, for the ruler committed an act that is contrary to Islam and he should be considered an infidel and an apostate. Based on that, there are several obligations, including rejecting him, revolting against him, and toppling him. Here the scholar is being very hypocritical.

(It seems to me that one needs to be careful with these issues, especially because these words are coming from a Shaykh and a leader who is a role-model. He should lead, make sure of the accuracy of each statement, avoid giving people illusions, and not cause divisions through his words. This is especially true because many of the youth of our nations and others are receptive to radicalism, isolationism, and divisions, due to several reasons including the bad and frustrating situation of the nation and (TN: the problem) of the class of scholars. What I mean is that such talk about bad scholars who work for current apostate governments in our countries is very sensitive issue that should be addressed in detail, with extreme care, and fear of mistakes. We should do great job, otherwise we would be accused of injustice like we are accusing them. In the past, this lowly servant wrote about this issue in some short responses. I might move some of them to attachments folder. I go back to commenting on this paragraph. It would be best if the paragraph on a scholar contains some restrictions and reservations, such as, "If the scholar knows that the ruler is a non-believer, he would be considered a hypocrite.")

Page 3

Abu-Yahya:

There are many actions with specific ruling on them in the Shari'a that the rulers kept away from the ears of people (and strived to lessen them to the best of their ability). They might deny their existence because they are not used to hearing them. For example: if a ruler supports an infidel country against Islam and its people, and the scholar later claims that he is in charge (should be listened to and obeyed and should not be disobeyed), then I would call things in their Shari'a names, for the ruler committed an act that is contrary to Islam and he should be considered an infidel and an apostate.

Based on that, there are several obligations, including rejecting him, revolting against him, and toppling him (and working hard on that). Here the scholar is being very hypocritical.

Note:

No doubt that these words are not against the approach because the scholar might have the right starting point based on true and legal jurisprudence, but was mistaken in the conclusion like anyone would in scientific and practical issues. Confusion could happen, based on the evidence used to build the argument. It (TN: confusion) also might occur in the application of the Shari'a ruling to the situation. So mistakes can happen in understanding the evidence and in the application of the ruling. You cannot say that any scholar who issues a fatwa, such as the ones that the Shaykh mentioned, is a great hypocrite. I also think that using such absolute language can open a wave of excessiveness against us by some of the enthusiastic youth. Such waves are not desired and they would take us back to debates that, through the generosity of God, we feel that we are beyond them. I think that we should pay great attention to this and if this sentence has to be used, I suggest that it should be as the following:

The scholar who issues a fatwa on the obligation of obeying the ruler even in the presence of evidence of the ruler's apostasy, he would be clearly contradicting the truth. As result, he should not be followed and should be responded to in order to show him his mistake and deviation from the truth. That is the case even if he has an excuse for his decision, for having an excuse does not mean that he should not be criticized.

Page 4

This is especially true on clear and obvious issues that most evidence and scholars agree upon and the educated and the ordinary people know the answer to, such as the issue of declaring anyone who supports the infidels against Muslims as a non-believer and the ruler should not be followed as soon as he becomes an apostate and he should be toppled.

Abu-Yahya:

So, let us study the issue of our faith and let us review together these words (note: a large section of this was removed and I do not think that it should be added, especially because the intention here is to show the truth about these names, and not to judge and divide the people. Categorizing people in such fashion–even when it is accurate-might be used by some youth for incitement and for starting things that they know nothing about. When we address people, we should be careful to this segment of the youth which can be more harmful to jihad and al-Mujahidin than anything else).

On the definition of worship and Islam, I say:

'Atiyah:

So, let us study the issue of our faith and let us review together these words. First I want to confirm that the overwhelming majority of the children of our nation are worshipers of God almighty, and the mosques that are full of worshipers are evidence of that. These people are divided into two sections:

Page 5

One section worships God alone. Notice the word "alone" here. These people are on the right path and they are the ones who were promised paradise. May God make me and make you among them. The other section, worships God almighty and something else, even when they do not feel that they are doing so. These individuals have lost the true path and conducted some acts of polytheism. May God save us from polytheism. The reason for (here it is best to say: among the reasons are so and so. The reason is not ignorance only; it is greater than that. It is not accepting the truth and the guidance, and not searching for it at the first place, because they are busy with life and loving it and preferring it. This means being satisfied and pleased with life. This meaning was mentioned repeatedly in the Quran. Most of misguidance and non-belief by the people happens because of love life and preferring it over eternity. In my opinion, it would be best here to point out that these reasons collectively should not be ignored) this is that the meaning of worship and the meaning of "there is no god but God" has been badly damaged. Fixing this damage is the heart of what we are talking about. (It would be better here to right something like: regardless of the ruling, whether they are declared as nonbelievers, outside the nation, or continue to be within the circle of Islam, it would require guidelines and details. We should look at all issues related to it, including its forms, its conditions, and things that would prevent it, but I am just describing the unfortunate situation.)

On the issue of defining worship and Islam, I would say:

Abu-Yahya:

Page 6

Then we come to the meaning of the testimony that there is no god but God, I say: this testimony is a great statement and it contains a call to all people and it is the greatest words that a human being can say. These words are the line between non- belief and believing, and through it one enters the faith of the truth if he was aware of its true meaning and determined to do what it takes.

(Note: there is no need to mention these two conditions, even though they are true, because they might be misused by some who look for anything that could be misinterpreted. They might be interpreted as not accepting Muslims as Muslims when they state these words, instead we will wait until we make sure that they know the meaning of it and do what it takes. The idea here is to be specific in your selection of words and in your sentences so that you express the intended meaning and not to become a target for the immature and the shallow.)

Abu-Yahya:

(This is not strongly tied to what was mentioned previously; it was talking about the issues of legislating, permitting, and prohibiting, and then it moved to the issue of supporting the infidels against the Muslims and it mentioned some of the forms of that support. Even the statement went beyond Yemen to include other countries, such as Pakistan and others. This might be a known contradiction to Islam, but it is a totally different from the issues of legislating, permitting, and prohibiting. Here, I think that you should not get into small and detailed issues, and instead stay generic by saying that those oppressors gave themselves the right to legislate, and deciding on things to permit and prohibit, and oppressed those who disagree with them and try to revolt against their god-like authority.

Page 7

This is a known issue and proving it does not require getting detailed and into micro details which might weaken this research. I also do not like to mention al-Zindani, because in spite of all the ugly things that he did, many admirers and supporters of Jihad inside and outside of Yemen respect him, honor him and might seek his advice. To be fair, a significant number of al-Mujahidin who reach the jihadi arena here were instructed or prepared by him, especially the new Russian converts to Islam who moved from Russia to Yemen and stayed for a while at al-Iman University and then moved with their families to the field of Jihad. We do not think that there is a need at this time to open a front against him and against his followers. This issue is not too complicated or a heavy weight in our war against the crusaders and their tails. We have to choose between being silent or outspoken in a way that can achieve the goal without getting into unnecessary wrangling. This is my thinking on this issue. I suggest that you delete the part that talks about the sergeant of Yemen unless you want to mention some of the things that they did and were contradictory to Islam in a different paragraph, you should talk about their support to the infidels in their war against the Muslims. As for al-Zindani and al-Iman University, I think that should be deleted completely.
God know best.

'Atiyah:

PART THREE: LETTERS TO/FROM MEMBERS AND LEADERS

…..who tried 'Abid-al-Razzaq who killed the evangelists in Yemen who were spreading Christianity and were able to convince some families to convert to it. The Yemeni justice system sentenced him to death in accordance to the religion of 'Ali-Bin-'Abdallah Saleh in order to appease the Americans. When one of the lions of Islam killed one of the great heretics of socialism, who is known for his heresies inside the council of representatives, the president of al-Iman University stood up to defend him and said that he prays.

Page 8

Prayer did not preserve the blood of those who refused to allow alms (and the atheist heretics), so why would it preserve the blood of those who deny that the authority is in the hands of God (and competes with God with through his rule and arrogance)?

O director of al-Iman University, did your confusion on the issues related to faith reach this extent?

(Is it appropriate to point to the director of al-Iman University through this strait forward statement? If your intention is to talk about al-Shaykh al-Zindani, perhaps you should soften the statement and delete the end of it. It would be enough for you to say, "Did the confusion on the issues related to faith reach this extent?" At the beginning of the sentence you can say, "Some got up to defend him.")

Abu-Yahya:

He said about the battle of Muraysi', "We returned to the city in order for the proud to push out the lowly." He said this in front of members of his tribe and his companions, including Zayd Bin-Arqam who was a young man. He told his uncle, the prophet, while 'Umar was with him. 'Umar said, "Order 'Abad Bin-Bishr to kill him." (Note: there is no doubt that a segment of youth might understand the sentence "Order 'Abad Bin-Bishr to kill him" as a call to kill the misleading scholars, while I know very well that al-Shaykh, may God protect him, did not want that and this never came to him mind.

This sentence might be valuable find for some extremists who are carefully looking for someone to agree with their desires. I think that this sentence should be completely removed and make the words on dealing with them clear and precise. They (TN: words) should call for disregarding their fatwas, not listen to their absurdity, warn people about their misguidance, and refute their false arguments which they mix with some truth in order to give their arguments some credibility to be able to promote them.)

Page 9

This is the duty of the Muslims and the way that they should deal with the scholars who appear on TV channels (I think that you should remove this sentence because not everyone who appears on TV channels is the same. It would be enough to use the shaykh's next sentence) today and the official and unofficial scholars of the sultans who lie to God and to people and discourage people from Jihad in Afghanistan and Iraq.

Abu-al-Hasan:

In order for the Muslims to know how to treat those individuals and anyone like them, they need to look at how the companions of the prophets treated the leaders of the hypocrites, 'Abdallah Bin-Abu-Salul, who used to stand every Friday and used to say, "O people, this is the Prophet of God. God honored you through him, so support him, aid him, listen to him, and obey him," After he did what he did and disappointed Islam and the Muslims by returning with only one third of the army, he got up to preach as he is used to, but people grabbed him and asked him to stay seated and told him that he is the enemy of God and that he is not worthy of that. He left and walked away in anger.

God said in the Quran, "What ye suffered on the day the two armies met, was with the will of God, in order that He might test the believers, and the Hypocrites also. These were told: come and fight in the way of God, or (at least) drive (The foe from your city).

Page 10

They said: Had we known how to fight, we should certainly have followed you. They were that day nearer to Unbelief than to Faith, saying with their lips what was not in their hearts, but God hath full knowledge of all they conceal." (1)

(Important note: the paragraph on al-Murisi' battle and the sentence "Order 'Abad Bin-Bishr to kill him" were removed because it could be interpreted as a call to kill those official and unofficial scholars according to the part that says, "This is the duty that should be..." This is a very dangerous matter that requires a legal review to determine if it is permissible or not. Also, it is not appropriate if you consider the situation of the al-mujahidin at this time, especially in the shadow of the unjust media campaigns against jihad and al-Mujahidin. These media campaigns are directed toward the Muslims to convince them that al-Mujahidin are takfiris, killers, and people justify the shed of Muslims' blood. Therefore, I think that you should accept this change and keep the next paragraph as it is, in order to let the readers understand from the incident of Ibn-Salul who stood up to preach, but was silenced, grabbed by his clothes, and pulled down by the companions, that it is their duty to respond to the lies of those agents and silence them as much as we can by exposing their collaboration and the collaborations of those in charge them to the Muslims. Also, that it is their duty to warn Muslim to not listen to them and alert them of their danger to the doctrine of loyalty and disavowal and to Jihad and al-Mujahidin. God knows best.

This is the duty of the Muslims and the way that they should deal with the scholars who appear on TV channels today and the official and unofficial scholars of the sultans who lie to God and to people and discourage people from Jihad in Afghanistan and Iraq.

1-Surah of Al 'Umran 166 – 167

Page 11

There are other important paragraphs that contains comments by the brothers, may God reward them greatly, such as their comments on the paragraph related to 'Ali 'Abdallah Salih, the paragraph related to "abiding to the Muslims and their imam (TN: sic), and many other ones."

Praise be to God the lord of the universe for the success that he granted us. We pray to Him to grant us His blessings. Amen.

God's peace, mercy, and blessings be upon you.

Mahmud
Rabi'ah al-Awal 1429
(TN: March 2008)

PART THREE: LETTERS TO/FROM MEMBERS AND LEADERS

5. Letter to 'Abd Al-Latif

Updates on security are requested (ID cards, etc.). It is indicated that there had been little communication from this author due to a lack of safety. Pictures of martyrs were requested.

Date: 29 December 2009

From: Khalid

http://www.dni.gov/files/documents/ubl/english/Letter%20to%20Abd%20Al-Latif%20dtd%2029%20December%202009.pdf

Full translation begins here:

(Page 1)

In the name of Allah the most gracious the most merciful.

I praise God, peace and prayers be upon our Prophet Muhammad, his family and all of his companions.

To my generous brother 'Abd Al-Latif,

Peace, mercy and the blessings of Allah be upon you.

I hope that this letter that I have sent to you finds you well and in good health, as we fear Allah.

I urge you to write to me in detail about your security news. We are fine, thanks be to God and, (('Abdullah)), (('A'isha)), ((Usamah)) and ((Siham)) are all doing well, thanks be to God.

'Abdullah is pursuing his studies as well as 'A'isha, however Usamah always asks when he is going to go to school with them. The first thing Siham does when she wakes up is ask, where is my maternal uncle? May God protect them all and may he unite us with you, because he is our master and capable of doing so.

My generous brother,

With respect to the I.D. card, I sent you my picture and pictures of my father because we need them quickly, if possible

(Page 2)

Lastly, I told you we had previously been unable to send letters because we were busy with the father involving the statements.

With respect to this letter, I took advantage of the opportunity to write to you; we did not forget you – so don't be sad. All there is to it, is that we were busy with the jihad and the nation's issues

Important point:
Please send me the pictures of my brother Sa'ad before and after his martyrdom, as well as pictures of the floods in Jeddah from the internet (Youtube site) or (facebook)

Your brother in Allah - Khalid

Monday, 12 Muharram 1431 HJ (29 December 2009)

6. Letter dtd 18 July 2010

The document provided is a summary of the original letter. Addressed to Abu-Basir, the letter asks for opinions on the situation in Yemen and the Arabian Peninsula. It is suggested that a peace treaty with local forces/tribes be signed in order to focus more on America. It is recommended to strike America internally. The author recommends members take extra security measures in addition to forming a committee to address publications.

From: 'Atiyyah

http://www.dni.gov/files/documents/ubl/english/Letter%20dtd%2018%20JUL%202010.pdf

This is a letter dated 18 JUL 2010 by 'Atiyyah asking Abu-Basir for his feedback on a very sensitive matter which is still in discussion with Abu-'Abdallah [T.C: UBL] about the war in Yemen and the Arabian Peninsula and only to be handled by very few such as Anwar al-'Awlaqi besides the recipient. The opinion is to keep the status quo in Yemen [No war and No peace] with the government by signing a truce under the cover of the tribes or sending messages thru mediators to leave "us" alone in exchange of focusing on America. The purpose is to focus on striking inside America and its interests abroad especially oil producing countries to agitate public opinion and to force US to withdraw from Afghanistan and Iraq. The letter recommends extra security measures for Anwar al-'Awlaqi that requires him to change his way of life and to write a letter in English to Adam Ghadan for cooperation in Jihad media efforts. 'Atiyyah recommends not repeating the mistakes by AQIZ against the tribes in Iraq and assures that he signed treaties with tribes in Yemen and they are harboring al-Qaida, stating that similar mistakes have been made in Yemen by attacking the tribes. 'Atiyyah is referencing to the attack on the US embassy in Yemen recommending more experienced persons, and to carry out future suicide attacks by more than one individual for moral, cover up and backup inside airplanes and elsewhere. 'Atiyyah recommends forming a committee of Abu-Basir, Shaykh Mahmud, and Shaykh Abu-Yahya to filter the products of As Sahab publication.

PART THREE: LETTERS TO/FROM MEMBERS AND LEADERS

> ## 7. Letter dtd 09 August 2010
>
> The letter contains information on the family history of 'Abd-al-Rahman, himself, and his involvement with Al-Qa'ida. Additionally, a list of shaykhs that instructed al-Rahman is provided.
>
> From: 'Abd-al-Rahman
>
> http://www.dni.gov/files/documents/ubl/english/Letter%20dtd%2009%20August%202010.pdf

In the name of Allah the merciful and compassionate

The poor servant's translation (TN: he means Allah's poor servant.. In Arabic is 'Abd-al-Faqir)

My name is 'Abd-al-Rahman Bin Muhammad al-Husayn Bin al-Shaykh Muhammad Salim Bin 'Abd-al-Jalil al-Mijani al- Abyiri, aka Hajji Walid 'Abd-al-Jalil.

(TN: In the beginning of this document, 'Abd-al-Rahman gives a history of his family tree that goes back centuries.)

My father memorized the Qur'an and studied some of the doctrine of al-Maliki ideology, and sought more religious learning. He ran a commercial business (nfi) from a young age. As for my grandfather, he was a pious scholar who taught many of our tribe's children.

I come from a middle class family, religious and conservative. I have four paternal uncles and four paternal aunts. I have eight brothers; six of them are alive. I am number nine of the children. I am the second oldest male. I have eight sisters, six of them are alive.

I have two wives and two boys. Ahmad, aka Ayman, was born in 2004 and 'Abd-al-Wahhab who is born in 2010.

I was born in the sanctified Mecca, on 7 October 1981, at sunset, in al-Muna city at al-Mu'allah Bridge. I was premature, born at the eighth month. I spent the first years of my life in Mecca, then my father sent me with my brother and cousin to Mauritania from 1986 until 1992 to memorize Qur'an and study 'Uthmani writing. After that I returned to my family in Mecca in 1992, and remained there until 2003, continuing my religious studies. In 1994, I frequented my friend's (nfi) library to read religious and ideologist books and follow-up on news and media, because my father would not allow us to watch television. As Shaykh Usama announced the foundation of the worldwide front, I followed it in the newspapers that my father brought home.

I studied in Mecca Institute and graduated in 2000-2001 with high grades.

I discussed with my father the idea to start some projects such as to revive my grandfather's library to teach scholars and plant them in the government in order to initiate revolution and consequently apply Shari'ah. I began on the project and established a library. As the Intifada of al-Aqsa began, I started to follow the news via Al Jazeera. I followed discussion programs and read books to learn about the Intifada. In 2002, I decided on the pilgrimage to pledge allegiance to Muslim Brotherhood in 'Arafah. That year, Tahir aka now as al-Muthanna, a Mauritanian brother who lived above my place, invited me to his house for dinner. This latter could not get a visa to Pakistan; so I met him after he has been in the country seven months.

In 1994, a Mauritanian brother who returned from Afghanistan insisted that we (nfi) watch a film regarding mujahidin. Until that moment, I hadn't heard of mujahidin, and the idea of become mujahid haven't ever occurred to my mind. However, my paternal cousin

Part Three: Letters to/from Members and Leaders

told me that his friends in Mecca proposed the idea to him, to go to Afghanistan to receive training; but I did not pay much attention to it.

Likewise, my father had a friend named Nur-al-Din al-Jaza'iri who proposed to my father to go to jihad in Afghanistan. However, my father apologized due to the fact that there is no Imam (nfi), but Nur-al-Din headed to jihad and became a martyr.

I remember when Al Jazeera began to promote Shaykh Usama's interviews. My father obliged us to go with some family members to Jeddah, despite our will. For that reason, we missed Al Jazeera televised programs and didn't learn much about Usama, until after the attacks of 9/11.

As soon as we returned, I borrowed the movie from the Mauritanian brother and watched it. I was moved and influenced by it. I admired the activities, beliefs and bravery of the mujahidin. At that time, I stopped my daily studies and began to go to the friend to watch movies and discuss issues regarding Afghanistan and Shaykh Usama. Shortly afterward, I asked the Mauritanian brother to find a way for me to go to jihad, so he did. I travelled to Pakistan based on my acceptance to Karachi University. Then, I went to Afghanistan and joined al-Faruq camp, a month and half before 9/11. I suffered from asthma as a child, and I had an attack after so many years, on my way between Quetta and Karachi.

I met the Shaykh and the Doctor (Zawahiri) 8 to 9 days before 9/11, when they visited the camp to give lessons. The lesson of the Doctor was about Qur'an and religion, as the lesson of the Shaykh was about the importance of martyrdom, obedience... The registration of our names in the organization was managed by Abu-Muhammad (nfi).

The following day, the Shaykh gave a lecture about the reality of the nation, the near attack against the Jews, a new historical chapter that will rise the nation, the enemy's developed technology, Mas'ud's role in the Crusader's war, booties of the Northern Alliance, the Al Sa'ud family conflicts, in addition to information that the attack is going to be in 10 days. I have greeted the Dr. twice, and the Shaykh only once, due to the big entourage around him.

My father had mentioned to me before, that he had met the Doctor several times in Mecca, at Mahmud 'Abd-al-Latif's place.

When I returned to the Peninsula, I discontinued my reading of jihadist news and media, and regained my scholar studies until 2003. Two days after the fall of Baghdad, we (nfi) moved to Mauritania, where I got married. Khubayb may Allah release him, and I found two ways to jihad: One to (join) the Salafi group in Algeria and the second to go to Afghanistan. A brother who allocates the brothers requested that Khubayb goes to Afghanistan and I go to Algeria to learn the core of the organization, which I did at the end of 2003 until end of 2005.

Exactly a week after London's bombings, I went (nfi) to arrange to go to Afghanistan to pledge allegiance. During that time, I participated in great and terrible events (nfi). I completely changed my personality; I had the same task there (nfi) like the one here (nfi), I completed it without having a rank/title, and I also participated in leadership missions without having an official title.

I went to convey the issues, returned to them (nfi) and conveyed my message to the brothers (nfi). In 2006, I went to visit my family, on the same day I was expelled by the Mauritanian authorities due to a long story. I became on the wanted list of the Mauritanian government and other countries (nfi). The Mauritanian government has two pictures of me, dated 1996 and 2003, in which I looked completed different. Then, I travelled to several countries using different documents, but my passport remained new because I only used it once for my travel.

Until 2007, the only language I knew was Arabic. I now know French at an academic level, a good level of Farsi, good knowledge of Urdu grammar. I am learning to read Pashto now, and can speak it little bit.

I began to understand the philosophy of languages, which I found very easy. Since I was expelled from Mauritania, I went to the brothers and lived alone. I had a limited interaction with people, only a couple of them who would alternate their shifts to provide me services. I began to write in French and about administrative issues. During my isolation, I wrote a book about international budgets and another one on the philosophy of countries. Fortunately, the enemy did not know about my location, as well as the brothers (mujahidin), my fathers and family (TN: possibly, he means wives?); only those who were directly present with me to assist me. I used to plan for the assistants my appropriate moves and locations. I used to just inquire about the region and safety.

On the other hand, at the same time I was active and calm in Waziristan (nfi).

In the beginning of 2007, I returned to the brothers in Algeria and stayed there for several months. Then, I obtained new travel documents, which I used to travel to the brothers here (nfi) until these latter entrusted me to pledge allegiance (nfi). Due to the problems among emirs in the desert, we (TN: possibly he means I) participated in conciliation. Then, based on Shaykh Sa'id's orders I had to go back (nfi). So, in 2007 I returned during the Red Mosque event and remained there until this day. The time I spent in Algeria and here requires a lengthy description; perhaps I will recount it in the future.

Shaykhs who taught me are as follows:
- Shaykh Muhammad Walid al-Mukhtar Walid Al (Waymin)
- Shaykh Ahmad Walid 'Abd-al-Qadir
- Shaykh 'Abdallah Walid 'Abidin
- Shaykh 'Abdallah Muhammad 'Ali Barnawi
- Shaykh 'Ali al-Sanusi Ahmad
- Shaykh Musa Sukkar Bu-Qas (var. Buqas)
- Shaykh 'Abdallah al-Hajj al-Tanbakti
- Shaykh 'Abd-al-Rahman Bin 'Abd-al-Rahman Shumaylah al-Ahdal
- Shaykh 'Abd-al-Rahman Walid Dadadah
- Ahmad Walid Ahmad
- Shaykh 'Abdallah Walid Shaykh Muhammad
- Shaykh Walid Dayfallah

- Shaykh Muhammad Walid Sidi Habib
- Shaykh Ibrahim Walid Ibn
- Shaykh Sami al-Jihani
- Shaykh 'Ali al-Hikami
- Shaykh Muhammad al-Mandili (TN: possibly, Fath al-Majid)
- Shaykh Yahya Bin Fahd al-Makki
- Shaykh 'Abd-al-Rahman al-'Ujlan
- Shaykh 'Abd-al-Rahman al-Somali
- Shaykh Muhammad al-Amin al-Hirrari
- Shaykh Muhammad 'Ali Adam al-Ethiopi
- Shaykh Muhammad al-Ruqibah
- Shaykh Sid Ahmad Walid al-Imam
- Shaykh Fawwaz al-Qa'idi
- Shaykh Ikramallah
- Shaykh Sidi Muhammad al-Ansari
- Shaykh Mansur al-Da'jani
- Shu'ayl al-Lahyani
- Muhammad Iqbal
- Shaykh Wasiyallah Muhammad 'Abbas
- Shaykh Ahmad al-Sanusi Ahmad

And many others, whom I don't remember at this moment.

Written on 09 August 2010

PART THREE: LETTERS TO/FROM MEMBERS AND LEADERS

> ## 8. Letter to Shaykh Abu Yahya
>
> A request for communication to Shaykh 'Atiyah is made. According to the author, difficulties should be suppressed by locational movement. 'Abd-al-Qayyum requests updates on Libya and the Fighting Group leadership.
>
> Date: 20 March 2011
>
> From: 'Abd-al-Qayyum
>
> http://www.dni.gov/files/documents/ubl/english2/Letter%20to%20Shaykh%20%20Abu%20Yahya.pdf

Full Translation Begins:

In the name of God the merciful the compassionate

To Shaykh / Abu Yahya, may God save you

Peace be upon you with God's mercy and blessings

I have received your generous letter and may God bless you. I only would like to give you a message for Shaykh 'Atiyah. We have waited a long time for his reply, considering to the ramifications of the events near us, and as a fighting group which is still standing and will stay so with God's permission.

Being the only person in charge here, and committed to its members and their activities, I was very sorry for this delay. I and my group reserve the right to make a stand by not accepting its reasoning. I expected all to be on the level of the events in Libya and its acceleration. I consequently bear, in front of God, the responsibility of not awaiting his generous response. I consider him responsible in front of God and in front of Abu 'Abdallah and the Doctor and in front of the Fighting Group leadership. He is responsible for any bad encounter that we may face us along the road, resulting from what he considered to be directly connected to him, without committing himself for a while.

As for yourself, I think you did what you could, and I and the members are committed to move soon, so that matters will not egt worse.

God is behind our intentions

The one who loves you

'Abd-al-Qayyum

Sunday 20 March 2011

PART THREE: LETTERS TO/FROM MEMBERS AND LEADERS

> ## 9. Letter dtd 5 April 2011
>
> This letter begins with a discussion of how to move Hamzah to either Baluchistan or on to Peshawar. The author mentions the detainment of Abu al-Harith by Pakistani intelligence services. Additionally, it is suggested that a statement be issued regarding revolutions in the Arab countries, among other topics. Finally, various countries and individuals are discussed, with a mention of Libya and its organization of brothers.
>
> From: Mahmud
>
> http://www.dni.gov/files/documents/ubl/english/Letter%20dtd%205%20April%202011.pdf

To the honorable Shaykh, may God protect you and guide you,

Greetings. I pray to God for this letter to find you well and in good health.

We are doing well and recently things have been calmer. The brothers are more careful and keeping low profile.

Shaykh Abu Muhammad is fine and communication with him continues, but he told us that for two months his carrier will not be coming. Hopefully we will communicate with him towards the end of April.

-Regarding ((Hamzah)):

I am embarrassed to talk to you about this. I hope that you will understand my point of view. As you know, I do not have an interest in this and all I want is safety, security, and success. You are his father and you are our Amir and we will obey. I have the feeling that you are not aware of the security situation here. I tried to find a way to send him to you on the main road, but I was not able to find one due to the intensified security procedures and searches. We can look into sending him by smuggling him in like the Mujahidin brothers. We can arrange for him to go to Baluchistan and from there we can arrange with the brother ((Abu 'Abdallah)) al-Sindi and his friends to receive him there and then decide if he should stay there or send him to Peshawar as you wanted.

In summary, there are three options:

-The first option: We can send him to you through our middle-man, but this is bad option and should not be utilized due to the security situation and because it might lead to the capture of our middle-man. So this option doubles the risk.

We can alter this option by sending Hamzah with an individual other than our middle-man (he will have nothing to do with our middle-man). We will give him the phone numbers of your middle-man (Aslam or someone else) and he can call him once they get there and hand him Hamzah.

The second option: Is for me to send him to Peshawar through other individuals (other than our courier) like all the brothers who go from our area to Peshawar. It is a smuggling route. They go from the Waziristan region, Federally Administered Tribal Areas, Pakistan towards the Khyber tribes and from there they go down to Peshawar (they go down to Bara, I believe, or somewhere nearby) and then enter Peshawar. This route is dangerous, but less dangerous than the first one. This way, our carrier will avoid any danger because Hamzah will be taken by other mujahidin brothers.

Page: 2

The question is should we tell the brothers who will be escorting him who this individual is in order to take the matter seriously or should we just say take him to Peshawar and he will find his way there? Even with that, people might know who he is.

The third option: is to send Hamzah to Balochistan. This is easier for us and we can send him from south Waziristan. We can send him to people there and he can stay there until 'Abdallah al-Sindi arrives and gets him. This is the least dangerous option and the easiest. I recommend this option. As I told you, you can arrange with 'Abdallah al-Sindi (directly or through me if he sends his phone numbers).

Notes: I talked to brother ((Munir)) about sending Hamzah, and he agrees with me that we should not send him due to the situation that I described to you. I did not discuss this with ((Abu Yahya)) because we did not meet for the last three months and I did not write to him about this in our correspondence.

-Here, we are talking only about Hamzah as a man. As for the family (his wife and two children), there is no problem in sending them the regular route (first option). The idea is to send Hamzah and his family separately.

However, If we decide on the Balochistan option (third option), he can go with his family.

-Brother 'Abdallah al-Sindi sent me ((Khalid))'s identification documents and drivers license and they can be used by Hamzah when he moves. You either tell us what to do with the identification documents or I will give them to Hamzah to use if you go with one of these options.

Attention: If the decision is to go with The Baluchistan route, I will need some time to complete the arrangement (not too long). I want to warn you and remind you of the difficulty of the situation here and for you not to get worried.

As for Hamzah, he and his family are fine. He wants to receive training and to learn. I wanted your permission to give him some space to move in a manner that we will carefully arrange for, in order for him to attend some special training. Anyway, he took his family to the house of our brother ((Abu Khalil)).

Other topics:

-Sorry to inform you that more than two months ago, brother ((Abu al-Harith)) al-Sindi (the brother-in-law of Abu 'Abdallah al-Sindi) was detained by the Pakistani intelligence in Karachi.

Page: 3

-So far I did not get any responses from the family of B M (TN: sic) in spite of the fact that I received a response from brother Abu 'Abdallah al-Sindi and Khalid's identification documents that I told you about earlier. Brother, 'Abdallah al-Sindi did not give any more details, but promised to soon send the phone numbers that we asked him for.

-I sent the Quran of (('Um Hamzah)) and hopefully you received it.

Also we started transferring ten million rupees to brother Aslam. I wrote to him and asked him to exchange them to dollars, euros and keep them so that you (TN: in plural form) can have them.

Regarding the money that we have, we exchanged a large part of the rupees to gold, dollars and euros.

Of course, there are lots of expenses that we paid for in rupees directly in support of several jihadi groups in the tribes (Shura Shamali, Ms'udis, Khalifah Haqqani, Tehrik e-Taliban Pakistan, and others. This is in addition to groups of immigrants) because we have to support people. Everyone heard of the deal. We also paid for the expenses of sponsorships. We do not have many debts. Praise be to God. We also bought weapons, ammunition, and equipment in preparation for any possible war. We also renewed some of the budgets for some workshops and collaborating groups. We also raised some of the budgets.

Praise be to God, the flow of money from outside and from inside Pakistan these days is good.

-We are watching the Arab revolutions and the changes in the Arab countries. Praise be to God for the fall of the tyrants of Tunis and Egypt. Now we are watching the situation in Libya, Yemen, and Syria. Attached is some of what the brothers wrote to me about these revolutions.

In general we believe that these are major changes and have good things in them.

Did you think about issuing a statement to the nation to show solidarity with the people, express happiness for the fall of the tyrants, and support the revolutions against injustice, corruption, brutality and oppression? It should contain instructions and reminders to the youth and the entire nation. It should be generic and not go into details. It should also urge people to continue on the path of jihad, repentance, and return to God. It should also contain a warning about the deceitfulness of the Americans and others. It should also say that the Jewish state is about to end, and so on.

Perhaps you are waiting for these revolutions to mature and see what shape they take. I am sure that you will talk about these revolutions on your tape for the tenth anniversary of 11 September 2001.

Attached are some of the thoughts and reflections on the major changes. This is a paper that I wrote to the brothers here in order to discuss it.

Page: 4

I will attach some of what I wrote and what was published here on that issue.

I will also attach two letters from ((al-Tayib)) Agha and my response to them, and the latest correspondence with Algeria, Somalia, and Yemen, and my response to the brothers in Algeria. Attached also is my letter to the brothers in Somalia and another letter to ((Abu Basir)). As you can see, the brothers in Somalia are suggesting that you write letter to brother Hasan ((Zahir)) (variant: Dhahir) to encourage him and lift his sprit. Also, attached are some administrative books and other files from the internet.

Reagrding Shaykh ((Yunis)), he is fine and I sent to him your latest letter, and God willing he received it. A month ago, he wrote to me and told me that he might go to Somalia directly if he can make the arrangement. Through the Baluchi, they found some trusted smugglers to get them there directly (during their stay in Balochistan for the last ten months, they got to know the sea routes). He and his friends decided that going to Iran and staying in it is not appropriate. That is a summary of what he wrote to me. I wrote to him a response a few days ago and asked him to confirm the security of the route. I also suggested an idea for him and his friends to study and consider. The idea came to me in light of the popular revolutions. The idea in short is to distribute his brothers in Tunis and Syria and other locations. This is going to require the Syrian brothers to wait until the revolution succeeds and the Asad regime falls and the country turns into chaos.

Just to remind you, Shaykh Yunis has three Syrian brothers, one Tunisian, and one Algerian (used to live in Germany) with him. The Tunisian can travel to Tunis now and he can easily enter Tunis. Some of people from here traveled to Tunis and were able to get in. The three Syrians hopefully will be able to get in soon. All that remains is him and the Algerian brother. It might be appropriate for them to go to Somalia or easily hide in Iran or some other place since there is only two of them.

The changes that took place in the Arab region are big and many things will change with them.

Regarding Libya, the latest that we received is that the brothers are starting to organize themselves and they have activities and role there. Brothers from the Combating Group who got out of prisons and others in East Libya (in Binghazi, Darnah, and al-Bayda' and its surroundings) say that there is an active Islamic jihadi revival

PART THREE: LETTERS TO/FROM MEMBERS AND LEADERS

and that they have been waiting for this chance for a long time. I believe that the brothers' names, activities and recordings will start to appear soon.

Also regarding Libya, as result of the excitement among the brothers with this opportunity for Jihad in Libya, brother ((Anas al-Subay'i)) al-Libi and other brothers asked for permission to go to Libya.

Attached is a letter from Anas (whose name here now is 'Abd al-Qayyum). He wrote to Abu Yahya and Abu Yahya forwarded it to me. He accuses me of being late in responding to him. I have a very good reason for being late. I am trying to stay away, lower my profile, and decrease my communications and movement. Also, so far, I did receive those letters that he talks about.

At any rate, I made a copy of his letter for you to look at. I also attached what I wrote to Abu-Yahya in order to inform him and other brothers there.

In short, we gave him permission to go to Libya.

For clarification: Anas' morale has been very bad since he came to us from Iran, and you know that from Iran he sent his wife and children, even the oldest two ('Abdallah and 'Abd al-Rahman) who are young men. When he arrived here, he seemed upset, worried, and depressed.

Page: 5

In general, he is hard to get along with and he is not comfortable with most brothers. The brothers, with my knowledge and Abu Yahya's knowledge, always tried to give him an empty space to get him comfortable in and to have one or two brothers serve him. In short, his situation was worrying and he was calling his wife in Libya, in spite of knowing that communication was banned and in spite of knowing that he is considered dangerous and wanted by the Americans. He used the phone repeatedly. When the current Libyan revolution started and when he learned that brother 'Urwah al-Libi, aka Abu Malik al-Libi, who was with him in prison in Iran and travelled there and called him and encouraged him and informed him that route was easy, he got very excited and wrote what he wrote.

We ask God for success and aid to us and to all the brothers.

Did you read the file that I sent to you a few months ago under the title "Terrorize Them" and did you comment on it? The brother has thoughts, requirements, and activities. He needs some instructions from you or Abu Muhammad because honestly, he does not listen to me or to others here.

Regarding the brothers in Iran, a coordinator for me there sent some generic news without details. He said that some of the higher brothers got out and they are wondering what to do with them. I responded to him immediately and asked him for details and told him that all high brothers should come to us and we are waiting for them.

Brother ((Abu al-Samah)) al-Masri left and now he is in Iran. It seems that he resumed media activities and communications under the title "Jama'at al-Jihad" as you can see in an attached file.

Also, brother (('Abdallah Rajab)) al-Libi (previously known as Abu al-Ward) left and he is in Iran too.

Also, Abu Malik al-Libi, who is one of the prominent brothers in the Combating Group, left to Libya. He stayed in Iran and he did not come to us. About a month ago, he traveled to Libya and he got there safely. He called some of the brothers. We are also in touch with him through the internet and we await his messages. He is one of the important brothers in the field and we expect him to have a role in Libya.

I believe that in the past, I told you that the sons of ((Abu al-Khayr)) al-Masri and their families (one of them is married to the daughter of ((Abu Muhammad)) al-Masri and he is the brother-in-law of Hamzah. I do not know who the other one is married to) left and they are now in Baluchistan. We made arrangement for them there and told them to disappear in there until further notice. I sent a letter to them and explained our situation to them. They are in Baluchistan with one of the good and trustworthy brothers. We might take Hamzah to them and keep him under the Baluchi brothers.

This is the summary of the letter.

Page: 6

I wrote to brother 'Urwah in my response to him that we can think about this and can reach something acceptable on this matter. I will forward the idea to the leadership. He might have already informed the Libyan brothers and they might have informed the Brits. We do not have confirmation, of course. Perhaps 'Urwah will have something new in the next message, despite of being very busy in Libya.

This is what happened.

Note: I got rid of all the cards (chips) that were between us in the past. I broke them and destroyed them. Now I use new cards with you. Please, I need you to break and destroy the previous cards and use new ones. We should do this each time we change the cards.

Also, please forgive me for sending a short letter to brother Aslam, which I need you to give to him. It states that the sum of money that I sent to him with your letters is his agreed upon sponsorship.

We await your letters and news

God's peace, mercy and blessing be upon you

Mahmud

5 April 2011

(End Text of Letter)

10. Letter to Brother Hamzah

In this letter, Khalid discusses Hamza's travels to meet with him in Peshawar. The author elaborates on further travel arrangements for Hamza, particularly the need of an ID card for movement between Baluchistan and Karachi.

Date: 26 April 2011

From: Khalid

http://www.dni.gov/files/documents/ubl/english2/Letter%20to%20brother%20Hamzah.pdf

(Page 1 of 2)

In the name of God the merciful the passionate

Thanks to God the Master of Heavens and prayers and greetings on the faithful messenger Muhammad Bin Abdullah, his kindred and all his companions.

Thereafter:

My generous brother Hamzah, may God preserves and guide

Greetings to you by the Islamic greetings, the greetings of Heaven dwellers

Peace be upon you with God's mercy and blessings

To start with, thanks God for saving you from the prisons of the Rejectionists (TN: Shi'a) the wicked Magi. We were following your exit with great patience. I am awaiting your arrival as the path in front of us is long and the tasks are great and plenty.

My brother, Sheikh Mahmud got my ID with driver's license. We asked the sheikh to give it to us or to you, so that you can go to the outskirts of Baluchistan. We wrote to Sheikh Mahmud to give it to you, so you can come to us with God's permission. My generous brother, immediately after arriving at Baluchistan, inquire about the security situation in the place where you are; be very cautious and say many prayers. If the security situation is alright, you may send your photo to Brother Abdullah Al-Sindi, so that he can extract for you an original ID, so that you can move from Baluchistan to Karachi. The road is difficult to move without an original ID. If it is possible to move without the original ID, then use my ID, with God's blessing, to Karachi, then to Peshawar by air or train. When you arrive safely, contact this number. Inform him that you are Hamzah and stay with him; he is informed that you are coming and we will arrange for you to come to us later.

Note: If the ID and the license will delay you from leaving the region or you do not need it, kindly return them to Sheikh Mahmud so that he can return them to us.

Finally: (Page 2 of 2)

May God facilitate your coming to us so that we can be assured about you.

I apologize for the short message, because of my occupation with the father, who sends you his greetings.

Your brother Khalid
April 26 2011

Attached with this message is another message to Brother Abdullah Al-Sindi

> ## 11. Letter to Um 'Abd-al-Rahman, 26 April 2011
>
> The author discusses an impending meeting with the receiver. The contents of a previous letter referred to as "Four Months" will be discussed at this meeting. Finally, the author instructs this letter to be destroyed after it is received.
>
> From: Unknown
>
> http://www.dni.gov/files/documents/ubl/english/Letter%20to%20Um%20Abd-al-Rahman%20dtd%2026%20April%202011.pdf

(Full translation begins here)

Page 1

(TN: The paper on which this message is drafted has a watermark that reads, "My sister in Allah.")

In the name of Allah the merciful and compassionate

My dear sister Um 'Abd-al-Rahman, May Allah protect her

Allah's peace, mercy, and blessings be upon you

I hope that this message brings you best wishes and supplications for you to be in the best health, safety, and secure conditions from Allah Almighty.

We congratulate you for the falling of the tyrants in Egypt and Tunisia and ask Allah to purify the rest of the Muslims' countries. We hope for the spread of prosperity, safety, and control of Allah's Shari'a.

To begin, my beloved sister, I give you the good news that a new dawn has shined on us and the stress of meeting you, thanks to

Allah, has been removed after we, with Allah's help, have overcome the security obstacle that delayed meeting you for sure, with Allah's permission. We are waiting for a message from the brothers that will include the arrangement for the final step to meet you. The brother who is in charge in your area will inform you soon, God willing. My son will be in your reception in a safe location in Peshawar area to materialize our reunion, which our hearts have been looking forward to and our tongues have been constantly supplicating for its completion.

My son thanks Allah, who answered his prayers and his wish will come true soon, God willing. He waits impatiently for the day when we meet, when the matter is complete, and our two homes and our two lives are illuminated. It has been said that with patience you gain what you want.

Page 2

He also thanks Allah who granted him success in that. Allah's messenger said, (TN: Following is a loose translation of the Hadith, "Gain the religion otherwise your hands will be stock to dirt." (TN: The Hadith talks about four reasons for which a woman is married: For her wealth, beauty, lineage, and her religion; in this order. Hands be stock to dirt refers to poverty.) This is how he (TN: His son) counts her (TN: Possibly the bride); her advocate is Allah. This is out of Allah's grace upon him. He prays that may Allah gather him with you soon. He says that, with Allah's permission, he will compensate her for what she missed and she waits for him. May Allah gather him with her in happiness.

My beloved sister,

I hope from Allah that this will be the last message that precedes meeting you. (TN: When we meet) we will be able to clarify for you all the confusion in the previous messages, on the top of which is the message of (The four months) (TN: The phrase "four months" is underlined.) I hope you will consider it completely canceled. I wanted to include in this message some words to clarify part of it. Allah knows our stance of finalizing the matter as it is, especially my son, who is the concerned (TN: party). We have been through difficult security circumstances; God only knows it. The matter is not hidden from you, my precious sister. However, by the grace of Allah, things changed and every day that goes by our situation is from good to better; thanks to Allah.

My beloved sister, you did not fall short with us, may Allah reward you. May Allah help me in returning the favor in words and in action.

(TN: Underlined text begins here)

Before concluding:

My virtuous sister, Allah knows that we have things in our minds that would take long (TN: Time) to explain; the situation does not permit mentioning them. Soon, we will meet with you and will have the opportunity to clarify all the confusion of the "Four Months" message as well as others. Thanks to God that the length of time has increased love. (TN: End of underlined text)

To you (TN: I send) my best regards and my son sends his greetings to you.

Page 3

Please transfer my greetings to all my beloved daughters, especially the precious bride, for them my longing increases day after day.

All from here send their greetings, especially my daughters and my grandchildren.

Security note: (TN: Security note is underlined)

Please do not let anyone know about the correspondents and that the meeting between us is near. Allah's messenger, peace be upon him, said, "Seek secrecy to accomplish your things."

Please destroy this message after reading it.

Tuesday 26 April 2011

We wait for a message from you, and for the meeting to take place immediately after it, with Allah's permission.

(TN: End of full translation)

12. Letter to Shaykh Mahmud

After discussing the revolutions of the Arab Spring, the author explains that al Qa'ida has a responsibility to provide guidance and to re-establish the "law of God." Meetings, updates, and requests of member duties are requested, too.

Date: Unknown

From: Unknown

http://www.dni.gov/files/documents/ubl/english/Letter%20to%20Shaykh%20Mahmud.pdf

(Full translation)

Page 1

In the name of God the most merciful

To Shaykh Mahmud, may God bless him,

Greetings,

I hope that you receive this letter while you, your family, and children are in good health.

Perhaps you have been monitoring the surprising and fast-moving developments. Ten days after the fall of the tyrant of Tunis, the Egyptian revolution started and more than four million people gathered in Cairo demanding the removal of the greatest and strongest agent of the infidels in the area. Before his fall, the revolution in Yemen started, and before things settled in Yemen, the revolution in Libya had begun. I believe that the end is going to be for the benefit of the Muslims soon, despite the craziness and brutality of the ((Qadhafi)) regime against the revolutionists. Before things settled in Libya, the revolution of Oman had begun. The land of the two sanctuaries decided on 11 March as the day for demonstrations. This is in addition to the demonstration in Algeria, Morocco, Jordan, and Lebanon.

These events are very great and grand. Based on ground truth and history, one is led to believe that this will affect the entire Muslim world. Things are moving in the direction of getting the land of the Muslims out from under the dominance of the US. Americans are very worried about these successive revolutions.

The secretary of state expressed this concern by saying, "We are afraid that the area could fall into the hands of militant Muslims." She said this before things had gotten to where they are after the revolution in Egypt had begun. Egypt is the floodgate, and its fall means the fall of all the tyrants in the area and the beginning of a new era for the entire nation. In spite of that, the international environment did not allow the West to back ((Mubarak)). They are also showing the same weakness in their position toward Libya. This position led many intellectuals around the world to criticize politicians and accuse them of being spectators and not rising to the level of the events. This has shown the world the weakness of the West and the retreat of its role in the world.

These events are the most important events that the nation has witnessed in centuries. While asleep, the nation's religion and holy sites were being desecrated (except for the Afghan Jihad and today's Jihad).

Page 2

Two decades ago, some of the sons of this nation tried to get up and these were the events in Syria, Algeria, Egypt, and Yemen. However, these attempts failed to achieve their goals due to various reasons that I should talk about in an article. Those movements were not the size of today's movements. Today's movements are in danger of falling into the trap of creating a system that is different from what God has ordered us to implement.

Our greatest duty is to provide guidance. This guidance should be disciplined and guided by Shari'a. In the past, I called on the honest in the nation to nominate a number of scholars to form a Shura council that would monitor the issues of the nation and provide guidance, opinion, and counsel. However, their failure to respond to that call and the situation that the nation finds itself in dictate that we, al-Mujahidin, should perform this duty and try to the best of our ability to fill the great gap. We should also be gentle and compassionate toward those who were misguided for many decades.

No doubt that al-Mujahidin have many responsibilities, but this great duty should have the greatest share of our efforts to prevent the current revolution from becoming like previous revolutions against the Western occupation.

Jihad in Afghanistan is a duty to reestablish the law of God in it. It also is the way for liberating a nation of 1.5 billion people and the way to regain its holy sites. While we were fighting in Afghanistan and draining the head of the infidels, it became weak to a degree that enabled the Muslim nation to regain some of its self confidence and courage. It also removed the overwhelming pressure to not revolt against the agents of the US. As this pressure gradually vanished, the people started their revolutions.

Page 3

Keep in mind that those streams that call for half-measure solutions, such as the Brotherhood, have gained a better understanding, especially the youth in them. This phenomenon was addressed in a long question to Shaykh ((Abu-Muhammad)) by a member of the Brotherhood. Also, it was mentioned in media outlets that there is a strong Salafi stream within the Brotherhood.

Based on the above, we should not be consumed with the front in Afghanistan where we are witnessing a robust jihadi movement, while the heart of the Muslim nation is witnessing popular revolutions. The front in Afghanistan brought some great benefits and destroyed the image of head of the infidels. This does not mean that we should stop

Jihad there; instead we should focus our efforts toward the direction that is most likely the path for liberating the nation. As I said, history and ground truth show that these revolutions are the path for restoring the Caliphate.

We should work on increasing media productions. Our efforts should be focused on guiding the nation through a specific plan that we all have discussed. The next phase is very important and dangerous and cannot tolerate any contradiction in our instructions. In principle, it seems to me that the most important steps to take during the next phase are:

1- To hold the hand of the people and encourage them to revolt against the tyrants. We should touch on the fact that this is a religious obligation. We should talk about toppling the tyrants without talking about issues related to the Caliphate.

2- The phase after the toppling of the regimes; it is the phase for building awareness and correcting understandings.

3- ....

Due to our effort to fill the gap and to prepare a plan to guide the nation, we should deploy all capabilities and skills in literature (normal text, poetry), audio and print. We should dedicate these capabilities to guiding the youth of the nation. We should leave the management of the work in Afghanistan and Waziristan to individuals who have administrative and field capabilities but do not have writing skills.

Based on this, receiving this letter will mark the end of your administrative work in Afghanistan and you should appoint ...... to replace you. You should work as soon as possible on arranging a safe route for getting out on a cloudy day in the area to Peshawar and the surrounding areas until we find you a house in the area that I am in.

Page 4

In your previous letter, you wrote that the unstable situation and the commotion can reduce the brain's ability to think and can reduce productivity. This will allow you to monitor the media better and will facilitate correspondence between us to exchange opinions and to increase our speeches to the nation. It will also allow us to exchange visits to verbally discuss our thoughts on these great events. Before I finish talking about this issue, I would to say that my words are contradictory to what I said in previous letters, but the magnetude of the events dictates that we implement a full mobilization.

Please let ((Abu-Yahya)) know about what I said in the letter above and ask him to go out of the spying area in order to be able to closely monitor the events of the nation. Also, please convey my words on this issue to the rest of the brothers who can write; ask them to do the same thing that I asked Shaykh Abu-Yahya to do. Do not exclude any one of them, for each voice counts at this phase; the work is going to be a joint effort.

Regarding what you mentioned in your previous letter about the general motto of the brothers is that martyrdom is better than detention, and based on that, one should not go out of the secured area. My response to that is that if the foundation is true, that does not necessarily mean that what was built on it is true. The facts prove that the American technology and advanced systems cannot capture a mujahid if he does not make a security violation that will lead them to him. Commitment to operational security makes his technological advancement a waste. Security procedures in our circumstances should be practiced at all times and there is no room for mistakes. Some people are not disciplined and cannot do this, and these people should be treated differently - perhaps a job in the field might be best for them.

As for those who are disciplined, you arrange houses for them at the edge of a neighborhood due to their relative distance from people. This reduces many security risks. They should be kept with trustworthy companions. These companions should have a cover, especially those who have neighbors watching them.

One of the most important security issues in the cities is children. They should not be allowed to go out unless it is necessary (medical treatment). They should be taught the local language.

Page 5

They should not be allowed to be in the yard unless they have an adult with them to control their noise.

General points:

1- Regarding the eruption of revolutions ....brothers, Yemen, Algeria, Iraq .... keep them unallied through awareness for them and for the Mujahidin. This means that operations by us against the army and police should stop in all areas, especially Yemen.

2- Regarding what you mentioned about al-Ilham magazine, please send a reminder to the brother and ask them not to repeat this.

3- Enclosed is a statement.

4- Somehow, please issue a statement on the matter.

5- Please let me know if Tunis (TN: sic) can come and live in one of the cities in the province of Sarhad to help with the work plan and in correcting understandings among the children of this nation. I also need your opinion about him leaving his work that I tasked him with and appointing a qualified brother to do it.

- Regarding the Shura, I am sure you know the importance of this. Please send me your opinion on the issue. Also, I am waiting for Abu-Yahya's research on the matter. If hearts and intentions are pure, all disagreements will be resolved.

- Regarding Hamzah, thank you for your assessment of the situation. If you can send him with his mother, then I want to emphasize what I said before. Perhaps what you said about arrangements for getting him out to him has been done. In any case, please tell him not to leave the house unless it is absolutely necessary. Guests going to him (TN: sic).

We should not be just an aiding factor in the issues of our nation; we should take ownership of these issues. This is the most important point in our history, so we need to focus on it and pay attention to it.

Page 6

- Please follow up on the file of targeting the French that was previously mentioned.

- Please ask the brothers in the media to send the living will statements of the 19 brothers - that were not broadcast and that we did not receive - so as to get them to us before the 10th anniversary of our blessed attacks.
- Regarding what you said about the file that I sent to brother ((Abu-al-Nur)), you were correct and for that reason I did not ask everyone to do what he mentioned. I just wanted to encourage anyone who provides advice in a gentle manner.

- Regarding the letter from Khaled to ((Abu-al-Harith)), you did a good job. As for the Khaled's call to brother 'Abdallah al- ((Sindi)), it will not happen and Khaled is with us. That would have happened if he went to live with his brother.

- Regarding the warning that you sent in the "Dangerous Warning" file, such important issues should be sent inside the file that contains your letter to me to guarantee that I receive it and review it.

- Regarding your efforts with the Taliban, praise to God for what you were able to accomplish. Regarding the statement that I asked you to publish, it is good that you did not mention Tehrik. I also think that you should publish it in Arabic because we want all the Arab Mujahidin in all the fields to benefit from it. As you know, there are lots of operations that were attributed to our brothers in Iraq in which civilians got harmed.

Regarding the companion, please expedite the arrangements for him. On 15 January 2011, we agreed in writing with our companions that we would arrange to have them replaced within six months. You know that the issue of arranging a safe place after selecting the appropriate individual requires time. Please update me on the companion in each letter that you send to me.

- Regarding your meeting with the brother to arrange for the companion, you should not meet with him at all. Arrangements can be arranged in a generic manner by lettes. In your previous letter, you talked about the incident in which Brother Riyad became a martyr. I do not know what happened, but this incident shows that the security precautions that I asked you to implement were not implemented. Please pay attention to implementing the precautions that I mentioned, including meeting only two people and reducing your movements to the minimum.

Page 7

- Regarding the operation in which Taliban targeted one the tribes, this operation is unjustifiable because it killed innocents and it contradicted the general policy.

- Regarding the France statement, Al Jazeera has published it.

- Regarding the letter of my son Sa'd (may God rest his soul), I think that you should delete the copies of it that you have.

Next time, I will send you a copy and I will delete from it what needs to be deleted, and this copy should keep in the archives of al-Sahab due to its content that can expose the truth about the Iranian regime.

- Regarding what you mentioned about the picture of Sa'd (may God rest his soul), his after-death picture should be deleted, and it is okay to keep other picture in the archive.

- Regarding the poem, may God bless you for it, but I do not think that you should send it to the brothers.

13. Letter from Hafiz

From brother Hafiz, this letter gives an update on communications with a negotiator and contact with the Iranians.

Date: Unknown

From: Hafiz

http://www.dni.gov/files/documents/ubl/english/Letter%20from%20Hafiz.pdf

(TN: One handwritten page)

And I have told the negotiator that getting a personally signed message from the mayor is an extremely difficult issue, and that we can get a message from his agents. Additionally, we are still not sure or knowledgeable of the situation of the patients until this moment, and that in such conditions it is difficult to work in such circumstances. I insisted on the subject of sending one of the patients, so that we can evaluate the situation before we enter any issues or dialogue.

I am going to call the intermediary after three days, and I will ask him to initially allow me to talk by phone with some of the patients, like Muhammad, the son of the mayor, and some of the shaykhs there; at a minimum, so that we are assured of the seriousness of the intermediaries and those whom they represent, and to evaluate the size of importance and level given to that issue by the Iranians.

In my personal opinion, they are in a hesitant situation and are afraid of complications, so they want to establish a relationship and activate that relationship in order not to incur any harm on the people who are allied with them. I say that we talk to them because of the patients and the possibility of getting material support from them, without entering into long-term agreements or giving promises that we may not be able to fulfill.

Please respond and advise what to do.

And if the brothers want to send a representative to negotiate, I propose Shaykh Abu Husayn, due to the ease of his movements that his features allow, in addition to the other factors, and Allah only knows.

Regards
You loving brother,
Hafiz
5/6

> **14. Letter Addressed to Atiyah**
>
> In this letter, updates are given and requested. There is a focus on the Islamic Maghreb, and Atiyah encourages them to uproot local American forces. It says that American embassies in African countries should be attacked. However, members of al Qa'ida should swear their loyalty and be sure not to attack army and police forces. And, in time, the Islamic state should be formed.
>
> Date: Unknown
>
> From: Unknown
>
> http://www.dni.gov/files/documents/ubl/english/Letter%20Addressed%20to%20Atiyah.pdf

3 pages translated where necessary from Arabic

Letter addressed to Atiyah on list of names

Translation begins here:

PAGE: 1

In the name of God, Most Gracious, Most Merciful,

To my good two brothers Hajj (('Uthman)), and Shaykh ((Mahmud)), may peace and the blessings of God be yours.

I hope that you, your family, and all the brothers are well and enjoying good health when you receive my letter.

I hope that you are giving your attention to store the provisions, especially wheat and dates (TN: underlined text)

- I hope that you will inform us about all of the Yemeni brothers who are with you.

- I hope that you will inform us about the leakage of the news covering the martyrdom of our son Sa'ad; may God have mercy on his soul.

- I hope that you will send over the Pashtuni mediator.

- I hope that you will request the regional (TN variant, Qatari) curricula from Ahmad ((Zaydan)) and maybe you can copy them from the internet.

I hope that you will write a letter to our brothers in the Islamic Maghreb to inform them with the previously mentioned concept (NFI), and for them to consider themselves as the army of the Muslims in the Islamic Maghreb whose job is to uproot the obnoxious tree by concentrating on its American trunk, and to avoid being occupied with the local security forces. Also they have to differentiate between those who go over to their location to fight them, the Imams who occupy themselves for that purpose, and those they (the brothers) seek to attack in their own headquarters. By fighting the local enemy we don't get the result that we deployed for, which is to reinstate the wise Caliphate and eliminate the disgrace and humiliation that our nation is suffering from.

You should ask them to avoid insisting on the formation of an Islamic State at the time being, but to work on breaking the power of our main enemy by attacking the American embassies in the African countries, such as Sierra Leone, Togo, and mainly to attack the American oil companies.

They also need to give their attention to extend specific training to curry external operations, and they shouldn't be stingy in the quantity of explosives to be used or the number of martyrs. You are to pass to them your experience on this subject, and warm them about the mistakes that Mujahidin did in their operations against the Americans; some of which were mentioned in our previous letter.

- I hope that you send a letter to the brothers in Yemen to have them implement security measures, avoid moving about except for dire need. The same is true for the leadership members who appear in the media outlets, who should also avoid meeting people (in restaurants and gas stations).

- After informing them with above mentioned concept, you should also warn them against the dangers behind a bloody fight with the tribes (as previously mentioned by us)

NB: Of importance is to have one of the important Tanzim (TN: al-Qa'ida) leadership member to be from the south.

PAGES: 2 AND 3

- They should avoid targeting the army and the police force quarters, and often declare that they aren't targeting them, but are after the Americans who are killing our families in Gaza. Also they should clearly tell the military to avoid serving the crusaders, and that they shouldn't fight the party that doesn't fight them, and that they are defending themselves and wouldn't shoot anyone except if they are coming to fight them. This is an important issue that will have the Mujahidin gain the sympathy of the people, and will also weaken the morale of the soldiers.

- Try to have the people who are with the al-Qa'ida swear allegiance (TN: to al-Qa'ida), and if they don't then don't shun them, be open minded, agree to their working with you, and with the passage of time they will appreciate your tolerance, which will make them close to you, and they will join up with you.

- The high rank leadership should be well scrutinized to avoid any doubts.

- Some of the names of the old-timer brothers are, ((Abu Ghazwan)), ((Abu Hurayrah al-Yafi'i)), ((Abu Rihanah al- Yafi'i)), ((Abu 'Umar al-((Wasabi)), and in 'Ubaydah there is 'Abd al-Qawi al-((Jad'i)).

- You should deal with the President's proposal in a prudent way that will show that your enemy is the party that is insisting on escalating the issues and that its action will result in fighting to take place; which fact will have the people sympathies with the Mujahidin and judge the enemy to be the party that is responsible for the fighting consequences. It will also show that we are keen on having a strong foundation for the unity of the Muslim nation and for the safety and security of its people. The issue of abandoning our weapons is totally unacceptable because it (TN: weapons) is part of our existence and history, and we rely on it to safeguard our life. A man is incomplete without a weapon, and the people who laid down their weapons are now worthless.

- We hope that you will send a letter to the brothers in Somalia to have them avoid declaring their solidarity with the al-Qa'ida, and to give their full attention to collecting ransom money and hijack ships.

General comments:
We have to consider the situation of the brothers who are in the midst of the fighting arena, as is the case in Algeria and Yemen. It might be difficult for them to understand and accept our proposal to avoid attacking the army and the police force, and for that reason, we have to draw their attention to the Shari'a evidence and the logical assessment (TN: to avoid attacking such countries as) Syria, Egypt, as well as Sudan. Sudan was under pressure to neglect implementing the Shari'a, and thus it deviated from its set path. However, the pressure increased on it (Sudan) and it had to cede the south (TN: vague, translated as is).

Every arrow and every explosive mine can be used to destroy an American vehicle, and there are others (TN: mines/gear) that should be disbursed to target and bomb American vehicles and prioritize them over NATO vehicles.

We should consider an exception to the rule (TN: of not targeting the military) when an Algerian or Yemeni military unit (not a regular patrol) is on its way to the locations of the brothers.

In other words, any action that is carried at this stage to defend the Mujahidin group in "that country" and allow it to carry its main mission of attacking the American interests is excluded from the general rule.

We should stress on the importance of timing in establishing the Islamic State. We should be aware that planning for the establishment of the state begins with exhausting the main influential power that enforced the siege on the Hamas government, and that overthrew the Islamic Emirate in Afghanistan and Iraq despite the fact this power was depleted. We should keep in mind that this main power still has the capacity to lay siege on any Islamic State, and that such a siege might force the people to overthrow their duly elected governments.

We have to continue with exhausting and depleting them till they become so weak that they can't overthrow any State that we establish. That will be the time to commence with forming the Islamic state.

(End of translation)

PART THREE: LETTERS TO/FROM MEMBERS AND LEADERS

15. Letter to My Beloved Brother

In this letter, the author discusses a number of topics, including the communication between the author and the Algerian Salafist group. The group is encouraged to join "the leading Brother," and an offer of funds is mentioned.

Date: Unknown

From: Unknown

http://www.dni.gov/files/documents/ubl/english2/Letter%20to%20my%20beloved%20Brother.pdf

In the Name of Allah, the Merciful the Beneficent.

Praise be to Allah. Prayers and peace be upon the Messenger of Allah.

Your message arrived… May Allah bind you with His protection and care. Allah knows that we miss you all very much and that we ask Him, in His glory and His many names, with His supreme attributes, to protect you all and watch over you and make all of your decisions correct.

My beloved Brother, My greetings and longing for the two leading brother Shaykhs. We pray that Allah protects them both… Please inform them that we are doing very well, God willing, and we will not listen to but what they tell us, with the grace of Allah.

In regards to what you mentioned (TN: possibly, "what I mentioned"; unclear with the lack of short vowels) regarding the issue of the head Brother's delay in knowing about what happened between us, God willing, please do not worry yourself with the matter, as long as the Doctor is in the picture… However, I wanted him to know about the issue, so that the matter would be completely clear. As you know, my

Brother, the issue is with the psyches and individual thought, and our strategy here differs from any other location.

For this reason, we sent "Ja'far" to you all to express this. We have waited for this period, such that if something were to happen, everything would be clear, because there were some opinions that oppose the nature of our work here… There is no doubt that there will be disturbances and differences and we are well aware of this during these difficult times. We would not accept this matter if it weren't for the good of victory of this religion and the rise of our two head Brothers, for this is a symbol of Islam and there is no exception but to be victorious in overcoming its enemy.

In regards to your (TN: plural) blessing on this matter, Allah knows, there is no exception but for this to take place such that the picture can be clear for the Ummah and so that we may sever the path of the atheists and the hypocrites. Perhaps you have heard some of the malicious analyses that this issue is to weaken the two parties, God only knows… There is a note we would like to bring to your attention: There is communication between us and the "Algerian" Salafist group. It was our intention to send them a message to spur them to join with the leading Brother, God willing. This is what we were thinking of. What is your (TN: plural) opinion, such that we may do this?

In regards to "Muhajir Ibrahim," as Ja'far mentioned to you all, praise Allah, we are making natural and good arrangements for the future, God willing.

As a final matter, are you all in need of funds? We have, praise Allah, some available, such that we could send some of what we have to you all.

We ask that Allah protect you all and keep our Brother well. Tell him, by God, that we will not resign and we hope to pass on news that will make him satisfied.

Your Brother.

PART FOUR: AL-QA'IDA'S INTERNAL ISSUES AND CONCERNS

1. Letter to Muhammad Aslam, 22 April 2011

Positions in the organization are discussed, as is convincing a man to join al Qa'ida under the cover of a fake job.

From: Unknown

http://www.dni.gov/files/documents/ubl/english2/Letter%20to%20Muhammad%20Aslam%20dtd%2022%20April%202011.pdf

(TN: begin Full translation)

(TN: page 1 of 1)

In the Name of God, the Merciful and Compassionate

Praise be to God, the Lord of the worlds, and prayers and peace be upon our Prophet Muhammad and his family and companions, all of them.

Now then…

To the noble brother Muhammad Aslam. May God have mercy on him.

May God's peace, mercy and blessings be upon you.

I hope this letter of mine reaches you and that you are well and in good health.

Now then…

With regard to the brother whom you recommended be our associate (TN: possibly partner) and your mentioning the things that are preventing him from leaving his position, we suggest that you propose to him that he be self-employed (TN: in business) and that he convince his relatives that self-employment is better than a position and that he found a partner to work with (<u>even though the salary of a position is steady</u>).

And these are some of the choices that he might work at, and please let me know about the brother's experience, and what kind of work he is inclined to like, if none of these choices are suitable to him:

1- A real estate office
2- An automobile spare parts store
3- A household appliances store
4- A grocery store
5- A small chicken farm

Do you have any other suggestions if he declines to be our associate, let me know.

We learned from Hajjah Um Hamzah that you have school books. Please send them with the courier from our side, to copy them by scanner, so as to help her and then we will return them, God willing and may God reward you well.

Your brother,
22 April 2011

(TN: end of translation)

2. Terror Franchise

This letter gives a very extensive report of the ideological and operational goals of the Mujahidin. The first part consists of a discussion of ideology and methodology necessary to carry out desired missions against the west. It contains the message, mission, and operational history of the Mujahidin, as well as necessary operational tactics and technology. It discusses in length the preferred methods of offense, giving the reader instructions and references for explosive material and other tactical war methods.

Date: Unknown

From: Abu-Salih Al Somali

http://www.dni.gov/files/documents/ubl/english/Terror%20Franchise.pdf

Terror Franchise

THE UNSTOPPABLE ASSASSIN

TECHS Vital role for its success

AL-QA'IDA'S MYSTIQUE EXPOSED

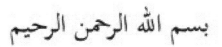

In the Name of Allah the most Gracious, the Most Merciful, All Praise and thanks are due to Him alone, I thank Him and seek His help, assistance, forgiveness and guidance. And I seek His refuge from the evils of our selves and misdoings. Whoever Allah Guides there is no one that can misguide and whoever Allah misguides there is absolutely no one that can guide, and I bare witness that nothing is worthy of worship except Allah, and I bare witness that Muhammad (may the peace and blessing of Allah be upon Him) is the servant and messenger of Allah.

O Muslims with scientific and technical Backgrounds:
Engineers, Doctors, Biologists, Pharmacists, researchers, hobbyists, Handymen and women, experimenters, discoverers, The courageous, Experts in all fields, Amateurs, and all of you who care and **realize** that you are a part of **an Ummah**..

Here is how **YOU CAN** easily, safely and **anonymously** engrave your name in history by assisting us with the **KNOWLIDGE** and **KNOW-HOW** of how to counter Islam's enemies' technology-especially (Laser guided weapons), and how to be able to make **death,** in its **explosions** form- especially (the Oxidizer part of it) and **toxicants** in an easy, practical and improvised way anywhere on earth..

As I am about to write this letter, my heart beats hurry in excitement and I am looking forward to every word and letter, that I beg Allah to enable me to write in a manner in which he is pleased with and I ask Him the Lord of the heavens and earth to place **Baraka** (blessing) in what I write and that He the sustainer of life makes these words the reason for you-who read it- to **ACT NOW**, without any delay or procrastination...For it's **very late already**, but not too late, yet!! Because you are still alive and breathing...

What makes me even more and more thankful to Allah and even more happy and thrilled is knowing that the actual writing of these words and the very effort of seeking to **communicate** with those with experience and technical skills, and the undertaking of **exchanging of technologies**, expertise and best practices within the Global Jihad Movement, and seeking to enhance and **adopt new technologies** through **Allied coordination, innovation** and **pursuit of extra knowledge**, <u>regardless of all difficult circumstances</u>- all of the mentioned are **the very BLESSED ACTIONS** that the Zio-Crusaders and their think-tanks **hope** the Mujahideen would **never be guided to!!!**

Why?!![1] Because they **know as they have confessed** that the mentioned above are (after the aid of Allah-of course) the **key sources** of success for the Mujahideen, through which they **improve** their overall **capabilities, increase** their **operational range globally** and become even more **LEATHAL**, **effective, adaptive, secured, successful, zealous and victorious**...Al-hamdu-lillah.

They hope with all their sinful hearts that the Mujahideen would be just overwhelmed under their loosing-trillion dollar crusade, just waiting inactive to be killed. They yearn so badly that if only the Mujahideen (individuals and Groups) would be tangled in **energy draining, achievement crippling,** and **delaying shackles** of unawareness, fear, individualism, egoism, distrust, **routine**, impoliteness, and other traps that their commander **Satan** throws in the path of those who **struggle against him and his plans**.

---

[1] Studies by the -US Homeland security backed research cooperation -**RAND** titled: Sharing the Dragon's teeth, Terrorist Groups and the Exchange of New Technologies. <u>A must read for Mujahideen</u>!!

Part Four: Al-Qa'ida's Internal Issues and Concerns

I wouldn't be exaggerating, if I declare that what I am about to write maybe is the **most important** thing I have written **in my life**, and that it is the most important thing the reader may come across in a very long time...Why? Because Allah willing it's the key to entering Al-Firdaws Al ala, It is the door to be written in history's few lines of the loyal, honorable, pious, and those who desire a life and memory **beyond** that of speaking mammals....!!!

It is the key and vital requirement to **stopping** evil, greed, genocide, corruption, immorality, slaughter, inhumanity, robbery, bondage and **suffering on a global scale**. Moreover, as you'll soon see, what I am about to reveal to you is the way (By the permission of Allah) to goodness, piety, justice, sovereignty, freedom, safety, and honor for **all of the inhabitants of this globe**.

It's frankly what you -**technical people**- **CAN DO** to take the **bigger share** of this Jihad and holy struggle against America, Israel and its friends' Ziocrusade, against Muslims and all that stands for morality, justice, and honor. It is **very simple** for you to do, if you **decide not to deprive yourself** the blessing of pleasing Allah and being saved from the torments of this life and the last.

Yes **YOU, CAN**- Allah willing-change history right there from your home town, under the cool air of your air conditioner, safe and sound away from any danger or fear.. I am not joking!! Not only that, but even though I am writing to you right from the battle field under the explosions of bombings and continuous humming of Predator UAV"s, B52s, jet fighters, Apache helicopters and the rest!!!......You-O technical man or woman- **CAN SHARE** and have the **same reward** if not more from Allah **If you help us fight this Battle** which effects your present and future and the very existence of every living being on Earth...

Knowledge is power: These pig eating invaders and their loyal dogs are too **scared of death** to fight us face to face. By Allah, let it be clear brothers and sisters that the Greedy, blood thirsty enemies of Allah have not succeeded in killing Muslims and inflicting calamity on the Muslim Ummah, and steeling their lands and resources because of their might and power and sophisticated technology as much as it is the result of **YOU technical people** of the Muslim Ummah abandoning us – your Mujahideen brothers- in the battle filed, fighting, and facing fear and death to protect your security, honor, chastity, children, family, wealth, and life!!

The main reason they **continue to kill us** is because nor do we have the knowledge and resources to counter the technology they are using against us, nor are we-in the battle filed-in a position to research and seek the **know-how** needed to counter the enemies tactics, nor are you assisting us with the answers to do that!!! **YOU** have a big chance **NOW** to **STOP** the savageness and arrogance of America and its allies...Yes you! And I am going to tell you how...so straight forward... so easy....so safe...so much rewarding in both worlds...

I am going -Allah willing- to give you **THE CREAM** of our thirty year global fight with the enemies of Islam...Be it the west itself or its western grown agents, and how you **technical people** out there can **play the most important role** in the close-to-end stage of this battle between the **Party of Satan** and the **Party of Allah** the Almighty.

<u>**Important introduction:**</u>

Today's War:

After Allah the Almighty destroyed the communist empire on the hands of minimally equipped Muslims' youth who **sold their souls for His pleasure**. <u>**The whole WORLD now has become A BATTLE FIELED,**</u> America and its Nato allies get their money, authority and soldiers from their **VOTERS**...**those drunkard selfish** serial tagged **infra-human** Americans, and Europeans who consume the- well advertised and marketed- filth of their Zionist capitalist masters producing the money and manpower which their masters utilize to seek to destroy Israel's enemies and to rob the people of the globe of their minds, honor, land, resources, chastity, minerals, oil, and lives!!!

It is the **VOTERS,** who choose their leaders who deploy their armies against Muslims, and pay billions of (their produced tax money) to Israel to massacre our brothers and sister. It is the voters who vote on laws against the purity and chastity of **Hijab** and **Minarets**..While they are the ones who vote in favor of human alien satanic practices such as homosexual marriages and infant butchery in the wombs of their selfish heartless prostitute mothers. The voters are the ones, who demanded America's **pullout from Vietnam**, and they are the ones who **pulled out their Spanish troops from Afghanistan** and they are the ones who **turned the evil Tony Blair into a lame duck** and ended his ten year carrier of arrogance and American subordination with disgrace!!

The American and European citizens are **the switch** to **shut down** this heartless damned Zio-crusade machine of Evil and greed...!!!

Allah guided the leaders of the Mujahideen, to this **marvelous effective secret**...And they refused-**as the west had wished**- to exhaust their selves and limited resources in side battles with the poodles of America and Israel be it the apostate regimes or the idol worshippers or the many other Jews shoe lickers...They refused to be fooled into tackling the servants, while the **commander in chief and protector of infidelity, Zionism and evil, (America)** stays intact and safe freely keeping on generating and nourishing more and more of its loyal agents...whom it has given the duty of protecting the **cursed Jews**, by taking upon themselves the continuous humiliation, disgrace, brainwashing, tormenting and starving of the Muslim youth and Ummah, So that the *living hells* (the Muslim majority countries) which they control can be the examples against which the western **so called democratic heavens** can be compared to.

As Allah the Almighty guided Muslims who lived in the west to the path of Jihad, He the Glorified opened the chests of the Honorable Mujahideen such as Ramzi Yousuf, Aymal Qansi and the leaders of Jihad- commencing with Al-Qaeda's leaders sheikh Osama and Doctor Ayman Al-zawahiri to the efficient idea of **shutting down the source of energy** from which the ziocrusade invaders keep on refueling with money, soldiers, and support....The Mujahideen started thinking **beyond hitting America's many tails** and Decided that this coward **swine** –hiding **in B52 bombers and behind the controls of remotely operated, spy planes**- is only killed by blows **directly to the head**.. **That is America's homeland, its interests and its institutions and economical building blocks ALL OVER THE GLOBE**.

The Mujahideen answered Allah's call **to terrify His enemies and theirs,** and with Allah's help and assistance **began the effort of producing death and fear** in the drunkard sinful hearts of **American Voters**, so it may be a shocking awakener for their brains drugged by Alcohol and sexually driven media, to wake up and smell not the coffee **but the blood**...**OUR BLOOD**...but from now on... **mixed with THEIRS**..!! As Sheikh Osama declared: As you **kill us** you will be **killed**, and as you **bomb us** you will **be bombed**!!!!

PART FOUR: AL-QA'IDA'S INTERNAL ISSUES AND CONCERNS

Mujahideens' Message:

The message is clear and not vague..**Americans** and their blind allies must clearly understand, memorize, and develop an un-doubtful conviction that they must **fear the actions** of their governments against **Islam** and **the Muslim** world as they <u>fear DEATH it self!!!</u> The same as every American relates cancer tumors, heart attacks and AIDS with loss of limbs, end of life, coffins, graves and the inevitable payback in the pits of Hell, Every **American** should see and feel **REAL DEATH** with **every penny paid** from the taxpayers' money to **Israel**. The **Americans** and their NATO allies' citizens should **perceive FATALITY** with **every missile** fired on our brothers and sister in **Gaza**, they should envision **MOTRTALITY** with every step their evil soldiers take towards our lands. The Americans and their European allies need to imagine, visualize, and comprehend **DEATH, amputation, blood, pain, depression, bankruptcy, misery and** <u>**TOTAL DESTRUCTION**</u> with every drop of ink or (bit) used to ridicule Prophet Muhammad (may the peace and blessing of Allah be upon Him) or Qura'n or any symbol of Islam. They should wait for the same with every second our sister Afia Siddiqi or our blind sheikh Omar AbadRrahman spends in American jails.

Global Mujahideens' Mission:

The mission of the Global Mujahideen of today is to **KILL** a few tens, or hundreds or thousands of the infidel citizens of America and its western ally countries in their **HOMELANDS** and **wherever they are sited** on any spot on the planet until they **FEAR** participating in or supporting any actions against Islam and the Muslims as they **FEAR DEATH ITSELF**!!! The **VOTERS** in America and its ally countries should know that their lives and the lives of their loved ones are going to be the price paid for the evil actions of those who they **VOTE FOR** (against us and our loved ones)!!.

Moreover, the mission of the Global Mujahideen is to **destroy the American economy** by targeting American economical targets **globally**.

They must **KNOW** that if they choose to **LIVE** for **ISRAEL**, then for it **THEY SHALL DIE!!**

Global Mujahideens' Executed Missions:

In accordance with this creed and successful strategy the Mujahideen carried out many painful operations against the previously mentioned lawful targets, such as the first world trade center bombings in New York and the American embassy bombings in Kenya and Nairobi and the bombing of the American warship USS Cole in Yemen and the historic catastrophic blessed operations of September eleven which destroyed the world trade centers and a large part of the Pentagon when nineteen young men used four passenger planes and by the help of Allah transferred them into human guided missiles. After that, and even when the Muslim Ummah was tested with the destruction of the Islamic Emirate of Afghanistan on the Hands of America and its NATO allies supported by the essential role of the apostate government of Pakistan lead by the western agent Musharraf and then the bandit Zardari, and regardless of all of the horrific difficulties endured by the Mujahideen, they **continued** (All praises due to **Allah**) **steadfastly** with their **life's mission** and <u>proven plan</u>.

By the grace of Allah, **the honorable Global Mujahideen** struck the **Spanish railways** with multiple deadly explosions at rush hour which by the grace of Allah lead to the Spaniards getting the message. They had enough intelligence-opposite to the stupid arrogant

Americans and Brits- to immediately sack their American subordinate government and pull their troops from the battle field. Then, similar deadly martyrdom operations against **the London subways** were executed, which trashed the haughty Tony Blair and started (By the grace of the Almighty) a chain of tribulations and disgraceful revelations in the British governing parties.

However, seemingly the British were too arrogant and stupid to have had learned quickly enough and are asking-like the Americans, Germans, and French for **extra lessons**!! Following the London bombing and before it, there were several blessed operation against American and European targets in Indonesia, Pakistan, Egypt, India and elsewhere[2], such as the brave bombing of a bus carrying **French nationals**, the **Marriott hotel** massive bombing, the bombing of the Denmark embassy in Islamabad, the massive Bali bombings, and lately the heroic Fidai operations **in Bombay**-India's economical capital- in which several western targets were struck in which many Americans and other westerners were killed. Following that, was the beautiful huge bombing-also in India- of the western **German bakery** mainly visited by Jews and western nationals in general...And not to forget of course the latest detrimental martyrdom operation in Khost on several CIA senior officers in a military base in Afghanistan.

America and its allies knew that the **SPREAD** of this (**SUCCESSFUL STRATEGY**) adopted by the Global Jihad Movement leads un-doubtfully to the **rapid demise** of its satanic evil gang comprised of America, its allies and its institutions (named the **international community**).... This meant that they won't be able anymore to **suck the blood** of their long tamed victims to satisfy their never-ending greed for wealth and power!! This meant that they would be deprived of the money, land, man power and military might they (the party of Satan) have throughout history sought to seize lands and install their **Satan approved man made laws**.

On these lands and living under these laws, Allah's creations are transformed into **obedient consumers**-in a huge farm-like crowd called- the Market economy. The inhabitants of these human farms are deceived into **PAYING FOR** heart killing, moral demolishing, faith disfiguring, in humane evil obscene products...under the attractive banners of freedom, human rights and equality. Moreover, in these **cursed gatherings**, man marring man and woman marring woman are signs of modernity, advancement, and success.

Just a perfect plan (as they had hoped) to distract humans from their **PLOT** and ultimately fulfill the promise of **their original commander SATAN** to **drag** the sons and daughters of Adam with them **into Hell**!!

America and its foolish followers or allies came with all their might and CIA agents and propaganda to the land of Khurasan thinking that they would be able to siege and quarantine this **Ideology** and **Methodology** which <u>**threatens their unquestioned control of this globe**</u>. The battle began on two fronts, the traditional on land combat-which the Mujahideen are familiar with- The other new front was the proven-lethal **selective covert war** against the Mujahideen, their leaders, their technical personal and supporters among both the Islamic emirate and Pakistani Taliban commanders and Pakhtoon tribes.

---

[2] For extra information on Global Mujahideen executed missions: *see MIPT Terrorism Knowledge Base*, and the previously mentioned rand study.

Part Four: Al-Qa'ida's Internal Issues and Concerns

The battle on Land:

As for the front of land combat, the Americans, NATO, ISAF, UN, and their dollar-purchased supporting mercenaries among the (Shia' Hazara majority North Alliance) and apostate local Afghanis were continuously (by the help of Allah) cut to peaces by the deadly explosions of countless non stopping **Istishadi (Martyrdom- operations)** against their fortified high wall Camps, their vehicles -which the cowards rarely stepped out of any way- and their rare foot patrols.

The other **WEAPON** that filled most of their corpses' bags and just ripped their yellow sinful hearts is what they call **IED's**...Improvised explosive devises –mainly made of different ordnances' shells or basic **two substance (Oxidizer+Reducer)-mixtures** armed with shrapnel sometimes which ripped through their so-called armored vehicles and bodies, which ended up in Afghanistan dogs' tummies just as Dr Ayman Al zawahiri (may Allah protect him and all the Mujahideen) had warned them before. These [**ACd's**) **(Anti Crusader) devices** were in this case either detonated with (Improvised-simply built Pressure switches, and booby traps) or remotely detonated either via radio controlled switches (RC) or using the more common and easier to make **FLASH** attached to several hundred meters of doubled enamel wire. The **FLASH** is basically a simple (Mujahideen improvised Circuit-built totally from easily available China components). The circuit produces high voltages (up to 250-700 volts) utilizing four AA batteries connected in series. The high voltage enables the current to pass through the wire to the detonator overcoming the resistance of the long wire. Among the Mujahideens' Main tactics in Afghanistan also, were ambushes, Fidai operations, target killings, poisoning, artillery operations and others.

The result by the help of Allah was that the crusade collation came to realize-from the ground troops up to higher ranking officers that, if they wouldn't run way fast enough they would un-doubtfully **all die**. As a result, Obama downgraded his declared ambitions or to be exact his (Zio-Christian Lobbyist masters') day dreams from eliminating Taliban and transforming Afghanistan to a (*Democratic Country*!!) to what they would like to imagine as achievable goals: stated as eliminating Al-Qaeda, and depriving it and their Allies of safe heavens from which they can plan operations against the west and its allies such as China, and India.

ISI-CIA Deadly Covert War:

Having said that, **there was a battle hidden behind the scenes**!! There but not there!! In a nut shell Pakistan's ISI sold or surrendered to America its 60 year old (already prepared) infrastructure of senior agents, Informers, recruiters, bases, Political parties, airports, logistics, and all that the Americans demanded from them. ISI dogs gathered the somewhat freely available Info from their countless –money worshipping tribal agents, or from the many captured-among the Mujahideen and civilians, in check posts, sudden ambushes, and sudden raids on houses during the preparation stage through 2003-2006. Their American Masters would choose the targets, and then give out the **IR transmitting Designators and invisible ink markers** to the many **spy contractors** who then try to get the job of placing the designator on the selected target done with the least spent (on the many **disposable agents**) leaving most of the money for themselves and their coordinators among the Government, Army, and ISI officials. After the designator is placed on the targeted compound or vehicles (mostly when **left unguarded** in market places) the only thing left is for the UAV to **track the IR signal or invisible ink** flashing from the target or near to it, shoot a (near to IR laser beam) on the target then fire laser guided missiles towards the reflected laser energy. This is what happened with most of the Mujahideen killed in khurasan.!!!

Taking advantage of repeated mistakes:

Apparently, The Mujahideen in the targeted khurasan region-surrounded by different enemies from all directions did not –may be- have the chance to adapt to ground realities as quickly as the enemy changed its tactics to an unusual one with the arrival of Robert gates as America's defense minister to a selective **long-breath covert war**. Selective laser guided bombings of specific **individuals one at a time** or selective **groups one at a time**, later bundled and broadened with time, and spaced by some intervals, and now and then exchanged with different warship bombings-sometimes even on useless targets and mass ground operations which displaced millions of civilians, all of the mentioned and a mixture of other mind and heart stressing aspects-not to mention-the painful fact that the Mujahideen and the tribal inhabitants were just looked at from the rest of Muslim Ummah (including those with **technical knowledge**). All that, compounded with the severe lack of financial resources, and maybe at sometimes the **not so efficient (learn and adapt)** attitude added to somewhat improvable organizational skills related mainly to coordination, enemy tactics assessment, communication, inter-exchange of knowledge and technology and decision making. Add to that, as a senior Mujahideen strategist states: The Mujahideen getting too caught up with the **offensive aspect** of the battle and not giving the **crucial defensive** aspect of it the absolutely **vital attention it requires**, as a result overlooking a major **building block of success** in gorilla warfare! All of the mentioned and many maybe un-controllable or controllable variables (Allah knows best) may have weighed towards the Mujahideens' **weak and slow counter strategy against the technology** deployed by the Americans against them.

To summarize, the great-history making, honorable Jihad in Khurasan with all its countless blessings and rewards (Allah willing) for those honored to be part of it and the whole Ummah and world, wasn't different from any human endeavor- and has had a lot of room for improvement, advancement, adaptation, and innovation, but there has been and continues to be an **ENEMY** guided by some of the neighbors of the Mujahideen waiting **patiently** for the chances in (recurring) **faults and mistakes** to **betray** and **kill**!!

Allah's enemy's waste of life, wealth and effort:

Having mentioned, that the American Zio-crusade collation -totally facilitated by the **ISI's** already established infrastructure-**took advantage** of the weak points of the Mujahideen and was able (after Allah's permission) to kill some of them, this of course, still does not change the fact that the party of Satan are **loosing on an enormous scale on all fronts**, and **still did not and will not** (by the Help of Allah) achieve their goal of attaining security for the citizens of America and its ally countries unless –as Sheikh Osama told them- we live it in reality in Palestine and the world over. As for those killed, American missiles have been the means for them to gain **Shahada** (martyrdom) (so we consider them and to Allah is their *reckoning*) which is the ultimate dream of every Mujahid, by which (Allah willing) the winners guarantee success and security and the highest ranks and infinite joy in *Jannatul Firdaws* which Allah has prepared specially for those who sell themselves for His pleasure. As for **Israel's battalion**, they As Allah the Almighty have said in Quran, spent trillions of their money and what they have spent became a source of sorrow for them and after that they **shall be defeated**.

Part Four: Al-Qa'ida's Internal Issues and Concerns

Allah- their creator and the Lord of the universe who defeated Firown, and the destroyer of the people of A' ad, Thamood and the many disbelieving nations before and after them **will definitely** punish, humiliate, disgrace and destroy the American gang, however, as He the Almighty has declared- He will **grant a group of His loving slaves** (who **pass the tests,** do the required work and become **eligible**) the honor and pleasure of **being the means** for this **GREATEST ACHIEVEMENT**. I Pray to Allah and beg His bounty and mercy to grant me and **YOU** who are reading these words the honor to be among the fortunate who **rid** this world of evil and lead Allah's creation from the darkness, sorrow and anxiety of disbelief to the **light** and **gladness** of **Islam**.

TERROR FRANCHISE: The UNSTOPPABLE ASSASSIN!!.

America and its foolish allies based their so called **war on terror** on a few expired (wishful thinking) principles. Summed in: 1) that terror operations must be directed and planed by a specific person or group from one or two spots on the globe!! 2) Stereotyping those who execute such operations!! 3) That the means (knowledge and material) used to inflict death and terror can be narrowed and hence either be blocked or watched over in markets!!

To the despair of the crusaders, regardless of all their efforts in countering terrorism the Global jihad movement have in the (face of counterterrorism pressure) thanks to Allah, rather transformed, and revolutionized into a **MULTINATIONAL, TRANSATLANTIC FRANCHISE**, or as techs call it an **OPEN SOURCE TERROR PROJECT**. The Mission is clearly and boldly known and **it's the right** and even more the **duty and obligation** of every Muslim to **take upon him or her self the responsibility** to serve in **a module or unit** of this **MISSION**.

Let us (1) divide into **completely disconnected**, **INVISBLE**, **INFINITE TASKFORCES** (2) every taskforce completes the part of the mission which it is best at (3) Then make the ready **component[S]** available by all means, resources, options and methods so that the final **Executing Taskforces** all over the planet earth can easily assemble the effective product (DEATH AND TERROR), and distribute it (in the **market economy**) to those who **DESERVE** IT!! This paper is not going to deal with **why we should terrify Americans** and their blind allies, for there are countless history-long records in all forms known to mankind that answer this (somewhat silly-outdated) question!! This Paper is concerned with the vital aspect of **HOW we CAN ALL TERRIFY** Allah's enemies.

Terror operations usually fall into three or four broad categories (1) assassination using (common or improvised) weapons or more effectively toxicants (Cyanide, Ricin, Phosgene etc) (2) seizure (e.g..highjacking Planes, buses, remote civic hauls etc) (3) explosive destruction of a major asset, usually accompanied by substantial loss of life (4) unconventional operations (such as ramming rock filled trucks into high speed trains rail crossings) etc.

Terror tools:
As it seems clear from the previously stated categories, that in addition to the **correct and truthful ideology and methodology** required to execute such operations, an operation **CAN NOT** be done without **the crucial** requirement of **THE SCIENCE, THE TECHNOLOGY** and **TOOLS** or **EQUIPMENT** which is **utilized** by the executing taskforce to attain the desired result in the form of (**dreadful, eye opening and oppression stopping death, fear and terror**!!). No matter how brave or truthful and sincere the Mujahid can be,

he, she or they in addition to completing the **Sharia requirements** for victory such as (seeking Allah's pleasure alone, relying on him alone, hoping and expecting success from Him alone, humbleness, piety etc), they must also **fulfill the requirements** that go along with **the universal rules** and ways Allah has made this world work according to. **Terror tools**, after Allah's help were, are and will be the main source of achievement on both the conventional battle filed and the most vital **Transatlantic City terror** warfare. No wonder, Allah has ordered His slaves in Quran to give this **crucial necessity** the utmost attention as He the Al Mighty says in Suratul Anfal, verse 60:

*(And **make ready** against them all you can **of power**, including steeds of war (tanks, planes, explosives, missiles, artillery) to **threaten the enemy** of Allah and your enemy, and others besides whom, you may not know but whom Allah does know. And whatever you shall spend in the cause of Allah shall be repaid unto you, and you shall not be treated unjustly)* [8:60]

Simple, but DEADLY:
Contrary to what the western media keeps on signing on their media, **Terror franchises** and **taskforces DO NOT** need neither nuclear bombs nor radio active material (even though it would be nice to have) to **achieve their goal** !! A few grams of Cyanide (easily manufactured and sold by the kilo in third world countries) or Ricin diluted in water and injected randomly in anything ingested on super markets shelves, picnics, restaurants etc, or a few kilos of sodium chlorate or any other oxidizer-grounded properly- and mixed in the right ratio with a reducer (according to Oxy-red mixtures rules[3]) and armed with shrapnel or for example a U-HALL truck filled with rocks and driven on high speed rail tracks crossings- all of the previous are just examples of what **multinational Terror Franchises** need to disseminate **NONSTOP, UNPREDICTED, INVISIBLE SUDDEN DEATH** even for one, two or a handful of VOTERS to **create the right atmosphere of terror and fear of the unknown** for them to **STOP** (the rat race for a while) and RETHINK (THE PROS AND CONS) of their elected governments' policies, alliances and actions!!

Techs Taskforce: Research and Documentation.
This unit consists of those mentioned in the head of this paper. **YOU** have the **utmost vital part** to complete.

Research the needed information, there are many sources **to begin with** mostly found in the **literature and websites** of specific interests groups such as, rouge science, civil rights, hackers, knowledge freedom, hobbyists, Anarchist, Survivalists, alternative fuel-energy, **pyrotechnics**, invention Patents, video sites, anti government, DIY, How to, evil scientists, MIT fab-lab,(applied science, chemistry, etc), appropriate technology, information unlimited etc. As for chemical related material, a good approach is to see how this substance was produced when it was first discovered or invented, new industrial methods are based on energy efficiency, mass production and low cost, which does not matter to Terror Franchises, Producing **one kilo** of (**any oxidizer or toxicant**) a week for example is very much acceptable. Key aspects of concern to Terror Producers are improvising, small scale, onsite, starting martial based on consumer products, and home built or purchased apparatuses (even from another continent).

Performing the procedures :After the research is completed, the second **even more important part** is actually performing the procedures (synthesis, assembly etc) and

---

[3] For example: any chlorate + motor oil (44:6) ratio also Hydrogen peroxide 70-80% + (honey or black pepper or flour etc) (4:1) ratio are very powerful explosive mixture...Look at shiekh abu khabbab's training manual for many other mixtures.

Part Four: Al-Qa'ida's Internal Issues and Concerns

explaining it in an easy(step by step, foolproof) practical manner on video (preferred) and-or PDF format document and any other media used in the civilian arena such as Flash, PowerPoint etc. Reviewing presentation skills' and watching already available instruction-oriented material of the previously mentioned groups gives a good idea of the **best practices** to make use of while preparing such material such as **ALSO** mentioning alternatives from house hold and consumer products, car parts, garden, hardware, plumbing, building material, and every and anything around that can be brought or improvised **regardless** of the **original field** and purpose it is **used for.**

The information and tools needed are related to two main aspects of this war and a third one connected to it and serves its end results. These categories are (1) Defensive (2) Offensive (3) General development.

Points to bear in mind:
1) You can undertake as much as you can from the following lists or even one of the topics listed is also **very beneficial**. The researcher should be careful of falling into hindering; achievement blocking traps such hesitation, procrastination, undermining oneself, **just do it**, begin the first line and the rest will just flow and you'll enjoy it. Trust me.
2) Not to consider any information not important or too obvious. What might be obvious to someone maybe is not to the other, and we are working here with an entire nation and generations to come. Allah willing.
2) Include a lot of illustrations, pictures, sources, etc. Try to be persuasive and encouraging.
3) While video recording a mask can be weared, voice changed etc.
4) If for some reason (hopefully not) the research wouldn't be followed up with the actual explained application, then at least the research should be suitably propagated, so it could be built upon and completed by others.
5) No doubt there is going to be a lot of effort, money and time put in **this crucial work of Jihad**, however, there needs to be **also great** effort in making sure that the information is disseminated to all Terror Franchises and Taskforces **Globally**. **Anonymously**, upload your (long waited for) work to web sharing sites, Jihadi discussion forums, and send emails advertising about the material and request effort be made to get the info to the right hands or you can even send the info (on DVD) by mail to someone you think would get it to where it needs to go.
6) If the whole project takes a lot of time, maybe it is better to make it into parts and upload it one after the other as soon as one is ready. At the end, maybe the whole project can be uploaded all in one piece again.

Offensive tools: I am going to begin with this topic because I think it is the most important part in our mission: Many operations failed in the preparation stage primarily because the tools were not available in a secured and easy way. Working on **making Terror tools available to all**, Allah willing, no doubt increases exponentially the number of those willing to **execute operations globally** .The needed information is arranged according to its importance:

Explosions: Immediately needed
1) Preparation, synthesis of (Oxidizers) especially substances in **class 3** as categorized by the NFPA (look at the provided files in the terror franchise folder).
2) Hydrogen peroxide via fuel cell, electrolysis of an aqueous solution of sulfuric acid or other compounds. Or electrochemical reduction of Oxygen using [gas diffusion electrode ...what is this?] or [packed bed electrode...what is this?]...or absolutely any other option. And best way to raise its concentration to 35-80%

3) Producing Hydrogen (Via water electrolysis or whatever is best) for either usage in fuel cell? Or in a (downscaled *anthraquinone-what is this- process*).
4) Utilizing apparatuses such Ozone Generators, electrical arc, furnaces, electrochemical cells etc in the production of Oxidizers or its starting material such as sulfuric cid for electrolysis.
5) (k,Na) Chlorate, Chlorite, perchlorate, manufacturing on a small scale.
6) 65% calcium hypochlorite production via hydroxide and chlorine or other.
7) Chlorine production and storage for hypochlorite etc.
8) The effectiveness of any of the other peroxides, oxides, chromates or <u>any Non-nirate oxy</u>. (Look at the **Pyrotechnic composition** file, and ***Detect*** file in **terror tools** folder).
9) Synthesis of Sodium, Potassium or other (elements Ca etc, substances) that **react explosively** with **water** or to be burnt (Oxidized) in air (simple-how) into peroxides and either used directly with a reducer (How-which)? Or reacted with (water or diluted sulfuric acid?) to form hydrogen peroxide.
10) New options for primary explosives (used in detonators).
11) Production of Carbides, for acetylene, how to explode?
12) Production of Oxygen, storage how to best utilize?
13) Nitric Acid via Ozonator or other procedure. And raising its concentration to anhydrous form.
14) Small scale improvised mechanical nitration of (hexamine, etc – to rdx, petn) including temperature control options etc. also Bachmann process.
15) Other alternatives for Acetone as a RDX solvent.
16) Producing lead dioxide plates (lead is available in (lead acid) batteries' plates) etc to be used either as an oxidizer (if it works) or as anodes in electrolysis.
17) Producing iron oxides (rust) utilizing it as an oxidizer? Other than thermites?
18) Fuel air explosions (Butane, methane, benzene) sprayed in air? gas leaks?
19) HHO bombs, gases from water Hydrogen, Oxygen... explode through ignition?
20) Sulfates as oxidizer (How?) examples.
21) Hydrogen producing reactions (caustic soda or hydrochloric acid + metals (zinc or aluminum) how powerful if contained in sealed containers.
22) Water based, and solvent based binders, Plasticizer for powdered material.
23) A Non liquid (solid or jelly) mixture using the great 70%Hydrogen peroxide oxidizer.
24) Any other option (energetic compounds, devices etc) to create a kinetic **MOVING FORCE**, with enormous heat, eye opening massive glow, and deafening; brain awaking loud noise.

Toxicants: Immediately needed
1) Actual improvised production and testing of Cyanides, Ricin.(immediately needed)
2) Preparation and testing (rabbits is ok) of any lethal (delayed and immediate) ingested toxicants.
3) On Camera production of any of war gases (Phosgene, VX, etc)..Look at NbK file and scientific principles of improvised home warfare. (onsite production apparatus also).
4) Actual production and testing of Biological toxicants (Anthrax, Botulism, clostridium, endotoxins, Exotoxins etc)
5) Production of (HCl) or whatever is needed in the production of toxicants.
6) Any other options that can be used as toxicant ....plants, etc...detailed, local names pictures, incidents, cultivation...Insects...etc...read scientific principles of improvised home warfare volume 2, 5, 6.
7) Bacteria based weapons....how? detail. Any other practical options.
8) Airborne substance that when sprayed in small quantity or mixed (tablet form) with water, tranquilizes the entire inhabitants of a hall or plane. And its antidote.

Part Four: Al-Qa'ida's Internal Issues and Concerns

Rocketry: Flying death.
1) Step by step manufacture of improvised rockets, including propellant, Fixed and erectable fins etc.
2) 90% H_2O_2 propelled rockets system, tanks, pumps, catalyst.
3) Simple improvised **inertia switch** for after flight switching of timer in rockets.
4) Improvised home made mortar, grenade launcher, rocket launcher, etc.

Electronics oriented:
1) Remote switching options: simple 2-5watt radio frequency based remotes. Fm, Am etc. even better PLL controlled. Digital code options. etc...anti jamming procedures.
2) Utilizing light frequencies in high power (laser, IR, etc) modulated or not transmitters and sensors to switch on, off circuits in the 1500 meter range, in daylight.
3) Utilizing ultrasound, infra sound etc through strobes in the ground or air etc for remote switching.(un-jammable options)
4) **Most importantly** devises to disable, incapacitate or destroy enemy electronic devises, sensors, equipments, communication etc. Stingray?
5) Ultra sonic *(Acoustical)* phasor, Pain generating incapacitating (Non lethal-or lethal) devises.
6) 5-15 watt FM (88-102 MHz) transmitters for radio transmission of Dawa and anti kufr messages. Step by step assembly and tuning.
7) Options for generating electrical energy, and fuels for vehicles in all situations.
8) (Vibration, magnetic (metal), sound etc) activated switches (circuits). And any improvised booby trap, tripping methods etc. (triggering IEDs) etc.
9) Utilizing HHO electrically produced gas mixture for projectile propulsion.
10) Any idea about utilizing any common appliance, thing etc in an uncommon manner, with some tweaking.
11) Passive systems for detecting plane positions in the air, and auto aiming of weapons (launcher) accordingly.

Mechanical oriented:
1) A six by six inch launching pad, utilizes gears, pistons and motors etc to move 360 degrees on the horizontal axis and maybe 90 degrees on the vertical axis, something that looks like a ground-tennis ball thrower. Operated remotely either with wire or wireless. On this pad we can either fit multiple rocket launchers or any other weapon with a camera, to be able to aim the weapon (remotely) on helicopters, UAVs, military convoys etc.
2) Non explosive (mechanical based) throwers for projectiles such as crossbow, leaf and motor operated slingers.
3) Options for mechanical **timers** (triggering, security) (gear system etc).
4) Propeller driven gliders, for flying Fidais and Istishadis..into their forts and compounds.
5) (Universal) Scopes for artillery, horizontal increments of 60 and every one devided to a hundred, 360 degrees divided to 60 minutes and every minute into 100 seconds. Vertical 90 degrees divided to 15 minutes and each 100 seconds. Mills scope

Documents Forging: Pass to anywhere.
1) Information and methods of improvised security printing forging.
2) Monogram production, chip cloning, picture changing, info erasing on both water based and regular new type passports.
3) Other methods and skills to produce whatever security documents governments produce. Passport, certificate, license, passes, etc

4) Available and prospect smuggling roots and methods.
5) Information on America and Europe's borders and its weaknesses.

Additional related Info: Big goals need BIG teamwork.
1) **Camouflage**: manufacture of artificial rocks, camouflage for IEDs, and makeup science for changing appearance.
2) **Molds, casts**: making molds for pourable material, molding shoe soles, statues.
3) Any ideas for hiding or better integrating mixtures into consumer products manufacture.
4) **Any and every idea that exposes weaknesses** in the west and how to exploit it.
5) Small scale manufacturing process of everything humans use. Machining, casting, molding, pressing, forging, finishing, bending...processes...pro...?
6) Any beneficial info applied to life, alternatives in energy, medicine, innovation, mechanics, communication, weaponry, etc...

Defense Tools: Primarily, research is needed in the **crucial field** of the methods and technology deployed by the party of Satan against the Mujahideen on **the battle field** and in **the city**, then completed by the research and documentation of the measures and tools to counter such enemy tactics, For example.
1) Laser detection and jamming
2) IR detection (wide range).
3) Invisible ink, color (used by the enemy for target designation. How to detect it?
4) Detection and jamming of satellite communication. Used by spies and to remotely control UAV, and transmit video footage.
5) Mobile and communication scanning and positioning (triangular etc) counter measures.
6) Utilization of HF etc Transceivers in transatlantic sound and data communication.
7) Applicable Hacking, phreaking etc skills for ground line, mobile, internet, wireless etc and utilization in secured communication and other useful (non-regulated!) activities.
8) Utilizing Tesla coil, plasma devises in jamming laser guided missile?

Media, Propaganda Task force: *One for EVERY one.*
Remember Allah says: "*And incite the believers*", and Prophet Muhammad peace be upon Him says: "*Fight the polytheists with your wealth, your hands **and your tongues***". And He said to Omar al Farooq" *I swear by in whose hand is my soul **his words** (Ibn Rawaha's) is even **more hurting** on the disbelievers than the strikes and blows of arrows!!*

This unit consists of mostly computer and internet savvy people. The Motto *"1 for EVERY one"* means that the main mission of this unit is to (Anonymously) send at least one message (text, voice, video etc) to every Kafir (non believer on the globe. (especially in America and NATO alliance countries) and send the same to every Muslim on this globe via the net, mobiles even bulk mail and flyer and street stands-as applicable- (why not) etc. Some ideas...
1) It is all about wining attention!
2) Utilize the same methods used by **massive** marketing and spam campaigns.
3) Social sites, blogs, etc twitter, face book, my space etc All and every, influential persons and groups...learn from marketing firms, same method...different message!
4) Customize the message to the *language* and *norms* of every country being sent to.
5) The message could be one line for the Kafir's for example: *Do you want be saved from the coming sep/11?* Link to already prepared material Bow Bregdal's video, Adams messages Siddeq Khan's message and all His brothers.

Part Four: Al-Qa'ida's Internal Issues and Concerns

6) Prepare statistics of American's filth...Rape, murder, prison population, cheating, adultery, alcoholism, drug addiction, sodomy, child sex, abortion, robbery, homosexuality, aids, sexually transmitted diseases, trillion budget deficit, etc, etc. let them remember how evil and disgusting they are and why the Mujahideen will do anything to kick them out from the Muslims' lands. Huge posters, wall writings, road video displays, pamphlets etc...Ok....innovate...**DO IT**!!
7) Prepare statistics of America's crime thru out history against humanity beginning with red Indians, Vietnam, Hiroshima, Nagasaki, and Palestine......., Abu Guraib,....,....!!.
8) Prepare statistics of America's servitude to lobbyists, banks; Show their governments' subordination to AIPAC and similar Zionists.
9) Mobilize already anti government groups. Tea party, coffee party etc.
10) Message to Muslims could be for example, *do you want to be the next sep/11 hero. Or do you have a HEART? That cares for our brothers and sisters in Gaza?* Connect **them to this file** and the Arabic version (ارهبوهم|*terrify them). ***Extremely important...*** guide, direct, refer, show, take, point, funnel and channel them to **Jihad**...

For you or against you:

Here, with these words I have showed you the *Highway* (Allah willing) to rescue your self and Ummah from disgrace. **You** can't say:"*I did not know what to do!*" you can't say: "*the roads were blocked to the Mujahideen, I couldn't meet them.*" You can't say :" *but I am scared or my children, my wife, husband, my job, my...*" **brother, sister** you don't need to come!!. If you are going to do what we have requested, your place (for now) is right there **were** you can **get the job done**. Allah will ask you: what have you done with the knowledge, health, youth, wealth, time and chances you had? This paper is going to be on the Day of Judgment either for you-*if you act upon it*- or against you-*if you just set it aside to gather dust*!!! **NOW** is the time to prepare an answer for those inevitable questions!

With these words **YOU** have received **your mission,** it's your honor, your Ummah, your dignity, your destiny, your religion, your family, your life, your chance....Don't wait!!**Make a DIFFRENCE**!!!You can...you will **succeed**... Allah is with us..

End Note: Kindly make it your first duty to get this paper in its digital or printed form to everyone you know, **including sheikhs and preachers** and those who you think **can help** and will pass the word on, They don't have to be Mujahideen, let them read it and make du'a that Allah opens their hearts, He alone is the guider to truth. Add to it the terror tools folder if you can.

Please translate to Urdu, Arabic, German, and all possibly beneficial languages.
The meeting is in Firdaws by the mercy and generosity of Allah.
O Allah I have proclaimed, O Allah be my witness.

And at the end we proclaim all praises and thanks are due to Allah the Lord of the worlds.

Your brother in Islam
Abu-Salih Al Somali
Khurasan

3. Spreadsheet

This is a detailed record of al Qa'ida's finances. Expenditures and deposits reveal names and organizations of all contributors to the organization.

Date: Unknown

From: Unknown

http://www.dni.gov/files/documents/ubl/english/Spreadsheet%202.pdf

Part Four: Al-Qa'ida's Internal Issues and Concerns

Full Translation

Monthly Accounting in Rupee

Gross Receipts		48,652,950
Gross Expenditures		48,652,950
current balance		

date	Description	Receipts	Expenditure	Balance
April	Opening Balance or forwarded from the previous month			500,000
	From the group of the late Harun received from Shaykh Mahmud	500,000		500,000
	From Shaykh 'Abdallah ((Sa'id))	234,000		734,000
May	The brethren share in the vehicle of the late Abu-Khabab	100,000		834,000
	From ((Nasir-al-Din)), friend to 'Azzam al-((Lubnani))	195,000		1,029,000
	From ((Abu-al-Harith)), from Bismallah, at Hajji Muhammad	325,000		1,354,000
	From ((Abu-al-Harith)), from Dr. Ma'az at Hajji Muhammad	37,000		1,391,000
	From ((Abu-al-Harith)), from Bismallah, at Hajji Muhammad	89,000		1,480,000
	From Ghana'im al-((Fatih)) (TN: also means spoils of the conqueror) with Hajji Muhammad	5,000,000		6,480,000
	From the part of Ghana'im al-Fatih, with 'Abd-al-Hafiz ((Sultan))	5,425,000		11,905,000
	From Shaykh Ilyas, three months budget received by Shaykh Abdallah Sa'id	2,500,000		14,405,000
	From a friend	195,000		14,600,000
May	From Kuwait, Abu-Ayyub, 2,000 Dinars exchanges to Rupees	533,600		15,133,600
	From 'Abid al-((Binjabi)), received by Hajji Muhammad	60,000		15,193,600
May	From 'Abd-al-Razzaq, after withdrawal of 50,000	200,000		15,393,600
	From Abu-Hafs of the Emirates, from a friend	396,000		15,789,600
	From Kuwait, Abu-Ayyub	120,500		15,910,100
	From the Indian brother in Madinah	292,400		16,202,500
	From Abu-'Umar al-Dabli, received by Hajji Muhammad	175,000		16,377,500
	From father, may God protect him	300,000		16,677,500
	From 'Abid al-((Binjabi)), received by Hajji Muhammad	295,000		16,972,500
	From Anwar, received by Hafiz sultan	1,000,000		17,972,500
June	From Abu-Hafs of the Emirates, from a friend	195,000		18,167,500
	From Abu-Hafs of the Emirates, from a friend	395,000		18,562,500
	From a friend	295,000		18,857,500
	From Hamzah al-((Tablighi)), sent by Abu-Ayyub the Kuwaiti	135,000		18,992,500
	From Hamzah al-((Tablighi)), sent by Abu-Ayyub the Kuwaiti	193,880		19,186,380
July 2009	From Abu-al-Harith, (TN: probably a title), for budget allocations	1,314,385		20,500,765
July 2009	From Kuwait, Abu-Ayyub	138,000		20,638,765
July 2009	From the Indian brother in Madinah, the messenger received 5,000 Rupees	335,000		20,973,765
July 2009	From a friend	195,000		21,168,765
July 2009	From Abu-al-Harith, 2,000 Euro, 25 Pounds, and 500 Dollars	276,575		21,445,340
July 2009	From Hajji Idris the Pakistani an; received by Hajji Muhammad for the bails	500,000		21,945,340
July 2009	From Jawid, a friend of Ahmad ((Khan))	200,000		22,145,340
August 2009	From Muhammad Qasim, Emirates	50,000		22,195,340
August 2009	From a friend of Abu-Hafs	395,000		22,590,340
10 August	From Abu-al-Harith, Jawid	1,140,000		23,730,340
10 August	From Abu-al-Harith, Farhanah, Niim, and Nillo	135,000		23,865,340
10 August	From Abu-al-Harith, Muhammad 'Adil	26,000		23,891,340
10 August	From Abu-al-Harith, Niim, Nillo, and 15 grams of gold with Abu-al-Harith	62,000		23,953,340
10 August	From Abu-al-Harith, 'Arif Qasmani	300,000		24,253,340
10 August	From Abu-al-Harith, Muhammad 'Adil	250,000		24,503,340

AL-QA'IDA'S MYSTIQUE EXPOSED

Date	Description	Amount	Running Total
10 August	From Abu-al-Harith, Fadilah's sister	47,000	24,550,340
10 August	From Abu-al-Harith, Bismallah	400,000	24,950,340
10 August	Umran the incarcerated	230,130	25,180,470
July 2009	From Abu-al-Harith, Bismallah, dispensed for associated bails	1,000,000	26,180,470
July 2009	From Abu-al-Harith, 'Umran the incarcerated, dispensed by them	300,000	26,480,470
July 2009	From Abu-al-Harith, from 'Ammar, dispensed by them	258,535	26,739,005
7 September 2009	From father, may God protect him	849,000	27,588,005
	From Abu-Jamilah the Kuwaiti for Shaykh 'Abdallah Sa'id, budgeted receipts	1,400,000	28,988,005
29 September 2009	From a friend of Sadiq Nur	295,000	29,283,005
29 September 2009	From a friend of Sadiq Nur	295,000	29,578,005
29 September 2009	From Abu-al-Harith, 'Abdallah 'Abdallah	1,356,500	30,934,505
29 September 2009	From Abu-al-Harith, Bismallah	1,000,000	31,934,505
29 September 2009	From Abu-al-Harith, Shaykh ((Diya'-al-Din))	350,000	32,284,505
29 September 2009	From Abu-al-Harith, 'Ala'-al-Din, and 1,000 Dirham	814,250	33,098,755
29 September 2009	From Abu-al-Harith, from a virtuous sister, 100,000 dispensed for rent as per her instructions	250,000	33,348,755
29 September 2009	From Abu-al-Harith, from Muhammad 'Uthman, and 300 Sterling Pounds	150,000	33,498,755
29 September 2009	From Abu-al-Harith, and sister Nahid	50,000	33,548,755
22 September 2009	From the group of the late Harun, received from Zuhayr al-((Maghribi)) 70 measure of gold, given to Hajji Muhammad		33,548,755
01 October	From the group of the late Harun, 2,500,000 received by Shaykh Mahmud (TN: amount discrepancy)	250,000	33,798,755
	Month of Shawal budget for Abu-ak-Wafa'	100,000	33,898,755
15 October	From Muhammad Qasim, 500,000 Rupees received by Shaykh Mahmud	500,000	34,398,755
20 October	From sister Mansurah, 500,000 Rupees received by al-Hafiz Sultan	6,261,500	40,660,255
23 October			40,660,255
23 October	From Abu-Ayyub the Kuwaiti, 500 Dinars for the treasury, and 5,000 Rupees for the carrier	141,000	40,801,255
25 October	From a friend of Sadiq Nur	445,000	41,246,255
25 October	From Abu-al-Harith, Kamal	100,000	41,346,255
25 October	From Abu-al-Harith, Ibrahim	77,315	41,423,570
25 October	From Abu-al-Harith, the value of the gold from a virtuous sister	129,000	41,552,570
25 October	From Abu-al-Harith, Abu-'Umar	400,000	41,952,570
25 October	From Abu-al-Harith, Nahid	98,500	42,051,070
25 October	From Abu-al-Harith, Dr. Dawud	146,000	42,197,070
25 October	From Abu-al-Harith, 'Ala'-al-din	442,660	42,639,730
25 October	From Abu-al-Harith, Bismallah	1,200,000	43,839,730
25 October	From Abu-al-Harith, Nasir and Mansur	946,180	41,606,435
	From the group of the late Harun, Shaykh Mahmud received 100 measures of gold kept in the house of 'Abd-al-Rahman Albi Umm (TN: unknown type of measurement)		40,660,255
30 October	From Abu-al-Harith, 'Ala'-al-din	81,500	40,882,755
November	From Abu-al-Harith, from Nahid	52,000	41,298,255
6 December	From Faruq Siraqah	500,000	41,846,255
13 December	From father may God protect him, 6,500 Euro approx 800,000	780,000	42,203,570
18 December	Unclaimed $7740 dollars under the name of 'Umar al-((Faruq)), dated 8 November 2007, added to Gen Fd	61,790	41,614,360
20 December 2009	From the family of the late Ibrahim al-Yemeni	391,750	42,344,320
22 December 2009	From sister Mansurah, received by al-Hafiz	2,000,000	44,051,070
		48,652,950	-
			48,652,950

229

Monthly Accounting in Euros

Gross Receipts.	€ 29,420
Gross Expenditures	€ 29,420
current balance	€ 0

date	Description	Receipts	Expenditures	Balance
April	Opening Balance or forwarded from the previous month			€ 0
	From Abu-Riyan, al-Doha care of Hajji Muhammad	€ 16,770	€ 16,770	-
	From a Levantine brother in Pakistan care of Hajji Muhammad	150	150	-
8 October	Received by al-Hafiz Sultan from Abu-Riyan of al-Doha	12,500	12,500	
		€ 29,420	€ 29,420	€ 0

Monthly Accounting in Dollars

Gross Receipts: $40,180
Gross Expenditures: $40,180
current balance: $0

date	Description	Receipts	Expenditure	Balance
April	Opening Balance or forwarded from the previous month			$0
	From 'Abad	$12,000	$12,000	
	From the mother of the late Shaykh Ibrahim, care of 'Abd-al-Hafiz Sultan	3,000	3,000	-
May	From Abu-'Umar al-Dubli, received by Hajji Muhammad	50	50	-
June	From Turkey, kept with Hajji Muhammad for bails	12,000	12,000	-
31 August	From Abu-al-Harith, 'Umran the incarcerated, exchanged in Rupees (TN: "sic")	3,130	3,130	-
25 October	From Abu-al-Harith, Bismallah	10,000	-	10,000
13 November	Six months support the family of the late Ya'qub the Kenyan	-	1,700	8,300
	To Mawia Sabir, $800 exchanged for 63,200 Rupees through Shaykh Abu-Yahya		800	7,500
25 November	$7,500 exchanged for 623,100 Rupees, added to general fund		7,500	-
		$40,180	$40,180	$0

4. Letter Regarding Abu al-Hasan

A concern is expressed over brothers who are aging and what should be done with them. In addition, the regulation of brothers and their movements is addressed.

Date: Unknown

From: Unknown

http://www.dni.gov/files/documents/ubl/english/Letter%20regarding%20Abu%20al-Hasan.pdf

Full Translation

God has spoken of it in his magnanimous book, and He knows what is in the hearts. Kindly, interpret the meaning in good intention as in the story of Yusuf (TN: Joseph) and his brothers, Prayers and Peace be upon them, that God reminded them of his suggestion in five places.

Regarding the subject of our late brother Abu al-Hasan, May God have Mercy on him, and our condolence is we are from God and to God return.

I was meeting with the brothers and asked how many leaders they have to realize the matter. It was apparent to me that they were all princes, and Jihad is their rights; one of them stated that he (TN: Abu al-Hasan) was touched (TN: touched spiritually), prompting a newly added, less than a year, brother to ask if Abu al-Hasan is bewitched. The Prince said if we refuse him, he will do it (TN: "sic"). I noticed from his talks that he was planning for something, and I decided not to talk with him to avoid any embarrassment because this matter was not allowed without the Shaykh's permission. When I learned the he had told you of the matter, I could not work with them and other things before it were decided by God. I was away from them; I only worked with them for one year, and would like to work away from them if you so permit me, and My God reward you with prosperity.

Another matter is the senior brothers, who are approaching the age of 50; discussed with me, they said "We are at the beginning of the seventh year, thank God, and the Shaykh does not ask about us, and we are still on the same line, this is nothing and you are our big brother", I told them that this was not the Shaykh's behavior, and we knew your kindness and mercy on your brothers; for the Prophets, prayers and peace of God be upon him, asked what did Ka'b do? And when Abu-Zir, May God be pleased with him, was late and people saw him coming from afar, the Prophet, prayers and peace of God be upon him, said "be Abu-Zir". Also, it was written in the Book of God about his Prophet Sulayman, prayer and peace be upon him, that during his round visiting the birds, he asked about the Hudhud (TN: Hoopoe), and when he said…

PART FOUR: AL-QA'IDA'S INTERNAL ISSUES AND CONCERNS

5. Letter to Shaykh Abu-al-Layth, Abu-Yahya, Shaykh 'Abdullah Sa'id

This is an inquiry about joining al Qa'ida. According to the author, this is an exciting step.

Date: Unknown

From: Unknown

http://www.dni.gov/files/documents/ubl/english2/Letter%20to%20Shaykh%20Abu-al-Layth%20Shaykh%20Abu-Yahya%20Shaykh%20Abdallah%20Said.pdf

Page 1

In the Name of God, the Merciful, the Compassionate

Praise be to God, Lord of the Universe, and prayers and peace on our Prophet Muhammad and all his descendants and disciples.

Peace be with you, and God's mercy and blessings.

To my dear brothers Shaykh ((Abu-al-Layth)), Shaykh ((Abu-Yahya)), Shaykh 'Abdallah ((Sa'id)) and Shaykh (TN: blank)

I pray you are all well and good.

Dear brothers, your messages about joining the al-Qa'ida Organization is fabulous (TN: news), and I pray to God that He helps us all be successful in aiding our religion. Your joining us will further encourage the mujahidin, and it signifies your sense of responsibility and fulfilling your duty. May God be accepting of us all.

I have a proposal for you.

Regarding some of the things that you mentioned on the unique characteristics of Libya, I want to say that men of reason and understanding should carefully consider the unique characteristics of every country.

My proposal is that you join (TN: al-Qa'ida) the same way that the Jihad Organization did under Shaykh Ayman al-((Zawahiri)), and the Monotheism and Jihad Organization under its emir Abu- Mus'ab al-Zarqawi, God rest his soul, and the Salafi Group for the Call and Combat under our dear brother, ((Abu-Mus'ab)) 'Abd- al-Wadud.

I expect you know about the (TN: high) standing you have in our hearts, which is greater than what you enjoy in any one country, and you are surely aware that in this sea of worldwide fighting against Muslims, they now feel they belong to the greater Islamic community in a universal sense, by the grace of God, so this trend must be encouraged.

This is how it seems to me. I am waiting for your (TN: reply) message.

Peace be with you, and God's mercy and blessings.

PART FIVE: SELECTED COMMUNICATION WITH EXTERNAL BODIES

> ### 1. Letter to Ansar Al-Sunnah Group
>
> Messages are given to brothers of al Qa'ida, martyrs, and Muslims everywhere. Dedication to Allah is reiterated.
>
> Date: 9 June 2006
>
> From: Abu-'Abdullah al-Hasan Bin-Mahmud, Prince of Ansar al-Sunnah Group
>
> http://www.dni.gov/files/documents/ubl/english/Letter%20Ansar%20Al-Sunnah%20Group.pdf

Page: 1

Ansar Al-Sunnah Group

(From Abu-'Abdullah Al-Hasan Bin-Mahmud, the emir of al-Ansar al-Sunnah to the noble brothers in al-Qai'da organization)

In the name of Allah, the most compassionate, the most merciful Praise be to Allah, the mighty and best prayers and peace be upon the Prophet of mercy and Prophet of battle and upon his family, his companions all and those who follow them until the day of resurrection.

To the noble brothers in al-Qa'ida organization,

Praise be to His name said, "So lose not heart, nor fall into despair, for ye must gain mastery, if you are true in faith." Al-'Imran: 139.

With hearts accepting the wishes of Allah, if He promised His mujahidin worshipers one of two good things and with tears that combined happiness and sadness at the same time,

We bid farewell to our brothers in Allah, headed by our beloved brother Shaykh Abu-Mus'ab al-Zarqawi. We ask Allah to accept him and those with him among His martyrs and provide them what He promised them and deliver them to paradise.

There is no need for offering condolences for the death of martyrs.

Page 2

The blessed journey of jihad requires blood and bodies to continue, and there is no purer blood than the blood of those who lead the march, and become the fuel to motivate the people and strengthen the determination.

And to our brothers the mujahidin, who intend to continue despite the rush of the enemies from every place and every direction.

And to the Muslims everywhere,
The battle continues, and it is fiercer. God willing, the next phase is to defeat the new plans like the old ones, which aimed to cut off the vein of the nation and its arm that beats the enemy to achieve justice for the Muslims.

Let the worshiper of the Cross and their supporters hear our thunderous anger that will deafen their ears and paralyze them. Allah's anger is with weapon and bombs, not with words and pens. Allah is the greatest. Praise to Allah, and glory to His messenger and to the believers

Abu-'Abdullah al-Hasan Bin-Mahmud
The Prince of Ansar al-Sunnah Group
09 June 2006

2. Letter to Mujahidin in Somalia dtd 28 December 2006

This is a letter to the Mujahidin in Somalia. There are many quotations from the Qur'an and there is a call to fight and fulfill pledges previously made. According to the author, this cell has a lot to learn, and it should take notes from more experienced cells. Notes on Ethiopia and youth are given as well.

From: Atiyatallah

http://www.dni.gov/files/documents/ubl/english2/Letter%20to%20Mujahidin%20in%20Somalia%20dtd%2028%20December%202006.pdf

(Fully Translated)

In the name of Allah, the most merciful, the most graceful

The Magnification of Hope in the Somali Jihad

(They have lied, the fight has come)

Praise be to God, Who denied his followers humiliation, magnified their small numbers, and supported the oppressed, though it comes later, the Almighty who says, "That (is so). And if one has retaliated to no greater extent than the injury he received and is again set upon inordinately, God will help him: for God is One that blots out (sins) and forgives (again and again)" [Partial Qur'anic verse –Surat Al-Hajj 22:60], peace and prayers be upon him, our prophet Muhammad, the chosen, the prophet of the epic and the mercy, the Imam of the Mujahidin, the commander of the unique, and on all his family, companions, and those who followed his path.

Henceforth:

To you, the Mujahidin brothers in Somalia, steadfast and patient, God is with those who patiently preserve the pious, for God is with those who restrain themselves, and those who do well. He is your Protector, and the nonbelievers have no one to protect them.

God Almighty says, "God is the Protector of those who have faith: from the depths of darkness He will lead them forth into light. Of those who reject faith, the patrons are the evil ones: from light they will lead them forth into the depths of darkness. They will be companions of the fire, to dwell therein (forever)." [Partial Qur'anic verse Q–Surat Al-Baqara 2:257]

There is no harm that you are distorted or siding with a certain side or group, as God willing, will make you the ones on the attack and not the ones who run away. You are the people of resolve. We heard your wisdom and that you are geared up for a long war. We ask God to strengthen you, to be present with you, and to provide you His reinforcements, God Almighty says, "It is He Who sent down tranquility into the hearts of the Believers, that they may add faith to their faith, for to God belongs the forces of the heavens and the earth, and God is full of knowledge and wisdom "[Partial Qur'anic verse – Surat Al-Fatah 48:4].

Therefore, depend on God and do not be discouraged. I swear to God that the nonbeliever enemy is more despicable than what you think and so easy for God to handle...!

This enemy is fighting the followers of God, God Almighty says, "Those who resist God and His Apostle will be humbled to dust, as were those before them: for We have already sent down clear signs. And the unbelievers (will have) a humiliating Penalty..." [Partial Qur'anic verse – Surat Al-Mujadalah 58:5]

And, "Those who resist God and His Apostle will be among those most humiliated." [Partial Qur'anic verse – Surat Al-Mujadalah 58:20]

Part Five: Selected Communication with External Bodies

And, "Who attacked someone I protect, I will allow him to be counterattacked."

O brothers, now is the time to go fighting, the entitlement has become manifest, so fear God and be patient. God will fulfill His pledge if you complete yours:

"So lose not heart, nor fall into despair, For ye must gain mastery if ye are true in faith." [Partial Qur'anic verse – Surat Al-'Umran 3:139]

And, "And slacken not in following up the enemy: If ye are suffering hardships, they are suffering similar hardships. But ye have Hope from God, while they have none. And God is full of knowledge and wisdom." [Partial Qur'anic verse – Surat Al-Nusa' 4:104]

And, "O you who believe! When you meet a force, stay firm, and call God in remembrance much (and often), that you may prosper. Obey God and His Apostle, and fall into no disputes, lest ye lose heart and your power depart. Be patient and perseverant, for God is with those who patiently persevere." [Partial Qur'anic verse –Surat AlQ-Q Anfal 8:45,46]

O Mujahidin! Depend on God and hold on to the land, as Usama advised you, dig the trenches, prepare safe bases, get the explosives ready, plant mines in the entrances, the roads, and in the buildings. focus on setting up traps, hit hard on the enemy as they are tired and terrified. They entered your lands like doubtful bandits. Establish strong detachments from your youth, be united like one person, be cautious of disputes and conflicts. Cut the roads on the enemy, disrupt his logistics and supplies; they are pretty vulnerable. Be mindful that victory means taking booty. Do not forget the sayings of your Prophet, "God made my livelihood under the tip of my arrow."

The mujahidin in Somalia should ease the work of the immigrated mujahidin and direct them to fight the enemy of Allah, as the mujahidin have warm hearts and their eyes are directed to paradise.

The mujahidin in Somalia must learn from their brothers, the mujahidin in Iraq and Afghanistan.

The mujahidin in Somalia should be careful of the air bombardments and should benefit from the art of gathering and dispersion experience, as well as movement, night and day transportation, camouflage, and other techniques related to war tricks.

Good luck comes only from God.

To you, the mujahidin in Somalia, you should not give the enemy the chance to hit from a distance. Be careful of taking things lightly and beware being careless. You should be firm and considerate in pursuing causes. To you, the mujahidin in Somalia, you should never care about the enemy's number or the enemy's equipment, or who's behind the enemy, whether it's the United States or the infidel West. The United States is definitely with them, and the planes that are shelling Mogadishu are no doubt American, but Allah is with us!

Our Prophet (PBUH) said "The believer who is strong is good and more liked by God than the weak one, seek goodness either way, maintain what is good for you, depend only on God, and never give up."

God is on our side!

God Is Great, God is Higher and Superior and Grandest.

God Almighty says, "How oft, by God's will, has a small force vanquished a big one? God is with those who steadfastly persevere." [Partial Qur'anic verse – Surat AlQ.-QBaqarah 2:249]

And, "God will certainly aid those who aid His (cause), for verily God is full of Strength, Exalted in Might, (able to enforce His Will). [Partial Qur'anic verse – Surat AlQ.-Hajj 22:40]

And, "O ye who believe! Be ye helpers of God. As said Jesus, the son of Mary, to the Disciples, "Who will be my helpers to (the work of) God." Said the disciples, "We are God's helpers!" Then a portion of the Children of Israel believed, and a portion disbelieved: But to those who believed, We gave power against their enemies, and they became the ones that prevailed. [Partial Qur'anic verse – Surat AlQ̣-Q̣Anfal 6:14]

And, "O ye who believe! If ye will aid (the cause of) God, He will aid you, and plant your feet firmly. [Partial Qur'anic verse – Surat AlQ̣-Q̣Anfal 47:7]

Therefore, stay with God, stay with your brothers and your nation, and beware of the people of hypocrisy among us. Victory is near, hopes and prayers to the mujahidin of Somalia. The attack of Ethiopia against the Islamic Somalia and the fact of having the crusaders and their allies advance to the Islamic countries will be cause for a new jihad assertion that you are not afraid to face. To the contrary the end of the enemy will come, so do not abandon jihad.

<u>O the Umma (TN: nation) of Islam, and to you the youth of Islam:</u> rejoice, be hopeful, seek salvation from God, after clouds the sun shines. Go willing, victory is near [So, verily, with every difficulty, there is relief], and be mindful, "Victory comes with patience, and relief comes after hardship."

The blaspheming, oppressor enemy is blind by conceit; his hatred has overtaken him and has caused him not to see the massive consequences of his actions!

Ethiopia's invasion of the Islamic Somali lands and the entry of the crusaders and their collaborators to the Islamic lands are a grave injustice and an act of immorality. God will fight them. All this creates a new wide arena for Jihad. I swear we are the nation of Jihad and martyrdom We fear no wars or fighting, we could die if we stop our Jihad...! God Almighty says,

"You who believe! Give your response to God and His Apostle, when He calls you to that which will give you life. Know that God cometh in between a man and his heart, and that it is He to whom ye shall (all) be gathered. [Partial Qur'anic verse – Surat AlQ̣-Q̣Anfal 8:24]

Now the real war will begin in Somalia, the nexus of Islam in the Horn of Africa. Now the people of Islam have the chance to have the enemies of God taste the scourge of war. The people of Islam will teach and train their generations in the school of Jihad; they are the ones to establish the souls and then the nation and the state, gradually but surely.

Soon enough you will hear and see.

The war between us and our enemy is a contest; it has its ups and downs.

Does the believer fear anything when he has been secured by God one of the two best: victory or martyrdom!?

God Almighty says, "Say: 'Nothing will happen to us except what God has decreed for us: He is our protector': and on God let the Believers put their Trust. Say: 'Can you expect for us (any fate) other than one of two glorious things - (martyrdom or victory)?' But we can expect for you either that God will send His punishment from Himself or by our hands. So wait (expectant); we too will wait with you." [Partial Qur'anic verse

– Surat AlQ.-Q.Tawbah 9:52]

The nation of Islam is proceeding ahead and slowly approaching, all with the blessing of God, and day by day, it is getting closer to getting better and over, and closer to a showing triumph,"And the end is (best) for the pious," "And the end is (best) for the righteous."

The prayers should multiply especially the insistence in praying is important, as praying is considered one of the great weapons knowing that the enemy doesn't possess any!

Anyone among you who is able to join the brothers, do not delay, particularly those in the surrounding countries, they are obligated surely, and God is the best aid.

O God, Here comes Ethiopia, the crusader, is backed by the United States, the leader of the crusaders, who is challenging and fighting the religion of the Mujahidin,

O God, give support to Your slaves the monotheists, the ones who went to Jihad for your sake and to raise the word of Islam in Somalia.

O God, get hold of the enemies by the throat, and we ask for Your help against their wickedness.

O God, with Your aid we can attack them, and with You we are able to move around, and with Your help we can fight.

O God, the protector of the believers, the protector of the pious.

Amen.

Amen.

And praise be to God Almighty,

'Atiyatallah

Wednesday, 7 Dhu l-Hijja 1427 (TN: December 28, 2006)

> **3. Letter to Special Committee of al-Jihad's Qa'ida of the Mujahidin Affairs in Iraq and to the Ansar al-Sunnah Army**
> It is said that the head of the organization is keen on unity, and the general love and loyalty for the brotherhood is very important.
>
> Date: 29 January 2006
>
> From: Special Committee of al-Jihads Qa'ida of the Mujahidin
>
> http://www.dni.gov/files/documents/ubl/english/Letter%20to%20Special%20Committee%20of%20al-Jihads%20Qaida%20of%20the%20Mujahidin%20Affairs%20in%20Iraq%20and%20to%20the%20Ansar%20al-Sunnah%20Army.pdf

Page 1 of 1

In the name of Allah, the Merciful, the Compassionate.

Praise is to Allah and prayers and peace be upon the Messenger of Allah and his family and followers.

From the brothers in the Special Committee of al-Jihad's Qa'ida of the Mujahidin Affairs in Iraq, to the honorable brothers in Ansar al-Sunnah Army, peace and God's mercy and blessings be upon you.

Praise is to Allah whom with his blessing good things are accomplished, and we praise Him for leading us to a single religion, single book, and one Prophet, and united us on one path and one program, the path and program of Jihad in His cause, to make His word the highest and the infidels' word the lowest. We thank Him for his victories over His enemies. We were very happy for the communications between us, and it is your efforts to be closer to us by sending an honorable brother before Abu Muhammad, and then sending two other honorable brothers these days and they are Brother

PART FIVE: SELECTED COMMUNICATION WITH EXTERNAL BODIES

Abu al-Darda'a and Brother Abu Muhammad. We were happy and honored to meet and listen to them and for giving us a detailed and précised picture about the situation around you. We recorded everything they said, and we sent a copy of it to the Doctor and we will send a copy to al-Shaykh, God willing. We are writing this letter to you, to present to you a number of realities and advice special for you and for us, and for the Mujahidin in general and they are:

1. You must know that our honorable Shaykh is very keen on the unity of the line with you and considers it of the first priority in this period, and he believes all the obstacles standing in its way must be removed.

2. You must know that our honorable Shaykh and the Mujahidin brothers here have great respect and appreciation for the Army of Ansar al-Sunnah, and they consider them and us one item, no difference between us. They also thank you for what you offered in the cause of Allah and in the path of uniting the lines and the views, and they pray to Allah to reward them the highest rewards for what they endured in this cause, and they ask from them more efforts, giving, and sacrifice in the victory of this great religion, and to strengthen it.

3. We want to relay to you that we have taken a blessed step toward improving the conditions and toward reaching for the better, and that was done by sending an honorable brother and a virtuous shaykh, you know him very well. We pray to Allah to keep him and give him success, and for him to be in our favorable judgment, and God willing he will be followed by other brothers, and Allah whom we ask for help and he who helps us.

4. We hoped that the brothers' stay with us would be longer to allow us to reach other steps in the path to unity and reforms, and you may know that this is a great matter that must be done in wisdom and deliberateness, and you must also know the circumstances of the Shaykhs and the difficulty of communications with them due to the security situations they are in, and you also know that the brothers

must hear from the green side, even if we have complete confidence in what the brothers relay to us, but for fairness and justice we must listen to the other side, and we asked for their presence, and few days ago we were told that they were on their way here. Anyway, the presence of the two brothers is a step forward, praise is to Allah.

5. We advise ourselves and you and all the Mujahidin to adhere to God's commandments and not to separate, as God ordered: "And hold fast, all together, by the rope which God stretched out for you, and be not divided among yourselves" and we advise them of making the Muslim and Jihadist brothers above all consideration and loyalty, and to let them know that regardless of the differences of opinions and diligence at the work, it doesn't affect the brotherhood, love, and loyalty.

6. We advise ourselves and all the Mujahidin to follow all the rules and rituals of Islam and not to leave any of them, according to God's order : "O ye who believe, enter into Islam wholeheartedly, and follow not the footsteps of the evil one; for he is to an avowed enemy," and they cannot do that without following God's rules and the Sunnah of his Prophet, the smiling, the fighter, the merciful; who was of the best manners, who called for the worship of Allah, and he is the shining light in which God said, "Ye have indeed in the apostle of God a beautiful pattern" and he also said, "Say that if ye do love God, follow me, God will love you and forgive your sins, for God is oft forgiving, most merciful."

7. And we center the advice following the Prophet's noble behavior and his praiseworthy character, as God described him and his companions (Muhammad, the apostle of God, and those who are with him, you see the kneeling and prostrating, wishing for God's blessing and satisfaction, they are merciful among each other but they tough on the infidels) and here we concentrate on the mercy for the Muslims and the humility and forgiveness, and to bow to Allah, recognizing His grace, especially in the time of victory over the enemies, as was the Prophet's situation when he entered Mecca victorious and a conqueror.

8. We advise ourselves and you to be patient, God fearing, and steadfast on this road and the complete confidence in God's victory that is coming, where he said, "It was a must on us to give victory to the believers."

We ask Allah to join us in what is right that satisfies Him, and our last prayer is praise is to Allah, God of all creations.

From your brothers in the Special Committee of al-Jihad Qa'ida of the Mujahidin' Affairs in Iraq

Sunday 29 Dhil Hijah 1426
29 January 2006

4. Letter to Hakimullah Mahsud, Leader of Taliban Movement

The Jihadist military is discussed, as are religious issues.

Date: 4 December 2010

From: Shaykh Mahmud and Shaykh Abu Yahya

http://www.dni.gov/files/documents/ubl/english2/Letter%20to%20Hakimullah%20Mahsud%20Leader%20of%20the%20Taliban%20Movement.pdf

In the name of Allah, the Merciful, the Compassionate.

To the respected brother/ Hakimullah Mahsud, Leader of the Taliban Movement, God keep him.

(TN: After the prayers to God to protect him and praising him, he writes)

We looked at the movement list you sent to us, asking us for our opinion. We have previously written to brother Qari ((Husayn) may God have mercy on him, and we informed him that we will send our comments to you soon. But he was killed a short time after that, and we had asked him to inform of the matter, but I do not know if he did, or not.

Anyway, as for the complete general evaluation of the list, we do not see that it is suitable to control the movement in many of its general or detailed issues. And based on experience, its results will be negative and different than what we need of control and agreement. It will become a reason for the flare up of many problems that you do not need now. This is a general evaluation of the list, and we have written some partially detailed comments on some of its issues, despite not comprehending all that it contained on issues, for they are many.

PART FIVE: SELECTED COMMUNICATION WITH EXTERNAL BODIES

God willing we will send you some of them. But what we see, in summary:

1- This list in general, its points are not suitable for becoming a reason for controlling the movements, or in uniting the word of the people to it, especially when it comes to the scientific application which is primarily intended.

2- There are some religious issues that must be corrected, and we have written some quick comments about that, and we did not continue for fear of taking long; the time is short, and there is too much work.

3- We will strive to send the rest of the comments and details in the religious issues we referred to previously, and we ask God to help us.

4- There are important issues which the document did not allude to, such as the military committee and its branches, although the organization is Jihadist Military, and also what is related to the Martyrdom operations and their rules, and the targets' rules used for targeting, and also the training committee and preparations, military, and educational.

5- All our comments about the list are attached to this paper, and we have indicated them by underlining.

Written by: Shaykh/ Mahmud and Shaykh/ Abu Yahya

27 Dhu-al Hijah 1431 (TN: 4 December 2010)

5. A Letter to the Sunnah People in Syria

The author addresses the Sunnah people in Syria and the Levantine region, calling attention to the oppression and injustice they face under the Alawite regime. A call is made for the Sunnah people to maintain their faith and seek victory over their oppressors.

Date: 24 November 2011

From: Abdullah Al-'Azzam Battalion

http://www.dni.gov/files/documents/ubl/english/A%20Letter%20to%20the%20Sunnah%20people%20in%20Syria.pdf

Page 1

(TN: Cover page)

From the series (and you will uncover the road of the criminals)

Report 2

A letter from the Mujahid brother Salih Abdullah Al-Qar'awi

May God bless him

To the Sunnah people in Syria

Abdul 'Azzam Brigades

Page 2

Part Five: Selected Communication with External Bodies

(TN: Repeats information on cover page)

Wednesday, 24 November 2010

Production: Al-Fajr Center for information

Page 3

In the name of the Lord the merciful the compassionate

Thanks to the Lord who makes the believers and workers victorious. Who made the Sunnah his worshippers {if you make the Lord victorious then he will make you victorious and will implant your feet}. And prayers and peace be upon whom the Lord gave victory with fear, and who made his living under the shadow of his spear, the Lord prayed over him and his people, and his Jihadist friends.

From the star of the news to his people, the Sunnah people in Syria, peace be upon you and his mercy and his blessings .....

Today, I am talking to you as that of a counselor to his people, the one who loves his family. I am talking to you like a son to his father, like a brother to his brothers. There is nothing prompting me to do this except for loyalty to the faith and inherent love, which make me want to leave the world to protect your religion and world. I carry the worries so you can free yourselves from distress. My desire is not a worldly thing that I want for myself. I do not desire a world for myself but I seek that you get more pride and elevation, and for you to protect your religion and world. The world will never look nice in my eyes even if I had the whole world, if I am seeing my people and family under the onslaught of their enemy. And the enemy keeps them from their religion and steals from them their world. How can someone sleep under these conditions, even if they are the king of the world? While his family is weakened, living the life of humiliation and degradation, their children are imprisoned and their elders are mistreated and they are expelled from their land and their entire rights are taken away from them. Our people of Syria, if we angered God and did not help you to achieve victory, then salvation would leave oneself, so how can he accept that for his family? So our support for your victory is a religious duty, and it is a mountainous defense, so listen to me and be hopeful with my speech. If you find my words good advice, then take it. If it is not, then ignore it. Your judgment should not be impacted by the devil that pretends to be your brothers; you would not see that their actions are for their own personal gains even if it is at your expense. And how many times were we fooled by a slick person who looked after our interests as long as it coincided with his interest; and if he finds his interest with the enemy, then he will go against us and it will not affect you, one thousand prayers. Rights and self respect will not happen to people without serious work and patience. Being tired requires long rest and working with the faith that is needed for the victory for God.

Our people, the people of the blessed Syria, the Lord said about the land you live in: "Praise the one who took his slave at night from the haram mosques to the Aqsa mosque, that we

Page 4

blessed." The interpretation of "That blessed us around him" is "He who made blessings around him, for the inhabitants and the residents." Some scholars say "around him" means "the land of Syria."

Al-Bukhari said about Ibn 'Omar, may the Lord bless them, that the prophet – Lord's prayers upon him – said, "Oh Lord bless for us our Syria."

And in the Sahihain about Sa'd Bin Abi Waqqas – bless him – the prophet – prayers of the Lord upon him – said, "The people of the west still with the truth until the Day of Judgment."

Mu'az Bin Jabal - bless him – said, "And they are in Syria."

Imam Ahmad – bless his soul - and other scholars said, "The people of the west are the Syrians."

And in the Lord's book and his prophet's Sunnah it mentions Syria favorably and its blessing and the need to hold onto the land and the migration to it and the truth and the work for the sake of God is part of its people, so bless you people of Syria. Since 'Umar – bless him - opened the holy house (TN: Jerusalem) they were the pride of Muslims, near the Christians. Their problems with the Christians and the Shi'ites and other fringes are known, as was stated by scholars. And these good things are for Syria and its people. And this is the history that is witness to their victory for Islam and the Jihad for God. To give the good news to the believers in the victory for God, and his blessing for their efforts, and his enabling them, with the condition that they make the Lord victorious, and they work for his religion, and they entrust in him expending their efforts to providing victory and the way for doors of enablement.

To make injustice taboo and the duty to return rights:

Oh blessed people of Syria, the grandest of religious duties is to lift injustice and the return of the rights and to take it by force from the despotic regimes. That way life will be straightened out, justice will prevail, and temptation will leave. As the Lord said:

"And for you not to fight for the sake of the Lord and those weak from men, women, and children that say to our Lord, get us out of this village with the unjust residents and give us a loyal one and give us victory. Those who believe fight for the sake of the Lord and those who do not believe fight for the sake of Satan. Fight those who are loyal to Satan because who supports Satan is weak." And the Lord said, "Fight them so there no temptation and the religion will be for the Lord and when it is over, then your enemies will be the unjust ones." And temptation keeps people from their religion and the non-believers will grow in numbers and every unjust one is a temptation.

Page 5

And religion will be for God and if injustice rises – from the Shi'ites and others – over Muslims and the land of the Muslims, and if it is not over the servants of God – believers and non believers – a ruler who is not for justice and right, that has no injustice neither for the believer and the non-believer alike, but all live with their rights that are guaranteed by God's Shari'a; to protect themselves, money, and honor and the victory for the oppressed ones. Some scholars said, "If they attack then they attack the whole nation and Jihad will be required and Muslims' money and souls will be spent for the sake of that, as God's Shari'a forbids injustice completely and this does not distinguish between Muslims and non-Muslims or Arab and a non-Arab." In Sahih Muslim, Abi Zirr – bless him – said the prophet – Lord's prayers upon him – with what he was saying about his God, said "Oh my subjects, I made injustice taboo for myself and made it taboo for you, so don't be unjust…" And the idea of the Lord saying "among you" returns to his saying "my subjects;" it is general and includes all of the Lord's subjects, so it does not matter whether the unjust person is Muslim or non-Muslim. And the one whose injustice is directed against them, it does not matter whether they are Muslim or non- Muslim, so we need to support those who are receiving injustice, regardless of whether they are Muslims or non-Muslims and regardless of their sex. And the unjust one needs to be pushed back no matter where, and no matter whether the unjust ones are a regime, organization, a fraternity, or individuals.

When we look at the situation of our people in Lebanon and Syria and the whole Levantine region, we find out that they are the most mistreated people of our times. Injustice is practiced against them in every way and at its worst. It is injustice in religion and in life at the hands of the various sects that intimidate God's servants in the land of Syria. They steal their wealth, they corrupt it from the 'Alawites and the Shi'ites. So I make my call to you my people, the Sunnis in Syria, with these questions:

- Why are calls to end injustice not answered unless these calls are coming from the leaders of the Shi'ite sect?

- Why do they ignore what happens to you Sunni people when you face crime and injustice?

- Why do they do not open investigations to find out the fate of hundreds who were killed from torture in prisons? And those who were killed in cold blood on the streets and were left to bleed at the hands of these sects, the unjust Shi'ites and their arms in the country?

- And why are the ones who killed the Sunni people on May 7th not held accountable, while their leader is proud of that day and counts it as a great day for the people's resistance?

- Why are the rights not upheld for the mothers whose children were killed by elements of the army, which is covered and supported by the Shi'ites?

- Why is the Alawite regime not being held for their crimes in Lebanon and Syria?

Page 6

Like the kidnapping of hundreds from the city of Tripoli (TN: Syrian Tripoli) in October 1986 and then his neutralization of the kidnapped people; their corpses were found by the scores, through Tripoli and its surroundings.

And what did the criminals do in what was known as the slaughter of Hama?

And what did they do in Tadmur prison?

And what happened in Saidnaya prison?

And this Alawite regime crushed the Kurds in north Syria. Where are the courts in all of this? So are these crimes so many that it is forgiven? And was their evidence lost and so it is forgotten? Or is it so many that it gets repeated always? Is it God's permanent Sunnah… so victory will not be possible without understanding God's Sunnah and to obey him… God did not tell us, "If you make them victorious they will help you be victorious." He said, "If they covet pride God has pride for all." Those who ask for victory from the enemies of God will receive increase in injustice and humiliation. There is no victory except from God and there is no pride without obeying his commands. If you make the Lord victorious he will help you be victorious. And to get rid of injustice and unfairness and getting rid of the unjust ruler and to bring justice to people you can only do it by force. The Almighty said, "Fight them until there is no distress and faith will be for the Lord" and if there was a method other than force we would have found it in the Quran. Because in light and calm there is complete faith. The Almighty said, "This is my straight line so follow it, do not follow the road that will divide you from this cause." And he is asking you for that so you may be good. Then he said, "This is a book that we sent so follow it, then you'll get mercy. If you say he sent the book to two sects before us and we were unaware of their studies, or you say if he sent us a book we will be wiser than them, so it came to you from God with guidance and mercy."

And so, we from the Abdullah 'Azzam battalion, ask to form legal councils, using scholars from honest judges, from any country who should rule according to God's law and return the rights to their legitimate owners and to raise injustice from the weak and to protect Muslims' blood, and their broken honor, and their stolen money, and their confiscated lands. They will rule about these things with God's guidance, and they should lead Muslims to the right path via the Godly rulings, until it becomes a well-known right, devoid of the goings-on.

So how long are we going to put up with what's happening to the Sunni people while their honor is violated and there is no voice from the Islamic people, who move a thing to help support their brothers and family?

Where is the work that I taught to Muslims with the duty to support the oppressed and to prevent his humiliation?

Page 7

Where is the work of the diplomats who allow the ruler to be above them and the people, and above the legal rulers? Don't the diplomats know or account for those who violate the Sunnah and who commit injustice, killings, and criminal activities? Where is the accounting? Why the cover-up?

And why do the people of Syria have to put up with such atrocities for many long decades, when no one seems to come to their support, and religious people do not defend them and there are no laws for their justice?

Why are the intelligence people not held accountable for imprisoning the innocent? And they torture them and kill them in their prisons. Why are they not held accountable and who supports them and backs them up?

And why are the unfair judges escaping from supporting the prisoners with their laws? When the prisoners complain about torture, the judges say that this out of the jurisdiction of this court. So what kind of justice do we expect when the judges do not deal with injustice? It is as if they are saying, "We studied and appointed him to the court, we spent the county's money to pay their salaries and to establish their courts." But there is evidence that our courts are not used to looking at evidence and ruling in a just way, and it is not for the security of the country and its citizens; they are appointed to mistreat the Sunnis and to issue rulings, such as the execution of our young people, oh Sunni people! And to waste the years of the lives of your children in the prisons, oh Sunni people!

Their rulings and behaviors say one thing and they speak of other things, but some of what they say is proof of their corruption and is evidence.

Don't the Sunni people know that those who cover the crimes of the military courts are the Shi'ites, and the ones who protect the intelligence officers are really Shi'ites, who continue to torture your children to this day?

Early operational steps:

Our people, the people of Sunnah, you heard what was issued by the so-called opposition lately with regard to their refusal to deal with the security forces, and they asked to oppose them and not to respond to them, as they are only a Mafia organization as they stated. And if what they said is true - about them being Mafia - it was their right to say that it was to their benefit. But, it was the opposition itself who agreed to these institutions – according to the famous Doha agreement – and they entered with them into a national unity government with their total agreement. And with what they desired from conditions, after that they turned on the agreement and they disagreed and as for the institutions, they have not changed. So what changed?

Page 8

So we ask our people, the people of Sunnah, a call that is not issued for political reasons or personal ones, rather it is for bringing justice and truth. It is not for a claim that we make and it can be true or a lie, it is for what you already know and live in and complain about and suffer from.

So we ask you to boycott these unjust institutions that do not respect your rights, as they took them away. Especially the military intelligence and their members, so you must refuse to deal with them and announce not to respond to their requests and you need to apply pressure in every way to stop their unjust arrest campaigns and the incidents of killings and torture. You need to work together in numbers for the sake of God with all your groups, a true concentration, real and operational, that its effect will be seen on the earth. You need to push the scholars and students and preachers and speakers and the Sunni groups that do not have suspicious associations; people who have no goal other than to help the cause of the Sunnah and to fight for their rights. You do not need any proof that these institutions do not work for the good of the nation or its security or to impose justice for the sake of the citizens. Why does the military intelligence not conduct any attacks except against Sunni areas? Why does the security apparatus only come to your areas and neighborhoods? Why do we never see the army or others covering Shi'ite areas like the suburbs, for example?

So we request a call for justice right now. We ask you to refrain from dealing with the military intelligence and their associates that are in your areas in large numbers and you need to start to refuse this obvious injustice that is falling on you. And that is – without a doubt – directed by Hizballah, which extends its arm to sensitive centers with the army. We also ask you to document the injustice that happens to you and the harm that follows, using sound and video whenever possible. Because good, accurate information is the strongest modern weapon. And what we say can be proved in front of the eyes of the sleeping nation. We have important facts and painful events that we are going to expose to you at the proper time, with God's permission.

To measure using two different measuring tools:

There is a strange separation among you that I hope you will see and understand. Are not the raids that you suffer from - Sunni people – and the killing and torture incidents, happening without any investigations? Aren't you not allowed to file even a virtual complaint? It is virtual because when you complain you're asking your oppressor to judge themselves and there is litigation and it is the legal action and the rule! And with that they don't suffer from the complaint - excessive injustice and humiliation from them - so how do you deal with that?

Page 9

If an explosion takes place in a Shi'ite area, they cover it completely, like in the suburbs for example. Or in houses that belong to the party in Southern Lebanon. If this takes place then what happens – by their own admission – is that the party (TN: Hizballah) establishes a security zone and keeps the people away from the site of the incident. Then the army comes in late, after getting permission from the party, to establish a zone behind the one established by the party. And that is what is witnessed by the people with their own eyes. Then after the party is done with cleaning up the place and after they make all the changes that they want, they ask for help from others, and then the Saiyid (TN: Possibly Hasan Nasrallah, the leader of Hizballah) deals with whomever is under his hands, and no one dares to challenge him, even with words.

And this joke, in truth, is an entertaining play; it proves that the law that they called the legal chief is only applied against the Sunnah. As for the party (TN: Hizballah) they are above all legal chiefs, whether they are local or from above. They do not submit except for external entities. They are alone with no partners. The basic rules that are known to lawyers and investigative judges and all law people, which they know based on Anglo-Saxon law or French law, which are used throughout the world; are that one of the conditions of investigations – if there is an investigation in the first place – is that the judge should be the first one to come to the incident site; keeping under his control those special units who specialize in such investigations. According to law, specialists are the only people who should take over an incident site for investigation. It is also a condition that the judge needs to proceed and take statements from witnesses. He himself should review the site of the incident and examine it. He should certify and secure all items that are found (TN: evidence materials) and anything that will help with the investigation, like the lifting of fingerprints and the like. This seems to never take place whenever there is an incident in Shi'ite areas. But what happens is what we mentioned; the party surrounds the site and they hide all evidence and everything, so what value does that have? Without a doubt it is meaningless. It claims that the law is applied against all, a rarity that people laugh at and a lie that wise people know.

Syria the prisoner:

I want to call on our people in Syria the prisoner. I want to remind them that their role – in the coming days – is very important and central in the direction of the Sunnah throughout Syria, to pride and elevation and more humiliation. That is because the criminal Alawite government is the main leader in the war in Syria, and in Lebanon indirectly. Lebanon's security and its stability are tied to the reduction of the Alawite government's influence in Lebanon. It is your role to help lift the injustice against your people in Lebanon, as you know. And

PART FIVE: SELECTED COMMUNICATION WITH EXTERNAL BODIES

Page 10

you should not leave your people in Palestine and Lebanon to the hands of the Jews and the Alawite government. And they get away with it – I mean the Jews and the Alawites and their followers – and they don't have to worry about challenge or reactions. To give the ability for some of us in Syria needs to be done by all. Fate is one as the religion is one. So if our heroic people in Syria started a movement, the balance between us and our enemies would be balanced, little by little. And if their situation became stronger, this would lessen the pressure on our people in Lebanon and would strengthen them. And if they became stronger, then it would be the beginning of the end for the corrupt authorities in Syria. Because the activities in different locations complement each other and it is not right that the Alawite government should feel safe from being held accountable and safe from punishment.

Najad (TN: president of Iran) and the Jews:

As for the inward group and the general leader of their occupation program, Safawi Iran, the whole world saw how their president was elected by the power of weapons! The whole world saw him with his repeated boring theatrics, when he visited south Lebanon, and his repeated empty threats to the Jews, and that is a repetition with his predecessors who were "if they find the ones who believe what they said they believe, and if they allowed their Satan(s) they said, 'We are with you but we are being mocked.' God mocks them and he extends them with their oppression (TN: Unknown word)," as he threatens the Jews and the Americans, and he does as he pleases and makes announcements, and if the Jews wanted to kill him they would have easily as their airplanes occupy Lebanon's skies and fly over it, but to protect him and not to threaten him. So why, if one of the Jihadist leaders announced his appearance like Najad? Jewish spies would uncover the movements of those who take precautions and they would kill him. They would even kill individual jihadists and not just their leaders. As they did repeatedly in Gaza, even though they are careful and stay out of sight. So is Lebanon's sky harder for them than the Gaza skies? No, by God. And are the young Jihadist people more important than the head of an enemy state the size of

Iran, who announces his appearance? Yes, if animosity appears on the tongue and is different from the acts and there is between them negotiations an agreements which make him an ally to them at this stage. So where are the knowledgeable hearts and the alert minds and the sharp eyes to expose these facts with the lies? I am sure today that the reports regarding the coming of Najad to Lebanon was not to support his party, but a sign that Lebanon is his province, like when the American leaders come to Iraq and Afghanistan, which they occupy with their military, they are equal in that regard. And what about Najad's wider movements in the area and the political understandings between Iran and other countries? They are only a preparation, and that is the reality and the fact.

Page 11

And remember, people of the Sunnah, that "the liar of the suburb," the head of Hizballah, was proud with the state of the knowledgeable and he repeated his accusation that the Mujahidin from the Sunnah were agents for the Jews and the Americans. Like this example. And know that the party is gathering weapons for use in internal conflicts, to kill the people of the Sunnah and the group. And that is what they threatened to do and it was repeated by their seniors, and they used the International Court as an excuse to do that.

And history is witness to their betrayal of the faith and their conspiracy against Islam and its followers from the beginnings of their religion, beginning with what was done by Ibn Saba' Al- Yahwdi and the problems he left, and then they conspired with the Al-Tatar and they handed Iraq over to them and the appearance of their slavish country in Egypt and the animosity to the people of Sunnah in it, and then the conspiracy of their Safawi nation with the crusaders in the killing of Muslims, and their conspiracy with the crusaders and the Jews in their mission against the Islamic nation - in Afghanistan, Iraq, and now Syria. They started with it by protecting the Jewish borders and they will finish it by swallowing Syria with the aid of the crusaders and the Jews. But we figure that the flesh of the people of Syria will be bitter "alqam" (TN: word unclear) against the bad people, with God's permission. God will make their plans fail against the Jihadist Sunnis. The Lord said in his precious book, "And remember when ye met, He showed them to you as few in your eyes, and He made you appear as contemptible in their eyes: that God might accomplish a matter already enacted. For to God do all questions go back for decision."

So what's happening is that the Shi'ites and their followers will meet up with the Jews in following Christ to fight the people of Islam till the end of time. Like it was informed by the honest – God's prayers upon him – as it came to a true Muslim about Ishaq Bin Abdullah about his uncle Ans Bin Malik, that the prophet – God's prayers upon him –said, "The Dujjal follow the Jews of Asbahan 70,000, they have pallium (TN: men's robe)."

The deceit of Hizballah and the Shi'ite party:

Hizballah is still very reckless and in their threats they are boisterous, and for their real hegemony over Lebanon is progressing and their tongue says, "We are the strongest." So we say, "Don't they see that God who created them is stronger than them?"

And the party's use of the military intelligence and its officers against the Sunnis continues and we should be afraid of despotic ones who are faking belonging to the Sunnis so they may cause chaos in Sunni areas. And to preoccupy the people of Sunnah with that, and they split them with those knowledgeable and those ignorant of their reality, who think they're good like the almighty Lord said, "And from the non-believers there are two groups and the Lord responded to what they gained" and the scholars said the meaning is, "What matters to you – oh

Page 12

believers – that with the nonbelievers there are two different groups." So the Shi'ites provide money and weapons to Sunnis, to make threats of their own for the benefit of the Shi'ites, but he who goes to the aid of the Sunnis will be threatened with death and dire consequences.

And we know from the party about their financing, honoring, and their direct orders; thinking that the Sunnis are asleep and not aware of their deceit. But the day of reckoning will come with God's permission and tomorrow for those who wait for it is near.

As for those who sold out their religion and nation and who agreed to become tools for the party against the Sunnis - an eye attempts to uncover their secrets with the party, and the devil spreads conflict between them; and there is the luring of the young people by telling them that they are supporting the resistance and they will lure them with money. They agree to do that to allow the party to succeed against the Sunnis; and for their money and to love the world more than the hereafter. They are traitors who betrayed their religion and sold their families and took sides with their enemies that fight Muslims in an open war. And they make non-believers out of the young people from those who hail from the prophet, God's prayers upon him, and they dishonor their pure wives and makes the blood of the Sunnis flow and threaten them in secret and openly.

Oh people of sound minds and wisdom, the enemies of Sunnis have two faces: The outside enemies consisting of the crusaders and the Jews and the two do not differ, other than he who becomes an agent for the enemy is a traitor to his religion and family. "They said to those who hate what the Lord sent, we will make you obey some orders," and if they are pushed to be traitors "They loved life in the world better than the hereafter" or they are apologizing "they say we are afraid that a circle will touch us," they are equal in the betrayal. And that is the second face of the enemy. They are the internal enemy that is represented by the wicked ungrateful Shi'ites. And he who becomes an agent for those in the justice scale, he is an agent to the past ones. The partnership between the two groups to fight the Sunnis and the greediness to make them change their religion and to rape their lands and to kill their youth, and whoever helps them with that is a traitor. "And whoever takes their side from your people becomes one of them and God does not lead the unjust people to the right path." And if the party's situation was not clear to some people yesterday, it is now very clear to the Sunnis and even the elderly know the truth! So how can the traitors apologize to their families if they are discovered? And what kind of apology do they have for their despotic work? So every traitor who joined the enemy of the Sunnis needs to review his actions and repent to his God before it's too late.

Because maybe his mistake was because of someone who sold out his religion, and I look here at a wing in the Murabitwn fighters who were recruited by the Shi'ite Amal movement. And when the Shi'ites achieved what they were looking for, they left them just like the Shi'ites would do, and the end of this group was at the hands of the Shi'ites themselves.

And that is the reward for those who sold out their religion and nation and the one who abandons gets abandoned.

Page 13

And today, the Hizballah Shi'ites wear new shoes. On their top is a man called Mustapha Hamdan, who was to penetrate the Sunnis by luring them with money and fooling them by claiming that it is their duty to support the resistance! And no one in Lebanon is fooled by truth of this alleged resistance movement. It is nothing less than a resistance against Sunnis that threatens with killing and humiliation, in order for them to carry out their sectarian goals. So we say to that and those like them: What resistance do you need in Beirut and the areas where the Sunnis are? If you want to resist, as you claim, we challenge you and your party to shoot one bullet against the Jews! So show us the Jews as your targets if you were telling the truth.

And you should know that after a while, his masters will exchange for another set of shoes:

(TN: appears to be a poem)

"You are not but a shoe easy to ride,

And if you looked around, the leg of the rider will toss you out"

That is what the Lord provided. But he will not escape punishment before that with God's permission, if he does not repent, and the abused sect, the Sunnis, will start moving, no doubt, to conquer the enemy from its head, the head of the snake, and his cheap tools in Lebanon.

And we want to warn that there are Sunnis who will be held accountable as they play the same role that was done by Hamdan, and for the same corrupt excuses, and we say to those: This is the last warning to you and you should repent. And they should be discouraged from doing so, as Hamdan is an example. And they say about their misguided behavior and their deeds, that they are for the sake of Shi'ites, along with and the betrayal of their families. We will uncover their names and their deeds in helping make the Shi'ites victorious against the Sunnis, so that our people may know the ugly deeds and they can be treated like traitors. The Almighty said, "And those who repent before you get to them will be accepted by God for God is forgiving and merciful." And for those who repent we are obligated to keep their secrets and to help him get things straight.

I want to remind our people that we are from the Abdullah Al-'Azzam battalion, and we do not take political sides and we don't care about the dirty politics of Lebanon. We rise above it. And we do not ask the Sunnis to stand behind this or that. The Sunnis, however, matter to us in their religious, political, and economic interests. We want them to rise, and take this as serious work And we seek to protect the five necessary things for the Sunnis of Lebanon and Syria. So it is essential to protect the religion, oneself, honor, mind, and money. We will not harm anyone who leaves the Sunnis alone; those who dare to go against any of these five items and want to attack the Sunnis

Page 14

should beware of the consequences. And there will be no animosities except against the oppressors, and we do not accept injustice against anyone on this earth regardless of their sect or affiliation, and we know that we need to help the oppressed if we can, but our priority is for our own people with whom we share the same faith. We will not accept that our people, the Sunnis, are afraid and do not feel safe and their rights are taken from them by Hizballah and their apparatus. And the attacking Shi'ites feel safe in their homes with themselves and living conditions. Justice is eye for an eye and a tooth for a tooth and he one starts it is the oppressor.

As for the traitors, they need to know that he who promises them with victory and protection is giving them empty promises. Because they will not be able to protect their own sects and keep them from harm if the oppressed sect rises to take its rights and to lift oppression against its children. So can they protect the agents (TN: They won't be able to protect their own much less their agents)? So they're better of repenting and they need to repent before they are told, "Now that you were bad before and were one of the despots." And the wise one is the one who takes advice, and the poor one who becomes an example to others.

Conclusion:

In conclusion, I ask my brothers who carry the faith and want to make Sunnis victorious, that he should make efforts for our voices to reach the scholars and the students of knowledge and thinkers, and to anyone who has influence in their society; to spread our reports and essays to all sects and Muslims. I also ask them to be patient with non-receptive scholars and to be polite in dealing with them and being with them, because the call is from the lowest point to the highest; it is essential to stick to the civility of the call and most importantly, to be patient. They need to plead with their brothers and to win their trust and sympathy and to make them want to help making Islamic causes victorious. And they need to be able to accept harm while doing this. And those who cannot be patient and thick-skinned, need to work on something else and leave this to those who can stick to civility and who can take it. There is nothing good in any work where the people cannot stay with the message for the sake of the Lord and his prophet - Lord's prayers upon him.

I ask the Almighty Lord to gather our word for the truth and the straight path. And may he align us and gather our hearts. And

Page 15

may he make us like the ones he said about, "hard ones against the non-believers and merciful among themselves" and the ones he said about "and the Lord will come and he loves them and they love him, humble with the believers and above the non-believers, and the struggle for the sake of the Lord and are not afraid of the blame of others and that is what the Lord gives to he who wants because the Lord is large and knowledgeable." Lord lead us and our Sunni people to the victorious path and the roads of possibilities. Allow us the ability to lift injustice from ourselves and the taking from us our rights, so we may live in our lands safe and secure, with no rulers from your servants above us, except for the ruler who follows your rules and who will not mistreat under the shadow of someone.

And the Lord prayed and blessed your servant and prophet Muhammad and his people, friends, and wives, and all.

And our first prayer, Thanks to the Lord the Lord of the Universe

Abdullah Al-'Azzam Battalion
Al-Arba'a, 18 Dhu al-Hijja 1431
Wednesday Nov 24 2011

Source: (Fajr Center for Information)

PART FIVE: SELECTED COMMUNICATION WITH EXTERNAL BODIES

> ### 6. Ideas as Discussion with the Sons of the Peninsula
>
> Americans in Riyadh and Jews in Morocco are targeted, for they follow the word of Bush and are therefore misguided and corrupt. There are questions of what to do with those in the Arabian Peninsula.
>
> Date: Unknown
>
> From: Unknown
>
> http://www.dni.gov/files/documents/ubl/english/Ideas%20as%20discussion%20with%20the%20sons%20of%20the%20Peninsula.pdf

Full translation

(TN: First line is red handwritten note.)

From here we can suggest these ideas as a discussion with the sons of the Peninsula

After they distanced themselves from the true religion and followed the unjust nation, hell called upon the rulers of the area.

For those who follow the declarations by the ruler of Riyadh and his deputy and ministers in this difficult period, since the killing of Americans in Riyadh and the Jews in Morocco it can be surmised that these people follow the words of Bush and his program. They fight Islam in a clear war. There are announcements by King Fahd that the true believers, the scholars and those who struggle for the sake of God, the King states that they are misguided and corrupt, with poor thinking. These are the people who observe Islam in detail, without any prejudice, just like it was sent through our master Muhammad, God's prayers upon him. In truth, he means that this is outside the religion, and outside the law, and by that he is denying the verses that call for Jihad, and he names it corrupt thinking. What did the Mujahidin do except that they answered the call of God and the Prophet by resisting the occupying non-believers and the denigrating of their Jihad. It amounts to denigration of the belief and not to them personally, and that is what was discovered during these events and the declarations by Prince 'Abdallah; whoever justifies these operations against the Crusaders in the name of Islam is a partner with those criminals, as he claimed. This shows a clear indication that the regime has a religion, other than that sanctioned by God. They do not want a religion that urges pushing the occupiers and killing the non-believing Crusaders. If it were Islam, then he would have known in advance that the religion orders him to conduct such operations and does not hide the verses about Jihad from him.

The salvation for this nation is God's book and his Prophet's Sunnah, and not the rulers and their followers. Only God knows who is on the right path or the wrong path (and Moses said, my Lord I know what comes with wisdom from him and who has consequences of the region and he will not give tyrants success).

So who are the ones with the straying minds and the corrupt factions, those who follow what God and the Prophet had said about the obligation to expel the Jews and the Christians from the Arabian Peninsula, or those who opened the Peninsula to them and gave them military bases? The Almighty Lord said (those who allow partners for God are unholy and they should not be allowed near the forbidden mosque after their year) and the God's Prophet, prayers be upon him, said as was stated by Al-Bukhari about Ibn 'Abbas…

(TN: cut off.)

PART SIX: SELECTED SPECIFIC TOPICS

A. Islamic Emirate

> **1. Lessons Learned Following the Fall of the Islamic Emirate**
>
> This is simply a list of the current state of affairs after the 'fall of the Islamic Emirate.' Arrests, bombings, and killings are discussed, reported, and reviewed.
>
> Date: Unknown
>
> From: Unknown
>
> http://www.dni.gov/files/documents/ubl/english/Lessons%20Learned%20Following%20the%20Fall%20of%20the%20Islamic%20Emirate.pdf

(Fully translated)

In the Name of Allah, the Merciful, the Beneficent.

Lessons learned via incidents following the fall of the Islamic Emirate

1) The bombing of Muhammad ((Salah))'s house a half an hour after arriving to it in Khost (Var. Khowst).

2) The bombing of mujahidin assemblies at the former Ministry of Defense [facility] or the al-Aman Palace in Kabul, killing 40 mujahid.

3) The bombing of the al-Tayyib Agha house in Qandahar after its satellite communications and the brothers were rescued with Allah's grace.

4) The bombing of our house (Sayf al-(('Adl))'s) after our departure two days prior due to heavy traffic of people in the region to take funds from the United Nations after its departure. This is what Sayf al-'Adl noted. He told me that the people knew of the house and it was expected that it would be bombed.

5) The arrest of Khalid al-((Shaykh)), which was carried out by recruiting an agent and by using money and what we needed as far as food for Mukhtar.

6) The arrest of ((Abu Zubaydah)), due to our opening up so much to Lashkar-e Tayyiba or to use the phones and the Internet.

7) The arrest of the Yemeni group, due to the excess in their departure, their communications, and their outward appearance that differs from the outward appearance of the [others].

8) The arrest of Firas and Waqqas, due to finding that they had weapons.

9) The arrest of ((Abu Yasir)), due to his excess in responding frequently on the Internet, or the treachery of Lashkar-e Tayyiba.

10) The killing of the brothers in the Dawigar operation because the location was discovered and the [information] spread and due to brothers from distant locations [parking] at the house. [Due to] the brothers not acting once they heard of the disclosure [of their location].

11) The arrest of ((Abu al-Mundhir)), due to observing him in Mir Ali. He was arrested after he left Banu, Allah knows.

PART SIX: SELECTED SPECIFIC TOPICS

12) The slaughter that took place Lawdar due to the use of vehicles in departing and in gathering in one location after having heard the sound of the khabith – C130. (TN: Khabith meaning "malicious," is often used in reference to American aircraft.)

13) The killing of Nawwab and his family after not heeding warnings that he received prior to his death and due to his openness to people and his refusal to leave Mir Ali and to change his penetrated crew, God knows.

14) The arrest of ((Abu al-Faraj)) due to his lack of precaution when his associate was late and didn't come, with this being the first time that he sent someone as his deputy.

15) The arrest of Sharifallah al-((Masri)) due to his interactions with individuals he knew to be penetrations with contacts to ISI.

16) The killing of 'Ikrimah (Var.: 'Akramah) and his brothers due to a lack of changing residence after it was discovered and became well known to everyone.

17) The killing of Shaykh al-((Kindi)) after not taking the attack on Pakistan seriously in a campaign against the mujahidin.

18) The arrest and killing of a number of loved ones on [unclear] (TN: transliterated: al-Batkat) due to the easy-going nature of the brothers and indifference to the infidel factions regarding their movements, the pot is not safe each time it falls. (TN: Arab saying meaning, "you may get away with it once, but not every time.")

2. Letter to Islamic Emirate of Afghanistan

> Written to the Mujahidin brothers, this letter conveys the importance of martyrdom and the need to carry on without certain leaders. Victory is said to be near.
>
> Date: Unknown
>
> From: Unknown
>
> http://www.dni.gov/files/documents/ubl/english2/Letter%20to%20Islamic%20Emirate%20of%20Afghanistan.pdf

Page 1

In the name of Allah, the Compassionate, the Merciful.

Islamic Emirate of Afghanistan
Political Commission
Media Division

No. (TN: blank)
Date (TN: blank)

Condolences on the occasion of the martyrdom of Shaykh Abu-Yazid al-Mustafa, may Allah bestow his soul.

God has said, "Think not of those who were killed in the way of Allah as dead. Nay, they are alive, with their Lord, and they have provision. They rejoice in what Allah has bestowed upon them of His bounty and rejoice for the sake of those who have not yet joined them, but are left behind (not yet martyred) that on them no fear shall come, nor shall they grieve. They rejoice in a Grace and a bounty from Allah and that Allah will not waste the reward of the believers." (Qur'an: Surah Al 'Umran, 3:169- 171).

Part Six: Selected Specific Topics

With hearts filled with patience, hope, and the belief in God's judgment and acts, we received word of the martyrdom of the heroic fighter and veteran leader, Shaykh Abu-Yazid al-Mustafa, together with a group of the knights of jihad and faith. May God rest their souls, all of them, and make them to live in the highest paradise with the prophets, the true believers, the martyrs, and the righteous, as they are the best to be friends with.

In the name of the Islamic Emirate of Afghanistan, we offer our condolences to our brothers the mujahidin of al-Qa'ida and to the Islamic Nation in general for the loss of this heroic fighter. As God said in condolence to his faithful worshipers, "If a wound (and killing) has touched you, be sure a similar wound (and killing) has touched the others. And so are the days (good and not so good), we give to men by turns: that Allah may test those who believe, and that He may take martyrs among you. And Allah likes not the Zalimun (polytheists and wrong-doers)." [Qur'an: Surah Al 'Umran 140].

O mujahidin! The death of the heroic leaders will not impact the course of the jihad against unbelief and falsehood negatively.

When a single knight is dismounted in the battle between the soldiers of God and the guardians of the devil, God opens the doors to unexpected victories for the Muslims with his blood.

We ask God to receive him into the highest heavens and to recompense the mujahidin and send them blessings. We ask that his pure blood become the cause of the mujahidin's victory and the defeat of the occupiers everywhere.

We commend our brothers the mujahidin to walk in the way of your righteous martyrs. Be a comfort to the believers and a punishment to the unbelievers, and bring yourselves into accordance with the word of God: "Among the believers are men who have been true to their covenant with Allah: of them some have fulfilled their obligations, and some of them are still waiting, but they have never changed in the least." (Qur'an: Surah Al Ahzab 23).

Page 2

O mujahidin brothers!

We bring you the good news that victory is near, and the crusader enemy will be defeated. We must all observe precision and preparation in managing the matters of our jihad. We must keep our ranks free of divisions and selfishness. We must be alert against all the conspiracies which are contrived to harm the reputation of the mujahidin. We must focus our efforts in the field of resistance on striking the usurping enemy. We must not become preoccupied with anything that distracts us from the original goal. Turn your attention to the most important goals. We are sure that victory is on the side of the mujahidin as long as they are true in their jihad and in their dealings with God, as God said, "O believers! If you help the cause of Allah, He will help you and establish your feet firmly." (Qur'an: Surah Al Qital 7).

Continue your jihad and your fight against the occupiers and their cowed helpers. Order your ranks, and God will be with you and will not abandon you and your works.

Peace and blessings be upon you.

Website: www.pol-islamicemirate.com
Email: Politicalpress1@yahoo.com, Politicalpress2@gmail.com, Politicalpress3@hotmail.com

(TN: End of Translation)

B. Islamic Nation

> **1. Message for General Islamic Nation**
>
> More revolutions are discussed, as are the situations in Tunisia and Egypt. A history of revolutions is mentioned, as are leaders. A few poems composed by the author are included as well.
>
> Date: Unknown
>
> From: Unknown
>
> http://www.dni.gov/files/documents/ubl/english/Message%20for%20general%20Islamic%20nation.pdf

(Fully Translated)

Page 1

Praise be to God, we worship Him, turn to Him for help, beg His forgiveness, and seek refuge in Him from the evils of ourselves and our bad actions. He who is guided by God will not go astray, and he who is misguided has no one to guide him. I witness there is no God but Allah, no partner for Him, and I witness that Muhammad is His servant and His prophet.

Thereafter,

To the general Islamic nation, peace be upon you with God's mercy and blessings…

The people of the world in its entirety got out from their enslavement by their despotic rulers. The most recent of them are the people of Eastern Europe who had lived for many decades in the slavery of global Communism until the Soviet Union began to sway on the peaks of the Hindu Kush. As it (TN: the Soviet Union) showed its weakness to the entire world, the people of Europe seized upon that weakness, revolted, and freed themselves from the slavery of global Communism. Today, we live in similar days. Our countries have lived for decades in unpleasant religious, social, cultural and economic conditions, due to the Western domination of them. In these critical times, God Almighty willed that the American-led Western camp become tied up in Afghanistan on the very peaks of the Hindu Kush, swaying and showing its weakness to the entire world. As it (TN: Western camp) showed its weakness and lost its prestige, and as the injustice of authoritarian leaders piled up over the people with the support of the Western camp, the regional and global climates became ready to topple the agents of the West. This was a rare, historic opportunity for the entire Islamic nation to take initiative and free itself from the slavery of Western domination.

At this pivotal point, the light of the revolution in Tunisia shone and ignited the Muslims' emotions in Egypt. Egypt, with its revolution, ignited the emotions of the Islamic world entirely. The success of the Tunisian revolution in overthrowing tyranny brought down the injustice, despair, inaction, and fear, and sent the spirit of courage, glory, zeal, and audacity, and convinced the people of the Islamic nation that when they advance in large numbers, they make the hearts of the tyrants tremble.

My Muslim Nation: After faith, it is among the most important of duties to work on seizing this great opportunity and to exert the effort to maintain these embers in the land of Egypt. Among the most important reasons for the success of the revolutions, after the will of God Almighty are:

First: Raising public awareness. It has been established by the previous events that public awareness is among the most important factors in carrying out a successful revolution. Therefore, I call upon all believers in the Islamic nation, particularly those with opinions, words, and money, to call into battle their efforts to enlighten its children.

Page 2

Don't hold back anything you can deliver for its course, either by word or by accomplishment. The best of what was written about this is the book, "Concepts That Should Be Corrected," and the book, "Our Present Reality," by Shaykh Muhammad Qutb. To help us understand this further, it is necessary to look at the documents and testimonies by witnesses from the inside these organizations, such as former ministers and officers. (Some of those testimonies came to light in some episodes of "Witness to the Era" and "Life Experience" (TN: Al Jazeera Network television programs) by Haykal, a previous minister who knew a great deal of facts from behind closed doors. He reported many of those facts in two chapters of his book, "Political Talk," one chapter on Jordan and the other on Morocco. It is advisable for people of every country to become informed about what concerns their country so they may understand the truths and undertake their duties toward them.)

Second: Taking lessons from history, particularly from the history of the revolutions and what pertains to them, and studying the reasons for the success or failure of these revolutions. An example of this is the Muslim revolution in Algeria more than two decades ago. The masses were ready to carry out the revolution. However, the leadership made a fatal mistake in that it stayed in Algeria without a sanctuary from arrest or the practice of severe pressures, which denied it freedom to make crucial decisions. This is a matter of utmost importance. Likewise, it changed its mind about the demonstrations to protect the blood of Muslims. This is what happened over and over again in Egypt and Yemen when the masses gathered in Cairo and the million-man march in Sana' demanding the overthrow of the ruler. However, the leaders of the revolution talked with the rulers and believed their promises, fearing Muslim bloodshed. So, they dismissed the masses and then were betrayed. In the process, Shaykh 'Abd-al-Qadir 'Awdah, God have mercy on him, was killed, as well as so many innocent people after him. We ask God almighty to have mercy on them all. It wasn't long before the situation in Yemen returned to what it had been before. Fearing bloodshed in a country such as Yemen is a grave mistake. According to statistics, 70,000 people die each year in Egypt alone from the injustice and despotism of the regime, due to water pollution emanating from the factories of big businessmen, the allies of the authorities. This means the death of hundreds every day.

Third: People who are seeking liberation should have the psychology of the kings and their nature. They [the kings] are among the cross sections in which killing inside the family occurs, where the man kills his father or his brother, strongly due to the desires of the kings. This shows the extent of their concern toward the blood of their people. Also, treachery is a feature that accompanies many of [the kings] if faced by an event that threatens their kingdoms, forcing the ruler to lose his sound judgment and bring about his greatest desire for revenge from those who jolt his kingdom. The greatest example of this is the event involving 'Abd-al-Malik, when he betrayed the peace with Ibn-al-'As [from the early Islamic era], despite the reconciliation and treaties signed by both parties before the scholars and the problem solvers.

Page 3

He didn't keep the peace with him, as he decided to return after three days and kill Ibn-al-'As. And that was the first treachery in Islam.

Fourth: The revolution must be led by powerful, trusted men who are not afraid of dying. They should take into consideration the importance of accuracy in measuring the appropriate conditions to begin the revolution, without haste or delay. Haste could abort the revolution and delay could waste the opportunity for many decades. Here it is worth indicating that some Islamic countries today need weeks to prepare and to conduct awareness before beginning the revolution, and some need months. Toppling the tyrants needs a conditioned leadership capable of bearing the necessary costs for change. Freedom isn't achieved without a heavy price, and blood is a component that cannot be separated from the other components to achieve it. I am well aware of the fact that exposing the people of the Islamic nation to death is a very difficult matter, but there is no other way to save them. No other way.

Part Six: Selected Specific Topics

(TN: Poem begins)

I advised and we are of different houses
But between us there is ancestry and linkages
We drew close even if our countries were far
Shari'a of our Lord is just and true
The kingdoms are built on victims
The right approach and will not be brought down
By the dead will be life for generations
And by the captives, ransom for them to grow up
For the red freedom is a door
With every bloody hand, knock on it

(TN: Poem ends)

Oh, sons of my Muslim nation, you are at a dangerous crossroads and have a rare historic opportunity to get out from the subjection of slavery. Seize it and break the shackles to become free of the global Zionist oppression. It is a great offense and huge ignorance to lose this opportunity for which the Muslim nation has waited many decades.

In closing: Oppression has wreaked great havoc in our countries and it must be disavowed and changed. God's prophet said "Those who engage against them in jihad..." And he also said "[Men rewarded for a great deed are] the master of martyrs, Hamzah Bin 'Abd-al-Muttalib, and another man who was killed as he stood up against an unjust ruler advising him to do goodness and refrain from wrongdoing." So accolades to he who goes out on this great purpose, and if killed, he will be a great martyr. If he lives, he will be in happiness, so say the truth and don't worry about it.

(TN: Poem begins)

Tell the truth to the tyrants.
It is the power it is the good news.

Page 4

It is the path to the world.
It is the path to the hereafter.

If you want, die as a slave.
If you want, die as a free person.

(TN: Poem ends)

The battle today between the people and the ruler is a battle of wills, and the revolution is a revolution of glory and dignity. Most of the rulers today still think with the mind of Abu-Juhhal [a person from the early era of Islam]. They don't realize the gap between them and the rising generation in values, principles, and beliefs that are blended with them and mixed in their hearts. After the people inhaled the scent and sampled the taste of freedom and dignity, their blood and spirit were infused with pride, the same pride that changed the souls of the oppressed in Mecca, may God be pleased with them. The face of the earth changed when they stood up to the tribe of Quraysh [from the early era of Islam], a raging giant that amassed around them all sorts of suffering, brought down on them all types of torture, and repeatedly had them sampling the bitter taste of death. However, they could not make them forget the taste of faith and pride. Taking away their souls was much easier than taking away their freedom, so they would go back and worship the tyrants and not God. Those rulers did not understand the meaning of faith and pride, which were rooted in the hearts of the oppressed.

It is beneficial for them to learn from the outcome of the tyrants who came before them and to realize that it is impossible for them to stay in power as long as they continue to suppress the free, be responsible for the chaos and the bloodshed, and dominate the Muslim people.

PART SIX: SELECTED SPECIFIC TOPICS

2. Message for all Muslims Following US State of Union Address

This message discounts the message of President Bush in the State of the Union Address. The author assures the Islamic world that al Qa'ida is still just as strong and that America and its friends are both liars and delusional. This message seeks to expose the lies told by Bush and his officials in an effort to defame the American government and it's objectives against al Qa'ida.

Date: Unknown

From: Unknown

http://www.dni.gov/files/documents/ubl/english/Message%20for%20all%20Muslims%20following%20US%20State%20of%20the%20Union%20Address.pdf

(Page 1 of 4)

In the name of God, and praise to God.

Peace and prayers be upon God's messenger, his family, companions and followers

My fellow Muslims everywhere,
God's peace, mercy and blessings be upon you,

Bush has delivered his State of the Union address before Congress, and his speech was filled with lies and misguidance. One wonders how the leader of the most powerful nation on earth is not ashamed of all of this deceit and lying, and how could anyone from his nation's leaders and warlords cheer or applaud him? It is a phenomenon that requires a lot of thinking and reflection. Did Bush reach such a low level that he ridicules the intelligence of his audience? And did all of his audience reach an extent that they accept this belittlement and mocking of their intelligence? Does the most powerful nation in the world enjoy such baldness that they accept this misguidance and mislead, promote, and spread it everywhere? In any case, this might be outside the scope of my subject, and so let's get back to the Crusader Bush who is full of lies.

In his speech, Bush made four broad claims, broader than the distance between East and West:

His first claim: That his forces are spreading freedom and security in the world.

His second claim: That Iraq has gained its freedom due to the help of the Coalition Forces.

His third claim: That his government has captured more than two thirds of al-Qa'ida.

And his fourth claim: That the situation in Afghanistan is stable.

Along with these claims, he repeatedly insisted on requesting more money and funds to support his forces and security agencies.

We want to remind the whole world and the American people, who are led behind this lying Crusader-president, and recall a number of crystal clear facts, that even Bush and his lies cannot hide. The first thing we would like to remind Crusader- Bush with is that his forces do not spread freedom or security, but oppression and fear, and install corrupt rulers who are protected by his forces, who plan and show them how to brutalize and scavenge their people, while allowing them to inherit their powers from tyrant to descendant tyrant.

A quick look at the Islamic world, from Morocco to Indonesia, will reveal to you what sort of rulers the US supports and blesses their efforts in a war against Islam which it calls "The War on Terror."

Where is the freedom that the US is spreading through its agents such as Egypt's Husni Mubarak? That tyrant, who admitted to taking Egypt out of the Islamic-nation battle against Israel, disarmed the Sinai, and held the Sharm ash-Shaykh conference. He has always exercised pressure on the Palestinian Jihad organizations for the sake of Israel. Husni Mubarak, whose

(Page 2 of 4)

prisons are overcrowded with tens of thousands of honorable freemen that only demand the just rule of Shari'ah and resist surrendering to Israel as they fight against corruption, moral and financial deterioration... that Husni Mubarak who is preparing his son to succeed him in subjugating Egypt.

Where is the freedom of the Al Sa'ud family, who consider the country and the people in it as their own personal property, those who propagate a Saudi religion that calls for the complete and blind obedience to the ruler, who support Jews and Christians who brought their hordes of armies to the land of Islam which filled the land with corruption, deterioration, theft, immorality, and assaults against sanctities.

Where is the independence of Pervez Musharraf, who allows the FBI to frolic in his country with freedoms that they cannot even enjoy in America? Where is the independence of Pervez Musharraf, who helped America to kill tens of thousands of people and to annihilate the Islamic Emirate of Afghanistan, and who is now seeking to achieve America's, Israel's, and India's goal to annihilate Pakistan, by allowing the American, Israeli and Indian intelligence to interrogate the scientists of Pakistan's nuclear project and jail them like criminals. It is a campaign that will only benefit Americans, Jews and Indians.

Wasn't he the same Musharraf who America called a dictator tyrant, then announced later that he is a sincere friend when he helped them to shed Muslim blood in Afghanistan and to suffocate Jihad in Kashmir, and set the FBI free to roam in Pakistan, and last but least - allowed the Americans to get hold of the scientists that worked on the nuclear project, to torture them and to make an example of them for the sake of America's War On Terrorism?

Aren't America and all of its friends and allies similar to him in their war on Terrorism, those that spread fear, coercion, theft, corruption, despotism and treason?

The second thing we would like to remind the liar-Crusader Bush of, is that Iraq does not enjoy freedom or security. The only thing that happened was a power transfer, from the control of a tyrant dictator-ruler who was secular and hostile to Islam, to a Crusader occupation that fights Islam, kills, detains, and tortures whoever they like and that steals anything and whatever they want from Iraq on the pretext of a lie which would make a bereaved woman laugh; that the US troops in Iraq are searching for the lost phantom Weapons of Mass Destruction.

It is an occupation that seeks only to divide Iraq into torn pieces that serve the interest of Zionists and Crusaders. You liar deceitful Crusader: Why didn't you mention one word in your speech about those that you massacred in the hundreds, in a holocaust of the struggling Iraq?

Why didn't you mention a single word about the "delusion" of the Weapons of Mass Destruction?

Third, we would like to tell Bush, the liar-Crusader, that he did not destroy or annihilate two-thirds of al-Qa'ida. On the contrary, it is still here – with God's grace – alive and present in the Jihad arena raising the banner of Islam in the face of the Zionist-Crusader campaign aimed against the Islamic nation. You liar-Crusader, your battle is not against al-Qa'ida, but against Islam and the entire Islamic nation, which considers al-Qa'ida to be one of its fighting vanguards that – with God's help – will defend its dignity, honor, and sanctities.

(Page 3 of 4)

In regards to the one-half, two-third or three-quarters... whatever delusions or false rumors you may have, I say that you and your criminal security agencies know better than anyone that al-Qa'ida – with God's graciousness and generosity – are increasing, growing and expanding, despite what you and your Zionist allies say. You of all people should know best that the Islamic nation embraces al-Qa'ida and its Jihadists, and provides them with aid and support, because they realize that al-Qa'ida fights you and everyone that stands under your cross, and that it defends Islam and Muslims. We promise to God Almighty to pursue you as long as we still have a beating pulse in our veins. Just like the Prophet (PBUH) and his companies actively pursued Ibn-al-Haqiq and Ka'b Bin-al-Ashraf, with God's help and support.

Two years of war on the Mujahidin were sufficient to convince any rational person of the extent of the folly of this war against Islam and Muslims, but you are a foolish liar who cannot reflect on the past, to learn what happened to the fate of the Russians and the British that preceded you.

Therefore, we don't have any ploy to offer you or your herds, except to kill and send all of you to hell for an everlasting evil unfortunate fate. We have made up our minds to make you, your Crusader-herds, allies and traitor-agents a lesson to criminals in history, with God's help and strength.

The motives that led to 9/11 are still there, even increasing and escalating due to your crimes and stupidity, and the 19 individuals who made you taste the worst defeat that history has seen in the attacks on New York and Washington, are not exceptional freaks of history, but are the vanguards of a nation that rose up for Jihad, and there are millions of their brothers eager to seek the same path.

And we say to you and to others of your Crusader kind, similar to what Hassan Bin-Thabit - may God be pleased with him - said to the polytheists of Quraysh (TN: the prominent tribe of the Prophet): (TN: A poem meaning that: if you get lost, we will continue our pilgrimage business and everything will be ok and things will be bright again, or else you just wait for the hangman who will show you a day that only God will be Merciful to whoever He wants.)

Bush, you liar-Crusader, fortify your targets, strengthen your defenses, and intensify your security, because the Jihadi Islamic nation which sent the previous clandestine companies to New York and Washington has made up its mind to send another bunch of companies, one after the other, carrying death and mayhem and seeking heaven.

The fourth thing we would like to remind the liar-Crusader Bush of, is that the situation in Afghanistan is still unstable. Otherwise liar-Crusader, how could we - with God's help and strength - launch attacks against your forces and your traitor- bandit agents, and from where can we – you liar-Crusader – send you our letters that challenge you and expose your lies and falsifications? Can your puppet-agent Karzai hire Afghan guards to protect him? Or does he get protected by American soldiers? Could the United Nations forces be deployed outside Kabul? Why do your forces retreat from one location to the next? Why do you have to depend on hired gangsters that filled the country stealing, looting, ripping-off, and disgracing its honor, besides the narcotic trade and that's based on your confessions? And why do you, liar-Crusader, admit that after two years of your Crusade the Taliban is still the greatest threat in Afghanistan?

(Page 4 of 4)

Can you, the liar-Crusader, answer all of these embarrassing scandalous questions?

The messenger of God, Prophet (PBUH) said: (TN: A quote from the Hadith which means – what people realized as words of early prophecy was saying if you don't feel shame then do whatever you want.)

In regards to the American people who Bush addressed in his speech, we have a few words to say: To the mothers and fathers of U.S. soldiers, whenever they receive a coffin arriving back home, they should remember the US crimes in Iraq, Palestine, Afghanistan,

Part Six: Selected Specific Topics

Chechnya, Kashmir, Guantanamo, and all of the detention camps belonging to American friends everywhere. People of America, whoever plants thorns will not reap roses.

I congratulate the Islamic nation, for the return of your masses to fight in the Jihad arena carrying the Prophet's (PBUH) victorious banner. So, increase your enemy, and rush your martyrs to heaven, and don't be hesitant in massacring those Zionist-Crusader criminals, and as God said: (Do you fear them? Nay, it is Allah Who is more deserving of your fear, if you are true believers.)

Finally, we pray and thank God Almighty, Lord of all worlds, and God bless our Prophet Muhammad, his family, and companions, peace be upon them.

(End of Translation)

C. Afghanistan

> ### 1. Summary on Situation in Afghanistan and Pakistan
>
> The motivations of al Qa'ida, its "knowledge, jurisprudence, wisdom, reason, intelligence, and maturity," are reinforced. The author believes the idea of Jihad as an ideology should be spread. Movements in Pakistan are said to be self-sufficient. Despite issues with spy infiltration, immigrants, and finances, these areas are still seen as successful.
>
> Date: Unknown
>
> From: Unknown
>
> http://www.dni.gov/files/documents/ubl/english/Summary%20on%20situation%20in%20Afghanistan%20and%20Pakistan.pdf

Page 1

The first attachment: A simple summary on the reality of the situation in our arena in Afghanistan and Pakistan

1- Praise be to God, we are well and in good health. We are enjoying God's blessings, generosity, and kindness in our life, faith, security, and jihad against the enemies of God. We are also enjoying the pride that God blessed us with in these circumstances. The rest of the brothers are fine, praise be to God. We believe that there are many good things going on in our arena, but like all jihadi arenas and jihadi experience, it has problems, negativities, mistakes, deficiencies, shortcomings, and so on. These things might happen because of problems caused by some. (God does not oppress anyone). Many men came to the arena but did not stay patiently after they saw mistakes, shortcomings, administrative errors, and so on. Some even turned around and spoke angrily against the arena; however, these individuals are very few. The majority are good, praise be to

God. We believe that our arena is the most deeply rooted arena in terms of knowledge, jurisprudence, wisdom, reason, intelligence, and maturity. It is a mother or an older sister to all arenas through the generosity of God.

2- Jihad as an ideology, belief, approach, practice, application, desire from the heart, and passion has spread among people in a way that would cause the enemy great anger, make them lose sleep, and disturb their tranquility in their country. May God humiliate them, extend their sleeplessness, and dim their future. God is the greatest! A complete jihadi generation in Afghanistan and the tribal areas of Pakistan is more wholesome, tight, mature, and kind. As for the problems, they are there, as I mentioned before, and the matter is up to God. However, do not have fear for al-Jihad. As beloved martyr Khalid al-Habib said once, "If we all get killed, there is no fear for jihad, for the message was delivered (to the nation)." This generation, through its awareness and maturity, has transcended above many issues that others have and continue to stumble over and be puzzled by, including fighting apostates, loyalists to the crusaders, and other issues.

3- We (the mother organization here) are working on the two sides, in Afghanistan and Pakistan. This is in addition to missions by immigrants and local supporters, raising the generation, conducting external work, leading, supplying, and supervising the branches, protecting the organization, and other large requirements.

Work in Pakistan is almost self-sufficient. There are many operating groups and local Taliban groups who have joined, and there is Tahrik Taliban or those who did not join. Those who did not join are no less (TN: effective) than those who have joined (TN: sic).

We are participating in the work in Afghanistan, and we have to do that, but praise be to God, Taliban almost does not need us. We are providing only moral and symbolic support, but in spite of that, our participation is good and important.

4- Among the problems that we suffer from:

Over the last two years, the problem of the spying war and spying aircrafts benefited the enemy greatly and led to the killing of many jihadi cadres, leaders, and others. This is something that is concerning us and exhausting us. God is our guardian, to Him we complain, and our fate is up to Him. God willing, we are patient, constant in our exertion of efforts, balancing out this war, and adapting to the situation. Therefore, we need to cooperate, exchange expertise, especially because we expect the enemy to transport these experiences to your arena and to the Somali arena, for they (TN: the enemy) tasted their sweetness. May God humiliate them. We need to cooperate quickly. God willing, we will gather what we have on this area that can benefit you and send it to you in our next letter to you.

Also, there is the financial problem, which is a problem in jihad whether or not it is a time of hardship. God is the giver and He knows what we need.

There is also the problem of managing the many components of the immigrants' presence here. We have Arabs, Uzbeks, Turks, Turkistanis, Balkans, Russians of all kinds, Germans, and others. Unfortunately, there is so much chaos on the ground, but we try to remedy things.

Also, there is a problem with some immigrants, especially the Arab ones. I will try to shed light on it through help from God. In our jihadi arenas in general we suffer from unjustified divisions and alliances, which I call the "fake commandants." This is the case even in our arena in Khurasan, in spite of being the mother arena and the best arena, as I mentioned before. Despite the weaknesses, shortcomings, and challenges, it continues to be the strongest, most symbolic arena, and so on. Due to our incomplete strength and control, we get inflicted with people who conduct jihad according to their moods or as they wish. They come to the arena and live it, but they do not abide by the rules and they might not like the established system. Usually, these people are impulsive and might be active, skilled, smart, and capable, but problems arise and they start saying things such as "We are marginalized," if they see, for example, that we did not appoint them fast enough in the positions that they want. Of course, we have our own methods, which are partly based on great caution in recommending individuals and not giving them any positions before they spend some time in the arena, working and giving. Sometimes they also say, "I have energy to work and produce, but they are restricting me."

Page 2

Some have purely bad demands that are not based on an argument. They just refuse to be ordered and refuse to listen, obey, or stay where they were placed and insist on being the head. There are many examples of this, and if you add to them our visible mistakes, shortcomings, and weakness, you get the ingredients for divisions. You find these people leaving the group and becoming a burden on the arena. They become a source for damage, whether they know it or not, because they are not disciplined in their movement, communications, relationships, and so on. They do not take into consideration the interest of the jihadi community. Also, their individualism and independence might cause quarrels and frictions that are harmful, embarrassing, and upsetting, and this might lead to bickering and exchange of insults. May God help us. We have a few groups and individuals who repelled from each other, including brother Ghazwan al- Yamani (aka: Abu al-Husayn), who was killed about a month and half ago, and who came to us about two years ago and told us then that he came from your side (I am not sure if he came from your side or from the side of al-Qa'iti, may God rest his soul). There are others, including brother Safwan and a young brother named 'Isa Bin-Maryam. They are both Yemenis, and they were both captured in Quetta, Pakistan, while on their way to Iran last year. Safwan is the one who was in correspondence with you, and through him we received your video message last year. We pray to God to break their imprisonment and change them. Also, among them is brother Hamzah al-Jawfi and a brother named Dhabbah al- Ta'ifi, who was detained in a tribal area near Peshawar last year and was handed over to Saudi Arabia. We pray to God break his imprisonment and change him. He has friends who are still here, including 'Ukashah al-'Iraqi and others.

Among them also is brother Najm or Najm al-Khayr (Salih al-Qar'awi) al-Qasimi. Unfortunately, he is a great example of these individuals for he does not belong to us completely and does not listen or obey us. He says, "I am with Shaykh 'Usama and the Emir al-Mu'minin Mullah Muhammad 'Umar, but I am not necessarily with Mustafa Abu al-Yazid, 'Atiyyah, or others. Jihad is big and I do not need to be limited to a group." Unfortunately, that is almost exactly what he used to say. Such talk is ignorance and is wrong without any doubt. This also applies to those who lightly establish jihadi groups whenever they wish to do so with total disregard to guidelines and restrictions. We should be uniting the existing groups in the first place. We should only allow those who have a shari'ah-based reason for working individually in an arena or in a field. It seems that now he has group that consists of individuals like him, and he always tries to lure young men from the Peninsula and cause us problems, may God help us. He is a very simple man and does not have the qualifications to lead jihadi work or jurisprudence. He was supposed to be a soldier for Islam and a mujahid for the sake of God. He was placed in a trustworthy jihadi group under renowned and wise leadership that supervises him until he quietly matures. Once God allows him, the Muslims accept him, and his time comes, he can even replace 'Usama without a problem! But, everything needs to happen properly and he cannot be an independent leader because he is not qualified for it. That is our opinion, but he is not convinced. We failed in containing him because of his insistence on being something! Two weeks ago, al-Fajr Centre conducted an interview with him. The brothers in al-Fajr should not have conducted it. They did not consult with us or ask us. As a semi-official jihadi media organization that belongs to us, they should come to us and consult with us on any operation for promoting and sponsoring leaders in front of the nation. For that reason, you will see the great gap in the words of brother Najm during the interview when he was asked the following:

-Najm, what is your position inside al-Qa'ida organization? He did not mention al-Qa'ida at all, not in praise or criticism. He also did not talk about his position in it.

PART SIX: SELECTED SPECIFIC TOPICS

-Al-Qa'ida organization has a branch named al-Qa'ida Organization in the Arabian Peninsula under the leadership of Abu-Basir Nasir al-Wahishi. What is your position in it? He did not mention this or get close to it, of course, because he cannot. He avoids these speed bumps. He is a "commander" and that is it!

Our point of view toward this issue or any similar issue is that the group, represented by its leaders, should look at this brother and ask if this person is qualified for this work or not. Is he qualified to be at this place at this position or not? If he is, then on God we will depend and move forward, but if the leadership thinks that he is not qualified or is operating in a fashion that is not acceptable, it should go to him and tell him that he is not good for this work and this work is not acceptable. The brother should obey and say, "Your wishes are my commands. I am a soldier and you can order me with whatever you want and whatever you deem appropriate." He should accept without any conditions.

As for the brother to come to you and tell you that he has a group that wants to work in the Peninsula, Lebanon, or anywhere else and that he has special and unique circumstances and that he wants to impose this on the organization, this would be inappropriate.

The organization might accept this in some cases because the organization understands that it needs to accommodate people to the best of its ability and that it includes and employs the pure and the immoral, but these are difficult balances and decisions.

Honestly, in my personal opinion and assessment, these things are nothing but illnesses, and we pray to God to heal us from them. However, we are in a real predicament; it is a problem if we stay silent and it is a problem if we speak out. People do not know what is going on while these individuals feed on our silence.

Page 3

Sometimes they might turn the issue into personal quarrel, may God save us. O God, grant us martyrdom for your sake that would please you and save us from divisions.

As for the Battalions of 'Abdallah 'Azzam, it is a small group of brothers in Lebanon who fired rockets against the Jews once, twice, or more. They are also trying to attack the convoys of the UNIFIL there. May God greatly reward them. This group was in communication with us at one point, but once our communications were disconnected, they established a link with brother Najm. He linked up with them, accommodated them, and supported them through the support that he collects. He became like a supervisor over them who speaks on their behalf. He says that he has group this and that, when in fact, he did not establish the group. At any rate, among the latest developments is that we are trying once again to contain brother Najm and have him become a disciplined member while we give him the responsibility to officially oversee the work in Lebanon alongside the brothers at the Battalions of 'Abdallah 'Azzam under al-Qa'ida. However, there are problems and challenges in dealing with him. That is our assessment of him and of those who work with him who are known to us. May God help us and He is the giver of success. This was a short glimpse to give you a picture of our arena at the current phase.

God is our and your supporter and he is the best supporter and advocate.
O God, correct our situation, o lord.

PART SIX: SELECTED SPECIFIC TOPICS

2. Undated letter re Afghanistan

The importance of martyrs is reiterated and the author believes the Islamic government should be put in place in Afghanistan. According to the letter this will protect the Afghani people from the Pakistani government.

Date: Unknown

From: Unknown

http://www.dni.gov/files/documents/ubl/english/Undated%20letter%20re%20Afghanistan.pdf

Full translation begins here

Page 1 of 1

In the name of Allah the most gracious the most merciful

Thanks be to Allah, the Lord of the Worlds, Master of the Day of Judgment, peace and prayers be upon our mujahidin leader, the imam of the prophets and the messengers, Muhammad Bin 'Abdullah, on his pure family, his companions and those who followed their paths to Judgment day

My generous brother, May God protect you – Peace, mercy and the blessings of Allah be upon you

I hope, praise and glory be to God, that you and all the brothers are in the protection of Allah and may he grant you his blessings, in health and success for what satisfies him. I hope that he would receive all the martyrs who offered their pure souls to glorify his word and set his authority

My generous brother: As you may know, international disbelief is today facing a resounding defeat in Afghanistan due to the jihad and the sacrifices for approximately ten years. It is now attempting to find a way to egress as it also attempts to intensify the situation in Afghanistan with crises like in 1992; and for the parties and the people to fight each other following its egress. In an effort to achieve this outrageous purpose, it attempts to exploit the subservient countries in the area to ignite the civil war fire in the country. Consequently, these subservient individuals shall attempt to maintain their authority on the border areas to find problems to erect an Islamic government. Hence, the central government shall lose its credibility, a fact that would lead to dividing the country, exactly similar to the past. It would also lead to the launch of the civil war's fire. All this would hinder the erection of the Islamic government, the great goal from the jihad and from all these sacrifices. In an effort to achieve the goals of the jihad and the ongoing sacrifices for the last ten years and to protect this oppressed and proud people from other endurances - we therefore request your assistance in the following points. Rest assured that we shall not relinquish the principles of the Shari'a and the erection of the Islamic State:

1. For the proud Afghani people and the Islamic State to be protected from the oppression of the Pakistani government, I urge you to firmly establish the bases in the neighboring country rather than in Afghanistan; because this country is not only one of the biggest supporters of the international infidel, but is its guide and one of its main partners. I will also attempt in the future to find problems for Islam and the Muslims, as time goes by.

2. For the opposition in Afghanistan to appear before the world as united, I ask you not to appoint a future leader in the country.

3. For you and the known officials to attempt not to show your presence in the country now or in the future; although your carrying out the jihad would be ongoing with our mujahidin, exactly similar to what it used to be in the past. We do not have any objection to your presence in Afghanistan, neither now nor at the end, but the need to implement this wisdom in the interest of all.

Part Six: Selected Specific Topics

At last, I ask God the Almighty once more to protect you all and to grant you success for these points. I shall wait to receive a written or taped response; please send it to me from the same route.

Peace, mercy and the blessings of Allah be upon you

3. Afghani Opportunity

> This lengthy message traces back opportunities in Afghanistan, Tunisia, and Algeria. Reasons to blame for failure are security, psychology, and government regimes. Situations in many Middle Eastern, Gulf, and African countries are explored, as well as physical resources and war strategy.
>
> Date: Unknown
>
> From: Unknown
>
> http://www.dni.gov/files/documents/ubl/english/Afghani%20Opportunity.pdf

In the name of the Lord the merciful

Thanks to god the lord of the universe and prayers and peace be upon our prophet Muhammad and his flock, Amen.

...

There was a good opportunity when Afghanistan had Jihad but we were not able to take advantage of it ... we need to talk about it in detail.

The Afghani opportunity was lost in 1399 Islamic calendar which equates to 1979

The last opportunity for Muslims to get free from the west, before the Afghani Jihad, was when there was a military occupation that was obvious to the Arab world because it provides the reasons for the people to move and fight, but awareness was weak of the liberation as from military occupation only.

Part Six: Selected Specific Topics

One of the last opportunities was in Algeria in 1962 and I am sorry to say there were no benefits from 1962 till now, 38 years, so when the opportunity to free Algeria came, it did not happen for four decades.

We recommend to the people to go out and establish operation rooms but we do not depend on people to do that as we are Al Qa'ida and we establish operations rooms to manage the events and the situation is dangerous and whoever is looking at the situation right now cannot imagine what we are doing for the sake of god, and we have the Internet and the like.

The strong word that can be carried out.

A way to a Caliphate or a way to liberate the nation.

We need to ask analysts and the educated in Tunisia and outside of Tunisia to study the Tunis experience in detail and to point to how we can use it and copy it elsewhere.

What happened in the recent past is that a new factor entered the equation and that is the information revolution technology which was not available in the past. Television was controlled by the regimes so it was an added tool for them to use to occupy our minds; and now with the new revolution which pulled the threads from the rulers and this information revolution since the Arab world was able to watch all of the satellite television and people were able to see with their own eyes what's going on instead having to hear about things from others. This resulted in changes at the root level especially after the appearance of the Al-Jazeera news channel and the appearance of the Mujahidin along with it, Al-Jazeera came on the scene in 1996. Then there was the spread of the Internet and it became available to the masses. The volume of information on the Internet is vastly larger than Al-Jazeera in terms of freedom of information.

They have the security forces and the army who think that they are righteous and whoever comes out against them spreads lies. It is important to note that security people are part of the people and when the people's awareness increases, their awareness increases too and that loosens their grip.

There is a space between the ruler and the people. The people's (space) area increases as they become more informed and aware. The ruler's area does not stay constant. As the people's space increases it is at the expense of the ruler's. This forms a tightening around him and he finds no space for himself to stay in power and then they run like Bin Ali did. He asked the army's chief to fire on the demonstrators but the latter refused the orders, so the president asked him to resign but he refused to do that also. This forced Bin Ali to run away. Even the police did not follow his orders to shoot at the demonstrators like he wanted them to. As a result, the shooting and killing of the demonstrators was by Bin Ali's security apparatus and that is why, relatively speaking, the number of victims was somewhat low as compared to revolutions where the people rise against a ruler.

The Tunis situation can be copied throughout the region.

We point to the awareness that a ruler will not scare us as long as we are able to convince his security people, and as a result he will find no option but to step down.

We need to change the idea that security forces are the first enemy of the people…. But this can be changed.

The study of psychology is very dangerous and very important, and they say that the Jews were able to control world forces with these two sciences, sociology and psychology.

So, whoever studies psychology knows that a military person's ability to kill people is limited -especially when he is asked to kill his cousins and that is why, in most countries, when someone is sentenced to be executed by firing squad seven people are used to fire at him with only one having live ammunition; in that way everyone assumes that they were not the one who did the actual killing.

To discuss this issue in detail is very important so that people know the security forces' abilities are limited.

Kuwait is very ready for the quiet fall of the ruling family. What will be helpful is to simplify the issue of monetary corruption in the minds of the people. As we mentioned in the examples about the petroleum and oil, while pointing out that what the Emir spent on each citizen was the result of the Tunisian revolution and his fear that it would be repeated in Kuwait. This money can be cut off and even if it becomes permanent it can always be pulled back if regional things quiet down.

The connection between the situation of the people and the oil petroleum revolution

Whoever asks for comfort becomes comfortable and whoever looks for misery is miserable.

- It is necessary to repeat the discussion about the revolution leadership and we need to write in detail about the revolutions of Egypt and Algeria and the coups and how the situation had settled.

- Revolution leadership. Even though bravery needs live models there are many issues that man needs live models to benefit from. And under these circumstances, a leader needs to take responsibility for the people and needs to take positions that will subject some of them to being killed. This will happen because people are not used to this process and especially since they did not get to this stage gradually nor train to take on responsibilities.

The companions, bless them, they were the Arab atmosphere, the battling atmosphere (TN: verbatim) and one of them took on the responsibility and there is a responsible person that the prophet, lord's prayers upon him, accepted and who took his orders. Therefore the whole weight of the decision will be shared when a decision that may cost military members' lives is taken and, after training, this individual will be ready to be the first ruler (the one who starts the decision making process) and he will be able to take such decisions.

As for these leaders, Abd al-Qadir 'Awdah, bless his soul, and Zandani, and 'Abassi Madani, they did not train and, as a result, opportunities were lost.

The first incident in Egypt was not criticized and the problem was repeated and Zandani returned and repeated it and it was not studied and then Abbasi returned and repeated it.

As for me, I knew the reason because, when I tried it in Afghanistan, because I was not trained I could not …..

From here the problem was repeated and we will not be able to establish an Islamic Nation with this attitude because there is a missing episode.

(TN: Author is not articulate and he puts down thoughts lacking good clarity and flow. Translation is verbatim).

The Algerian government was able to take the position that whoever goes out will get killed and the leader of the army had behind him officials and external powers and they ordered him and he is with a non-believer and his heart is hard and he holds ill feelings towards Muslims.

The Algerian people were ready to do what was necessary but there were problems with the leadership.

It was that the leaders of the revolution were under the control of the regime so they were arrested and they were supposed to be outside; the leader that took over from them fell under heavy pressure that any untrained Muslim would fall under because there were more than one million people who were ready to come out and demonstrate if the decision were made; -even though the army announced that anyone who comes out would be killed. So he imagined the streets being full of blood and he backed down. This was to the advantage of the regime and since then the situation has settled down for 18 years.

For leadership to be under the control of the regime is counterproductive and good administration.

We mention these trials so it may become a complete plan so we won't have failed the revolution.

Part Six: Selected Specific Topics

- The reason for the success of the Tunisian revolution is that it had no obvious leader, and if there were one then the mistake with Abd al-Qadir 'Awdah, bless his soul, would have been repeated. And the mistake of the Algerian leadership is that the senior leadership is the Labor party and if there were no head then there would be no one person to take responsibility for the report. This needs to be explained in detail so revolutions can succeed. (TN: verbatim)

- The scholars in Najd insist that there be no demonstrations and their excuse is that the ruler is a Muslim and based on the best of martyrs, Hamza, it occurred to me that if the despotic ruler achieves the best levels after the prophet and martyrs levels (TN: verbatim)

The best level for martyrdom is the position of being a leader of martyrs (TN: Unknown word) very strong until the individual sacrifices himself and says a word in front of the unjust Sultan what is there to stop three people who say the truth and their numbers could rise.

The basis of every rule is generality and whoever from among you sees something wrong should change it and the advice to the Islamic world is that with anyone that leads and resists they need 10 to go against the despotic leader (TN: verbatim)

And those who resist, what are their excuses when we are talking about a ruler who is a non-believer.

(It is a duty to go against the non-believing ruler; the Tunis situation shows that when the crowd goes into the streets they can remove him).

<u>Sunday 18 Safar 1432</u>

I am following the file and I delegate to the brothers that they need to organize and specify dates in their areas to get the largest numbers and popular leaders. <u>Can you lead?</u>

We talked about psychology and that the military person falls apart after a while and when he leaves the killing arena he starts to hallucinate, and the strongest proof of that appeared in Iraq during the war with Iran. The Iraqis dug foxholes at the border with Iran and when Khomeini sent his people in like sheep the Iraqi military opened fire and killed Iranians before they crossed into Iraq; and when the Iraqis killed so many they started to hallucinate even though they were not killing their own countrymen or their brothers in religionm but rather those who were attacking their country and wanted to occupy them; so killing them was a duty but man cannot continue to kill in large numbers.

We are clarifying this point to make people know that if they go out to protest against a ruler, they will not all be killed because that is not possible.

A reluctant ruler, if he gives in to demands a little, then he is ready to give up more as far as possible just as we note that when America pressures countries it does not accept the first offer like what happened when they asked Sudan to expel me. After that it was the first comment they made in a long line with Sudan and steps that have not ended to this day.

Today, we have a number of rulers who gave in to people's demands: The Jordanian monarch gave in to some demands and Mauritania gave in as well as the Emir of Kuwait -also Yemen and the president of Algeria and the regime in the land of the two mosques (TN: reference to Saudi Arabia) responded by opening jobs.

So people need to understand that the psychology of the rulers is to know that they take rights of people forcibly but they are ready to compromise so there is no right that cannot be discussed and negotiated.

Warning and beware of meeting them in the middle of the road, as it is important to take back all of the rights and notice that if you don't take all of the rights from these rulers then he will take everything back at the nearest opportunity and he will not hesitate to do that.

Part Six: Selected Specific Topics

- We will talk about the Tunisian experiment and how it was executed and the reasons for the uprising so we may know how to bring down the regimes based on points that we will specify with differences from one region to the other.

In most Arab countries they need many months to fill the people so they become like Tunisia but there are adjustments to meet the situation of each individual country.

The common theme of the Jordanian demonstrations was: we, the police, and the army, we're all together for the loaf of bread for life.

Important note: Neutralize the army and the police and that can be achieved in three stages:

1- Absorb their reaction when we go out against the regime.
2- Make them neutral
3- Win their support -meaning we should stop operations against the army and the police in all regions especially Yemen.

This is the second section based on winning their neutrality with awareness between all sides and the Mujahidin and that is with civil treatment.

I think I mentioned that we need to mobilize all of the truthful voices with those who have opinions and those who use the pen and the Internet to simplify issues to the masses.

To raise awareness: The subject of oil, we need to simplify this to the people in various ways.

Trucks

And the rivers in our lands the Nile river and the Tigris andEuphrates, and the Jordan river, and the 'Assi and Litani in addition to the large valley in the Arabian Island (sic). (TN: Seems like Bin Ladin refuses to call it Saudi Arabia, he calls it the Arabian Island).

To calculate the amount of oil that leaves the Gulf and Algeria boggles the mind. The Nile runs all year and the Aswan Dam has the power of 7 billion cubic meters and the length of the Aswan Dam lake is 400 kilometers.

The petroleum that exits our lands exceeds the amount of water running thru the Nile or the Euphrates -not to mention the Arabian valleys during the rains.

- We mention that and the transport vehicles and then we live in humiliation as other nations attack our holy places and we suffer from poverty and unemployment

- Become simple and allow people to talk

- If we do not take advantage of the situation we will remain in the middle ages along with our children and grandchildren.

And whoever tries the comfort is comfortable and whoever tries misery is miserable.

- The revolution needs to be led by men of faith, who understand the world and who do not distinguish between life and death.

And beware of those who clutter their minds and say how they are going to benefit after getting killed by the ruler, because this is dangerous talk and is contrary to what the prophet, god's prayers upon him, said.

He will use a heaven that is as wide as the sky and the earth so he cannot put forward the talk of the people with that of the prophet, GPUH (TN: God's Prayers Upon Him).

This is the biggest guarantee to keep the Muslim ruler from being unjust and tyrannical, by a gentle expert approach that the people need to introduce and as we said, killing moves the people and blood produces more blood so whoever denies the ruler will have his blood spilled leading to the blood of others.

Impose peace over war, and as long as blood was spilled over time,

Arabs say that killing denies killing

My enemy is the enemy of god, even if it be my cousin and relative

And the closest one to me is the one who is loyal to him, far from my eyes and my house and my in law

(TN: Poem, verbatim)

- America is in the last decade of the last century. In reality you saw how the ruler of Tunisia escaped from those who came out to deny him his injustice and despotism.

- Avoid branches to the right or left and avoid anyone that claims that they are saying that to bring awareness to people.

- America, in the last decade of the last century based on study centers did research and planned for the 21 century. This is the American century but with god's largess its horn was broken in the first year of the first decade of the century (TN: eluding to 9/1).

  And in the first year of the second decade, the circle of the Crusader/Zionist necklace that was around he Muslims' neck was broken. This is the century of Muslims with God's permission.

- Review what we wrote before with regard to excuses and we need a charitable and self support and we are witnesses to you and what hit you in calamity. If we have an issue we will search within ourselves and will leave excuses for every mistake / the excuses program by Al-Kilani (the program of the Islamic training) … with euhoric drugs to point sound amplifiers that is directed against the ears of the enemy

We look at sections of the Kilani book and we respect it.

This program makes a person not come up with anything. Al-Arabi said it gave them too much cussing and they escaped by camel (TN: verbatim!).

- You are more knowledgeable in your religious affairs.

- The nation is drowning in a big way with the justification program except for who asked for god's mercy and what he did, did not work with the self supporting program which is what happened with Abd al-Qadir 'Awdah, bless his soul, he did not critique so it was repeated with Al-Zandani and 'Abassi Madani and 'Ali Al-Hajj. Reading about this program is with Al Kilani from page 63 to 75.

- The justification program is met with the advice and the self criticism programs.

- Praise program

- A thing that the lord sends this nation at the beginning of each century.

- There are rulers and scholars and writers who justify the sins of the rulers and his injustice and as a result …..

- The first people to encourage advice and self criticism are the rulers and the loyalists according to 'Umar, bless him, Amra give me my eyes and received from the nobles information or the history of the Caliphates.

- The justification program goes hand in hand with ignorance

- "Support your brother whether he is treated unfairly or even when he treats others unfairly" is a wrong thing to say since the prophet clarified that to support the one who is treated unfairly is to support justice.

- Justification program produces yes-men scholars for the Sultan. They are yes-men and they want other people to be like them.

Part Six: Selected Specific Topics

- The program for justification is born and I am one of its victims. And this is what generates dependence and opportunism.

- The program of meeting at the middle of the road: It is a sickness that spread in the region and many of the scholars want to pass rights so they compliment the despot so he may allow them to pass the rights. This is a dangerous program that need to be avoided

- The importance of using victory to raise the nation.

- The Mujahidin plan. First weaken the west then their agents and with god's largess the west has reached the level of exhaustion and preoccupation and that is an opportunity dismantle the nation

- Paying attention to the matter of Somalia

- Giving a realistic view of the enemy

Part of the war is undoubtedly to know our enemy.

Know your enemy as we are at war. It is necessary that we know our enemy. He was our enemy before Islam and who increased his animosity after Islam. It is the western civilization that occupied our land for 1000 years. The Greeks 400 years, the Romans 600 years. If the opportunity came and we had the chance and we became free with the coming of Islam then our enemies came back with the crusader and then we became free with Salah Al-Din (TN: Saladin), bless his soul, then they came back in the year and occupied most of the Islamic world until the Muslim people rebelled and they were freed from the military colonialism; but because of their ignorance at the time of the great powers' intentions, it was not really freed from political and economic and educational colonialism. sThe nation remained divided and split into sections between agents for the occupation executing their plans; so this is a long history written with blood, corpses, and the injured -so be cautious!! The present reality and the western civilization as they stand with regard to Gaza is what the French foreign minister said - that if we imprison a Jew in France then it is a war crime and yet there are more than 10,000 Palestinians imprisoned by the Jews.

The truth about the west became clear and what they claim with regard to spreading freedom -because the day that Bin Ali escaped (TN: from Tunisia) there were French airplanes that were heading for Tunisia to deliver tear gas bombs so Bin Ali could beat on the Tunisian people. This is western civilization.

To the Nation in general and to Yemen specifically.

Ahmad Shawqi said, he asked for victory without a price then he embarrassed the people of the nation.

We need to talk in the name of formal and mind obligation, no one should spare anything that he can offer to further the advance of the nation and protect it from the domination of the west and their agents even if it is just a word or a Dirham, and before that and after it the prayers against the enemies of the nation and their agents and the prayer that the nation will be victorious and the establishment of god's rule upon the earth.

- The events call for speeding up the issuing of a report to show the key points and clarifications will follow.

The situation in Yemen is moving very fast towards revolution and a regime that lost its legitimacy and the situation of the people needs encouragement and warnings.

1- Convince the military and remind them of god and that the return to justice is better for them in their religion and their world and that the ruler is corrupting their religion and world
2- Continue and the regime will fall
3- The leadership should be safe from the hands of the ruler
4- There needs to be a spare leadership general and in the field.

They need to be able to absorb the anger of the security forces then they can turn them around (TN: co=opt them)

For the matter to succeed, I am leaning towards calling for the situation to be corrected and I draw up the map for the work of the correction work and formal group and they have a right to call for demonstrations; and if they ask us to demonstrate, then they will tell the people that the demonstrators are Al-Qa'ida and that will hurt the people's cause in Yemen. If I enter the minute details like specifying the time then they will look at the letter vey selectively. If we select a date to call for civil disobedience and demonstrations then the activists will think that we want to pick the fruits of their labor without them. So let them pick the fruit because our fruit is bigger.

The fragmentation in the region after the fall of the regime will make the area ripe for a positive response.

We are giving general instructions and we warn against being fragmented in the middle of the of the confrontation as this will be like repeating the mistakes of Abd al-Qadir 'Awdah and Zandani and the Algerian leadership who were under the control of the regime.

It is necessary to sacrifice some so there might be liberation and victory with god's permission.

After the fall of 'Ali Abdallah Salih, in this environment after Tunis, the Saudi regime and the Americans will not respond positively with regard to Yemen, but it will be very weak, so reform in this environment will be strong and we need to increase awareness and America and Saudi Arabia will have a low hand in the matter.

The Salafi program is already known among the brothers as a generation not far from the brothers and they will produce reforms.

Brothers in general politics at this stage will be supported to help bring on the regimes that follow America and then everybody will be on the move, and we will focus on spreading awareness and the correct understanding of Islam.
For sure, the Yemeni constitution is Islamic and it appears that way but the president does not follow it.

- We are in front of a new generation that is affected by education and the new information revolution; this is outside the current pattern by necessity and the Salafi line is the prevailing philosophy in Yemen. There are many Ansar brothers as they've been with us for a long time.

- The difference between Yemen and Algeria is that the Reform Party in Yemen is very strong while the security service is weak. In Algeria the security services are weak (TN: sic, but original must be in error. Should read "strong") and the Islamic parties were suppressed for more than 19 years.

- We need to spread information that we are against break up (separation) and patience is a virtue.

- The reading of the door to the happenings, in the Arabic speech by 'Abdul Baqi, page 250 and what's after it, has a very important observation with regard to this topic: Unity is not only a legitimate request, but it includes everything economic and political. If the south separates it will hurt them along with the north.

Unity is a legitimate duty for all and if unity is not established then no one will be able to resolve the unemployment problem.

Reformers are against separation and Saudi Arabia is supportive of that.

Al-'Umari said, the lord organized a lot of the steps for awakening and failures as desired by man …

Maybe because of the self and its inability and the lack of will, it is necessary to sacrifice ….. page 272-274

- It is important to avoid opening any side fronts that focus on the direct agent of America

- Send speakers to school and college students.

Part Six: Selected Specific Topics

- The most important condition for the living is victory for the living

- It is important to return the idea of Arab unity to the Arab consciousness because it is needed for the present and the future and the need for awakenings

- Some Arab intellectuals think that Arab unity is a necessary and basic program for the Arab civilization; it will free it from backwardness and monopoly and it will lead it to growth and production -page 299 and what follows this page.

- Arab unity will not be realized

   For example, if Kuwait wants to establish a car factory, this will not be possible since the numbers will be so small and the matter of cost is based on the numbers. But at the national level, we can open large factories so the number is important. (TN: the Arabic word used for national refers to "the greater Arab nation")

   Unity is important for Qatar itself because it is only natural that we should be one nation and this situation is for the society. So it is a matter of existing or dissolving by being invaded in the mind and politics and within decades we will stay or perish. ….necessary!…..

- The future of the Arabs will be hostage to what the Arabs can do in the way of practical steps in cooperation and complementing each other, and unity.

- Unity is not a romantic concept but a necessity that needs to be worked on in terms of planting it in the Arab mind … without true unity there will be no progress or growth…..

   Al-Mahdi said: there is a call for the Arab officials, it is not a problem….

It is a life or death situation, existing or dissolving

- General rules an suggestions for the movement:

1-All should forget their differences and should focus efforts on removing the greater enemy.
2-A basic change, and beware of meeting in the middle of the road.
3-Do not accept some off mainline (partial or divisive) changes and we should not allow others to trick us.

And this revolution has many points the most important ones are:

1- The size of the peoples' strength .... New to the people ....

(End of Text)

PART SIX: SELECTED SPECIFIC TOPICS

D. Arab Spring

> ### 1. Undated Message re Egypt Demonstrations
>
> While the Egypt revolution is discussed, this message talks about revolutions with respect to three different topics: the psychology of kings involved in these revolutions, the meaning of revolutions, and the leadership of the revolutions with particular attention to leaders concerns for loss of life. Examples of the Algerian, Iranian, and French revolutions are cited.
>
> Date: Unknown
>
> From: Unknown
>
> http://www.dni.gov/files/documents/ubl/english/Undated%20message%20re%20Egypt%20demonstrations.pdf

(Full Translation)

Praise be to Allah, we praise Him and seek His assistance. We seek His forgiveness and seek refuge in Him from our own evils and shortcomings in our deeds. There is no peace for anyone who strays [from Allah]. I swear that there is no God, but Allah alone. He has no partner, and I attest that Muhammad is His servant and His Messenger.

Today is the twelfth day of the demonstrations in Egypt and the battles and revolutions are having a psychological effect on [the events] . There is benefit from the [continued] experience. On the twelfth day, conditions have shifted, and Mubarak has exposed his [true] situation to the people in that he wishes die on Egyptian land.

As the experts in the fields of social science and psychology perceive, demonstrators will gradually begin to fall off the bandwagon for the revolution.

The youth led the revolution after it was ignited and there have been many that have entered [into their ranks] with just reasons for answering [the problems].

It is appropriate that the individual to intervene from our ranks be a man of Egypt, and this is al-((Zawahiri))

The result in delaying this matter is known.

Disagreeing [on this matter] is bad for all.

Dialogue regarding assaulting the palace has frequently been discussed for the past five days; however, carrying the responsibility for exposing the Muslims to death is a very heavy [burden] that would be heaviest upon the youth if the decision were given to raid the palace. [It would lead to] internal separation within the country.

An example of such is al-Hadrami, in advising on [one who] died. There are hundreds of other reasons that make it difficult to make this decision given the current climate.

Mubarak has stated that he is not concerned with the words of the people and that he cares only about his country, as he stated, "We are concerned with those sects of the population that have become mad, whereas their hearts have turned to stone, or worse." It appears as though Mubarak, [himself] is from this sect [of the population], and there is not a teardrop on his face. Vehicles are running over [demonstrators] and when asked about it, [all he can say] is that he is "Saddened to see Egyptians attacking one another."

We shall talk about the events and their indirect meanings.

We would like to briefly address:

1 - The psychology of the kings

2 - The meaning of the revolutions

3 - The leadership of the revolution and the fear of blood [loss]

PART SIX: SELECTED SPECIFIC TOPICS

For each point, there is more detail.

To [he who] fears blood [loss], this is corrupt ungodliness from within this citizen. The poet al-Nil stated ... (TN: sic; The author likely intended to insert the quote in a later draft.)

As for the nature of the kings, they are the ones often responsible for killing within their family ... his father, his brother, due to their intense desire to become king. For, without your family and the sons of the youth, the matter goes through very [easily].

As for betrayal, this is an attribute carried by many of them. If they are to be shaken from the throne, there is nothing that infuriates them more than this. For, he loses his rule when he is knocked down, and there is nothing of greater importance to him than to carry out revenge on he who shook him from his throne. He views this as the greatest of insults.

An example from eras past is when Ibn al- 'Aas overthrew 'Abd-al Malik ...

'Abd-al-Mali k was not pleased and was not satisfied until he returned three days later and killed [Ibn al-'Aas]. We are now living in similar times, and this was the first betrayal of Islam.

We then remember the revolution decades ago when the Egyptians expelled the tyrant military [commander], from which there was the opportunity to free Egypt. If it weren't for Shaykh 'Abd-al Qadir 'Awdah, Allah have mercy on him, who believed the lying military [commander] who then betrayed him, arrested him, and hanged him.

The Algerian revolution, due to the corrupt ungodliness that resulted in lost efforts for the revolutionaries.

More than two decades ago, the million-strong demonstration went out [to the streets] of Sana, where they then lost their opportunity [for revolution] when dialogue was opened between the President and the head of the opposition, Shaykh 'Abdallah Bin Husayn al-((Ahmar)) and Shaykh 'Abd-al-Maj id al-((Zandani)), when they believed [the President] and left the people out to dry. It wasn't long before matters returned to their original state regarding many of the items they agreed upon.

With regard to the corrupt ungodliness, hundreds die daily in Egypt due to the injustice and tyranny of the regime. [They die] from disease, due to water pollution from the factories of the large businessmen aligned with the authorities. From which, 70,000 die annually based on statistics. [In addition], tens of thousands [die annually] due to environmental pollution.

Thus, the regime destroys the souls of the people from the palace, just as an unarmed man is killed by gunfire. He does as he wishes with the blood of the Muslims in Egypt.

What will advance the country from the water crisis[?]

Freedom will be achieved only at a high cost. The door will become red from the knocking of bloodstained hands [to achieve] freedom.

Attention must be paid to the corrupt ungodliness. I understand completely that exposing the children of the Ummah to battle/death is extremely difficult; however, there is no other means to rescue them ... (TN: sic; The author likely intended to insert a verse from the Qur'an in a later draft.)

One must review contemporary revolutions by looking at the reasons these revolutions faltered and the success in [preventing] such. This faltering is due to the leaders [of the revolutions] fearing blood loss and believing that it would be possible to expel the tyranny from their countries with dialogue.

Likewise, the Iranian revolution succeeded because its leadership insisted on freeing the country of the regime completely. Even after they expelled the Shah, leaving matters to the Shahbur, where the people were calling for the return of the Shah, they did not stop the revolution. When this continued, despite shedding the regime of their blood supply, [they were insistent] on removing the entire regime.

Part Six: Selected Specific Topics

The French revolution, which continued until the ruling party (TN: Begin underline) was uprooted. (TN: end underline)

It is not our intent to express our position regarding "this or that" revolution, but rather, we are talking about the reasons for success or failure by the opposition in today's revolutions, and how this rare historic opportunity should not be wasted. We warn against the reliance upon the corrupt ungodliness, for bleeding out [the enemy] does not separate their vital [organs].

To my Muslim Brothers in the Islamic world, after the success in Tunisia and attempts to expel the rest of the tyrants, [I tell you] that this is the right of the Muslims and a religious duty.

(TN: Message is undated and unsigned.)

E. Revolution

> **1. Suggestion to End the Yemen Revolution**
>
> This letter calls for the end of the Yemen Revolution. Suggestions are proposed to accomplish this: movements to support local Muslims, a transitional government, and a payment for individuals who stop supporting the 'tyrant.'
>
> Date: Unknown
>
> From: Unknown
>
> http://www.dni.gov/files/documents/ubl/english/Suggestion%20to%20End%20 the%20Yemen%20Revolution.pdf

Translation Starts:

(Page 1 of 2)

And while searching for an exit for the people, I offer a suggestion to end the longest of the ongoing revolutions, the Yemen revolution, for the sake of developing and enriching it to be used as an example that could be modified to suit the situation in every country. This would include the details of its realities.

First of all, I should note that solving the crisis requires popular movements to support the Muslims there. The official initiatives have included unjust items, and those who proposed them stated that they are final and not open for negotiations. This suggests that they were initiatives to save the ruler and to circumvent the revolution, so that the neighbors of Yemen would not be influenced by the success of its revolution. (TN: begin underline) Otherwise, the wise people would know that he is not qualified for negotiation, after he has presented many cheating maneuvers and dishonored the promises and lost the people's trust. The documents have proven his collaboration with the Americans to kill his people, as what took place in Ma'rib and Shabwah, then falsifying the facts. (TN: end underline)

Returning to the initiative, I say: That the most important factor giving the ruler of Sanaa his strength in the last instances were the masses that he is producing on Friday and the military organizations that have not joined the revolution yet.

As for the masses that he is producing, it is a phenomena that needs a close look, to know the reasons behind their coming out to support a man who has betrayed the faith and the nation, having inflicted all kinds of harm.

This violates the normal situation of a human in dealing with those who harms him. But those who are well informed, about the details of the Yemeni situation under the current regime for the last quarter of a century, realize a bitter fact... A lot of those masses are in a situation similar to the captives of a ruler where the people have not taken the stand to impeach him, when his reign has fallen legally. He was supposed to be impeached, because he committed an act incompatible with Islamic practice, unanimously agreed upon as such by Muslim scholars, when he was red-handed in supporting the infidels and supplying their military destroyers to kill the disadvantaged Muslims in Iraq. That was more than a decade ago. That means that approximately one third of his reign passed after it became evident to all, his committing of acts incompatible with Islamic rules. Not being condemned for that great crime has lead him to continue his path of violating the Islamic Shari'ah and subjecting the people and destroying the country. This led the masses to reach a degree of tyranny, poverty, and ignorance which cannot be described. Then he resorted to relying on their poverty to buy their support. He exploited the sentiment, the feeling of the father for his children, and the supporter for those whom he supports.

The innocent children have the right, and it is the duty of those sons of this nation who could supply their demands. The parents have the right to relieve their children's poverty and ignorance that were imposed on them by the tyrant. All Muslims in Yemen have the right to save their blood, and relieve themselves from the crisis that they are suffering from. Our search, therefore, to save all, would incorporate the role of all the merchants of the Islamic World, particularly the merchants of Yemen and the Gulf states, and create committees as those which the president is tying his supporters with. But this is only to untie.

(Page 2 of 2)

the shackles, rather than tightening them. This is accomplished by pledging to give weekly salaries, distributed on Fridays, for whoever quits going to the arenas of the tyrant in his governorate. This is to continue until a new government is established to fulfill their requirements. The cost of these tasks is attainable and easy to any Gulf merchant. (TN: begin highlight) In addition, the merchants should cooperate with the charitable organizations. The scholars and advocates should concentrate their efforts in the remote areas, where ignorance prevails. This is to salvage the masses from ignorance by activating to the preaching attempts in their surroundings. Ignorance is the line of life for the tyrant rulers where they find their solders. (TN: end highlight)

As for the military organizations: One of the ways to deal with them is to form a transitional government that will pledge to the members of those organizations that it secures for them their safety, if they decide to move to its camp, with their employment status and salaries. This is safer to their religion and daily life. He who repents, God will forgive him, and may God forgive what happened before. The salaries for the transitional government are to be provided by a qualified entity, that should pledge its support to give security for those who would join this government, so that there is a source to supply their salaries.

2. Letter about Revolutions

It is important that brothers recognize advancement of opinion and to address changing frontiers as a "religious duty and an intellectual necessity."

Date: Unknown

From: Unknown

http://www.dni.gov/files/documents/ubl/english/Letter%20about%20revolutions.pdf

(Fully Translated)

Page 1

And before concluding, I would like to remind my sincere brothers, theologians of the religion, and the world, that the establishment of a council to work on the advancement of opinion and advice to the Muslim people throughout this phase is a religious duty and an intellectual necessity. It is of the greatest duties during this phase. This is one of the most significant frontiers. Some of the Islamic intellectuals in the region, specifically in the Gulf, are entrusted by the wide-spread masses of Muslims. For it is the duty of these individuals to ensure that they get out and begin establishing a council with what they have been enabled by the trust of the believers throughout the entire Islamic world. This council must be in a location that provides freedom of speech about the Ummah. It must be supported by a center for research and studies, such that it may respond with astonishing speed to [worldly] events and those requests that require an immediate response. (The ideal and the ideal with keenness about purpose isn't managed from proficiency.)

Regarding the mechanism [for such a council], each member of the society in a region must take into account the false information used to benefit the success of a revolution. Thus, there must be a precise review [of the situation]. Delay gives way to the opportunity for failure and rushing simply compounds burdens and endangers the revolution. Success of the revolutions in atmospheres such as these require that [advice] is provided at the appropriate time, after the Almighty Allah has [allowed the process] to begin. [It also requires] that men of superior faith lead them, [even] until death, and that they remain constant on advancing the situation step by step. [We must be wary] of delays [in the revolutions] for abstention will creep in and the difficult [nature of the work] will overcome those who have given their vows for their faith and those who have proved their cause with their blood. As the saying goes:

"I swear that I will not die except that I am free. / I have found that death has a bitter taste / I fear that I may be humiliated or tempted / For religion of Islam will not flee."

(Methods to prevent penetrations)

Page 2

(TN: This page repeats the above message verbatim with the addition of the following line at the bottom of the page:_

(The ideal and the ideal with keenness about purpose isn't managed from proficiency.)

PART SIX: SELECTED SPECIFIC TOPICS

> ### 3. Message for Islamic Ummah in General
>
> This document primarily discusses revolutions and the achievement of liberation. The success of revolutions is discussed, as well as the goals that one should focus on. Revolutions in Tunisia, Egypt and Yemen are briefly mentioned.
>
> Date: Unknown
>
> From: Unknown
>
> http://www.dni.gov/files/documents/ubl/english/Message%20for%20Islamic%20Ummah%20in%20general.pdf

(TN: Religious introduction)

To the Islamic Ummah in general, Peace be upon you with the mercy and blessings of Allah...

[To] my Muslim Ummah:... The people of the world, who were previously held prisoner, have succeeded in escaping from the slavery of their tyrant rulers. In recent history, the people of Eastern Europe, which lived a long contract under the slavery of the global communist regime, [have done so]. When the Soviet Union was established, they staggered under the Hindu Kush, appearing weak to the rest of the world. This was until the European people began to feel this weakness and seized their historic opportunity, starting in a single country, the revolution against the corrupt communist factions. This was duplicated by the brothers in neighboring countries, where revolution spread until it reached Eastern Europe and the slavery in which they were living under the global communist wave. Today, we are living a reality similar to this. Our nations have been living for centuries under unsatisfactory religious, social, cultural, and economic conditions. This was, of course, due to Western dominance. For centuries the awareness and development of the Ummah's people went mute. It has come to a point in which, by God, Western [military] bases, commanded by America, have advanced throughout Afghanistan itself. Just as [those oppressed] under the Hindu Kush began to stagger [out of the slavery] which had been perceived as a weakness to the world, where they lost their prestige, [we too] have the rare historic opportunity to escape from this accumulation of tyrannical rule, where [we] are held prisoner. [We have] to take charge of the reins and free ourselves from the Western dominance. This opportunity was illuminated with the revolution in Tunisia, where the Ummah had been forgotten. The Muslim sentiment was ignited as well in Egypt, where the Ahl al-Kinanah (TN: Egyptians) took the coal [that had been ignited] from their neighbors to spread the revolution to oust those not working [for the Ummah] in their homeland. With the Muslim revolution in Egypt, this shall ignite the sentiments felt by [the rest of] the Islamic Arab World.

[To] my Muslim Ummah: The success in the Tunisian revolution in toppling the tyranny put an end to the thought that there could not be a change in the ruling party, aside from one of two means: Either a military coup or by the presence of <u>foreign</u> forces. The Ummah assured that, once the people entered the equation with such a force, [the revolution] grew and [began to] creep into the shuddering hearts [of the people], where they stood witness to those that viewed it as their legitimate duty to <u>oust those not working [for the Ummah]</u> and to restore what was stolen from them of their Brothers' rights… in the land of Egypt… Thus, it is upon the Muslim population within Egypt and elsewhere to join together and stand shoulder to shoulder in protection of this revolution and the fruits thereof. Each Muslim must exert him/herself to their full extent.

Among the primary reasons for the success of the revolutions is learning from previous experiences, particularly the history of revolutions. I stress this, not directly specific to studying the reasons for the success of these revolutions, but rather, to show the reasons for success, or the effect of reviewing [the past] and not wasting <u>this</u> rare historic opportunity. Among those <u>revolutions</u> which must be reviewed is a study of the escaped [opportunity] for a revolution when the Muslims in Egypt expelled the military [commander related to the] 'Abd-al-Mun'im Riyad square [incident]. This was a great opportunity to expel the regime which existed until today. However, the Shaykh 'Abd- al-Qadir 'Awdah, Allah have mercy on him, disgraced the blood of the Muslims and believed the lying military [commander] and persuaded the people to return and obey [the government's] orders. If the people were to have remained, rather than disperse... [if they were to have] betrayed the Shaykh, [they could have realized their revolution]. However, [the Shaykh] did them in and the thousands of innocent followers. We ask that Allah have mercy on all of them.

Among them: The Muslims' revolution in Algeria main... (TN: The author appears to leave space to edit in future drafts.) for the efforts of the revolution were lost due to the corrupt godliness.

Among them: The million-strong demonstration in Sanaa, for this opportunity was lost as well with the dialogue between the President and the head of the opposition, Shaykh 'Abdallah Bin Husayn al-Ahmar (TN: Deceased leader of the Yemeni Islah Party) and Shaykh 'Abd-al-Majid al-Zindani (TN: Former Head of the Yemeni Islah Party's Shura Council), for, at the expense of the people, they believed him. Then, it wasn't long before they realized that he went back on his previous pledges [for change] on many of the issues in which they agreed upon.

Among them: The French revolution, which continued until the ruling party was uprooted.

Among them: The Iranian revolution, whose leaders insisted on freeing the country of the regime completely. Even after they expelled the Shah, leaving matters to the Shahbur, where the people were calling for the return of the Shah, they did not stop the revolution. When this continued, despite shedding the regime of their blood supply, [they were insistent] on removing the entire regime.

The main areas of concern for those preparing to achieve liberation are as follows:

First: The psychology of the King, his nature. It must be understood that the greatest evil is that in which a man can kill from within his family. The man kills his father or his brother in viewing the severity in nature of the King. This is what explains their regard for the blood of their people's children, which their King is threatening.

Likewise, the betrayal characteristics that the majority of them (TN: ruling parties) display, which unsettles those whom they govern. [This betrayal is in the form of the ruling party's inability in] being balanced in their rule (TN: abnormal spacing). The greatest concern of theirs being revenge on those who threaten their rule. They view this as an insult above all other insults. Likewise, many eras ago, when Ibn al-'As (TN: literally, 'the disobedient people) expelled 'Abd-al-Malik… 'Abd-al-Malik did not welcome [the change] and was not satisfied until he returned three days later and killed him. This is during the time of successors and this was the first betrayal in Islam.

Second: The importance of a steadfast position in the leadership and its boldness and seriousness in fearing blood[shed]. If, for instance, in this citizen there lies corrupt godliness, for it is as the poet al-Nil stated: "They support the war of peace, as long as blood is shed in [what they perceive as] the time for bloodshed."

The Arabs say that killing prevents death. For in Egypt, one dies due to [his] corruption [within] the regime, as seventy thousand die annually due to the oppression [of the regime]. Based on statistics of illnesses, [citizens die] due to pollution of the water [supplies] as a result of the factories of the large businessmen aligned with the authorities, from which, hundreds die of daily. [Likewise}, tens of thousands [die annually] due to pollution of the environment.

Thus, from the palace, the regime destroys the souls of the people, just as though an unarmed man is killed by gunfire. He does as he wishes with the blood of the Muslims in Egypt. One must be cautious of the corrupt godliness and understand that freedom will not be achieved without great sacrifice. Bleeding out [the enemy] does not separate [the link of] their vital [organs]. I understand completely that exposing the Children of the Ummah to battle/death is extremely difficult, however, there is no other means to rescue them. There is no other way to rescue them. The Almighty [Allah] stated [...kill them...] For there is no one that may go into battle without being exposed to death.

> **4. Undated Statement**
> This statement discusses revolutions in general, with specific references to the Egyptian uprising. The letter touches on the meanings of the Arab revolutions and consequences for the muslim people.
>
> Date: Unknown
>
> From: Unknown
>
> http://www.dni.gov/files/documents/ubl/english/Undated%20statement.pdf

Thanks be to God, peace and prayers be upon the Prophet, and his family and disciples:

The sons of Islam made glorious days,
And Arab rulers lost their thrones

As the face of the Umma (TN: Islamic nation) approaches the victory whose good omens have appeared from the east, suddenly the dawn of the revolution shines from the west. The revolution started in Tunisia. The Umma was pleased with it and the faces of the people shone through. The throats of the rulers choked. With the fall of the tyrant came the fall of fear and despair and reluctance. The meaning of boldness and dignity and courage stood up. The winds of freedom and change fell. Strength revolted in "Midan al-Tahrir" (TN: Liberation Square.)

The revolution was not for food or clothing but rather a revolution of might and rejection that illuminated the capital city of the Nile from top to bottom. The people of quiver Egypt appeared in glory and their souls longed for the era of their ancestors. They began to have strong faith in course through their veins. They understood the situation around them.

They saw the head of global blasphemy bobble in the hands of their brothers, no longer able to abort their revolution as had happened with an Arab revolution (TN: the Ahmed 'Urabi's Revolution)in the past. They seized the opportunity and quoted the boldness of Muhammad (('Ata))(TN: the Amir of the 9/11 American Airlines Flight 11, attackers). They signed the treaty. Enthusiasm Concern is mounting, hard work helps, and the revolution is budding. To those free people I say:

Time stood for you as Tariq did, a hitting stop
Despair is behind and hope is ahead,
You answer with blood, a spot of which is taken
And die the lion without his den,
He who gives his noble soul to his Lord
Paying for their wrong, how can he be blamed?

Most of the rulers did not realize the extent of the gap in the consciousness between them and the rising generation. They did not realize the meaning of faith, humanity, might, and freedom. They still think with the mentality of the Abbi-Jahl, (TN: in the era of ignorance), that the sweetness of the faith rooted in the soul of Bilal and Al Yasir, may God be pleased with them, was greater than the bitterness of their torture.

If the rulers realized that, they would know that the free faithful do not endure life except by their faith and freedom. In this they find torture sweet and delight in difficult. They are the ones that change the face of the earth. Freedom is only achieved at a great price. Blood is an inseparable part of its components. I do not truly know the difficulty the sons of the nation are exposed to killing but there is no way to save them and no other way except this way. Here I mention my Muslim brothers with these verses from the Nile poet:

I advised, and we are in different lands,
But between us there is kinship and understanding (TN: we share same language),
We became close if the nations are distant,
The law of our God is just and true,
The kingdom is not build up like the victims,
The rights are not there and that is not right,
In the victims there are generations of life,
And in prisoners there is ransom and release,
For red freedom there is a door,
For every bloodstained hand that knocks,

So, youth of the Umma, it is up to you to complain of the matters that befall it. Believe in God and pray to him for hope, since with your revolution you raised our heads up to God and your heads. With your revolution our hopes are achieved, God willing. God achieved your hopes. You have already seized the reins of the initiative; cling to the reins of control. It is up to you watch and wait.

There is no fairness in revolution. There was fierce fighting in the day following your revolution in Egypt, fateful for the nation as a whole. The battle was decisive between the global blasphemy and the Islamic nation. This is a rare historic opportunity for liberation from subordination that the nation has awaited for centuries. Assign your skilled choice, unify your ranks. Such conditions are endurable, except for the strongest, most faithful men. They are ready to die. They stay faithful to their promise and faith, and they prove their sincerity with their blood. They continue onward and do not flee difficulty. The tongue of their experience says:

I have sworn not to die except free,
Even If I find the taste of death bitter,
I fear that I will delight or be tempted,
As my faith is Islam, I will not forsake it.

(TN: End of translation)

PART SIX: SELECTED SPECIFIC TOPICS

> **5. Undated Statement 2**
>
> The proper actions that leaders of revolutions must take are revealed alongside a number of other measures necessary for the success of a revolution.
>
> Date: Unknown
>
> From: Unknown
>
> http://www.dni.gov/files/documents/ubl/english/Undated%20statement%202.pdf

(Fully Translated)

Most of the rulers did not realize the size of the gap between them and the rising generation. They did not feel the meaning of faith, humanity, dignity, and freedom that mixed with the blood of that generation. So they came from ignorance, because they kept thinking with the mentality of Abu Jahl who thought that his torture of Bilal, Allah be pleased with him, could erase the sweetness of the faith. The only thing he got back from Bilal was him saying "One, One". So if the rulers today know that their attempts are like his attempts, they will know that that they are trying for the impossible, as he who tastes faith and freedom will settle for nothing other than a dignified life.

- (Concentrating the arrows on toppling the regime) as it affirms the evil, sheds the pure blood, and loses the historical opportunity.

- When revolutions erupt, they must be supported, or else the opportunity will pass and waiting will be to the next generation. Civilians cool down quickly. An example of this is Palestine: They stopped them and they did not stand up after this, despite presence of the same motives that led them to revolt in the beginning.

- Closing the ranks and rejecting the dispute.

- Forming a Council of Trustees before conducting any revolution, and avoiding inflation of one demand at the expense of the other demands. All the demands will be repeatedly presented to the people, so that the people are prepared for continuation, even after the departure of the president. One of these demands will be that the secretaries of the Council of Trustees will pick up the administration of the country during the transitional period and not the military.

- Warning the leadership that they must change, even after the triumph of the revolution, as these leaderships constitute a risk for them since their psychological make up is susceptible to pressure.

- We ask the leadership that cannot go out in the demonstrations to stay out of the scene and leave the people and their business alone; what happened in Morocco was a terrible mistake.

- [Members of the] leadership who are in their 60s and 70s are ruined because of the repression in that stage; we want young leadership [members who are] in their 40s.

- The revolutions are coming; well-appointed of the leadership.

- Hope

- Positive interpretation of events, as much as possible.

- The fatigue that exhausted the tyrants.

- Tunisia is the pioneer, which is a blessing from Allah. He gives [His blessing] to who he wants, and at the speed of lightening, the knights of Egypt took the torch from free Tunisia to Al-Tahrir Square, where it illuminated the cities of the Nile from one end to the other.

- Those who are kind stay kind to the people who are kind.

- Of the highest duties, after faith, is mobilizing efforts to enlighten the sons of the nation, support their advance, and of the best that was written about this (concepts should be correct) and (our current reality) by Shaykh Muhammad Qutb.

Part Six: Selected Specific Topics

F. United States

1. Letter to the American People

Usama bin Laden addresses the American people, letting them know how detrimental the war in Afghanistan is to America, its economy, and its soldiers. He allocates blame to Bush and Obama, as well as to other high-ranking officials. The Mujahidin will not stop until the United States leaves.

Date: Unknown

From: Usama bin Laden

http://www.dni.gov/files/documents/ubl/english/Letter%20to%20the%20American%20people.pdf

(Fully Translated)

Page 1

In the name of Allah, the Compassionate, the Merciful.

From Usama Bin Muhammad Bin Ladin to the American people,

I speak to you about the subject of the ongoing war between you and us. Even though the consensus of your wise thinkers and others is that your time (TN: of defeat) will come, compassion for the women and children who are being unjustly killed, wounded, and displaced in Iraq, Afghanistan, and Pakistan motivates me to speak to you.

First of all, I would like to say that your war with us is the longest war in your history and the most expensive for you financially. As for us, we see it as being only halfway finished. If you were to ask your wise thinkers, they would tell you that there is no way to win it because the indications are against it. How will you win a war whose leaders are pessimistic and whose soldiers are committing suicide? If fear enters the hearts of men, winning the war becomes impossible. How will you win a war whose cost is like a hurricane blowing violently at your economy and weakening your dollar?

The Bush administration got you into these wars on the premise that they were vital to your security. He promised that it would be a quick war, won within six days or six weeks; however, six years have passed, and they are still promising you victory and not achieving it. Then Obama came and delayed the withdrawal that he had promised you by 16 more months. He promised you victory in Afghanistan and set a date for withdrawal from there. Six months later, Petraeus came to you once again with the number six, requesting that the withdrawal be delayed six months beyond the date that had been set. All the while you continue to bleed in Iraq and Afghanistan. You are wading into a war with no end in sight on the horizon and which has no connection to your security, which was confirmed by the operation of 'Umar al-Faruq (Var.: Umar Farouk), which was not launched from the battlefield and could have been launched from any place in the world.

As for us, jihad against the tyrants and the aggressors is a form of great worship in our religion. It is more precious to us than our fathers and sons. Thus, our jihad against you is worship,

Page 2

and your killing us is a testimony. Thanks to God, Almighty, we have been waging jihad for 30 years, against the Russians and then against you. Not a single one of our men has committed suicide, whereas every 30 days 30 of your men commit suicide.
Continue the war if you will.

(TN: Two lines of poetry that say the Mujahidin will not stop fighting until the United States leaves their land.)

Peace be upon those who follow right guidance.

We are defending our right. Jihad against the aggressors is a form of great worship in our religion, and killing us means a high status with our Lord. Thanks to God, we have been waging jihad for 30 years, against the Russians and then against you. Not a single one of our men has committed suicide, whereas every 30 days 30 of your men commit suicide. Continue the war if you will. Justice is the strongest army, and security is the best way of life, but it slipped out of your grasp <u>the day</u> you made the Jews victorious in occupying our land and killing our brothers in Palestine. The path to security is for you to lift <u>your oppression from us</u>.

> ## 2. Despotism of Big Money
>
> This brief letter is addressed to the American people; the author states that had the United States not gone into Afghanistan and had it been more prudent in its statements, money and blood would not have been wasted.
>
> Date: Unknown
>
> From: Unknown
>
> http://www.dni.gov/files/documents/ubl/english/Despotism%20of%20Big%20Money.pdf

(Full translation of video)

Praise be to God who has demanded justice and benevolence and forbade tyranny and aggression.

Moreover,
O American people, peace be with those of you who follow the right guidance. The subject of my talk is the despotism of Big Money and its role in the current wars between us.

I begin by reminding you that if you had reflected on a little of what has been said, you would have been able to avoid wasting much blood and money.

A good example is what one of your former presidents previously warned you about with the despotism of the Big Money and about a day when you would become its laborers.

PART SIX: SELECTED SPECIFIC TOPICS

G. Europe

1. German Economy

This letter is a briefing on the state of the German Economy. The status of investments, boycotts, and trade relationships is explored. Damage to the Germany economy by way of boycotting is given attention.

Date: Unknown

From: Unknown

http://www.dni.gov/files/documents/ubl/english/The%20German%20Economy.pdf

(Begin Text of Translation):

The German Economy

- Germany is considered the largest exporter in the world.

- In 2008, Germany exported goods valued at 955 Billion E uros (Comment: At a 1 Jan 2008 exchange rate of 1 Euro to U.S. $1.5, 955 Euros was equaled approximately U.S $1385.)

- 40% of its economy and one third 1/3 rd of its Employment are connected to the export.

- The vehicle's division is considered the most important and the biggest part exports where it is 17% of 2008 exports.

- Germany is considered the economic engine of Europe.

Germany has suffered from the economic crises where its sales abroad have regressed, and the economy experts sa y it will regress this year at a percentage of 15%.

- The hope the Arabic market will compensate the fall of sales in some important markets, therefore, they are concentrating on some of the countries that are intending on investing huge amounts, such as

- Algeria decided to invest 150 Billion Dollars until 2014

- Saudi Arabia intends to invest 100 Billion Dollars

- And also Libya.

- And they are craving for Iraq and particularly the north, such the city of Arbil. In his last visit to Iraq, the former economic minister said, the security condition has improved in all Iraq, and not in the north only, and in this he wanted to encourage the German investor.

- Qatar for example, it imports German products more than Morocco despite its population is only equal to 5% of the popul ation of Morocco.

- Boycotting the German automobile means harm to the Automotive sector first and with it other companies will be hurt also, such as BASF the largest Chemical company in the world , and also the steel industry, both are important sectors in Germany. Boycotting the German automotive will lead to the loss of jobs, and shortage in tax income to the government and other damages, and this the in tention of the rosary in the tape, companies connected to others and their destiny at the end of the journey is one, called hope. (Dominoeffekt) Domino effect.

- In case there was a call for boycotting the German merchandise, it better to have a substitute to the German technology, and the substitute may be the Japanese or the South Korean.

First: Japan has a technology to cover the needs of the people, who want to dispense with the German goods,

Second: Japan is going through a destructive and fierce crises, this may be a clear message to Japan if this was suitable, this is a suggestion, and I do not know anything about Japan.

And it is almost the same situation in regard to South Korea, but it is distinguished by being far from participation in the Animosity against the Muslims, and it pulled its troops from Afghanistan, and other than that.

Advice: avoid talking about the Jews and Palestine when talking to the Germans. This subject is very sensitive to in Germany, and it will bring negative results to our goal. I think if we were able to tell the people that we are with Germany, we only mean to get them out of Afghanistan; the people will understand our position, God willing.

- Perhaps the double standard will serve you in encouraging the Muslims.

After the publishing of the caricatures insulting Prophet Muhammad in Denmark, the German Minister of the Interior called asked all the European Newspapers to publish the caricatures, and it has a weight since it was not said by a minister of some country, but the Interior Minister of a country that has the largest publishing house in Europe (Axel☐Springer Verlag) , and what is important to mention is, the same minister promised reporters from Der Spiegel a day before the first Summit of Islam that if any one described him in this Summit as a Kafir (Infidel), he will face problems.

Mentioning this will serve us in spreading fear among the Media personalities believing publishing them, means targeting them. If the Media is afraid, the barrier between the truth and the people is broken. Fearing for their lives, the media will publish what encourages the people to vote for who wants to pull the tro ops, and only God knows.

(End Text of Translation):

> ## 2. Report on External Operations
>
> In this letter, the author wants brothers to delegate operations to other affiliate organizations in order to help with the work "load." There were operations carried out in Britain, Denmark, and Russia. Also, it was said that there must be new and innovative ways to execute operations; also, security needs to be tightened.
>
> Date: Unknown
>
> From: Unknown
>
> http://www.dni.gov/files/documents/ubl/english/Report%20on%20External%20Operations.pdf

(TN: Qu'ranic verses)

Report on the external operations

First of all, any operation must have plans and goals that need to be achieved before it begins, and you can measure the successes of any job if it has achieved its goal. Therefore, we defined to ourselves three goals, since the brother had assigned us to this mission, which are as follows:

1- Carry out an operation before the end of the year in which we started the work.
2- Establish structure and basics for the work; we will explain what that means later.
3- Transfer the idea and its plan to another trusted group, who will carry some of the load for us, and we will help them with whatever we can help, because the goal is to attack the enemies in their territory, or attack their interests, because these infidels are concentrating on whoever has relationship with us, more than any other groups that never pursued this road before.

Part Six: Selected Specific Topics

That was our vision for the work, but have we achieved our goals? I will say the following:

1- First goal: I confess that we have not succeeded in meeting the first goal, due to many reasons. First of them was bad luck and God wasn't on our side; we had sent a number of the brothers to Britain and Russia and Europe to be prepared and ready to work before the end of the year, some of them were with us before, but they had left and came back to us and travelled again and they are Russia (exploding the gas line or the American Embassy), Britain (a number of targets, depending on what our brothers will determine what will be suitable (TN: of targets) that can fit what materials are available. According to our knowledge, the brothers have not faced any security problems except what the news had broadcast a few days before the apprehension of a few British individuals, and we are not sure if they belong to us or not, and these two factors were the factors that we were depending on, after God, to help reach our goal, but the situation didn't go as well as we wish.

But the other brothers are new and we had rushed to send them very quickly, before their security was exposed or their residency documents expired, and we had trained them as much as we could in a short period of time (like, for example, the brother who came to us and as soon as he came the Mas'ud battle started, and had stayed two months, he spent one month on the road and waiting and had siege with us for two when we gave him an academic explosive course and travelled back before his residency expired, and we have not heard from him since he left, because it is very hard to communicate with him from our end and the strong wiretapping from his side. We hope that we hear from him very soon.

2- Second goal: We are not asking for a convenient atmosphere to work in to reach our goal, but we think that to do good and be creative at work depends on chance and on what we can do and what is available to us, but God knows that we have not done our best to create the correct atmosphere of work to reach our goal. Upon that, we have discovered that to have successful work, you have to know the basics of the work:

A-Personnel: They must be prepared spiritually, militarily, and psychologically to carry out this work.

B-Communications: We have to have secured methods of communications with these people and a safe way for them to travel back and forth, and to follow up on their news and the world news

C-Documents: We have a large number of brothers who had spent a long time with us and they are ready to work anywhere. In addition, we have brothers who have some security issues but the big problem are the legal documents; therefore, we have to resolve this problem because the new brothers whom we have sent very quickly, we can't guarantee their patience and their firmness in handling any enemy propaganda and tribulations.

D-Execution: One of the big problems that we are facing, even if we have all that it required to reach our goal, is when the brother is unable to carry out the operation because of the lack of the required tools (materials, weapons); therefore, we have to think of a new way to obtain these tools or invent new ways of execution.

If we would like to implement what we have discussed above, first thing we have to face is establishing a complete organization, which we cannot to because the lack of finance and required cadres, and I think our job is executive work which has to belong to us. That is why we have thought to open an office for ourselves in Iran, to receive whoever comes to join us or someone traveling, but we have backed off this idea because it will be very expensive.

If we go over these points one by one, we will say the following:

A-The people who had spent a long time with us in the jihad battlefield, they are very well trained and prepared, but the new personnel whom we quickly deploy, we are trying to prepare them according to the available time and condition, and if there is another group that is willing to stay for 6 months, then it will be possible to give them more courses or to enter Afghanistan for more training. In the past we have bought some artillery pieces and electronics parts, so if someone comes to us we can train him very quickly, but in regards to legitimate and psychology matters, it is very easy for us more than the Sheikhs' visits.

B-Communications: Thank God that we had a secure method to communicate with our brothers whom we sent and we are still working to develop these methods. We are trying to be diversified in the method of communications and not use just one method, as well as use a coding program and decrease the amount of communications; trying not to send any messages from Pakistan as often as we can.

Transportation is a big problem and for that reason we are trying to open several offices in different places, for example, in the near future we will send brothers to Somalia to run the business from Somalia and we have been trying to open another office in Turkey, but we unable to find the suitable brother for this office, and we had sent a brother to Iraq but he has not arrived yet.

Follow up on the news: We used to have an office to watch the news but it got bombed. Since then, we stopped watching the news; therefore, we are satisfied with listening to the radio and with what we receive from the media, in addition to some programs that belong to our work that were prepared by some friend from Pakistan. But watching TV news channels to know new ideas and enemy's tactics and his tricks, also to follow up on the international situation and discover the weak points, I think it is very important to our work; but it is very dangerous. That is why we live tribal lives; their news and their worries are not world news, where our work is. But we spend our time in reading intelligence files that have been prepared on the forum's site.

C-Documentation: we have renewed the machines and added some new personnel.

D-Execution: we have tried to solve this issue with several ways:

1- Manufacturing the materials from raw/primary materials, such as chlorate from salt
2- Transport the materials overseas by smuggling, after changing their shapes and camouflaging them.
3- To make the brothers use new methods like using house knifes, Gas or Gasoline or diesel tanks, and other means, such as airplanes, trains, cars as killing tools.

4- Try to benefit from the brothers who were previously convicted in trying to obtain weapons.
3- Instigating other groups and cooperating with them in this field is a good idea, because it is better for us that someone will share this responsibility with us and also to disperse and scatter the enemies' efforts, instead of concentrating only on Al-Qa'ida, and we thank God that there are some groups starting to cooperate with us.

Finally, in regards to targeting Denmark and Jews as per the orders, the situation is as follows:

- Denmark: we had sent a European group formed of 3 brothers a long time ago to carry out an operation in Denmark and the targets were American, but we lost our communication with them. But we heard that they had been captured but we're not sure; in addition, we have another brother who has been in jihad for long time.
- Jews: To be informed on who we had sent previously, and who had the capability to work in putting the Jews first (TN: he made the Jews his priority) on his list; also, we have been cooperating with two groups who are working in the same fields and there is progress and we are asking God to help.

End of the message

PART SIX: SELECTED SPECIFIC TOPICS

H. Africa

> **1. Letter dtd 07 August 2010**
>
> This lengthy letter discusses Somalia and issues that remain important to the country including poverty, education, Sufism, agricultural objectives, and trade. A plan to assassinate the President of Uganda is mentioned as well. Azmarai also discusses the Islamic Maghreb, the ceasefire with the Pakistani government, and finances. Coordination of movement under weather protection is mentioned as well as leaked documents from the Pentagon.
>
> From: Azmarai
>
> http://www.dni.gov/files/documents/ubl/english/Letter%20dtd%2007%20August%202010.pdf

(TN: Full translation; this letter was summarized previously.)

Page 1

In the name of God, the most merciful

Praise be to God, and prayer and peace be upon our prophet Muhammad, his family and companions. Amen.

Dear Brother, Shaykh Mahmud (May God protect him)

God's peace, mercy, and blessing be upon you

I hope that you receive this letter while you, your family, your children, and all the brothers are in a good health. May God help you and support you in carrying out all your responsibilities.

I received your good letter and I read its content and I read your suggestions regarding the regions. First, I will start by expressing my opinion regarding the regions and then I will talk about the other issues.

Regarding Somalia:

- I have attached a letter to ((Abu-al-Zubayr)) that contains a response to some of what was mentioned in his letter. I also told him that the response to the other issues will be in a letter from you, and a copy of it will go to Brother ((Abu- Muhammad)) and to him.

Regarding what you said about the issue of judges, it might be difficult for the brothers to implement this due to the vastness of the region, distance between people, and the difficulty of finding judges. Locating and appointing qualified judges is very difficult. Also, it is difficult to provide buildings and salaries for them. This issue is beyond their current capacity. Based on that, it would be easier for them to appoint a judge in each heavily populated area. These judges would provide rulings on all areas of life, except for trade issues, because as you know they are vast and would require a judge with distinct skills that require studying.

Page 2

This is especially true at this time, due to many developments in the trade business.

- Regarding the pledge of allegiance from the brothers in Somalia, it should be based on jihad for establishing an Islamic Caliphate.

- Regarding education for girls, I think that this issue should be left up to them.

- Regarding their request to mention them in our statements, this is good and we will do that.

PART SIX: SELECTED SPECIFIC TOPICS

- Please remind the brothers in Somalia to be compassionate with the people and remind them of the Hadiths on this. Regarding the Sufi groups, make sure to tell them to do their best to keep them unaligned, and if some of them refuse to stay unaligned, they should not treat all of them the same way. We do not want them to become an instrument for the enemy to use against us. Any provocation from our side would push them more toward the enemy.

They should be warned that there are differences between our enemies and they should distinguish between enemies with the conviction to fight us and those without conviction. These things should be considered for us to win the war.

- Please talk to the Somali brothers about reducing the harm to Muslims at Bakarah Market as result of attacking the headquarters of the African forces. Instead, they should focus on attacking them on their way to and from the airport. They should not carry out operations against their headquarters unless these are large, special operations or through digging tunnels that will allow them to reach the heart of the camp. Please study the matter and let me know.

Page 3

As a comment on the Uganda operation, they were supposed to arrange a good plan for assassinating the President of Uganda, ((Museveni)), for this can affect the war there. However, if they cannot, they should target vital military and economic targets.

I also suggest sending a Somali delegation of tribal dignitaries to the Gulf area to meet with businessmen and scholars to inform them on the poverty in Somalia, the death of children because of this poverty, and to remind them of their responsibility toward their brothers. They should explain the suffering of the people there, using pictures and statistics available to relief organizations. They should tell them that the poor people are waiting for some effort to save their lives. They should also present some ideas for irrigation projects.

One of the ways for completing a project is to start one and then take pictures of it and send those pictures to donors.

Page 4

The idea is to show the people that in spite of their poverty, they tried to start something, but they do not have the money to complete it.

Locals can also promise to rent lands for years in exchange for money to build the project. Keep in mind that one irrigation system can provide water for 40,000 acres. If the land is flat, as it is in Somalia, they can plant some very fruitful plants that can provide for people very quickly. They also can plant strategic plants, such as dates and fruit trees.

Other trees that would be appropriate for the area are palm olive trees, and they can be imported from Indonesia or Malaysia. Also, the palm trees are available around Somalia, but the trees that come from Malaysia are mutated and can be more rewarding economically. Each acre can bring 57,000 dollars and more. The land in Somalia is one of the most fertile in the world, and once used, the suffering of millions of Muslims will vanish, and people will start protecting the existence of the Islamic emirate. Also, building irrigation projects will create jobs for most Muslims. Also, we should plant things that need to be manually harvested so as to keep the jobs.

Page 5

Some of the brothers might think that their enemy might destroy these projects and the agriculture projects, but I think that it would be difficult for the enemy to do so, because they cannot enter in a direct clash with the humanitarian needs of the people. Also, these projects are not military targets, and attacking them would create great animosity from locals toward the collaborating government in Somalia.

The brothers working for the Islamic emirate should be warned against getting involved in the trade business because it could be very dangerous and contradictory to the mission of the state. People working for the state should be concerned only with security and justice.

Employees of the state should not compete for trade because this can destroy the Islamic state and movement and create a gap between the state and the people. You should learn from the Islamic movement in Sudan. The people there became distracted with business and trade and forgot about the implementation of the Shari'a. Today, Sudan is considered one of the most corrupt countries in the world.

Page 6

Also, among the important issues is that any matters or secrets that are discussed in the Shura councils should be kept as secrets, and people cannot discuss them with their children or relatives.

You should warn the brothers against cutting down trees on a large scale for the purpose of creating charcoal without replacing them. Cutting down trees should be limited to the needs of the people and local consumption and not for export.

I am sure that you are aware that climate change is causing drought in some areas and floods in others. The brothers in Somalia should be warned about this and they need to implement all necessary preparations.

Among the important preparations is to create an early warning system and establish an advanced monitoring system at the beginning of the river to be able to issue an alarm using a wireless system at the time of flooding.

Note: Be extra cautious and make sure that no letters or documents fall in the hands of the enemy. Communications with the brothers in Somalia should be handled like letters that contain secret and dangerous information.

Page 7

Regarding the Islamic Maghreb, I read a letter that talks about some entities that would like to reach ceasefire agreements with the brothers, and we believe that such agreements that are based on Shari'a principles are a good thing. We want the maximum number of entities to take the sidelines as we fight our greatest enemy, the US. As for the issue of the ten million euros per year, I do not think that we should be inflexible about it. The important thing for us now is to reach a ceasefire. As for the second letter, unfortunately, we were not able to open it. It is from brother Abu-Mus'ab (('Abd-al- Wadud)). Please resend it to us after you make sure that it can be opened.

Regarding Yemen, in your letter you mentioned that you are waiting for a letter from ((Abu-Basir)) that contains detailed information on the situation in Yemen. Please send it to me. You also mentioned that you will start the correspondence with Abu- Basir to facilitate for the new policy. I suggest that we wait on this until we see what they have on the matter, and then we can make the best decision.

Regarding what the brothers in Iraq mentioned about the disagreement between them and Ansar al-Islam, please continue to communicate with them and remind them to do their best to avoid disagreements and conflicts. Also, ask them to resolve their differences by using the tribal leaders and scholars and those who were members of Jama'at Ansar al-Sunnah.

Regarding what you mentioned about the situation where you are in Waziristan, I agree with what you said regarding cooling things down and reducing the movement for your security and safety and the security and safety of all the foreigners. Also, get some of the brothers out to the Sind area for a year or two, while focusing on continuing with special large operations in Afghanistan.

Please warn our brothers in Taliban Pakistan and Afghanistan to spread the prohibition of the shedding of Muslim blood among their members and to avoid the killing of Muslims. They should also implement an awareness campaign against punishing people based on suspicion.

Page 8

PART SIX: SELECTED SPECIFIC TOPICS

This issue applies to people working on counterintelligence. They should be reminded that they should not punish anyone without confirming their guilt.

I also wish to remind our brothers in the Taliban of the great importance of treating the tribes and villagers with compassion. Regarding the tribes that joined or intend to join the US awaking project, please warn them not to overreact in dealing with these tribes so as to not anger these tribes. Explain this to them and remind them of the experience of our brothers in Iraq with this.

Regarding the ceasefire with the Pakistani government, the continuation of the negotiations in the fashion that you described is in the interest of al-Mujahidin at this phase.

Regarding Shaykh ((Abu-Yahya)), I think that we should not get him busy with administrative issues and keep him away from his research, because they are very important. We need his efforts especially after the brothers in Somalia took control. This is an emirate on the ground, and it is real and has millions of people in it. It will require strong care and support in terms of religious research. Do not forget the magnitude of our responsibility since they decided to join us. He should dedicate a large part of his time toward this mission. As for the administrative issues, some other brothers can perform these duties.

Regarding appointing a deputy for you, please inform me of the capability of Shaykh ((Abu-Khalil)) at this time with regard to this mission. If there is no objection for him to become a deputy, then he should become one. You should inform him that he was appointed as a deputy for you for a year and that it can be extended. This year should start from the day when the letter arrives.

Page 9

As for the second deputy, I think that brother Abu-'Abd-al- Rahman al-((Maghribi)) (Var.: al-((Maghrebi))) should be the one, Please inform him of this and tell him that it is for a year and can be extended. If for some reason you are unable to appoint Shaykh Abu-Khalil to this position, then Abu-'Abd-al- Rahman al-Maghribi should be in that position and brother 'Abd- al-Jalil should be the second deputy.

Please send me the resumes of all the brothers who might be nominated for high administrative positions now or in the future. Also, please ask each one of them to write something about their vision of the jihadi work in general and provide their opinions and suggestions regarding any of the jihadi fronts.

I received from you the book, "The Points of Focus" by brother Abu-Ahmad 'Abd-al-Rahman al-((Masri)) with an introduction by Shaykh Abu-Muhammad al-((Maqdisi)). It is a very important book and we should make sure that all brothers read it. We should publish it widely on the Internet to benefit from it in building awareness among the youth in general and the youth in jihadi groups in particular. It should be spread all over the Muslim world and we should ask all the fields to spread it. It is a great instrument for good Muslims to get out from underneath the groups that recognize the regimes that are based on foundations that are contrary to true Islam. This book should be translated into Urdu, Pashto, Farsi, Turkish, Swahili, Malawi, English, French, and other languages.

It also would be a good idea to contact Shaykh Abu-Muhammad al-Maqdisi and ask him to get the permission of the author of the book to have it summarized. If he agrees, then we should send it to one of the shaykhs and ask him to summarize it and write helpful notes in the margins.

- We should be careful not to send big secrets by email, especially in Waziristan and the areas around it.

Page 10

We should also warn Shaykh Yunis about this. We should assume that the enemy can see these emails and only send through email information that can bring no harm if the enemy reads it. They should not trust it just because it is encrypted, because the enemy can easily monitor all email traffic to the al-Mujahidin area. Computer science is not our science and we are not the ones who invented it. I think that depending on encryption in sending secrets is a great risk. Encryption system works with ordinary people, but not against those who created email and the Internet. All sensitive communications should be done through carriers.

Example of the evidence that the enemy is looking at our messages is that after brother Abu-Basir sent a message in which he suggested that Shaykh Anwar al-(('Aulaqi)) (Var.: al-((Awlaqi))) should be the first man, the Americans stated that al-Shaykh Anwar al-'Aulaqi is the actual emir of the organization.

Regarding what you mentioned about the two million that you received and the four million that you are expecting from the Afghan government as a ransom for the Afghan diplomat, I am surprised by this because the Afghan government does not usually pay this kind of money to free its men.

There is a small chance that the Americans might be aware of the delivery of the money, especially because news in Afghanistan spreads very fast.

Page 11

They might have agreed to have the money within the aircraft monitoring area so as to reach the field commander in the area and the leaders that will receive that money. One way to find out the level of the accuracy of this theory is to know the importance of the hostage within the government or whether he is a relative of some high-ranking official in the government. In any case, you should consider yourselves under surveillance and you should change houses only on cloudy days.

I want you to be careful this time and in the future too.

With any amounts of money that you receive, you should make sure that you evade surveillance and you should exchange the money for another currency and at a bank in a large city, such as euros and then exchanging the euros to dollars at another bank.

The reason for this is for you to be protected from any harmful materials or rays that can be on the money.

Regarding the groups that asked you for money, I think that you should deal with them in rupees, and the total that you can spend is 100,000 USD. You can promise them that there will be more donations if we receive more money. If you see that you need more, then the total can reach 150,000 USD.

Page 12

Regarding paying the brothers their monthly salaries in advance, I think that we should pay them on time and not give them any in advance, because they could spend the money and then come back and ask for a loan, and we will find ourselves in an uncomfortable position with the brothers.

I would like for you to advance your knowledge in managing money and finances so as to be able to make the money last for a long time.

This money that God gave to al-Mujahidin might be enough for five or six years.

You should always be aware of the movement of money and the remaining amounts. You should ask for semi-monthly reports from the financial official. Please send me copies of these reports.

Please save the money in various safe locations with trustworthy individuals. Be prudent in the way you save this money. The amounts that will be kept with individuals should not be more than they can handle. Some brother can take up to fifty thousand, while other brothers can keep hundreds of thousands. Please pay attention to this matter.

Page 13

PART SIX: SELECTED SPECIFIC TOPICS

Please let me know what items related to the general policy get sent to the brothers in the fields. Also, please send me their responses to them.

You mentioned that one of the brothers that you consulted with after the letters from the field arrived is Bashir al- ((Madanis)). Please identify him. Note: In the past, I asked Shaykh Sa'id (may God rest his soul) to not change aliases unless it is important to do so.

Regarding our brother, the friend of the engineer, you should slow down and not nominate him until further notice. He should be mentored from time to time. He is close by and reachable, but the sickness of engineering has taken hold of him.

In your letter, you mentioned that you stopped the statement of Shaykh Abu-Muhammad (may God protect him) regarding Turkey and the Freedom Flotilla; is this the same statement? Please clarify and send us the statement, because the media published only small parts of it.

Please dedicate some brothers to translate the documents on Afghanistan and Pakistan that were leaked from the Pentagon because these documents contain the strategy of the enemy in the area. The US secretary of defense stated that the leak of these documents will negatively affect the war. The Website that published these documents revealed 92,000 documents and then another 15,000.

Please send us the speeches by Abu-Muhammad on a regular basis. Also please send me the speeches of Shaykh Abu-Yahya. Keep in mind that I asked him for all his previous publications.

Please send me the entire interview of Shaykh Anwar al-'Aulaqi with Sada al-((Malahim)).

Page 14

We are waiting for your responses to what we mentioned in our previous letter, which included a request to nominate a qualified brother to be in charge of a large operation in America.

Please let me know if you have brothers who are good with poetry. Also, please send books on poetry.

Regarding what you mentioned on the questions that Brother 'Abd-al-Rahman al-Maghribi sent, I will start answering the important questions on the list.

Regarding the media program that Ahmad ((Zidan)) is working on, please let him know that it would be better if it gets postponed until the tenth anniversary of 9/11. Also, one year for finishing it is not enough. He needs to create a vision for the program and review it several times. He will also need to interview a large number of people in various areas in the world, in addition to getting his questions to us and us getting the answers to him. Please get in touch with him and get the questions that he has for the program. We should not get involved in the scenario and the details of the program, except making sure to ask him not to interview anyone in my family.

As for the preparatory rights for Al Jazeera and Al Sahab, I think that we should negotiate to have audio materials for Al Jazeera and the written materials for Al Sahab. This means that some of the answers will be in audio and others will be in writing.

Page 15

Negotiations on this issue should continue until an agreement that will satisfy Al Sahab is reached. Please keep me posted on these negotiations.

Regarding the amount of money that was placed as a gift in my account, may God reward you for it. I will accept it, but as a loan. You should deduct this amount from my personal money when it arrives. Please send the money with the carrier.

Please send two copies of your letters to the regions: one to me and one to Shaykh Abu-Muhammad in order for us to be aware of what is going on.

Please convey my greetings to Shaykh Abu-Muhammad and to all the brothers. Also, please let me know how you are doing after the hard rain and floods. As for us, we are healthy and doing well.

In the past, I asked you to store an amount of wheat. Please let me know what happened with this.

Regarding what you said about trying to work with the Iranians on releasing my son Hamzah directly to Qatar, this plan might be threatening to the Iranians because of fear that their mistreatment of al-Mujahidin might be exposed to the media and cause them to not to release him.

Enclosed is a statement regarding the climate change, especially the floods in Pakistan. Please send it to Al Jazeera Television.

Enclosed are letters to Shaykh Abu-Yahya, Ilyas, Abu-Anas al-((Subay'i)), and 'Abd-al-Latif. Please have them send me responses to them.

Page 16

Please inform the middleman between us to be near the agreed-upon area on 27 August, because I intend to send a statement to the American people on the 9th anniversary of 9/11 to make sure that it reaches Al Jazeera Television before 9/11.

Finally, I pray to God to grant you success and protect you and help you with this great duty. I remind myself and you to be gentle and compassionate with the brothers. We should accept their good behavior and forgive their mistakes, and we should counsel them.

God's peace, mercy, and blessings be upon you.

Your brother, Azmarai
07 August 2010

2. Study Paper about the Kampala Raid in Uganda

This letter explains the thinking behind and results of the Kempala raid. Economic and governmental consequences are mentioned, as are the raid consequences in America as they relate to intelligence and Obama. Consequences in other nations are discussed as well.

Date: 11 August 2010

From: Al-Kita'ib Center for Monitoring and Reconnaissance

http://www.dni.gov/files/documents/ubl/english/Study%20Paper%20about%20the%20Kampala%20Raid%20in%20Uganda.pdf

(TN: The document is a study paper, possibly for propaganda purposes, about the so-called Kampala raid in Uganda, authored by Al-Kata'ib Center for Monitoring and Reconnaissance.)

Page 1

(TN: Map of Uganda with inset reading, "Bombs kill dozens of people," and pointing at Kampala.

11 August 2010.

(TN: Title) Consequences of Kampala Raid, 11 July 2010.

Al-Kata'ib Center for Monitoring and Reconnaissance

Page 2

(TN: All pages have the heading, Kampala raid, Al-Kata'ib Center for Monitoring and Reconnaissance.)

Part Six: Selected Specific Topics

In the name of Allah, praise Allah, and prayers and peace be on Allah's messenger.

After the blessed Kampala raid on eleventh July, its effects and consequences were different and simultaneous, whether in Uganda, Somalia, African countries, or the world, headed by the United States.

And according to study and analysis, these countries had only two choices:

- Either continue to support the weak transitional government, which only has control on limited parts of Mogadishu and the consequences of that.

- Or ceasing to interfere in Somali affairs and withdrawing their forces from there; accordingly, being defeated in front of the Mujahidin in Somalia.

The following is a narration of the consequences in the shape of points that will be detailed as needed, keeping in mind that these consequences have been spotted through monitoring the events from the date of the raid (11 July 2010) until the date of writing this report (11 August 2010). We start, in the name of Allah the most gracious the most merciful of Allah, seeking his help.

Page 3

The beginning of the raid consequences in Uganda:

- The raid created a condition of horror and fear never known before in Uganda; the timing, targets, and results were very suitable to wake the Ugandan people from their slumber, and get them to pay attention to the government decisions and actions.

- And of the most prominent popular responses was the rise of the opposition parties and their demanding Museveni to withdraw the forces from Somalia immediately, before the threats continued to demolish the prospects of the Ugandan future. These voices are still rising, while Museveni is still turning his back on them.

Page 4

- Also, worry has spread among the Western and Chinese investors equally, especially that Uganda and Kenya have borders that can be infiltrated with Somalia, and all the investors are looking warily to Uganda.

- The Ugandan currency UGX has fallen against the dollar after the raid.

- President Yuri Museveni found a chance for himself to hang onto the ruling chair, with the excuse of effecting revenge from Al-Shabaab movement and protecting security in Uganda, especially with the future of the oil that the Ugandans have been promised, which the analysts consider an important goal for Museveni; maybe he will not give it up by all possible means, which he actually started working on, like amassing the popular support and bringing forward what they call the extremists as a common enemy.

- Uganda did not withdraw its forces, but quickly, in a rash and angry response, sent two thousand more of its troops under American prodding; a miniscule number compared to the mission asked of them, in addition to begging the other African countries to provide, as Museveni invited the other African countries to share the military burden with him or else he would withdraw from Somalia.

- The explosions in Kampala has raised a question on many tongues, which is: Is there a peace to protect in Somalia? And they started to doubt the meaning of the mission to Somalia to start with.

- The explosions allowed opening a door about the violations of the Ugandan forces and their killing of the innocent in Somalia, so we started to hear reports from the humanitarian organizations and human rights groups, which were denouncing the haphazard bombardment at the residential areas day and night, and wrote articles

Page 5

and published the analysis, of which items were demands to control the Ugandan forces in their dealing with the civilians, or their withdrawal from Somalia.

- The Ugandan people want to withdraw their army and many voices are rising, saying, "We want our sons to protect us here in Uganda and not there to protect the Somalis."

- Concentrating the support for AMISOM has become the goal for the concerned parties.

Second: The raid consequences in America:

- Obama's reaction was fast and cunning and it looked like he was surprised, so he immediately sent a CIA team to investigate these explosions.

- The responses and speeches that Obama gave after the raid indicated imbalance in the American policy and indecisiveness, and he gave statements that were received with a lot of criticism in American circles, not to mention some of the analysts in the world; in which he classified the Al-Qa'ida people as being racists, in an attempt to create that impression with the Americans, which found rejection by their majority and was called short-sighted.

- Obama hurried to exploit the situation and pushed all the entities to send more forces to Somalia, but the issue with the African leaders is different than what it is with NATO, as the African leaders are criminals of the kind that exploit the situation in the worst possible way, and that is what awaits Obama and the American treasury of this conspiracy.

- Providing logistical and financial support to the soldiers of the AMISOM.

Page 6

- Pressure against the other countries, like South Africa.

- Increasing the monitoring of the Somali minority in America and travelers to Somalia. Also, the increase in numbers of arrest was recently noticed in America; the most recent was the arrest of two Somali women, one of whom was 63-years old, who were accused of sending 8000 American dollars to Al-Shabaab movement.

- It created a storm of media publicity that the terrorists were targeting soccer fans.

- Concentrating on the fact that the action was Al-Qa'ida- influenced, and that it was a manifestation of the increased influence of the foreign fighters inside Al-Shabaab movement.

- Attempting to project Al-Shabaab as a beast that wants to pounce on Africa and eat the green and the dry without a reason other than killing, while marginalizing the premeditated killing of Ugandan Muslims.

- The increase in worries against Al-Shabaab has become apparent.

- The American movement was mostly diplomatic, political, and intelligence.

Third: The raid consequences in the African countries:

- The most affected country was Burundi, where the academics hurried to attack the government for its erroneous politics, and the voices became loud about the integrity of that government. A journalist

Page 7

was arrested because of an article in which he wondered about the ability of Burundi to confront an attack like the one in Kampala.

- Security procedures doubled in Uganda, Burundi, Kenya, and Ethiopia, and fears in the other IGAD countries.

- Guinea and Djibouti came under pressure and negotiations to accept sending forces, estimated at two battalions of one thousand soldiers each, while the rest of the member countries refused to submit, like Botswana, while South Africa remained undecided.

- The analysts disclosed that the leaders and the people were not on the same path, as the leaders wanted to serve their own interests and accept the American bargaining, even at the expenses of their people; and the people were scared of death and destruction in their countries.

The raid consequences in Somalia:

- Increase in popular sympathy and support for Muslims in Somalia to the movement, which raised the American and the observers' ire, which they expressed on several occasions.

- Increase in the power and regional weight of the movement, with the infidels starting to account for it.

- Talk about development and increase of Al-Shabaab movement, and hinting that it is related to the connection with Al-Qa'ida.

Page 8

- The Somali government, as usual, is using the situation to beg for some money and support, in addition to the increase of fear in the ranks of the transitional government.

- The increase of fear in the hearts of the soldiers located in Somalia, with their management increasing their salaries from 500 to 750 dollars in order to silence them.

- The Ugandan forces did not discriminate between a Somali apostate and a Somali Muslim and treated all the Somalis equally, which upset some of the Somali soldiers in the Somali forces, and some of them left their weapons and surrendered and some of them deserted. The matter drew the attention of the politicians of the White House, who asked the Ugandans for discipline; and the transitional government to act so that they did not lose their already weak forces.

- Sending additional funds and support for the forces to raise their morale.

- The frequency of the daily bombardment has decreased to the level where they were before the Kampala explosions, even though they are still there.

- More light is being shed on the Somali issue.

- Many voices call for political dialogue and reconciliation instead of military intervention in Somalia.

- The suggestions went to the extent of planning to allow Al-Shabaab movement to get to power, and then work on toppling it and getting the government back from them in a different manner other than exploiting the Somali people.

Page 9

The Kampala raid disclosed the falsehood of claims that the Somali issue was merely internal fighting; the main entities of the struggle were uncovered: Crusader America and its cronies from one side, and the Mujahidin and the Somali people on the other, even in the eyes of some Christians and Ethiopians.

Fifth: The raid consequences in the world:

- The United Nations refused to handle the matter directly and wiggled out of responsibility.

- Refused to give offensive battle authorities (as they claim) to the soldiers of AMISOM.

- The ceiling of the force numbers remains variable; some experts say the number of soldiers available is enough, but financial and logistic support is unavailable.

- The first group of 200 soldiers is expected to arrive in September, with their bill paid by the White House.

- The rest are expected in time, but there are financial hurdles despite all the donations and the claimed American generosity.

- The Somali issue went abroad and AMISOM reputation was tarnished, which angered those who are working on polishing the reputation of these forces abroad.

- Al-Kata'ib publications were a reference for the observers and the analysts, and they used expressions that were coined in its publications, like "the African crusaders."

Page 10

Summary:

The situation have become as follows:

- With difficulty, AMISCOM forces are attempting to get reinforcements between some countries refusing to send their forces and some others that are hesitant, and some that are waiting for approval until they get the financial and logistical promised help. So it seems that there are 2000 soldiers ready to travel in September, and a remaining 2000 are getting ready, and Uganda does not want to find itself only with Burundi in Somalia.

- America is concentrating its intelligence on the immigrants to Somali and the Somalis themselves.

- America is strengthening its intelligence in the region, especially Kenya.

- Uganda asks the rest to share the burden and the opposition inside is strong and united, and the elections are looming close, while Museveni is preparing for his competition, and he holds in his hand the cards (revenge from Al-Shabaab).

- The battlefield has widened and can reach any country in the world, and it cannot be contained only in the capital Mogadishu. Now the enemy powers are scattered and they are looking everywhere to where the next hit will come.

- Economy and finances are the main worry for the African countries, and touching them is considered a great threat, which is why it raised the readiness status - to protect that specific sector.

- International Jihad is an expression that is becoming a reality.

Page 11

End of the summary of the Kampala raid consequences

11 July 2011

Any additions will be added, Allah willing.

Praise Allah

11 August 2010

Part Seven: Selected Religious Topics

A. Jihad

> ### 1. Jihad and Reform Front, 22 May 2007
>
> Religion is largely discussed. There is a miscommunication and a desire for al Qa'ida in Iraq to claim their disasters instead of letting them fall upon the Jihad and Reform Front.
>
> From: The Jihad and Reform Front
>
> http://www.dni.gov/files/documents/ubl/english/Jihad%20and%20Reform%20Front%2022%20May%202007.pdf

Page 1

Translation begins here:

In the name of God, most gracious, most merciful

Praise is to God to Whom we turn for help and ask His forgiveness, to whom we ask to be protected from our own sins and bad work, and whoever is guided by God will find his way, and whoever doubts God, there will be none to guide him.

I attest that there is only one God Who has no partner and I attest that Muhammad is His servant and Messenger.

"O ye who believe! Fear God as He should be feared and die not except in a state of Islam" (Quran 3:102).

"O mankind! Reverence your Guardian-Lord who created you from a single person, created of like nature, His mate, and from them twain scattered (like seeds) countless men and women; reverence God, through whom ye demand your mutual (rights), and (reverence) the wombs (that bore you): for God ever watches over you" (Quran 4:1).

"O ye who believe! Fear God, and (always) say a word directed to the Right: That He may make your conduct whole and sound and forgive you your sins: He that obeys God and His Apostle, has already attained the highest achievement" (Quran 33:70-71).

The best words are those in the book of God, and the best guidance is that of Muhammad, May God's blessings and peace be upon him, and the worst of things are those that are created (by man), each of which is a heresy, and each heresy is an aberration, and each aberration leads to fire (hell).

O God, the Lord of Gibrail, Mikael (Gabriel, Michael) and Israfil, the One who knows the unknown and knows martyrdom, You judge the problems that your people disagree on, O God guide us to the truth that people disagree on, O God you guide whoever you want to the right path.

God said, "O ye that believe! Betray not the trust of God and the Apostle, nor misappropriate knowingly things entrusted to you" (Quran 8:27). And the Messenger of God said, "All of you are guardians and are responsible for your subjects".

From: the Jihad and Reform Front

To: The honorable Shaykh Usamah Bin Laden and Dr. Ayman al-Zawahiri, may God safeguard you, protect you, and lead you to the road of Jihad to honor the word of God.

Your brothers at the Jihad and Reform Front strongly reproach you because we have sent you written and voice messages which we underwent the trouble of overcoming obstacles to deliver them to you. We did that as of the early days in which brother ((Abu Mus'ab)) swore allegiance to you, and in our letters we informed you of the consequences of his action, with the complications and the Shari'a breaches that took place, and with the escalating damage that is inflicting the Jihad progress in Iraq and is committed in the name of al-Qa'ida and in your name.

We sent you the evidence and the proof, and we kept on sending you our letters requesting that you personally intervene to solve the grave complications that are encompassing the blessed Jihad work in Iraq and are damaging your reputation. That said, there have not been any measures taken up till now to find a solution to the ongoing regression that forewarns of an imminent catastrophe if the situation remains as is. We demand that you send a clear reply to our previous letters indicating your own position on what is taking place, and it is for you to do that before we mention (variant, "declare") the ongoing catastrophes

Page 2

and disasters that are committed under the name of the Islamic State by the al-Qa'ida organization in Iraq. We believe that you don't value nor care for our letters and writings to you, and this will be the last complaint that we send to you, after which we will only complain to God.

Comment:

We refer to the first letter that Shaykh Usamah received three years ago via ((Abu al-Layth)) al-Libi and was sent by the Ansar al-Sunnah group, as well as their second letter that was handed over to brother ((Abu al-Darda')) who is well known to you when he was in charge of preparations and training in Camp Kharan and was killed after he delivered the letter to you. The letter was in the form of twelve audio tapes that were received by Shaykh Ayman who also received other letters addressed to you by al- Jaysh al Islami (TN: The Islamic Army) as well as by Jaysh al- Mujahidin (TN: The Mujahidin Army), and by other detachments.

You should be aware that in the day of reckoning, you are responsible in front of God for blessing the work done by the al-Qa'ida in Iraq organization without disavowing the scandals that are committed in your name.

If you still can, then this is your last chance to remedy the Jihad breakdown that is about to take place in Iraq, that is mostly caused by your followers, and let it be known to you that there are calamities taking place now that are much more severe than those of the past.

We ask you good Shaykhs to take action, and to do that through a speech that you air via the satellite TV stations in which you clear yourselves in front of God, the Mujahidin, and the Muslim people who believe that you are responsible for what is taking place in Iraq and the breaches that you didn't disavow, and which you can. We ask you to listen to the words of the good and truthful citizens who aren't your followers, to get true and clear information on what is taking place.

We pray to God to help you achieve your aim and to have you correct what is taking place.

We pray that God's blessings be upon our master Muhammad and his people and companions.

The Jihad and Reform Front

26 Jamadi al-Awwal 1428h (22 May 2007)

(End of translation)

B. Fatwas

> ### 1. Letter re Fatwas of the Permanent Committee
>
> Questions regarding marriage and young women are addressed and answered.
>
> Date: Unknown
>
> From: 'Abdallah Bin Ghadyan, 'Abd-al-Razzaq 'Afifi, 'Abd-al-'Aziz Bin 'Aballah Bin Baz
>
> http://www.dni.gov/files/documents/ubl/english/Letter%20re%20Fatwas%20of%20the%20Permanent%20Committee.pdf

(Fully Translated)

Page 1

The Fatwas of the Permanent Committee – The First Collection – (18 J / 18 S)

The second question from Fatwa number 12712:

Question 2: Is it allowed for the woman to prevent herself from marrying after the death of her first husband, or can a man order his wife not to marry another man if he dies before her? Please provide us with the answer.

Answer 2: It is not allowed for the wife to be prevented from marrying after the death of her husband, as that was exclusive to the wives of the Prophet, may God's prayers and peace be upon him. And it is not allowed for her husband to prevent her from marrying after him, and she is not obliged to obey him in that if he did. To quote the Prophet, may God's prayers and peace be upon him, "There is obedience in what is fair." (1) Through God there is success. May God's prayers and peace be upon our Prophet and his family and his companions.

The Permanent Committee for Scientific Research and the Issuing of Fatwas

Member
'Abdallah Bin Ghadyan

Vice President
'Abd-al-Razzaq 'Afifi

President
'Abd-al-'Aziz Bin 'Abdallah Bin Baz

----

(1) Sahih al-Bukhari al-Ahkam (6726), Sahih Muslim al-Imarah (1840), Sinan al-Nisa'I al-Bi'ah (4205), Sinan Abu Da'ud al- Jihad (2625), Musannad Ahmad Bin Hanbal (82/1).

@@@@@@@@@@@@@@@@@@@@@@@@@@@@

The Fatwas of the Permanent Committee – The First Collection – (18 J / 30 S)

The fifth question from Fatwa number 4921:

Question 5: Is it permitted for the young woman to abstain from marriage after the death of her first husband?

Answer 5: The (TN: Islamic) law strongly urges marriage and a desire for it, so the guardian of this young woman must advise her to marry and implore her to do so. If she refuses and does not fear she will be tempted, he can leave her be. Through God there is success. May God's prayers and peace be upon our Prophet and his family and his companions.

Part Seven: Selected Religious Topics

The Permanent Committee for Scientific Research and the Issuing of Fatwas

Member
'Abdallah Bin Ghadyan

Vice President
'Abd-al-Razzaq 'Afifi

President
'Abd-al-'Aziz Bin 'Abdallah Bin Baz

Page 2

@@@@@@@@@@@@@@@@@@@@@@@@@@@@ (TN: sic)

C. General

> ### 1. Undated Statement re American Conversions to Islam
>
> The author mentions how many American conversions to Islam have occurred and why this is good. This angers the United States, according to the author.
>
> Date: Unknown
>
> From: Unknown
>
> http://www.dni.gov/files/documents/ubl/english/Undated%20statement%20re%20American%20conversions%20to%20Islam.pdf

Full Translation

1,200,000,000—praise God, Comforter of His custodians. This is the testimony of the enemies. One of the unbelievers' broadcasts on BBC mentioned, a year after the events, that 120,000 Americans converted to Islam. After this year they haven't mentioned anything about this subject (may God humiliate them).

God said, "It is He Who got out the Unbelievers among the People of the Book from their homes at the first gathering (of the forces). Little did ye think that they would get out: And they thought that their fortresses would defend them from God. But the (Wrath of) God came to them from quarters from which they little expected (it)" (TN: Qur'an 59:2).

In this verse, both the faithful and the unbelievers were thinking about their strength, their economy, their machines, and their equipment. But God prevails over His affairs. God said, "but if it had been God's Will, He could certainly have exacted retribution from them (Himself); but (He lets you fight) in order to test you, some with others" (TN: Qur'an 47:4), so that He can distinguish between the wicked and the righteous.

God said, "God will not leave the believers in the state in which ye are now, until He separates what is evil from what is good" (TN: Qur'an 3:179), but to weigh the evidence against His servants and show mercy to the unbelievers. God said, "Do then those who devise evil (plots) feel secure that God will not cause the earth to swallow them up, or that the Wrath will not seize them from directions they little perceive? Or that He may not call them to account in the midst of their goings to and fro, without a chance of their frustrating Him? Or that He may not call them to account by a process of slow wastage - for thy Lord is indeed full of kindness and mercy" (TN: Qur'an 16:45- 47). Glory to God, for he is able to seize them in a moment, but He has mercy on them out of fear of impairing them, one after another, so that, in time, they can come under His mercy. The seal of the verses is that your Lord is merciful and compassionate. Glory to God—the Prophet brought the good news that he was His supporter. God said, "If any think that God will not help him (His Apostle, in this world and the Hereafter, let him stretch out a rope to the ceiling and cut (himself) off: then let him see whether his plan will remove that which enrages (him)! (TN: Qur'an 22:15).

2. Message to Muslim Brothers in Iraq and to the Islamic Nation

This lengthy letter serves as a motivational letter and a message to recalibrate and readdress the basis of Islam. It provides messages to Allah and mentions those who have died fighting. The author argues that it is important for the Mujahidin to unite and work on political elections.

Date: Unknown

From: Unknown

http://www.dni.gov/files/documents/ubl/english/Message%20to%20%20Muslim%20brothers%20in%20Iraq%20and%20to%20the%20Islamic%20nation.pdf

(Page 1 of 21)

In the Name of Allah the Gracious and Merciful

Praise to Allah, then praise to Allah, Praise to Allah who said:

(And what reason do you not have to fight in the cause of Allah, to rescue the helpless oppressed old men, women, and children who are crying: "Our lord! Deliver us from this town whose people are oppressors; send us a protector by your grace and send us a helper from your presence." Those who are believers fight in the cause of Allah and those are unbelievers fight in the cause of idolatry: so fight against the helpers of Satan; surely, Satan's crafty schemes are very weak) An-Nisa' 75-76

Peace and blessing be upon our Prophet Muhammad who said:

(Who will let down a Muslim man in his land, degrade him and violate his holiness, only if Allah lets him down in a land where he loves for him to be victorious; and no person will support a Muslim in a land where he degrades him and violates his holiness, only if Allah gives him support in a land where he is triumphant) told by Imam Ahmad.

To our Muslim brothers in Iraq specifically, and to the Islamic nation in general.

Peace, Allah's mercy and blessing are upon you.

My salute (TN: regards) to our patient people in Baghdad and its surround areas, the home of succession, and my salute to our Mujahidin brothers who are stationed there, in Ba'qubah, Samarra', Mosul, Kirkuk, Tikrit, al-Latifiyah, and its sisters in Bayji and Balad and all other towns and villages participating in Jihad. And most sincere regards to the free people in the land of al-Anbar, especially the people in Fallujah, a town that is standing strong and refused to be humiliated and subjected by all of infidel leaders. It taught them a lesson in consistence in principle and proved to them that the strength of faith is greater than that of planes and cannon shelling. It also exposed his (TN: President Bush) deceptive ways and democracy, and exposed him as a liar, a butcher, and killer. And what is the difference between Saddam's tyrant massacres in Halabjah, and Bush's massacre in Fallujah? Saddam killed several thousands of our Kurdish brothers, Allah have mercy on them, in the name of

(Page 2 of 21)

rotten nationalism. Also, this age's Pharaoh (TN: referring to President Bush) alone killed several thousands in Fallujah, and injured and disabled many more, and caused hundreds of thousands to migrate, all in the name of the Crusader Zionist movement, which is blood thirsty. Therefore, Muslims must fully realize the truth behind this war, that it is impossible to justify the blockade and siege of an entire town by arguing that hundreds of insurgents are located there. It is a war against Islam and all Muslims.

I ask Allah to accept all our martyred brothers, and to heal all of the wounded. It dismayed us, what happened to our people there. We were pleased with the great perseverance and the great results that followed. The spirit of Jihad, sacrifice, pride and refusal spread all over Iraq, like the spread of a wildfire. This Jihadi spirit reached the rest of the Muslim world, and it disappointed Bush's hopes, because he wanted to destroy this faithful city, to make an example to the rest of world that refuses the American slavery. And Allah provided it (TN: Fallujah) with pride and glory, and it remained standing in spite of his nose and insulted him, and it entered into history with honor through a wide door, and it became an example for resistance and steadfastness in the face of the American barbarianism.

And I am unable to describe those men and the people of this city, but I will try. A little description is better than none, and Allah gave them faith, and wove along the lines of brilliant stars. Their nineteen brothers, in fighting this age's Pharaoh, they did not only keep the heads of the Islamic Nation up high, but also the heads of all humans, in an age where the culture of slavery prevailed all over the world, and the culture of humiliation and submission under the banner of wisdom, interests and realism. They lifted up the heads of humanity in an age where the leaders of the world bow their heads in front of tyranny at the steps of the White House. The proud giants, who are pious and humble (that is what we think of them, but God is the ultimate judge), came higher than the world's glitter and decorations, waiting for Allah's promise, not believing in worshiping humans,

(Page 3 of 21)

and refusing to accept anyone as lord according to what they refer to as international law, or the new world order and systems which revolve within its orbit.

They came to remove the cornerstone in that oppressive order, which is established to enforce unjust resolutions by the Security Council and the United Nations against weak nations. That atheist organization, which regulates the relationship between countries that have veto power, led by the U.S. and the slaves of the General

Part Seven: Selected Religious Topics

Assembly. Then, it utters lies and fake statements about fairness, equality, and freedom.

Those great men did not waver in Fallujah, in the face of evil and arrogant tyranny, gunfire, and the destruction by airplanes, against the weak men, women and children. Then they (TN: the US) claim to carry the banner of freedom and humanity.

They (TN: People of Fallujah) stood up regardless of their small weak number, with their exposed chests, but in their hearts, they believed that the mountains will be moved, Allah is the ultimate judge.

This belief was rooted in the hearts of our ancestors, may Allah be satisfied with them. They (TN: ancestors) defeated the corrupted culture of the Crusaders with Allah's goodness in the past. Today we are holding onto this belief and will defeat them, Allah willing. They stood up to prove to the entire world the true meaning of faith, and the believer's meaning of glory and strength and adherence to a solid faith in Allah. They wrote a new line in a new glorious page in our nation's history, by their blood and bodies. They fought the enemy without any inhibitions, invaded the unknown, and nothing weakened them.

(TN: poem)
These are my ancestors, so bring me more like them. I hope to meet them again.

And I salute those strong men today, and in a time when Jihad is not a strange idea, and all of the Islamic nation greets you from one ocean to another, except those rulers whom are apostates, hypocrites, and the paid writers (and bad scholars who ask people not to fight the Americans, and call the great sin of not participating in Jihad "A peaceful resistance." They say fighting against the Americans is destruction,

(Page 4 of 21)

turmoil, holocaust, riot, and their hearts resembles the hearts of their ancestors, Allah said the following about them, "Those who ask Allah for a permission not to fight will end up in hell) al-Tawbah 49.

O men, yes, the Islamic nation sends you their regards today, and is watching you. Its heart is with you, and its tongues wish you the best, and have raised an anxieties by your great Jihad. It remembered the great pages of its history, also remembered Badr, Khyber, Yarmuk and Hittin (TN: famous Islamic battles) and held its head up high, and its hearts were cured. It reassured its heart and religion, and confidence returned to itself, and it spattered its desperation and sharpened its strength, with Allah's preference and by your Jihad and efforts. For a century, the nation was searching for you, like the search of a mother who lost her only child, and waited for you after long absence. So, you came like cold water to quench the thirst. It was waiting for you to raise its head, and unite its people, and reject the division, and silence its enemy. Rewards will be given, remember yourselves, and you can do that, Allah is your ultimate judge.

O people of Iraq who are carrying sharp swords, destroy the infidels' tanks, smash their heads, stab their throats, increase the prayers, and truly keep the promise and may Allah reward you with the best.

And then... glad tidings, the dawn started to loom, and the smartness of the believers began to appear, and the hopes of the infidel started to fade away. No doubt you remember that the arrogant said, "I will end this war in six days or six weeks." You also remember Bush saying, "The major operations are over," weeks after the start of the war. They think that the people are sheep, or that it is a picnic to Panama. They did not realize that the lions of the desert, who are willing to die, are waiting for them and urging others to be patient, for victory will bring happiness and death will bring martyrdom.

(TN: poem)
I will regain my honor at any price. I will do everything in my power.
I will get the head of the giant.
I will remind myself that it should fight. I will ask my soul to give praise and rest.
I will push away any harm and defend my honor.

Weeks and months have passed, and we are at the end of the second year, thanks to Allah who validated the believers, and humiliated the people of the cross. They estimated their dead as a hundred people before the war, but the number of deaths increases twelve times, by the hands of the people of the Qur'an and Sunnah, thanks will be to Allah.

Then I direct my speech to the Islamic nation in general. Hear me and learn, the matter is great, and it is the greatest and most important matter in today's world. This is a third world war, which was started by the Zionist-Crusader alliance, against the Muslim nation, and it is taking place in the land of Iraq, today's world revolves around the house of the Caliphate, Baghdad. Today, the entire world is watching this war, and is watching the two enemies, the Muslim nation on one hand and America and its allies on the other hand. Either good life and pride or suffering and humiliation. Today, the Muslims have a rare and precious opportunity to stop following the West and its slavery, and to destroy the restraints which the Crusaders handcuffed us with. Our nation has reached absolute bottom as a result of this following (TN: following the Western immorality).

It also led to retardation in many areas related to religion and life. The Crusaders put restraints on our Islamic world. They secured the ring at each capital city by appointing a stubborn agent of the West who suppresses the faith, life, manhood, and gives infidelity victory, and does not oppose immorality, and caused many of the people misery. They underestimated their people and themselves, they lacked the faith, and believed that there was no exit out of slavery to the West. They were under siege, and the following words of the poet can be applied to them:

(TN: poem)
The hardship became so tight, but later was resolved when I did not think that it would be

(Page 6 of 21)

The tails of disbelief called for mobilization on America's behalf, and hypocrisy became dominant. Rise, O servants of Allah, our enemy has come to our land. It isolated itself and broke the rings in its chain with its own hands. The worst thing was that it broke it in Bagdad. Allah made their destruction in it, and when they destroyed the ring, the entire chain became lost and the matter collapsed. This was contrary to what they had hoped for. The nation was in a big prison, surrounded by an iron gate. This is the gate that Chirac was referring to, when he said, "Hell's gate opened in Iraq." He meant that the chain around the gate broke loose; that gate around the Muslim word which their ancestors closed years ago.

This is why the Jewish artful named Kissinger screamed, saying to Europe, "Join us in the Iraq war, America's defeat is a defeat for the entire West." Also, in this context, Blair declared about this war, that it is historical. By God, it is historical, Bush and his administration stated in a clear language that Iraq is the main front in the war against Islam. He referred to it (TN: Iraq) as the axis of evil. In Christianity, this means that we are infidels and worthless. This explains all the actions of many soldiers at Abu Ghurayb prison against our captured brothers which shocked humanity. Then, he said, "We transferred the war to their land." Since when was Iraq a base for al-Qa'ida? It is a land for all Muslims. He also said that it is a Crusade.

Rice (TN: Condaleeza) said that they are making a historical change in the region. Isn't she the one who shares Bush's interest in spreading Christianity? Didn't Bush say that he wants to change our land to a Christian region? Is there pressure to change curriculums by deleting verses on Jihad and to promote their project for change under what they call "The Greater Middle East Project?"

It is nothing but steps to achieve their domination of the nation. After this statement, is there anything unclear about their intentions to fight the Muslims? Fear Allah, O Allah's servants, rise up to defend your religion, yourselves, your brothers, your honor and land. The most important duty after faith, is to support the Mujahidin and Jihad on battlefield against the Zionist Crusaders in Palestine, Iraq, and Afghanistan.

(Page 7 of 21)

Today Jihad is our duty, and it is known that scholars preached to the many that the highest duty after faith is to fight the enemy. This means that the nation should provide its resources, money, and children and whatever is needed to fight and kick the infidels out from our land. If you do not act upon this, sin will extend to all.

The enemy restricted the road for the Mujahidin to reach Palestine, therefore, supporting them financially is a must until they liberate their land from the infidels. The opportunity to attack the Americans, the allies of the Jews, is available. Jihad in Iraq is available via trusted channels and the opportunity to kill the Americans and their allies, and attacking their interest all over the world is also available.

Take advantage of this unique opportunity to take on this great duty, for in it is your glory in this life and eternity. Do not lose this opportunity and do not ignore it, like many who missed out on Jihad in the sake of Allah in Afghanistan one quarter of a century ago and who stayed in their small countries, whose borders were drawn by the Crusaders. Each one of them claims that he had an excuse and they lost this chance. They were reluctant to commit to Jihad in Afghanistan, in spite of the fact that all conditions were suitable for playing a major role in establishing a strong Islamic country. Instead, they were lazy and have fallen behind, which led to the weakening of the Mujahidin.

The lucky person is the one who stands and defends his religion. He who sits with the useless (TN: hopeless), away from the shadows of swords when Jihad is an obligation, commits a major sin. Remember the stories of the believers who sat (TN: did not fight/participated in

Jihad) before you, they cried and regretted it severely. In the story of Ka'b Bin Malik, may Allah be pleased with him, at Tabuk battle, is an example for you. He said:

The Prophet and the Muslims were getting ready. I knew that I needed to get ready too, but did not. I said to myself: I can if I want to. People continued to work and get ready, until the Prophet and Muslims with him started moving. By then it was too late for me to get ready. I wished I could, but it was too late.

(Page 8 of 21)

People should be serious before Allah, and the believers should race to Jihad. Allah's servant, take advantage of this opportunity, travel and catch up with them (TN: fight with the Mujahidin), so that you will not say, "I wish I had done it," so, hurry up. The Prophet said, "Do good deeds and do not sell eternity for a cheap earthly price." Abu Hurayrah.

What stops you from offering you financial support to Jihad, when you know that it is your duty?

And what stops from sacrificing yourselves for Jihad, when you believe that money is limited and life is limited and death will find you inevitably even if you were in a fortified tower.

O servants, fear Allah. Have you lost your mind that you do not give yourself and money for Allah? And why give reluctantly to Allah Almighty? God said the following about those who lost their honesty, lost their faith, became weak, and their faith became thin, "When they were commanded to fight, a group of them fear people as they should have feared Allah, or even more than that, and said: 'our Lord, why have you ordered us to fight? Could you delay its implementation for a while?' Tell them the enjoyment of worldly life is short, life of the hereafter is better for those who fear Allah, and rest assured that you will not be wronged equal to the fiber of a date-stone." al- Nisa' 77

Part Seven: Selected Religious Topics

This is the answer for those who fear judgment day. For those who let the Devil stand for them on the road of Jihad, and tell them, "If you commit Jihad you will get killed, lose your money, someone will marry your wife, your kids will be orphans," God said, "The enjoyment of worldly life is short, life of the hereafter is better for those who fear Allah, and rest assured that you will not be wronged equal to the fiber of a date- stone."

O servants of Allah, obey Allah and his messenger, if he called you; he will give you a life, and be aware of the inhibitors and disablers, who say to their brothers, "Come to us." Be aware of those who love the truth but do not do it, for they end up in the dark by praising and endorsing the tyrants. Those clearly are lost people and one should not pray behind them. They must fear Allah in their conduct toward themselves and the nation. They must repent their sins.

(Page 9 of 21)

Be aware of those who want to tell the lies, to do that they mix them with some truth. Jihad in Palestine and Iraq is a duty on those two countries. If there is an inability, shortness, or laziness, then the surrounding countries must take up Jihad, and then the next country, and the next one and so on until Jihad is spread all over the Islamic countries, and until all Islamic countries become one country.

This is the fatwa of scholars (may God have mercy on their souls), who did not take into consideration the moods of rulers, who are agents (TN: allies of the West) in surrounding capitals like Riyadh and Amman. It is clear that the inability exists in Iraq and Palestine and for that reason Jihad is mandatory on those who are near, such as the people of Saudi Arabia, Syria, Jordan, Turkey, Iran, and Kuwait. If they are unable, then other surrounding countries should take on Jihad.

Jihad in Palestine and Iraq is mandatory, discouraging Jihad is a sin. Be aware of those who teach it, and compete with divine teachings and prophecies through their teachings, who then claim that this is in the benefit of the faith. This is impossible. Allah said: (Those who oppose and do not follow His order will suffer) An-Nur 63

O servants of Allah, the road is clear, our messenger left us with a clear decisive message; as clear as day and night, and whoever deviates from it will be dead. Read the Qur'an and the Sunnah and you will find the straight path. Do not follow the opinions of those men, whatever they say, preach as long as their opinions are the opposite of Allah's word and the words of his messenger, even if they (TN: those men) were truthful and faithful. A mistake will not lessen their standing or good character, but do not follow their mistake.

Sitting and not participating in Jihad, which is mandatory, is an attribute of the hypocrites, may Allah curse them, and brings on them evil not like any other evil. He warned us about them and about not joining Jihad. God promised them suffering and pain in their hearts and denied them the knowledge and jurisprudence. Remember that the fruit of knowledge is fear of Allah.

(Page 10 of 21)

Learn and follow these verses, they clearly describe the only two paths toward mandatory Jihad. The first is the path of the Imam of the Mujahidin, of the Prophet, and the second is the path of those who stay behind. Make your own choice. Allah said: (When a Surah is revealed, they enjoy it and believe it and strive and fight along his messenger, but those with wealth and influence among them ask for exemption and say leave us alone we want to be with those who stay behind.) 67, 68, 86 al-Tawbah

O servants of Allah, this is from the master of mankind (TN: refer to Prophet Muhammad), who does not speak based on mood and whose past and future sins were forgiven. He is the greatest mediator and he and all of his followers performed Jihad through their money and themselves in support of the banner of "there is no god but Allah." During the battle of Tabuk, he fought the Romans, but you sat with women, then you claim that you follow the Prophet, and follow his path. May Allah fight the cowards.

(TN: Poem)

PART SEVEN: SELECTED RELIGIOUS TOPICS

The cowards will see weakness as the end, but that is not true. The winner is the one who makes sacrifices and work toward the afterlife.

And here I will mention some of the most important and dangerous rulings:

First: The ruling about whomever supports the infidels against the Muslims. Scholars declared that supporting the infidels against Muslims is a big sin against the religion, considered one of the ten acts that revoke the religion regardless if the infidel is an Arab or foreigner. The support of America, 'Allawi, Karzai, Mahmud 'Abbas, or other apostate governments in their fight against Muslims, is considered a great sin that warrants expulsion from the faith. This applies to owners of companies and workers who deliver the fuel, ammunition, food, and all other materials, and all who support them in any way. These people will be viewed as if they backed away from the faith and must be killed. Remember Allah's words (O you faithful, do not take a Christians and Jew as friends; they are the friends of each other, and whoever takes them as a friend becomes one of them, Allah will not guide the oppressors) Al-Ma'idah 51

You can review the book "The Rulings Toward Those who Aid the Americans), if you wish to the see evidence and words of the scholars. The Muslim should befriend Allah's servants even if they are foreigners, and fight the enemies of Allah even if they were Arabs. The Iraqi who performs Jihad against the American infidels or 'Allawi's apostate government, is our brother and friend, even if he is Iranian, Kurdish or Turkmen. And the Iraqi who is a part of this apostate government, and fights the Mujahidin who are resisting the occupation, is an apostate and infidel, even if he is an Arab.

And Muslims should not say, "This is a civil war and we should not participate in it." No, Muslims are our people, and we must repudiate the infidels. The Prophet fought his clan and cousins for the sake of Allah. Allah said: (O Noah, he is not of your family for he is not righteous. So, do not ask me for anything of which you have no knowledge. I caution you not to become one of the ignorant) Hud 46

Remember the story of Bilal al-Habashi and Abu Jahil al- Qurayshi. Bilal became a believer, so Allah was satisfied with him, and he was promised heaven, and Abu Jahil was a non- believer and Allah was mad at him and he is with the people of hell, and he became an enemy and his cousins fought him with their hands, may Allah be pleased with them. The linkage between the believers is based on faith in the first place and everything else follows. If faith becomes broken, then the linkage through in-laws and clan and homeland become invalid. Allah said, "You have an excellent example in Abraham and his companions. They said to their people plainly we disown you and your god that you worship. We renounce you and enmity and hate shall reign between us forever until you believe in Allah, the one and only God." al-Mumtahinah 4

Those Iraqis who are part of the 'Allawi's apostate government and fight for it, such as members of the army and the security forces, are like Abu Jahal al-'Arabi al-Qurayshi, their blood is permissible, are infidels and do not deserve to be prayed over, do not give or receive inheritance, their spouses will divorce them, and they will not be buried in Muslim cemeteries. And I say to them- fear Allah in yourselves and in your religion and the nation and stop supporting 'Allawi's apostate government, which was appointed by the American occupation.

(Page 12 of 21)

Everyone needs to think to himself, and ask why am I wasting my life and eternity for some money? Return to your faith and you will prosper, and you will become our brothers again, and reconnect the ties between us.

PART SEVEN: SELECTED RELIGIOUS TOPICS

Second: the ruling for participating in election in Iraq, Palestine, Afghanistan and others places.

Principally- It is not a secret that choosing emirs and leaders is a right of the people, but this right is restricted by conditions… We must seek to have a Muslim emir who will rule according to Shari'ah, and the most important condition is that he must be Muslim, and the religion that will be imposed on the people is Islam. This means that all laws and constitutions should be based on Islam.

And it is known that the constitution proposed by Bremer is an ignorant and manmade constitution. He insisted that it should not be based on Islam and that Islam is not the only source for legislation of laws and rule. Therefore, if we assumed that 90% of laws and rules are based on Islamic Shari'ah and 10% based on secularism, according to the Islamic scale this would be considered infidel and not a true Islamic constitution.

Islam is an approach that was revealed by God for people to strictly commit to in all aspects of life. Therefore, Islam cannot be overlooked. Allah said, "Fight them so will be no division and faith is only to God." Al-Anfal 39

He who believes in something and did not believe in other things, his prayers and fasting would not mean anything. Allah said, "Do you believe in a part of the holy book and reject the rest? So what other punishment do people among you, who behave like this, deserve, beside disgrace in this world and to be driven to grievous punishment on the day of judgment? Allah is aware of what you do" Al-Baqarah 85. If people commit to all of Islam's rules, but allow collection of interest by banks, for example, this country's constitution would not be considered Islamic, and whoever accepts this is infidel also. Because this behavior means that they do not completely follow Shari'ah, as Allah revealed it to us. This is a big sin that could cause the sinner to be considered out of the religion.

(Page 13 of 21)

Also, this election is being conducted by an order of America, under the shadows of its airplanes. Based on this:

Anyone who participants in this election, which was described previously, he would have denied Allah. There is no power but from Allah. One must be aware of the frauds who speak in the names of Islamic parties and organizations, and urge people to participate in this apostasy. If they were truthful, their main intention would be to repudiate this apostate government, urge people to commit Jihad against the Americans and their allies and if they cannot, they should renounce them in their hearts and avoid participating in the apostate's program or sit in their councils.

All that I mentioned about Iraq completely applies to the situation in Palestine. The country is under occupation, and the constitution is declaratory and ignorant, and Islam does not accept it, and the candidate Mahmud 'Abbas is an idiot and an apostate agent. They chose him after he and his friends wasted ten years of Muslim lives, through the Oslo agreement conspiracy and others. They chose him over others so he will lead people to a new maze, and will offer new concessions, and people will accept it, and he will suppress Jihad and armed resistance.

May Muslim fear Allah with themselves and their religion. Muslims should be careful about participating in this planned election. There is no difference between electing Abu Jahl (TN: Abu Jahl was an enemy of Islam at the time of Prophet Muhammad) Iyad 'Allawi or Mahmud 'Abbas or Hamid Karzai or Husni Mubarak or Fahd Bin 'Abd-al-'Aziz or other apostate rulers, even though the latter built and enlarged al Haram mosque, for Abu Ahl with Quraysh renewed the Ka'bah, and they walked around the old sanctuary and do the Hajj, and serve Allah, but according to the scale of Islam they still are infidels because they did not submit to Islam completely.

(Page 14 of 21)

Their non-belief was that they submitted to a legislative council which is like today's legislative council or what is called House of Representatives or the National Assembly. Allah said, "Did you make those who provide water to the pilgrims and maintain the Great Mosque equal to those who believe in Allah, the day of judgment and participated in Jihad? They are not equal in the sight of Allah and Allah dose not guide the wrongdoers" At-Tawba 19. Bin Kathir said the following Hadith, "God preferred faith and Jihad over serving water to people at the house of God."

In conclusion, Muslims must be careful with these elections, and they must rally round the Mujahidin and resist the occupiers. I remind myself and Mujahidin to fear Allah in secret and publicly, mention His name, read the Qur'an, and pray to Allah, as I remind myself and others to be patient, and avoid treason, for traitors will face their punishment at the last day. Also, be aware of the forbidden blood with exception to what the Shari'ah permitted in a very strict fashion which will be decided and studied by scholars of the Mujahidin. We gain God's support by obeying Him and distancing ourselves from sin. Also, I urge you to attack the lines of supply and the oil lines, and to plant mines, which kills everyone and murders the firm owners who provide the enemy with supplies, in Kuwait, Riyadh, Jordan, Turkey and other places. And you must participate in Jihad and get involved in martyrdom operations, which were effective in scaring the enemy, and confused them, and caused their plans to fail, and challenged them. These actions are most important.

(Page 15 of 21)

Then we have fought wars and learned about them. The worst thing is that America killed women and children deliberately, and the leader says it was a mistake. That is what had happened in Afghanistan, such as killing Dr. Ayman al-Zawahiri's wife, his daughter and his only son, may God have mercy on their souls. That is what Sharon practices in Palestine today, and what the White House killer of women and kids practices in Fallujah, al- Ramadi, Baghdad, Ba'qubah, Samarra', Mosul and other cities in Iraq. He kills the innocent when he fails to stop insurgency. So, be steadfast, be patient and be aware; whatever ability Allah gave you, you should do it We ask Allah to accept them as martyrs, and provide the wounded with healing.

I remind you that you are the first line of defense, to defend Muhammad's religion and nation. Allah will be with you. I wish that you do not cause any damage to Muslims. Know that the enemy's weakness and inability is exposed, and I heard that they were forced to use their emergency budget, and are facing hard times, and have countless problems too. Their economy is depleting, and the value of their dollar is continuously declining, and their debt is huge. In spite of all of this, Bush signed a law to borrow 800 billion dollars.

Also, they are unable to provide trained and qualified soldiers to fight this war. The reports states that 50% of the soldiers are from units that are not qualified to fight this war, such as the American National Guard. Also, they are unable to provide replacements, which is the reason for cancelling the soldiers' vacations. This caused an increase in the numbers of suicides and psychological illnesses among soldiers, and Iraq became a cemetery for Americans mercenaries, to Allah thanks and gratitude. And know, victory is for he who feared Allah and be patient, for one hour of patience will be followed by ages of happiness, Allah willing, and many good deeds will be gained.

(Page 16 of 21)

This fierce wars in Iraq and Palestine are most cruel, it is a war that will be decided only by a sharp sword or a brave lion. We praise you for your patience and stability in defending the religion, and performing Jihad. Allah said that it is either victory or martyrdom. Allah said, "How many of the Prophets fought in Allah's way, and with them a large bands of godly men, but they never lost heart if they met disaster in Allah's way, nor did they weaken nor give in, and Allah loves those who are firm and steadfast" Al 'Umran 146

The happy one is he who participated with his money or himself in this war to support his religion, and happiness to those (TN: women) who contributed through her children and money. Keep in mind that the expenses of al-Qa'ida in Iraq are 200,000 euros per week. This is in addition to the expenses of other organizations, so do not default in paying to help the Mujahidin.

This is a great war and has consequences; it has results and deep effects like the Badr battle (TN: famous Islamic battle). You still can hear and feel Badr's echo, the sounds of horses and swords, which strengthened the nation's spirit, glory, and Jihad. A Hadith says, "Gabriel asked the messenger who fought along your side in Badr? He replied: the best. Gabriel said: Was also watched by the best angels?" I think that Mujahidin today, who resist the American aircraft and tanks, and fight the missiles in Iraq and Palestine, represent the best of the nation today. May God grant success in Palestine's Badr, and Iraq's Badr, and Afghanistan's Badr, and Chechnya's Badr and other regions. And our Prophet said in a Hadith, "A group from my nation will fight for the truth righteousness until the day of the resurrection."

This group and the emir of Jihad, brother Abu Mus'ab al-Zarqawi, and other organizations that joined him, are the best, and they fight under Allah's orders.

(Page 17 of 21)

And their brave operations against the Americans and 'Allawi apostate government pleased us, as well as their response to Allah's and the messenger's order to fight, in unity and congregation and insist on Allah's teachings. Allah said, "Take shelter in Allah's rope and do not separate from Him." A'lay Imarn 103

In al-Qa'ida organization, we greatly welcome their unity with us. This is a great step, to unify all Mujahidin, to establish the righteous state, and destroy the void state, and we ask Allah to bless and accept it.

There is a great difference between the honest emirs of Mujahidin, who give up the emirate for their religion and to benefit the nation, and those leaders and kings who did nothing to unify the nation and did not cancel the borders that the Crusaders drew. Instead they were devoted to dividing and creating difference in the name of nationality, and they are ready to sacrifice their own people so they can keep the Emirate, and are willing to sacrifice their own sons, fathers, and brothers to maintain their power. The isolation of Hassan Bin Talal and Hamzah Bin al-Husayn, and marginalization of 'Abdallah Bin 'Abd-al-'Aziz and others is a great example of this. There is no hope that those leaders will unify the nation and care for its interest, in the midst of the global clusters...

Also, I remind the Mujahidin that uniting under unification is not a minor thing, but rather one of the most important duties. Therefore, it should be given attention, and the Jihadi organizations must unify and arrange among each other to get united, under one banner. The Shaykh of Islam, Bin Taymiyyah said, "When people stop following Allah's order, animosity and hate spread between them. Also, if they go different ways, they will suffer, and if they are united the will win, for a community is mercy and a division is torment."

The issues are going on in Iraq, with Allah's grace, in a confident and fast pace. The pace of escalation is promising, and the enemy is incurring many losses, in money, deaths and material.

(Page 18 of 21)

All of the enemies' plans have failed. Where did all their operations with the fancy names go? Names such as Iron Fist, Iron Hammer, Great Snake, and so on. All of it is gone with the wind, thanks to Allah. The Mujahidin, with Allah's grace, have the strength and ability which are necessary for conducting big operations in the middle of a day, in the middle of Baghdad as well as other places.

Also, the resistance, through Allah's grace, is growing and increasing, Allah willing we should not forget Bush and those around him who target the Muslim groups, Abu Mus'ab al-Zarqawi and his brothers.

(TN: Poem)

The Roman towers started to collapse
The Romans did not get their people out of those towers
Two battalions and their supporters armed with courage inflicted that damage.

O Muslim, the order for Jihad was issued. So, you must shake off the dust of despair, and feel the victory coming, Allah willing, and dedicate all your efforts to support the religion.

As for the apostate and hypocrite, I say to them: he who comes back to Islam and repents, Allah will grant him forgiveness, and that is good for their religion and world. And he who stabs the religion, and calls Jihad "terrorism" in context of condemnation, and supports the apostate leaders by his actions, writings or words has no right to live. He must write his living will, and they should not blame but themselves. The Mujahidin must follow the example of Muhammad Bin Muslim, may God be pleased with him, and catch those apostates to let them join Ka'b Bin al-Ashraf. Allah said, "They shall be cursed wherever they are found and they shall be seized and killed mercilessly." Al-Ahzab 60

I also say to the Apostate rulers: it is the nation's right to choose its ruler. So, give the people their rights. The weaknesses of the tyrant who appointed you in Iraq is starting to show his weakness. Today, events go by fast toward settling the account with you and your supporters.

(Page 19 0f 21)

- Take advantage of this opportunity before it disappears. The nation is awakened and sent their dear sons to Jihad in the name of Allah, to pursue the truth, and to revoke the wrong.

(TN: Poem)

History has witnessed Aws and Khazraj get defeated when the children of Islam created battalions for Jihad.

Where are Allah's good worshipers? Where are the patient people? Where are the people of Surah al-Baqarah? Where are those who pledge allegiance to death? Go ahead and destroy the American army and kill the Zionist battalions. Where are the young men of 'Adnan and Qahtan (TN: Arabs descended from 'Adnan and Qahtan)? Where are the young fighters of Rabi'ah? Where are the knights of the Red Mudar? Where are the grandsons of Salman al-Farisi and Tariq Bin Ziyad's lions and Salah al-Din valiant? Where are the grandsons of Muhammad al-Fatih and the heroes from the land of Syria? Where are the good people of Egypt? Where is the assistance from Yemen and the thousands of Aden?

This is a war happening between the infidels and the Muslims; between Muhammad's soldiers the soldiers of faith, and the Crusaders. He who does not wage war, will not get the rewards, and sin will surround him. Hurry up, hurry up to paradise, which is wider than earth and heaven. You will ride Allah's horses and paradise's wind will blow.

In conclusion: I pray to Allah to accept his heroes, who died fighting in Jihad, in every place, especially the heroes of martyrdom operations who tore up the American and Zionist army. I say farewell to those who joined the war and pray to Allah to give us and them stability. It was my honor to have known some of those who passed away, and I am saddened that I have not met the others. What comforts me is the fact that they died as martyrs of this great battle to support Islam. I ask Allah to accept the martyrs, and be compassionate toward them, and let their souls roam in heaven, and then latch on lamps hanging from Allah's throne. Also, I pray to Allah to give their parents patience and reward them greatly.

(Page 20 of 21)

Our congratulations to them, for they sacrificed their lives for Allah. We regard them, but Allah is the ultimate judge… Those heroes and the Mujahidin are considered heroes by the people.

(TN: Poem)

Part Seven: Selected Religious Topics

When you talk to them, you think that they are simple minded, While they are brilliant and faithful.

They sold misguidance for faith, They should be treated like the people of sincerity and loyalty. They submitted offerings for the Almighty, and submitted the valuable item to receive the rewards. They had a grasp of the matter, and understood that Allah has for them a good and long lasting life. They called their relatives and went saying:

(TN: Poem)

On the path of God we go
We wish to raise the banner
To restore the glory fo the faith
We will sacrifice our blood for that cause

They also said:

(TN: Poem)

Do not say that rest is nice for we made it impossible
Do not say that the path is tough for we dedicated our lives for it

And I say farewell to those heroes this poem:

(TN: Poem)

Farewell O hero,
The eyes are full of tears
The earth is saddened
And the heart is complaining
We met in this life
We hope to meet in the next life too
We pray to God
To meet you again
We hope that you are happy
In a place that knows no boredom

(Page 21 of 21)

In a paradise and a garden
Where the Prophets are
And where the loved ones are
The rivers are there
The virgins will call us
In a voice that has no parallel
The heroes of our nations will reside
And in it our martyrs will be

Allah, give us goodness in this world and in eternity, and save us from hell. To you we submit and in you we believe and in you we trust. In your name we fight and govern. Forgive us our sins. You are the provider and the taker, there is no god but you and there is no strength and power except through you. You have all the might and honor. Allah, you have all the might and honor. Enter the hearts of the young people and steer them to Jihad for your sake. Allah, link their hearts, make their feet firm, give them a high throne, and comfort their hearts. Allah, provide your victory to your Mujahidin worshipers everywhere.

Allah, comfort our brothers who are prisoners at the tyrants' jails everywhere, in American jails, Palestine, Bagdad, Riyadh, Morocco, Egypt, Afghanistan, Chechnya, India, and Pakistan. You have the ultimate power. Allah, comfort us with patience and make firm our feet and give us victory against the infidels. Allah will win, but many people do not know this. Allah's prayers and peace be upon Prophet Muhammad, his family, and companions. Our last prayer is praise be to Allah, the lord of the world.

(End of translation)

Part Eight: Selected Miscellaneous Topics

> **1. 06 Ramadan**
>
> This letter briefly discusses the relationship between the Taliban and Al-Qa'ida. The fall of the "Taliban State" is mentioned as well as an attack in Nairobi and a short note on the decision to carry out that attack.
>
> Date: 11 November 2002
>
> From: Unknown
>
> http://www.dni.gov/files/documents/ubl/english/06%20Ramadan.pdf

(Fully translated)

(TN: The original document is one handwritten page that appears to have been torn from a wire-bound notebook.

06 Ramadan 1423 (TN: 11 November 2002)

The beginning of the decision:

The enemy is the Crusader and Zionist alliance out to control the world. It is not the enemy from (TN: illegible). The Northern Alliance is merely one soldier of the many in this criminal army. We should not hold back our energies in front of this soldier and leave behind more than 98 percent of the nation to be violated by the Crusaders and the Zionists. The decision for the attack comes from this context. The strange thing about the Nairobi attack is that they agreed upon it, and we were imagining their reaction. When the American jets soar and annihilate the men, women, and children of al-Qa'ida, it becomes a state of nonexistence.

At that time, the brothers agreed upon the decision, despite the reaction, and the Taliban opposition wasn't apparent or even clear. However, when it came to the Cole, there was opposition from all the Shura members. They started seeing the reaction from Nairobi, the uproar, and the power of the media. The Taliban began to feel the weight, and then the Taliban opposition appeared. However, the opposition against the decision in the arena (al-Qa'ida) wasn't strong enough. The Jihad group was one of the supports, and at that time there was an alliance between the two of us. But al-Qa'ida's special Shura did object. And the American pressure on the Taliban led the Taliban to influence the brothers.

(TN: the following is written bottom of the page):

((Abu al-Walid)) spoke strong words about you in the newspapers, and the brothers' response was strong against him. He he was in a state of shock when he spoke, at that time the "Taliban State" collapsed. He knew that the State was going to fall. He couldn't find a place and began writing under a fictitious name, and he opposed the Shura council. The Emir Al Mu'minin (TN: Emir of the believers) ordered him, but he insisted on his remarks.

PART EIGHT: SELECTED MISCELLANEOUS TOPICS

> ## 2. Letter to Badr Khan, 3 December 2002
>
> In a brief note to Badr Khan, the author passes on his well wishes and instructs the receiver to coordinate an idea with 'Abdullah Khan.
>
> From: Unknown
>
> http://www.dni.gov/files/documents/ubl/english2/Letter%20to%20Badr%20Khan%203%20Dec%202002.pdf

Full translation

In the name of God, The Most Compassionate, The Most Merciful.

Dear brother Badr Khan, may God protect you.

Peace and blessings be upon you.

I hope that you and the respectable brothers are in good health, and may God reunite us soon, as it pleases Him.

1- We received an undated letter from you, and we thanked God to hear your good news.

2- With regards to what you mentioned about your dear brother, 'Abdallah Khan informed us that the issue was resolved between the two, and we agreed on everything he asked for. God is the one to grant success to what pleases Him.

3- With regards to your last idea, we hope you coordinate it with 'Abdallah Khan.

4- Please mention the date in your next letter, God willing. In closing, please give my regards to everybody, and let them know that they are in our prayers. May God accept your fasting, staying up late to pray, and your good deeds. Please remember us in your prayers in these blessed days.

Peace be upon you,

Tuesday 27 Ramadan 1423, which corresponds to 3 December 2002.

3. Gist of Conversation Oct 11

> This is a conversation between two people regarding the translation of literature into French and local languages. The author requests that brothers in the Islamic Maghreb not negotiate with the French on releasing hostages (journalists); rather, correspondence with Europeans should be about a withdrawal from Afghanistan. The distribution and publication of messages is also discussed.
>
> Date: 11 October (year unknown)
>
> From: Unknown
>
> http://www.dni.gov/files/documents/ubl/english/Gist%20of%20conversation%20Oct%2011.pdf

(TN: The file is an original message which was replied to by inserting blue text after each point.)

Gist begins:

(In the name of God the passionate the merciful)

Original Author: Stating that the message of Abu Mus'ab 'Abd-al-Wadud was opened and that he promised to respond to him. He was asking if someone had prepared an article about pacifying the renegades, to be sent to Algeria.

Blue response: I might have sent the message of Abu Yahya to them, but a complete research was not done.

Original Author: Hopefully if you direct al-Sahab people to translate the Jihadi articles into French, as mentioned by Shaykh Bashir al-Madani in his report on the Islamic Maghreb. Hopefully you should send a copy to Shaykh Abu Muhammad and another copy to al-Sahab.

Blue response: Have seen the text and will review it again and give copies to the brother as suggested.

Original Author: Emphasize to our brothers in the Islamic Maghreb to translate literature into French and local languages.

Blue response: Will do, with God's help.

Original Author: Kindly send us the names of the Tribes that were mentioned in Shaykh Bashir al-Madani's report of the Islamic Maghreb.

Blue response: Will do that in the next correspondence.

Original Author: Attached statement to the French people, please give to Al Jazeera Arabic and Al Jazeera International. Attaching another copy for our media people and a slide on the American statement to look at and give suggestions, then destroy.

(Page 2 of 10)

Blue response: I only got one slide and will send the brothers' response.

Original Author: Should send a message to the brothers in the Islamic Maghreb not to negotiate with the French on releasing the hostages for money ransoms. They should negotiate on the interference in the region and the request to withdraw from Afghanistan. Should also inform all that negotiations with Europeans should be on Afghanistan withdrawal. As for the Americans, it should be for stopping their support to Jews.

Blue response: We will do that and we have informed them that negotiations with Europeans are about Afghanistan withdrawal only.

Original Author: As for the French journalists, if it is proven that they are spies, their case is tied to the Afghani withdrawal, and if no

Part Eight: Selected Miscellaneous Topics

time table is given, they would be killed. If the case is not proven, then negotiation for a ransom.

Blue response: Have no information (My Shaykh), probably I should contact Haqqani; we'll ask and then suggest and advise on what you said.

Original Author: As for the book Reliance points (TN: Nuqat al-Irtikaz) I wish to be given guidelines on how to benefit from it. I have mentioned that in my message to Basir with the book. I wish this note to be removed if the message has not been sent.

(Page 3 of 10)

Blue response: I have already removed the note from the Somali message. I think we can benefit from the book without mentioning the author. The book idea is good but no need to promote the Egyptian author.

Original Author: After the last memorial of the blessed operations on the eleventh, a message was released for Shaykh Abu Muhammad. The way Al Jazeera handled the message was strange. they practically ignored it; you should give us your responses on the reasons, or maybe ask Ahmad Zaydan.

Blue response: By God My Shaykh, we do not know what to follow up on. We could write to Ahmad Zaydan, maybe they are taking their revenge on al-Zawahiri, this is possible, relying on the editor at that time.

Original Author: You sent me an article by Sayf al-'Adil (an article about al-Zarqawi) and after reviewing I feel it is not really written by Sayf al-'Adil and has some insults to al-Zarqawi….

(Page 4 of 10)

and to the rest of the organization. It has encouragement to our brothers in Iraq to establish their state without securing the means of its success. This shows that it was not Sayf al-'Adil, that he has taken authorization from me and Shaykh Abu Muhammad, to deal with the al-Zarqawi case. The unity has not yet come between us and the al-Jihad group, since Sayf took authorization from me and Shaykh Abu Hafs. Note that Sayf is now in prison and cannot defend himself. We feel that there some states who are distorting the mujahidin reputation.

Blue response: The article is old and published on the internet. Some have suspected its authenticity. I will ask some brothers to look into it and prepare a response. I know al-Zayat and Sayf, but know Abu al-Khayr only casually.

Original Author: Concerning using the internet for correspondence, it is ok for general messages, but the secrecy of the mujahidin does not allow its usage, as couriers are the only way.

(Page 5 of 10)

Blue response: The issue is highly complicated (My Shaykh). How can we correspond with brothers in Algeria, Iraq, Yemen and Somalia? Sometimes there is no other means after taking precautions. As for Iraq, we will try, but it is too difficult.

Original Author: Attached is a message from Sahib al-Tayyib; kindly read and distribute, and a copy of his and my message to al-Shaykh Abu Muhammad. The message of Abu Muhammad will come to you in the next message.

Blue response: I saw the letter of al-Tayyib and he said well as you did too… we will forward those messages to Abu Muhammad.

Original Author: We need information about two female journalists from Denmark working with the newspaper who insulted the Prophet (PBUH).They were expelled from Pakistan, then returned.

Blue response: Will do, with God's will.

Part Eight: Selected Miscellaneous Topics

Original Author: What about the information that I asked about, the brothers in Iraq. Have you sent them the general policy, and what were their responses?

Blue response: The general policy was not sent yet, will do after they respond to our message to inform us about their leadership. But have sent the policy to Yemen and Algeria and will send it to Somalia at the first chance.

(Page 6 of 10)

Original Author: Circulate to all brothers not to give interviews to Jihadi sites. The content is not always satisfactory. As an example, the interview of Abu Dajanah al- Khurasani, given before he was martyred, which did not give good impressions.

Blue response: We should develop the Jihadi media, and have an idea to coordinate with al-Sahab. We have to rely on Jihadi interviews. As for the Abu Dajanah interview, the interviewer was a British Pakistani who used to work with us and was also martyred.

Original Author: Hopefully you could send me the recommendations of the nineteen brothers which are available with the brothers in the media.

Blue response: Have asked 'Abd-al-Rahman to prepare it, to be sent when convenient.

(Page 7 of 10)

Original Author: Concerning the wheat, I suggest you choose two experienced men from the region to work in grain and sugar trade, and should have a silo on high ground and should reserve what is enough for one year. But the silos should be within reach of the brother when there is a necessity. As for the other method, if you move plenty you should use well sealed clean barrels.

Blue response: We will try to apply the first suggestion according to our abilities.

Original Author: Hopefully if you inform me about the program that Ahmad Zaydan will prepare for the tenth anniversary.

Blue response: Nothing happened; will discuss it with him and Shaykh Yahya,

(Page 8 of 10)

some technical suggestions from 'Abd-al-Rahman that such program only suits a program like a "Witness on the century" on Al Jazeera that takes many sessions. As for the suggested program, the Shaykh will not be able to talk more than 15 minutes. Will contact Brother 'Abd-al-Rahman about the matter. Also, we should ask Ahmad Zaydan and see his opinion.

Original Author: Concerning the companion.

Blue response: We will try our best, with God's help.

Original Author: Have sent you a message about the brother on the line and have not received your response about what took place.

Blue response: Probably you mean the message of condolence about Shaykh Sa'id, which I have distributed to a number of brothers. All were happy about it. Hopefully you could write a condolence message.

Original Author: Also, the message of our brother Abu Anas al-Suba'i and the message of the sons of Shaykh Sa'id.

Blue response: They received it all and I have not received a response. When I met Anas, I asked him what the news was about the Shaykh. He responded thank God may God reward him, as usual the Shaykh's message is short. That is what he said to me, may God protect you.

(Page 9 of 10)

PART EIGHT: SELECTED MISCELLANEOUS TOPICS

I usually do not read other people's messages, I don't know whether you have in your letter to him anything that needs a reply, and I will see him anyway.

Original Author: Also, the statement about the flooding, I have not received a message about your receiving it, and why it was not broadcasted. Please do not disseminate as it is late, and the second message do not broadcast if more than two weeks pass by. I would like to know why they were delayed.

Blue response: The first and second messages were published on the net, brothers were reluctant to publish the first one. The reason for its delay was because we sent it to Al Jazeera and they did not publish it after two weeks. I attach the response from our people on al-Sahab on the two messages. I gave my apologies that the Shaykh concentrated on a special angle and did not cover the side of the faith, since people alone have certain energy and capacity.

Original Author: The courier was delayed, as we agreed on the 20th of August.

Blue response: This is the explanation, as the courier said that he will be back on the 30th. I failed to read the message and awaited the message of Dawood. We got two consecutive days of curfew, so it is my mistake, and I should look harder at dates in the future.

(Page 10 of 10)

Original Author: Would like to get whatever available of books on strategy, and you knows it is available on the internet.

Blue response: With God's permission.

Original Author: Concerning sending money to me.

Blue response: Publish it by God's will, and may not be able to send you anything due to short time, maybe will prepare the required amount next time. Would you inform me about how to send it? We usually transfer money by an exchange office, to be received there in rupees. If you want to keep the value you let your representative take it in rupees, or if you want to transfer it to euros. Is sending it as such safe, security-wise? Will send you your account details as given to me by the late Dawood in mid-Ramadan.

Original Author: Would also want you to delete the old messages to them, with this message.

Blue response: Do not have any previous messages and will give them to (Hamzah) soon.

Original Author: Also I request that you ask Brother 'Abd-al-Latif to bring messages from them to us. Attached is a message from my son to the media.

Blue response: Did not arrive.

Original Author: Peace be upon you with God's mercy and blessings.

Blue response: And peace be upon you with God's mercy and blessings.

October 11 (as dated by the author)

Gist ends

PART EIGHT: SELECTED MISCELLANEOUS TOPICS

> **4. Request for Documents from CTC**
>
> The author is asking for papers from the Combating Terrorism Center from the US Military Academy.
>
> Date: Unknown
>
> From: Unknown
>
> http://www.dni.gov/files/documents/ubl/english2/Request%20for%20Documents%20from%20CTC.pdf

Please send all that is issued from the combating terrorism center of the American military.

(CTC, Combating Terrorism Center- Department of Social Sciences- United States Military Academy) (TN: as given in English)

You have sent some of them to me, thank you, but I lost one of the issues about a statistic of the items read in al-Tawhid wa al-Jihad web forum. I do not know the title. I also lost a movie about brother Muhammad 'Ali Abu al-Sa'ud, Allah affect his release, and the title as I remember (Al Qaeda spy in America) (TN: title as given in English), or something like that.

6- I also ask that you send whatever you can from the site of the Egyptian newspaper al-Sha'b (TN: the people), and al-Tajdid site for Dr. al-Mas'ari, especially his talks and speeches, also the site of al-Haraka al-Islamiyah Lil Islah (TN: The Islamic Movement for Reform) headed by Dr. Sa'd al-Faqih, and al-Maqrizi site. Forgive me for asking too much.

> **5. Instructions to Applicants**
>
> This is a copy of an application to become a member of al Qa'ida.
>
> Date: Unknown
>
> From: Unknown (appears to be a generalized application provided by al Qa'ida)
>
> http://www.dni.gov/files/documents/ubl/english/Instructions%20to%20Applicants.pdf

(Fully Translated)

(TN: Each page has a watermark that reads as follows, "The Security Committee – al-Qa'ida Organization" "O ye people of faith, be vigilant.")

In the name of Allah the compassionate and merciful

Important remarks before you fill in the application:

1. Please answer the required information accurately and truthfully.

2. Please write clearly and legibly.

3. If you do not speak Arabic, please answer in the language you know.

4. Please refrain from sharing the information you provide on the application with each other because it is a trust to Almighty Allah.

5. You should know that the review of this application form is limited to the concerned individuals only.

Part Eight: Selected Miscellaneous Topics

6. If you would like to discuss any further issue, please tell your direct brother supervisor.

(TN: The following is a blank form:)

Personal Information:

- Name:
- Today's Date (Hijri):..........Today's Date (A.D.): ....
- Nickname/Alias:
- First Name:
- Father's Name:
- Grandfather's Name:
- Family Name:
- Father's Occupation:
- Number of Family Members:
- Age:
- Marital status:
- Country:
- Profession:
- Address:........Country:.......City:.........Street:..........

- Date of your arrival in the land of Jihad:....................

- How long do you plan to stay in the (jihadi) theater?.........

Education Level:
Primary.......Elementary.......Secondary......College..........

When did Almighty Allah bless you with this gift?...............

How much of the holy Qur'an have you memorized? Did you study Shari'a? Who was your instructor?...............................

Which shaykhs do you listen to or read often?..................

Which shaykhs or Muslim dignitaries do you know?................

Have you invented or researched anything in any domain?.........

Any hobbies or pastimes?..

What other languages do you speak and at what level?.
Language:........Read:..........Write:...........Speak:..........

What is your fluency in these foreign language(s:)?
Poor..............Good.............Excellent..................

List the countries to which you have traveled and the purpose of the trip(s):..................................

Do you know anyone who travels to Western countries?............

What is your favorite material: science or literature?:..................................

List the experience or expertise that you have in any area:...................
....

Do you know any workers or experts in chemistry, communications, or any other field?...

Do any of your family or friends work with the government? If so, would he/she be willing to cooperate with or help us?..........................
....

How many trips have you taken to Pakistan and for what reas on(s)?..................................

Were you previously been affiliated to any group(s)? ....
....

Are you currently a member in a group?..........................

Have you been ever convicted by any court? When, and who convicted you? What was the offense?..........................

Have you ever been in jail or prison?...........................

PART EIGHT: SELECTED MISCELLANEOUS TOPICS

List your previous occupations:................................

Have you received military training?...........................

Have you ever joined the Afghanistan theater? If so, what year and which group?...

Are any of your relatives or friends in the jihad theater? ....
....

List the types of passports you possess. Did you use a real or forged passport for your current travel?........................

Provide details on how you arrived here:........................

Did you encounter any difficulties on the road to this place? ....
....

Do you wish to execute a suicide operation?.....................

What objectives would you would like to accomplish on your jihad path?...

What ideas and views do you, your family, and your other acquaintances have about jihad in Allah's sake here?............
Family members:...............Other acquaintances:................

Do you have any chronic or hereditary disease(s)?...............

Who should we contact in case you became a martyr?..............
- Address:...
- Phone numbers:..

Praise Allah, Lord of all worlds

6. Letter Implications of Climate Change

> This letter brings up issues found in the climate change area and its resulting implications for families, finances, food security, water, etc. In turn, the author looks at the advantages that may be drawn and the job of al Qa'ida to improve these situations.
>
> Date: Unknown
>
> From: Unknown
>
> http://www.dni.gov/files/documents/ubl/english/Letter%20Implications%20of%20Climate%20Change.pdf

(Page 1 of 4)

Indeed all praise is due to Allah and we pray for His assistance and forgiveness. We seek refuge in Him from the Evil of our souls and our misdeeds, for who Allah guides will not go astray and he who sends astray won't come to the right path except by His leave. I also bear witness that none deserves to be worshipped beside Allah, and that Muhammad is both His servant and Prophet.

My Islamic nation

Peace, Allah's mercy and blessings be upon you,

Henceforth:

Congratulations on the arrival of the Holy Month of Ramadan, the month of both the Qur'an and fasting and the month of the nightly prayers, alms-giving and Jihad, so let's strive in worshipping and avoid what keeps us away from glorifying Allah, Almighty.

Effects associated with the enormous climate changes (TN: begin footnote) using such expression without mentioning the view of Shari'ah concerning earthquakes and discord seems purely Western.

PART EIGHT: SELECTED MISCELLANEOUS TOPICS

The secularists maintain that these are natural disasters we must confront. In other words, they are saying, we are able to stand up to Allah and confront His judgment and they have neglected what is stated in the Qur'an concerning these events. (TN: End footnote) Indeed, what our Ummah is experiencing, of effects associated with the enormous climate changes and the great suffering the natural disasters are leaving behind that now become prevalent throughout the Muslim countries, renders the traditional relief efforts insufficient. (TN: Begin footnote) Relief work is mentioned as the only solution for these disasters, without warning that it is a plague or suffering from Allah Almighty, and the first solution is faith and correct deeds. One of the correct deeds is assisting Muslims. Once again, the speech is outside a required legal foundation. (TN: End footnote) Although the provision of tents, food and medicine will always be crucial, the afflictions are taking a larger shape and volume, hence, the quality, method and timing of aid must be equally improved.

Similarly, we are in need of making major efforts in our relief work, as those victimized by the current climate change is a very large number, expected to rise. According to the studies, this number is higher than the number of people victimized by wars, for which the states recruit their strongest men, offer their best training and slash major portions of their budgets.

Regionally, the countries are annually spending 100 thousand million euros on their armies, devoid of any effect on the Palestinian issue, and the relief work is still considered secondary while its resources could not be compared to that of the military. Had only 1% of such expenditures gone to relief, together with a sincere and experienced workforce, the earth's face would have changed, likewise the poor people's condition would have improved much decades ago.

On the other hand, what we are experiencing today (drought growth, particularly in Africa, and flooding in other regions, which in days left behind thousands dead and millions of victims forced to be displaced in Pakistan alone) imposes a moral duty upon the good-hearted and determined among the men, to move earnestly and rapidly in rescue of their Pakistani Muslim brothers. For the calamity is considerable and beyond description, whilst requiring massive means. To observe this you need to send delegations to look into this tragedy in reality.

You have seen one of your Muslim brothers in Pakistan, covered in water up to his chest while trying with both hands to hold two of his five or six year old children above water. So, have you wondered what might have happened to the rest of his children, or haven't you heard about the women who are imploring you by Allah, the Glorious and Almighty, divine right to come to their rescue. It is incumbent, upon everyone who is capable, to aid the Muslims in Pakistan and demonstrate concern towards their precious being.

Millions of children are left in the open, without a suitable living environment, including good drinking water, which has exposed them to dehydration, dangerous diseases and higher death rates. I pray to Allah Almighty to grant them both relief and mercy.

And owing to the high frequency of such disasters caused by climate changes, the effort must not become merely one of providing temporary assistance, rather, to set up a distinct relief organization (TN: Begin footnote) Kindly see the comment about the relief organizations at the end of the speech. (TN: End footnote) endowed with the knowledge, experience and financial capability crucial for the effective dealing with such more frequent, diverse and massive consequences of climate changes. It is therefore incumbent upon such an organization to shoulder the numerous tasks and major duties that would require the collaboration of those who are sincere. Among its duties, for example, would be…

(Page 2 of 4)

First: To research the residential compounds built along the banks of rivers and valleys in the Islamic World and the prospects of future disasters as a result of climate changes. For what disastrous floods have befallen the city of Jeddah in the past was expected for a simple reason, Jeddah and many other cities were not only built over the banks of valleys, many of their structures and residential buildings were constructed over the entire valleys' paths. I am not pointing to whose responsibility that was, for such may be discussed in a different time. Yet I am attempting to portray what took place, to avoid similar flooding disasters and to find fundamental solutions for the dangers that threaten people's lives. Additionally, it is essential that all dam and bridge safety regulations be examined and revised.

Second: What is also required is to do what is needed towards the countries that are or may be afflicted with famines resulting from wars or climate changes, for the famine most likely gives early warning a year or more prior to taking place; delaying the relief and essential aid would result in a large number of deaths, in particular among children, while those who may not die may not escape malnutrition and some form of brain damage.

Third: The establishment of development projects in the ravaged and poor areas, as there is excellent opportunity for establishing such projects since only modest spending is required. For example, the construction of regulators (TN: Or diversions) and canals in the countries where rivers or seasonal valleys are flowing, such as in Sudan, Chad, Somalia and Yemen. Based on field work in Sudan, the cost of a regulator (TN: Or river diversion) capable of irrigating tens of thousands of acres, together with the main and tributary canals, which also means providing assistance to tens of thousands of people, is about two hundred-thousand euros, more or less, based on the proximity or remoteness of the required construction material.

Fourth: Work towards realizing food-security, as the reports stated that if a calamity befalls any major wheat exporting country and causes a cease in exports, many countries worldwide, and in our region particularly, shall experience deadly famine in the full sense of the word.

At that point, the money would not stave off the deadly hunger as long as the bread, the main nourishment, is lacking. Whereas Sudan is endowed with rain-irrigated agricultural land of an area estimated at two hundred million acres, only little of that area has been cultivated. So, it is essential to raise peoples' awareness about such dangers and to encourage the merchants and their families to entirely devote some of their sons to relief and agricultural work; the merchants today are the field knights who may rescue their nation from the predictable horrible famines.

So, it is essential to focus on this aspect and avoid investment in unproductive sectors, while it is also wrong to rule out investing in agriculture based on the current circumstances and on the grounds that such requires great effort while the profits are small compared to other forms of investment - for the issue is not an issue of losses and profits, it is an issue of life and death. However, one must also observe that agricultural investment requires perception, while the contracts must secure the investor's rights and not impede his work. Also be informed that the main investment underpinning is the independence of the state, the state must not be involved in the administration. For instance, some of the investment experiences in Africa were encouraging and some were not, as there is association between the success of investment and the people where that investment is made. Some people have an advantage when working outside their country, owing to things like the association between certain workforces, or may have advantage within their countries when in other association with certain elements, provided that such elements control the upper departments and the most crucial division of work.

(Page 3 of 4)

Fifth: We need to raise Muslim awareness about the dangers associated with depleting the underground water used for agriculture that is not renewable, while it is crucial to establish a network of pipes that joins the agricultural wells with the main network of drinking-water, in order to be used in times of necessity.

And last, I encourage my Muslim brothers to be kind and give out all they could to rescue the weak and relieve their suffering. Whoever relieves a believer's suffering, Allah will relieve an Afterlife of distress for. So, we should work for that and ponder Allah's words, Glorious and Almighty: And whatever good ye send forth for your souls ye shall find it in God's Presence,- yea, better and greater, in

PART EIGHT: SELECTED MISCELLANEOUS TOPICS

Reward and seek ye the Grace of God. For God is Oft-Forgiving, Most Merciful.

I pray to Allah, the Great Lord of the splendid Throne, to grant the Muslims' martyrs mercy, whether those killed during wars and Jihad in Allah's cause, or who drowned in the sea of that flooding, and to ease for them inside their graves and admit them to Your heaven (to replace them in their families) and to compensate their relatives well. He is indeed the Patron of this and capable of it.

(TN: Supplication seeking Allah's forgiveness)

The comment about the relief organizations:

First: for your information, the relief organizations are all working according to regulations set forth by the United Nations; those which are inconstant they will not recognize or they may even outlaw on terrorism grounds or for not conducting their business in harmony with international relief work standards.

I know a person in charge of a relief organization calling itself "Islamic" and headquartered in London. He is the person in charge of all relief work for Pakistan. I have talked to him concerning the relief of war victims, e.g., in Waziristan and whether it is possible to use such an umbrella to assist the Mujahidin, for there is no contradiction since the Mujahidin are also victims and they have both sick and wounded families. He said that this is next to impossible, as they are watched by the intelligence and governments, and without recognition and facilitation they could not even breathe. He said that they are particularly subjected to a stricter monitoring owing to their name, which indicates their Islamic affiliation.

They even have to prove that their intentions are not incompatible with the United Nations laws pertaining to nondiscrimination based on religion, while every now and then have to provide assistance to non-Muslims, and hand-out gifts to and help Christians in their religious holidays!! They also have to provide aid to the poor Hindus, and are required to hire a certain percentage of females in compliance with the principles set forth by the United Nations that prohibit discrimination based on gender. Thus, no restriction for how females dress or appear is permitted. So, I have seen their females during Pakistani earthquake relief work, no different than the Western females, despite the fact that they are British Muslims who have Pakistani origins. However, in Pakistan, they are wearing tight pants, full makeup and are running side by side with men. Despite all of the above, the brother in charge claims it to be "Islamic" work.

Neither could the principles of the relief organizations possibly be Islamic nor could the services it provides possibly be good for Muslims and according to their needs, so how could we possibly call for establishing a distinct relief organization!?

Second

(Page 4 of 4)

Performing field studies and food-security development projects and establishing the pipes' networks, all of the above while there is no single Islamic state on the face of the earth, appears to be peculiar. So does the reality of Muslims permit them to accomplish this? That they resolve and confront the natural disasters -while such is basically both affliction and torture by Allah- having in mind that they have got no right to implement the rule of Shari'ah in their lands. Again and again, I have been thinking but could not reconcile my thoughts. What is stated in the speech seems to be discussing a very advanced phase and is assuming the Islamic state is actually established in one country, but advice is offered to another.

Third:

The expressions used, such as (the field studies, the development projects, the food-security and the establishment of pipes' networks, then the agricultural investment independent of the state, followed by the climate changes and disasters) in their entirety are expressions used by the West, and bear certain or special understandings. The speech is outside.

(End of Translation)

PART EIGHT: SELECTED MISCELLANEOUS TOPICS

> ### 7. Message from Abu Hammam al-Ghurayb
>
> This short note was written to provide religious support and discuss suicidal operations.
>
> Date: Unknown
>
> From: Abu Hammam al-Ghurayb
>
> http://www.dni.gov/files/documents/ubl/english/Message%20from%20Abu%20Hammam%20al-Ghurayb.pdf

Related to ID 22839

Full Translation

'Umar said to Asma', May God be pleased with them, "We are more worthy of the Prophet than you are", she replied "The Prophet, prayers and peace of God be upon him, was with you, comforting you, teaching the illiterate amongst you, and feeding the hungry amongst you", and we do not have one tenth of 'Umar or Asma', May God be pleased with them, in our midst. Same as what the Prophet, prayers and peace of God be upon him, said to comfort his companions in their calamities.

On the matter of the suicidal operations; it has become a cheap weapon after it was a weapon of deterrence and you could watch the video of our late brother Abu-Muhammad al-San'ani. He was a capable brother and you can judge the operation. Also, after the killing of our brother Abu al-Layth, an operation was carried out against Khisat al-Dar, and also other operations substituted with other military things. The final decision is yours, and this was a point of view and advice.

May God guide you to what pleases him, peace, mercy, and blessing be upon you.

You brother

Abu Hammam al-((Ghurayb))

(TN: source document was not dated)

PART EIGHT: SELECTED MISCELLANEOUS TOPICS

> ## 8. Undated Letter
>
> This letter contains a theological discussion in the form of parables. Topics such as believers and good/bad outcomes are discussed as well as the battles of Tabuk and Uhud.
>
> Date: Unknown
>
> From: Unknown
>
> http://www.dni.gov/files/documents/ubl/english/Undated%20letter.pdf

Full translation

…and Praise to Allah for the good and the bad, God said; (We afflict you with the good and the bad as an ordeal). He also said (You may love something and it is bad for you, and hate something and it is good for you). Do not think it is bad for you but it is good for you. And after God has told the stories of the Prophets (PBU them) in Surat Hud, he said, All that we relate to you of the stories of the apostles, with it we make the heart firm. In them there cometh to thee the truth, as well as an exhortation and a message of remembrance to those who believe. And in the story of Ayyub (PBUH) he ended it with; it is a reminder to the believers and to those who pray. And in the Prophet's tradition, the real believers say Praise is to Allah if they were afflicted by the good they were thankful, and if they were hit by the bad, they wait.

And in the story of our mother, 'A'ishah, God be satisfied with her, in the incident of Ufuk, some of them were mourned. Some of them said, he was better than I, and he told his wife, she is better than you. God said: If the believers thought that they are better, and they said it, it is a clear lie.

In the battle of Tabuk, when the Messenger was asked, What has Ka'ab done? Some said, look at his clothes, and others said, what a bad thing you said… we did not hear anything but good about him. And Joseph (PBUH) when he was released from the prison, he wrote on his door, among other things, recognizing the friends.

The second matter, God mentioned in his book about the battle of Uhud, and of those companions who were killed. There were seventy with Asadallah and the Messenger's uncle. God said (Of you, who wants life) and (You refused after he showed you what you desire) (And those who flee when the two forces met, the devil caused then to stumble, and the Prophet ordered them to be pardoned and asked God to forgive them, and to consult them in the matter so life do not stop and there will be confrontation between the two sides. Therefore God said (And consult them in the matter). I did not mention this for a thing but (TN: page ends.)

PART EIGHT: SELECTED MISCELLANEOUS TOPICS

> ## 9. Undated Letter 2
>
> This letter begins with instructions to pray and the importance of being humble to Allah. A lack of Afghan partisans and anti-aircraft are mentioned, as are issues between the United States, Afghanistan, and Pakistan.
>
> Date: Unknown
>
> From: Unknown
>
> http://www.dni.gov/files/documents/ubl/english/Undated%20letter%202.pdf

Full translation begins here:

This matter requires patience with piety and God the Almighty had said: (But if ye are constant and do right, not the least harm will their cunning do to you) and he also said: (behold, he that is righteous and patient,- never will God suffer the reward to be lost, of those who do right.) (TN: Qur'anic verses)

Also, increase the prayers and remembrance of Allah as in the story of Yunis, peace be upon him (Had it not been that he (repented and) glorified God, He would certainly have remained inside the fish till the Day of Resurrection.) (TN: Qur'anic verse). Here I mention the vision you had when you were in the Jalalabad complex and while you were killing a big snake with a bent stick; you were reading al-Kursi verse and you stopped at the end of the verse and repeated it while He was the most high. The matter requires a lot of prayers, supplication and humbleness to the Almighty, praise be to Him.

The other matter is not to be egotistical as God the Almighty had said to the people of Badr: (Call to mind when ye were a small (band), despised through the land, and afraid that men might despoil and kidnap you. But He provided a safe asylum for you, strengthened you with His aid, and gave you Good things for sustenance: that ye might be grateful.) (TN: Qur'anic verse) He said to those who came in the invasion: (God had helped you at Badr, when ye were a contemptible little force; then fear God. Thus May ye show your gratitude.)(TN: Qur'anic verse). The other matter is the oppression, as perhaps it exists amongst us and brothers were killed, May God have mercy on them, such as Shafiq who did not want to see the faces of the brothers and also amongst the living. Another issue was the problem of the lack of Afghan partisans and our weakness for not considering the reasons. The main reason being the lack of anti-aircraft – as the problem of the partisans was associated with it. If we had that we would have driven all the Afghanis against the Americans and our sole one was the Pakistani aviation. I believe this is a duty for their sake to form a committee; the purpose is to search for this weapon and you would have privilege over it until it is successful. I had written to the doctor some four years ago about the problem of the anti (TN: anti-aircraft). God only knows what happened; whether he received the letter or not. I have spoken with…

PART NINE: LETTERS TO FAMILY AND FRIENDS

To or From UBL

> ### 1. Letter from Zamray, 07 August 2010
>
> Zamray writes to the family of Shaykh Sa'id (who passed away as a martyr) and offers condolences. Zamray mentions the positive things their father accomplished in his life and recalls Sa'id's character.
>
> From: Zamray
>
> http://www.dni.gov/files/documents/ubl/english/Letter%20from%20Zamray%20dtd%2007%20August%202010.pdf

(TN: Verbatim full translation from Arabic to English.)

In the Name of Allah, the Merciful, the Beneficent.

Praise Allah, the Lord of all worlds. Prayers and peace be upon our prophet Muhammad, his family, and all of his companions.

To the generous Brothers, the children of the noble Brother, Shaykh Mustafa Abu al-Yazid, Allah have mercy on him.

'Abdallah, 'Abd-al-Rahman, Usamah, Ahmad, and their brothers.

Peace be upon you, with the mercy and blessings of Allah.

I hope that my letter finds all of you, your families, your children, and all of the Brothers well and in the grace of Allah. In the Almighty Allah may we fear and desire [to emulate].

I will begin my letter to you with my deepest condolences, for myself and for all of you, for [the death of] your noble father, Shaykh Sa'id, may Allah have mercy on him. May Allah have mercy on all of your family. We ask that the Almighty Allah honor all them in accepting them as martyrs and grant them patience and provide them with the strength, given their good deeds.

May Allah reward all of you and mend your hearts and grant you the patience and solace.

Your father, may the Almighty Allah have mercy on him, spent nearly three decades on the battlefields of jihad, victorious for the religion of Allah. We regard him and Allah will account for his duties. He was persistent in his resistance, upon the highest mountains of Waziristan, against campaigns of the enemies. He was gladly persistent and patient. He was content and satisfied. He [always] pushed through, as long as he had the Almighty Lord along his side. He did not complain. He did not anger, not even when his life was threatened. We commend him for this, may we praise him with Allah.

I ask that Almighty Allah bless all of you and your children. I pray that He keep you devoted upon the path of jihad, the same in which your father, Allah have mercy on him, was so devoted. I pray [that Allah] brings you piety and devotion. We ask that we are capable for Him and that we may be called upon. Praise Allah the Lord of all worlds.

Peace be upon you with the mercy and blessings of Allah.

Your Brother,
Zamray

Friday 07 August 2010

(TN: End of translation.)

PART NINE: LETTERS TO FAMILY AND FRIENDS

2. Letter to Sons 'Uthman, Muhammad, Hamzah, Wife Um Hamzah

Finances are discussed, as are travel plans. The author recommends his wife leave everything behind in order to not be traced. Abu 'Abdallah plans to reunite with his family, although it will take time and planning.

Date: 26 September 2010

From: Abu 'Abdallah (UBL)

http://www.dni.gov/files/documents/ubl/english/Letter%20to%20sons%20Uthman%20Muhammad%20Hamzah%20wife%20Um%20Hamzah.pdf

In the name of God, Most Gracious, Most Merciful

And praise God, the Lord of the universe, peace and prayers be upon our Prophet Muhammad, his family and all his companions…

Furthermore,

To my dear sons 'Uthman, Muhammad, Hamzah, my wife Um Hamzah, and my grandchildren

Peace, mercy of God and His blessing be upon you

I hope this letter finds you, your families and your offspring well, in good health, more devout to Almighty God and closer to Him.

We are longing to meet with you and hear your news, and praise God for your safe release (nfi). We have received good news concerning you and your children, may God take care of them and may Islam and the Muslims benefit from them. And about your pursuit for knowledge, I ask God almighty to bless your effort. We are getting ready in upcoming days to receive Um Hamzah over here, with God's permission. However, concerning 'Uthman, Muhammad, Hamzah and their families, unfortunately our security circumstances do not allow to meet up in one place at this particular stage. However, we will arrange a secure location for you to stay, with God's permission, and that would take us sometime to arrange. Therefore, we hope that you have arrived at a secure place. We are doing well, with God's grace, and waiting to hear from you so we could confer on what we should be doing in the next stage. Also, reassure us (TN: keep us posted) concerning Fatimah and her daughter, news regarding Asma' and Hamid after they departed, and news about Wafa' and her sons. We will try hard to send your brother Khalid to reach you, to see how you are doing and to consult with you.

Note: Before Um Hamzah arrives here, it is necessary for her to leave everything behind, including clothes, books, everything that she had in Iran… Everything that a needle might possibly penetrate. Some chips have been lately developed for eavesdropping, so small they could easily be hidden inside a syringe. Since the Iranians are not to be trusted, it is possible to implant a chip in some of the belongings that you might have brought along with you…

Note:

What you need regarding financial expenses, it could be arranged with Shaykh Mahmud or brother 'Abdallah al-Halabi, whereas Shaykh Mahmud has authorization to spend on what you need from my own personal account.

Your brothers, Um Khalid, and Um Safiyah send their regards to you all.

Peace, mercy of God and His blessing be upon you,
Abu 'Abdallah

Saturday, 26 September 2010

PART NINE: LETTERS TO FAMILY AND FRIENDS

> ## 3. Letter From Abu Abdallah to his Mother
>
> In this letter to his mother, Abdullah simply checks in and gives his well wishes, hoping to reunite.
>
> Date: Unknown
>
> From: Abu Abdullah
>
> http://www.dni.gov/files/documents/ubl/english/Letter%20from%20Abu%20Abdullah%20to%20his%20mother.pdf

Page 1 of 1

In the Name of God, Most Gracious, Most Merciful

Praise to God, the Lord of the universe, peace and prayers be upon the master of the messengers.

To the dearest and precious mother, may God preserve her.

Peace, mercy of God, and His blessings be upon you.

God willing, this letter finds you at your utmost health and wellbeing, and Happy Ramadan to you…

Glad tidings to you regarding the release of Hamzah, his mother, and his wife, praise God.

God willing, 'Abdullah, 'Aisha, Usamah, and Siham are not giving their mother Maryam a hard time. May God accept it from you and put that in the balance of your deeds, and may God bring us together for the best.

How is your wellbeing and what is your news and how about any visions or dreams? Good news, I saw that I had been chased by a huge black snake. Next thing, I was grabbing its head. I opened its mouth and I saw as if all the teeth had shattered. Praise God, there were brothers close by. I told them, "There is no harm" or "It won't hurt you because we smashed its teeth…" And praise God…

Attached is a message from Umm 'Abd-al-Rahman ((Al-Bi Em)) (TN: VAR, BM) to you, and they await the reply from you…

God willing, as soon as the programs (NFI) become available, I will send them to you, and may God reunite us with you for the best, sooner rather than later… O! Lord, Amen….

And my regards to all at your end and don't forget us in your prayers.

Peace, mercy of God, and His blessing be upon you.

Your negligent son, Abu 'Abdullah, 15th Ramadan

PART NINE: LETTERS TO FAMILY AND FRIENDS

4. Letter to Brother from Abu Abdallah

In this short and cordial letter, Abu Abdallah inquires about a suitable time for travel, communication, and a meeting.

Date: Unknown

From: Abu Abdallah (UBL)

http://www.dni.gov/files/documents/ubl/english2/Letter%20to%20Brother%20from%20Abu%20Abdallah.pdf

(Full translation)

In the name of God, the merciful, the benevolent

Praise be to God, the Lord of the here and the hereafter, and peace be upon our Prophet Muhammad and on his family and all his followers

Now then...

To the honorable brother (TN: no name given), God protect him

Peace be upon you and the mercy of God and his blessings.

I would like send my greetings of health and well being to you and those with you...

I wrote this message after it became difficult for Um-((Hamzah)) to come to our side, because of my companions. With God's permission, I will visit her. Are there any permanent, nightly, or time to time checkpoints there in the place where you deliver and receive messages in your area? In your opinion, what is the suitable time for movement from our area to your area? Is it after sunrise when movement is weak because of the extreme cold, or is it after sunset?

Is it suitable for the brothers to take me to the place where you all meet customarily, or [should they take me] to the other place where I met with the brother from our side a while ago in the neighboring city, and I prepared the goods in a bag for him? Know that Um-((Sufiyah)) and her two sons will be with me.

In conclusion, may God, the almighty, protect you all and charge you with the execution of what He loves and pleases Him. We call that praise be to God, the Lord of the here and the hereafter, and peace be upon our Prophet Muhammad and on his family and all of his followers.

Peace be upon you and the mercy of God and his blessings.

Your Brother,
((Abu-'Abdallah))

With regard to taking all possible security measures, in case any mishap should befall my two companions, I wish to arrange with you that my son Khalid will contact you and will name for you a known location, which you can recognize and come to, so that the situation can be rectified in a suitable manner. Please let me know of your capabilities in a circumstance such as this.

PART NINE: LETTERS TO FAMILY AND FRIENDS

Private Letters to Selected Individuals

> ### 1. Letter to Abu Sulayman
>
> Abu Sulayman is going to be marrying Umm 'Abd-al-Rahman. Details of the engagement are discussed.
>
> Date: 28 June 2007
>
> From: 'Abd-al-Latif
>
> http://www.dni.gov/files/documents/ubl/english/Letter%20to%20Abu%20Sulayman.pdf

(Fully Translated)

In the Name of Allah, the Merciful, the Compassionate.

Peace ,and God's prayers be upon you.

To my dear brother Abu Sulayman, God protect him.

How are you, and what is your news? I pray to God that you are well, as we are, Praise is to Allah.

I want to relay to you good news. I met with Umm 'Abd-al- Rahman's [maternal] aunt, and she told me, they do not object to your marriage to their daughter. She apologized for the delay in their answer to us. She told me that her daughter asked her to finish memorizing the Qur'an before the wedding and that was the reason they were late. Her daughter asks, if the marriage happens, God willing, will you come here for Jihad with them or what will the arrangement be? They will wait for your answer. I pray to Allah to facilitate his issue and allow what is good. I ask to supplicate and ask God for the proper guidance in everything. I am waiting for your answer. Pray to Allah to join us soon. Give my regards to everyone. 'Abdallah, 'Aisha, and Usama are all fine, and they send their regards.

Peace, and God's Mercy and Blessing be upon you.

Your sister, Umm 'Abdallah
2 Jumadi al-Thani 1428 H (TN: 28 June 2007)

In the Name of Allah, the Merciful, the Compassionate.

Peace, and God's Mercy and Blessing be upon you.

To my dear brother Abu Sulayman, the groom, God protect him,

I pray my letter will find you in the best of health.

Dear Brother, regarding the recent message, it had additional things and also the letter from beloved Mother. The additional things that I put into it messed up the letter, and I apologize.

Dearest Groom, My advice to you is to ask Allah for proper guidance. Your brother is waiting for your answer, and God greets you, O groom, God willing, He will assist to what is good. Do not forget us in your prayers.

Your brother, 'Abd-al-Latif
12 Jumadi al-Thani 1428 H (TN: 28 June 2007)

Peace and God's Mercy and Blessing be upon you.

PART NINE: LETTERS TO FAMILY AND FRIENDS

2. Letter dtd 16 December 2007

In this letter, Umm Khalid mentions the importance of martyrdom; he gives well wishes, and discusses a security situation involving a young girl.

From: Umm Khalid

http://www.dni.gov/files/documents/ubl/english/Letter%20dtd%2016%20December%202007.pdf

(Fully Translated)

In the name of God the merciful

[TN: Islamic greeting follows]

From the Umm ((Khalid)) to my dear sister Umm (('Abd-Al-Rahman)); may God protect you from every evil.

Peace be unto you all and God's mercy and his blessings.

I pray to God that my letter reaches you and that you and everyone are doing fine, are in good health, and are in favor with God. We, thank God, are doing fine. A gift from God, we give in sacrifice to God (in anticipation of our reward) the sweetheart that she was.

My most precious dear ((Khadijah))
She is my mature daughter.
She is the flower of the field.
She is my compassionate mother.
She is my smile and my wish.
In this vanishing life First one to call me
With that precious word.
O how painful the agony of separation.
If only I could be at your side again.

And despite this, thank God, we have a judge whose rule is just. He judges as he sees fit and his generosity grants us children. Indeed, God took what is his. However, the patience, praise, and thanks of his servant will be rewarded with a palace in heaven and a place in the house of praise as the Prophet so promised. So I hope from God that I be among the winners of this palace and that he compensates her children with goodness.

My dear sister, may God grant you success over your letter in which you explained to me the trying details of the little girl. God, may He be praised, puts one to the test and has a plan for each of us, and indeed, He took great care of me and gave me patience. To God be the glory and favor! We cannot say thank you enough for the effort you gave in washing, preparing, and covering the body. God was wise to make sure that I did not attend or see her. I will not bother you except to say may God grant you success and let not God see you as reprehensible. I will not forget you. I will call for you like I did previously before the days of the martyr Abu 'Abd-al-Rahman, and your son, the martyr 'Abdallah, and your in-law the martyr. May God have mercy and I ask God that he accepts them. By God I have not forgotten you all together in my prayers.

My dear sister, I love you, I promise. My sister who has loved me; you are in my heart as you have mentioned and more. O how I wish for and pray to God that a meeting between us is not far off in order to see you all together and see our dear brides Ummah al-((Hakim)) and her sisters. Regarding your condition that your dear daughter stay for four years next to all of you, we have no objections to that. We will make every effort to be close to all of you, God willing. However, as far as coming to all of you now so his brothers can participate, our security circumstances do not currently permit this.

Regarding the legal picture, as I mentioned, after a year, the situation will have calmed for all of you and for us. God willing, if the matters go away after a year, then it is so. Meanwhile, we are hoping for the good news that the release, God willing, will be before that. By

Part Nine: Letters to Family and Friends

God the grooms are gathering soon, God willing, and in the best condition.

Last but not least, greetings from me and girls, especially for yourself and for Ummah ((Allah)) and her sisters.

Khalid sends his condolences to his brothers for 'Abd-Al-Rahman and 'Abdallah.

My dear sister, I hope we can maintain correspondence between us through Abu 'Abdallah, her beloved husband, may God have mercy upon him.

07/12/1438 H, corresponding to 16 December 2007

3. Letter from Khalid to 'Abd-al-Latif

The security situation of Khalid and his family is reviewed, and he discusses previous correspondences. Khalid wishes he were able to bring 'Abd-al-Latif into the family sooner, and mentions some issues with marriage.

Date: 7 January 2008

From: Khalid

http://www.dni.gov/files/documents/ubl/english/Letter%20from%20Khalid%20to%20Abd-al-Latif.pdf

(Full translation)

In the name of God the Merciful, the Magnificent
All praises to God and peace be upon the prophet, family, companions.

Henceforth,

From Khalid to my brother 'Abd-al-Latif

Peace be upon you and God bless

I hope that you receive the letter and you are doing very well. Thank God, I have received your letter dated on 7 Dhi Al-Qi'da (TN: no year given, but possibly 17 November 2007, if referring to 1428, as below), which is one month after you sent it. We felt very happy.

First: Regarding our security situation after the kids' arrival right over here, I would like to let you know that it is good, and you do not have to worry.

Second: Regarding the contents of your letter
(Regarding what I and the precious, God have mercy upon her (TN: a female who passed away), this is our duty and, God willing, I will continue until God grant you a good woman. I feel that I did not provide you or your dad and mom anything. I feel that I am

shortcoming). I would like to say may God reward you, and your effort is appreciated.

You, my brother and my sister, have gotten me a fiancé, and an agreement was granted. You also have asked for a fiancé from my dad, and an agreement was granted.

There is nothing else to do, except praying to God.

My brother, glory to God! I and my dad have tried many times to bring you in here before my sister's death, God have mercy upon her. However, there is a problem that prevented us from doing so, and it is the same problem that is preventing me from getting married now. I ask God to grant us a solution, and God is capable of doing so.

28/12/1428 (TN: 07 January 2008)

4. Letter to Wife

> In a letter to his wife, the author declares his will. While he discusses escaping prison, he also communicates how much he misses his wife. Within this document is also a letter to his father, where he also declares his wishes were he to die.
>
> Date: 15 August 2008
>
> From: Sa'ad Ibn Usama bin Laden
>
> http://www.dni.gov/files/documents/ubl/english/Letter%20to%20wife.pdf

(TN: video letter) My last will

To my dear faithful wife

Praise God, and prayers and Peace be on the prophet of God, our prophet Muhammad, his family and his allies.

My dear wife, Peace be upon you, and mercy of God, and his blessings.

How are you doing? I hope you are well and all who are with you. How is my son `Usama and my two daughters, `Asma` and (TN: possibly, Duha)? I pray that you are all in good condition. And how is my sister Iman, and Um Hamzah, and how are my brothers and sisters? I ask God that you all are in good condition, and that he expedite your release and of all prisoners of the mujahidin to the shores of safety.

My dear wife, you know that I escaped from prison for my sister, you, Um Hamzah, and Hamid, but I found that the matter (TN: his situation after escaping) may take a long time. I know that you are in a psychological crisis, so I doubled my thinking to find a way out for you, so I ask God to speed up the resolution for you and to get us together on the shores of safety sooner and not later.

Part Nine: Letters to Family and Friends

My beloved wife,

Know that you do fill my heart with love, beautiful memories, and your long-suffering of tense situations in order to appease me and be kind to me, and every time I thought of you my eyes would tear for being away from you. I want you to know that I will not marry on you because I will not find a woman like you, and I will remain in the land of jihad until God will bring us together in this world to see you and enjoy looking at you and at my children, and to compensate you for the kindness and love you missed in prison, due to the tension and being occupied with the thought. Or if meeting in the world is not possible, then I will see you in the thereafter and that will suffice.

So be patient and strengthen yourself with faith so that you meet God with him pleased of you, and we meet in paradise between its rivers and luxuries, as that is the eternal life that remains because you are a good wife in this world, and I ask God that you will be my wife in the thereafter.

My will: If I get killed, and you want to return to your family, then that is okay, but you have to raise my children properly, and to watch them, and be careful of bad company for them, especially after puberty, especially the girls 'Asma' and (TN: possibly, Duha). So be very careful about them and if you can marry them to mujahidin, then that is best, or else to good people.

As for 'Usama, when he reaches adulthood, if there is someone else who cares for you, then send him to the battlefield at his grandfather's. I specify his grandfather because his path is clear and true without qualms on it, and because jihad is an obligated duty for all adults, so he has to conduct jihad.

As for you, you are the apple of my eye, and the most precious thing that I have in this world. If you want to marry after me, I have no objection, but I really want for you to be my wife in paradise, and the woman, if she marries two men, is given a choice on Judgment Day to be with one of them.

In closing,

Please forgive me for my shortcomings towards you, and that you pray for me, and remind my children to pray for me and to do charity for me, and to arrange for a continuous charity in my memory.

So, so long either in this world or in the thereafter, I ask God to protect you and my children from all evil, and to nourish you and the children with His unsleeping eye, and to give you the best of endings, and get us together in the upper heavens with the believers, prophets, and martyrs, and those are the best company.

(TN: a sentence that is possibly "I leave you with God in Sudan")

And peace be upon you, Your husband
Sa'ad Ibn 'Usama Bin Ladin
15 August 2008

To my dear father,

Praise God and prayers and peace be on the prophet of God, our prophet Muhammad, his family and his allies.

How are you doing my father? I ask God that you are in good condition.

For starters, I do not forget your kindness in raising us, and for deepening the meaning of jihad in our hearts, and spending on us, marrying us, and many many other things, so you have the credit after God in our adherence and guidance to that path, the path of dignity and winning of paradise. What a father you are; you are the greatest.

My dear father, I ask you to take care of my wife and children, to ask about them always, follow on their news, and arrange for their marriages and for their needs, as they are from me and I am from you, so they are your children also.

My dear father, I counted myself as a mujahid and immigrant in the path of God, so if I get killed, please pray a lot for me, and do continuous charities for my memory, as I will need all the push I can get to reach that everlasting home.

There is another issue, which is that when I got married, Abu Burhan (TN: cut off word) paid my marriage expenses, so if this money is not from your money, please pay him back so that I will not be imprisoned in my grave.

In closing, I ask God that if I am killed before you, that God accepts my vouching for you, my mother, my sons, my daughters, my wife, my brothers and sisters, your wives, and all of our family.

And I ask Him to make you victorious over your enemies and his, and to establish the Nation of Islam at the hands of the mujahidin sooner and not later.

And please forgive me if there is anything that happened of me that you do not like and relay my greetings to all our family, especially my mother, and remind her of the virtues, as God said "strengthen yourselves."

You son
Sa'ad Ibn 'Usama

15 August 2008

5. Letter from Hamzah to Father dtd July 2009

Written to Hamzah's father, the letter conveys a desire to meet, and a longing that has existed for eight years. Hamzah is imprisoned by the Mujahidin, all of which is for Allah. Martyrdom is something that must be achieved.

From: Hamzah (Abu-Usamah)

http://www.dni.gov/files/documents/ubl/english/Letter%20from%20Hamzah%20to%20father%20dtd%20July%202009.pdf

(Full Translation)

Page 1

In the name of God, the merciful

Praise God, the Almighty, I testify that there is no God but the one God with no equal, and I testify that Muhammad, his servant and messenger, is the honorable Prophet, God bless him, his family, and his followers until the day of judgment.

My beloved father,

Peace be upon you and the mercy of God and his blessings. How are you? What is your news? I ask the Master (TN: God), praise Him, that you are in more perfect health and better condition.

I write these lines to you, and I miss you very much. No one knows to what extent, but God, the Almighty, praise Him. I am filled with immense feelings, a sundry of emotions, and different sentiments at the same time. My pen is happy to write these lines to you, my tongue glad to greet you, and my emotions yearn for the arrival of your letter, so that I may know anything, but in my own manner. Just as my heart is sad from the long separation, yearning to meet

Part Nine: Letters to Family and Friends

with you, and worry from the increasing period of separation. I don't know when the Master, praise Him, will delight us with a meeting, but at the same time I don't know from where to begin or where to end, as the words jostle and the thoughts intertwine. I don't know how to begin in regard to the pain of the separation, or the hope of a meeting. I ask God, the Almighty, praise Him, to bring us together sooner rather than later.

My beloved father, I could not imagine the length of this bitter separation, when you left me, my brother Khalid, and my brother Bakr at the foot of the mountains that you went to near the olive farm. Eight consecutive years. My eyes still remember the last time they saw you, when you were under the olive tree and you gave every one of us a Muslim rosary, God remembers this, then you bid us farewell and we left, and it was as if we pulled out our livers and left them there.

My honorable father, how many times - from the depths of my heart - I wished to be beside you, specifically while I was growing up, which passed by, as I was 13 years old when you left and have now become 22. I wished to be beside you, to have your exquisite character impressed upon me, and to be as you want or prefer, as you have hoped for or more. When I had crucial situations (TN: hard times), I wished that I could see you, if only for a minute, to get your pertinent opinion on them. Every time I found bonds between you and I that prohibited me, but these situations taught me how to be a man. Praise God, we as brothers help one another, every one of us gives advice to his brother. We are all eager to have your commendable character, and we always remind one another of this, especially the brothers who were with you the longest. Fate has willed that we are in the hands of the people. There is no power and no strength except with God, due to the fact that we are still in their hands. But what truly makes me sad, is the Mujahidin legions have marched and I have not joined them.

Page 2

The Mujahidin have impressed greatly in the field of long victories, and I am still standing in my place, prohibited by the steel shackles. I have completed the period of adolescence and I am in this place.

Then, I began the period of young adulthood and I have impressed greatly in this phase, and I am still in the same place. I dread spending the rest of my young adulthood behind iron bars. This is the case for many of those we hear about in various places of the world, but I want to make a simple request of you, that I am completely certain you can accomplish. You wished for it before I wished for it, it is: make an attempt with the people (by all suitable means) to release us from their safe and secure hands.

My honorable father, a fact that comforts me from some of my pain is that after you make it possible, I will be sacrificing all of this for the sake of the glory of God, and for us with the authority of God, the Almighty, praise Him, in this highly rewarding tribulation for the glory of God. Al-Bukhari in Sahihah, narrated by Anis, God bless him, "That when the Prophet of God (God pray for him) returned from the battle of Tabuk and left the city. He said, 'There are people in the city that march with you and cross valleys with you.' They said, 'Oh Messenger of God, they're in the city?' He (TN: the prophet) responded, 'They are in the city, as they're confined with a reason.'" We here are confined with a reason, with the addition of another distinction, that we have confined ourselves in the place that we are, we are confined for the sake of God. Every time that I remember this, I find happiness and peace of mind, because we are here because of God, the Almighty, and we accept His decree, completely convinced that this is what God chose for us that which is the best and better for us.

My beloved father, I announce to you that I and everyone (I and my brothers), God be praised, are following on the same path, the path of jihad for the sake of God, which God, the Almighty, praise him, prescribed for us. As we have suffered a deep wound, our brothers killed, our shaykhs weakened, our women raped, and our children butchered... everywhere. There is no power and no strength except with God. By the grace of God, the Almighty, praise Him, we have a righteous group to follow on this path in a time of few followers. They serve H through jihad with immeasurable obligation to it (TN: jihad), they said, "They don't have an aversion to the free." We are followers of this path. We are going down this path with

Part Nine: Letters to Family and Friends

God's permission. The path of jihad for the sake of God is what we live. Be it we achieve victory or martyrdom, which is our utmost hope. The shaykhs who are with us, may God bless them with the reward, they spared no pain or expense in guiding us down this path, with the book, the customary procedure, the stand of the venerable forefathers, and some trials that we live with. Now we are not waiting until we are foreordained, with the grace of God's glory, soon we will have the opportunity to recompense for what we have neglected.

Page 3

My dear father, for several years, I have promised you good tidings, to fill your heart with happiness and joy, which I have failed to present to you. With this good news I have gained a portion of your absolution, through God, I have been elevated and endeared to the path of knowledge, praise be to God. I found before me a large void, He is helping me to devote myself to the search for knowledge. I found from the learned brothers one who helps me, directs me, and guides me on the path. Praise God, I began on it and attempted to gain all that I could from the opportunity. As I, praise be to God, have understood the word of God, and I strived to reach the highest level. I studied in jurisprudence science the book of "Subul al-Salam" (TN: The Path of Peace), and I studied al-'Aqidah al-Wasatiyah (TN: The Central Faith), a large portion of the al-Tahawiyah, and the book Fatah al-Majid. I studied two books on the generally accepted Hadith, and likewise, I studied how to extract from the Hadiths and their ascriptions. I studied two books on the origin of jurisprudence and I am now on the third book. I studied the fundamentals of jurisprudence, the introduction to al-Ajrumiyah, and the vast cultural treasures of the past. What has inspired me and encourages me to do so are the good deeds that I will do for God, the Almighty.

You will be happy with your son when you hear that he is on this path, and I honor you and my dear mother, who urged me to gain knowledge. By the grace of God, I am continuing to learn more, all of this is by the grace and glory of God, the Almighty, without whom I wouldn't have learned a tenth of this, if not for the innumerous blessings that He has bestowed upon us, that no one could count but Him, as well as the good upbringing and education that you and my honorable mother have provided, and also the guiding hand and the direction of the shaykhs who are with us. I thank God, the Almighty, for this blessing that he has bestowed. Likewise, thank you for the superior education you gave me and your excellent choices for us, may God reward you well, as a father. I ask God to create for me a son that He loves and you love. I have not forgotten your good wishes for God, the Almighty, to aid me in gaining more and more, from the origin to the apex, God willing, so I can serve Islam, Muslims, and this religion.

My beloved father, I was separated from you when I was a small child, not yet 13, but I am older now, and have attained manhood. You might not recognize me when you meet me, as my features have changed. Praise God, I live a stable life, and God has blessed me with a pious wife, and she has blessed me with a son who I gave your name, Usamah, and a daughter who I named after the mother, Khayriyah. I ask God to place their image in your eye. He created them to serve you. Usamah says hello to you. I ask the Glorious Master to bring us together sooner rather than later. Omens of victory have appeared. They manifest themselves in the long night and appear at sunrise as a lie. It didn't perish except in the rising of the true sunrise, and with its' approach. We will leave soon, with glorious God's permission, like my mother left and who was with her, to join the jihad troop that is waiting for us to join them.

Page 4

Before concluding, I bid to you, beloved Father, a hearty farewell. I remember every smile that you smiled at me, every word that you spoke to me, and every look that you gave me. I consider myself at this time to be forged in steel, and I come to my beloved father in a quick visit with this message. Several moments have let in some of my anxiety and it partners with my happiness, then I return once

PART NINE: LETTERS TO FAMILY AND FRIENDS

more to my same place. God the merciful, I hope very much you comfort us in our separation, and write for us our recompense with God, the generous. Peace be upon you all, the mercy of God and his blessings.

I have not forgotten your good wishes.

I miss you.
Your son,
Hamzah ((Abu-Usamah))
Rajib 1430 Hijri (TN: July 2009)

6. Letter to Aunt Umm-Khalid

Condolences are expressed for Umm-Khalid—her husband passed away (by suicide.) Umm Sa'd mentions she is pregnant and provides details on the operation that killed Abu-'Abdallah.

Date: 21 December 2010

From: Umm-Sa'd

http://www.dni.gov/files/documents/ubl/english2/Letter%20to%20Aunt%20Umm-Khalid.pdf

---

(TN: Handwritten letter)

In the Name of God, the Most Merciful, the Compassionate Upon God we rely

To my Dear [TC: Maternal] Aunt Umm-Khalid, may God protect you, and make paradise your last destination, may God enhance your rewards and ours. I express my sympathy for the demise of your loved one, he is indeed our loss, as well as the loss of the Islamic community; he was the secret soldier, the devout, who had superior manners and who was totally understanding and accepting of others (TN: The loss of Abu- 'Abdallah). May God accept him among Martyrs in the Supreme Paradise.

Dear Aunt, God does not take nor give; to God, everything is measured and preordained, according to fate. Thanks to God almighty, we cannot do anything except to say, just as the kind God's messenger has said, "The eyes tear and the heart saddens." We are very sad for the demise of Abu- 'Abdallah. Please forgive my poor sentences, the loss is bigger than anyone just giving consolation in few lines. However, God knows what is in the hearts; we have to be patient. I ask God to bless your endeavors as well as ours. I ask God that you

PART NINE: LETTERS TO FAMILY AND FRIENDS

are safe and in tranquility, protected by God the compassionate, the merciful, and that you are fine. How is everybody, and how are the children? I ask God the compassionate that they are fine, in good health. I inform you that I and my son Sa'd are fine and in good health, thanks to God. I am seven months' pregnant. God willing, if I am blessed with a boy, I will name him Muhammad, and if it is a girl, I will name her Khadijah, thanks to God. I was very happy to have received your dear letter, may God bless you. In reference to your inquiry about the circumstances surrounding the martyrdom of Abu- 'Abdallah, nay God accept him, he left my place following al-Fajr (TN: Dawn) prayer, on the 9th of Shawwal (TN: 18 September, possibly 2010). He was fasting; he had fasted four days in the month of Shawwal. He went out to do some work. I received his death news the following day. He was killed before breaking the fast, right before sunset prayer, on his way to us in his vehicle, together with Brother Sa'dun, may God accept both of them with His compassion. I ask God Almighty, the God of the great throne, to allow (TN: the demised Abu-'Abdallah) to have his Iftar meal (TN: Breaking the fast meal) in the Supreme Paradise. In reference to your inquiry regarding the wills following his death, may God have mercy upon him, I was keen in delivering the fiduciary items personally to Umm- Hamzah (TN: Hamzah's mother). However, the security situation did not allow that. So Shaykh Mahmud requested that I hand over the fiduciary items to him, and then he would deliver them to Umm Hamzah, and also deliver the fiduciary items pertaining to you, which are two boxes of Khadijah's gold, may God have mercy on her; two small boxes of gold; gifts to 'Aisha and Siham; a small suitcase that contains fiduciary items belonging to father, May God protect him and to Sa'd, May God have mercy upon him; Abu- 'Abdallah's ring; his family's numbers (TN: Possibly phone numbers), two video camera tapes; computer; pistol; pliers; four notebooks to include Abu-'Abdallah's wills, may God have mercy upon him; two iPods that were gifts to 'Abdallah and Usamah, May God protects them; and small gifts from me to the children, may the compassionate God protect them.

Page 2 (7FA051D32D004997B5B7D1090ED9031E)

I ask God that you receive these fiduciary items safely, and I ask God to bless your path, finally, thanks to God almighty. Do not forget us in your prayers and supplications, and peace upon thee with God's compassion and beneficence.

Your daughter Umm-Sa'd (TN: Sa'd's Mother)

14 Muharram 1432 Hijri
(TN: 21 December 2010)

[End of Translation]

PART NINE: LETTERS TO FAMILY AND FRIENDS

7. Letter to Sister Um-'Abd-al-Rahman

Um-Khalid sends notification of the death of 'Abd-al-Latif. Requests are made for a personal meeting within the next four months.

Date: 5 November 2010

From: Um-Khalid

http://www.dni.gov/files/documents/ubl/english/Letter%20to%20sister%20Um-Abd-al-Rahman.pdf

Full Translation

In the name of God the merciful the compassionate

Praise God Lord of the Universe, Peace and Prayers upon his Prophet Muhammad and his Companions

To My Beloved Sister Um-'Abd-al-Rahman

Peace be upon you

I hope my letter finds you well.

I apologize for not writing for a long time, because of the martyrdom of 'Abd-al-Latif on the nineteenth of September.

We hope you are comfortable where you are. Please communicate my greetings to my daughters and my grandchildren. (TN: This is the Middle Eastern way of saying that I love your daughters and your grandchildren like mine.)

We have been making every effort to meet your condition of providing a dwelling place for your daughter, in a location close to you for a period not less than a year. For security reasons, we were not able to achieve this goal. This has been going on now for three years. I am afraid that losing too much time waiting may result in missing the train for both of them. Therefore, I suggest setting a date for finding the right place, say four months from now. If we succeed in meeting your condition, we will go ahead with the marriage, otherwise we are sisters and your love is in our heart. (TN: Meaning terminating our marriage commitment.)

Please let us know of your comment on this proposal.
Greetings.

Your Sister,

Um-Khalid 5 November 2010

PART NINE: LETTERS TO FAMILY AND FRIENDS

> **8. Letter from Qari, early April**
>
> 'Uthman coordinates communications between family members for safety, and he seems to mediate the relationship between the recipient and his father.
>
> Date: early April, unknown year
>
> From: Qari 'abd-al-Salam ('Uthman)
>
> http://www.dni.gov/files/documents/ubl/english/Letter%20from%20Qari%20early%20April.pdf

Full translation

In the name of God. Praise be to God and prayers and peace be upon the messenger of God.

To the honorable brothers, Katrina and the uncle, God's peace, mercy, and blessings be upon you.

I pray to God for you to be well and in good health and I pray to Him to accept your good deeds, protect you, gather us in glory in this life, and grant us eternity.

May God reward you greatly for what you did on the issue of Sa'd and those with him. May God grant you success so that you can complete the matter and make your hands accomplish good things. Regarding the three things that you asked for in your letter, the link between us and Sa'd is disconnected for now and we think that the best way for this is through the people that he is with (we will call them the West). If your side agrees to get them out, in my opinion, the first step is to get their approval. If they agree, they should determine a way for us to contact Sa'd and those accompanying him, either through us using Shaykh al-Islam in Zahid or through you. We prefer the first method, for it is easier and faster for us.

As for the two conditions for accepting mediation: without anyone knowing about it, and for it to be from the father... we guarantee these two things for them and we can confirm this to them after the approval of the first step.

It is fine for you to write letters on their behalf until linking up with them.

We wrote this letter to you before we sent your letter to the father, in order to speed up the first step which is very important in any case, and because connecting with the father and getting his response might be delayed. God willing, we will send your letter to him as soon as possible. If his response arrives, we will send it to you as soon as possible.

May God reward you greatly.
Your loving brother,
Qari 'Abd-al-Salam ('Uthman)
Date: 27 Rabi' Thani (TN: no year given, early April)

PART NINE: LETTERS TO FAMILY AND FRIENDS

> ### 9. Undated Letter from Khalid Habib
>
> The short note, presumably written to Khalid's brother, mentions Khalid Habib's declining health.
>
> Date: Unknown
>
> http://www.dni.gov/files/documents/ubl/english/Undated%20letter%20from%20Khalid%20Habib.pdf

(TN: appears to begin in mid-sentence)

(5) ...of your promise with me and send the consent as soon as possible, my dear shaykh. Oh my, my health has declined quite a bit due to the successive wounds, the most recent six months ago. Praise God, God will grant me this as a badge on the Day of Resurrection. I ask him to accept me and you and all Muslims. I pray for us and you to be kept from Satan and man and the demons. May he protect you and the doctor with his safekeeping, which neither man nor demons can take away from us.

Your poor younger brother, at the mercy of his Lord.

Khalid Habib

10. Letter from Khalid to Abdullah and Abu al-Harish

An engagement is being coordinated.

Date: Unknown

From: Khalid

http://www.dni.gov/files/documents/ubl/english/Letter%20from%20Khalid%20to%20Abdullah%20and%20Abu%20al-Harish.pdf

Gist:

To Abdullah and Abu al-Harish

Perhaps you're wondering about my engagement to Karima al-Shaykh Abu 'Abd-al-Rahman (B.M.) and we informed (TN: unclear; VAR were told that) they are your side, and so we asked Shaykh Mahmud for your telephone number. I will call you to complete the matter, God willing, and to prepare what is needed. With me will be one of the brothers, and he will follow the communication with you to specify the place that we will meet. I ask of God for safety to facilitate the matter.

Keep me informed of your latest news and well being.

Your brother Khalid

PART NINE: LETTERS TO FAMILY AND FRIENDS

11. Letter from Khalid to his Son

Khalid requests updates from his son and gives him updates on family matters and status on education of family members.

Date: Unknown

From: Khalid

http://www.dni.gov/files/documents/ubl/english/Letter%20from%20Khalid%20to%20his%20son.pdf

Page 1

In the name of Allah, the Merciful, the Compassionate.

Praise is to Allah, and prayers and peace be upon our Prophet Muhammad, his family and all his companions.

My precious son, God protect him

Peace and God's mercy and blessing be upon you.

I hope this letter will reach and you are in good health. We received two chips from you, and I opened one with a lot of effort. It contained messages from you to us dated 17 Rabi' Awal, and a message from Umm 'Abd-al-Rahman, and also some films -- the most noticeable of them being "Firepower," and a voice tape; □"And the Unbelievers plotted and planned and God too planned and the best planner is God." And the second chip was not opened.

Precious son, I read your letter and God bless you and give you success, and only God knows how I feel about your stability, and this is my only son. Until this moment I do not know when his matter will be settled (TN: the writer began the letter talking to his son, and then he began talking to someone else), and I pray day and night to join you with your children, amen. They have not forgotten you, and they always ask about you. They are fine and well and we surround them with our love, and we shower them with all that we possess of compassion and affection -- why not, and they are a part of me, and "God have mercy on her." She was my mother, my friend, and my comfort in this life, but praise is to Allah, "We are to God and to him is our return." Oh Allah give me rewards in my misfortune, and compensate me better than her. Ten years ago, she told me, "Do not be sad. I see myself standing at the door of Paradise and knocking on the door. He asked who? And I said, I am Khadijah. And then I entered under a beautiful tree and all of you came with me." Yes, she preceded us, but we will follow her to heaven, God willing.

My precious son, please write to me your news, always to be assured that you are alright. But in regard to Abd Allah, he is almost done with the third chapter, and in the fifth part he received a grade of excellent. Also, we have established temporarily b programs for Abd Allah and 'Aisha, and praise is to Allah, their affairs are going very well. 'Aisha has finished the first book and began to study or read the second. She also completed the first math book and is about to finish half of a part on intelligence; remembrance and the ability to memorize

Page 2

appear to be part of her. Siham runs away from her mother and goes to school. She takes the books and reads BA TA and DA. She concentrates on BA, but Hamzah, he is busy playing with his Uncle (Maternal) Ibrahim, and he likes to make airplanes and ships from papers and he blows on them by his mouth to fly higher.

They all send their regards and their condition will please you.

And finally, my father sends his regards.

Peace and God's mercy and blessing be upon you.

Your mother who doesn't forget you in her prayers.

PART NINE: LETTERS TO FAMILY AND FRIENDS

In the name of Allah, the Merciful, the Compassionate.

Praise is to Allah, and prayers and peace be upon our Prophet Muhammad, his family and all his companions.

Dear brother Abd Allah al-Halabi,

Peace and God's mercy and blessing be upon you.

Your letter, dated 16 Rabi' Awal, has arrived, and I was very happy for it, and it assured us of your status, and we are fine, Praise is to Allah.

In regard to the ID card. Yes, father knows, and it would be nice if you send me the answer about it as soon as possible, and peace and God's mercy and blessings be upon you.

Your brother Khalid

The letter is a very short summary due to the tight time and it is late at night.

God rewards you for the films you sent.

12. Letter to Um Abid Al-Rahman

> The author explains why he or she has not been in communication—security issues had not permitted travel. A marriage is discussed.
>
> Date: Unknown
>
> From: Unknown
>
> http://www.dni.gov/files/documents/ubl/english/Letter%20to%20Um%20Abid%20al-Rahman.pdf

(Fully Translated)

In the name of God, the merciful, the compassionate

Thank God, the God of all gods for the grace of guiding, thank God for the grace of the hegira, equanimity, holy war, I witness there is no god but God and He has no partner, and I witness that Muhammad is his prophet and his best friend Adam until judgment day, God's blessing and peace be upon him, and his pure people, and the mothers of the faithful and to all the ones who walked that route until judgment day.

To my sister in God, the mother of martyrs, Um 'Abid al-Rahman, God bless her

God's blessing and peace be with you.

I have a feeling, no one knows how strong it is except God, that I will be meeting you through these lines after a very long time has elapsed for us and for the Islamic people, but as the saying goes, the rain starts with one drop, maybe after this letter we will meet in person, God is capable of that.

Part Nine: Letters to Family and Friends

I swear to you, since the day God blessed us by getting out of the infidels' fist on 29 Sha'ban 1431H (TN: 10 August 2010), I was hopeful that we would be meeting up with the ones we love, but the security situation didn't allow and permit us, as the poet said, "Not everything a person wishes for happens sometimes the current goes against the sailboats."

We took shelter with the supporters and we weren't able to meet with the family until 9 Rabi' al-Awwal 1432H, 12 February 2011. I met them alone, and I left Hamzah and his family with the supporters.

We rejoice after the meeting with them and seeing Khalid, the mujahid, who still has the hope to urgently marry into your family. He is trying very hard to reach you; he is trying to reach a brother to take the necessary steps to set up a meeting with you.

We consider this to be the beginning of a new era ,especially since our security is getting better and the signs for victory for our mujahidin have begun to be seen, at least after the latest problems, with which you are familiar, what happened in Tunisia, Egypt, and the surrounding countries. This is on top of the vision that came onto Khalid, and of which he previously informed you.

Maybe the delay in the marriage is due to reasons unknown to us, but God understands. Plus this delay played a role in their intellectual maturity and their understanding things in view of reality and which be reflected in their future.

13. Letter to Aunt

The author asks about his brother Hamzah and his children, and asks about his extended family. The author wishes for his aunt's company as well.

Date: Unknown

From: Unknown

http://www.dni.gov/files/documents/ubl/english2/Letter%20to%20Aunt.pdf

(Fully Translated)

In the name of Allah, the Merciful, the Beneficent.

Praise is to Allah, and peace and prayers be upon our Prophet Muhammad and his family and followers.

To my beloved Aunt:

Peace and God's Mercy and Blessing be upon you.

I write this letter to you after my heart was filled with joy for the happy news for which we have been waiting for many years, hoping that she would reach you in good health and peace of mind. I ask God to protect you, and to join you and Hamzah with us sooner and not later.

Dear Aunt, Please write to me about you, I have missed you since the day you left. Tell me about my brother, Hamzah, and Maryam and their children, God have them in his protection.

I also kindly ask you to provide with news about Wafa, my brother Sa'd's wife, and her children. I pray to God Almighty to have mercy on my brother Sa'd and my sister Khadijah and to accept them with the martyrs and to gathers us in them in the highest Paradise. Please

PART NINE: LETTERS TO FAMILY AND FRIENDS

inform me about my brothers and their children, and also about my sisters, Fatimah and Iman, and my brother Ladin.

Dear Aunt, we are all well and in peace, and we are all waiting for the day when you join us. In my rush, I do not want to forget to say that may God reward you with the best reward in the measure of your good deeds. and I want to write you about my younger siblings and the children of my sister Khadijah, they are with us and in the care of my sister Maryam; the only mother Suham knows is Maryam. And you know well the ages of 'Abdallah and Safiyah; Safiyah reminds me very much of my sister Khadijah.

My sister Asia is seven years old now, and 'Aisha is older by a few months, my brother Ibrahim is now six years and few months old, and Usama is a few months younger than he. Zaynab is four, and Suham is a few months younger, and Hussayn is two and a half.

I asked God to raise them and all my father's grandchildren well and to be good worshipers.

Finally: I ask God to make it easy for us to be united. Peace be upon you.

> ## 14. Letter to Brother Fatimah
>
> In this letter, 'Amir and Hammadah congratulate Fatimah on the birth of his child, and regret they were not able to attend the child birthing ceremony. In addition, well wishes are sent.
>
> Date: Unknown
>
> From: 'Amir and Hammadah
>
> http://www.dni.gov/files/documents/ubl/english2/Letter%20to%20Brother%20Fatimah.pdf

Full translation begins here:

In the name of God the merciful, the compassionate:

Praise be to God, and peace and prayers upon the Prophet, who was the last prophet.

Dear Brother ((Fatimah)), greetings and God bless you and be merciful to you. We ask the Lord of greatness and splendor to grant you and yours health. We ask him and give him glory to protect us in the world and the next, and to not give the blasphemers and hypocrites a path to us.

As for us, we are well, thank God, and lack nothing except seeing you and enjoying your conversation and your righteous prayers.

God knows we miss you. 'Amir tells you we miss you, dear shaykh. We would love to see you, to tell you three hundred million congratulations. God willing the new girl will grow with your prosperity. I wish that I had been there for the seven-day celebration (TN: after the birth of the child) and to talk baby talk with her. God willing she will grow to be a good daughter for you, with your love and affection. By the way, how is the boy Salah and his sister the

PART NINE: LETTERS TO FAMILY AND FRIENDS

little chick? We miss their mischief. May God keep them with you, and you with us, oh God.

We also bless the marriage of your two daughters. We ask the God of splendor and glory to make it a blessed marriage and to grant them good children.

This is what we have prepared up until now. We hope that we will be included in your righteous prayers. Send our greetings to all of the loved ones, especially the companion of the teacher who broke the wood (TN: SIC, NFI), tell him hello and ask him if he is still single or not.

Your younger brothers,

'Amir and Hammadah

15. Letter to daughter Umm-Mu'adh

> The author expresses how much he or she misses their daughter, and asks how other individuals are doing. The author communicates messages from his/her grandmother and hopes Umm-Mu'adh teaches her brother certain subjects in school.
>
> Date: Unknown
>
> From: Unknown
>
> http://www.dni.gov/files/documents/ubl/english2/Letter%20to%20daughter%20Umm-Muadh.pdf

Page 1 of 1

In the name of God, the Compassionate the Merciful

To my precious daughter, ((Umm-Mu'adh))

Peace, mercy, and blessings of God be upon you

How are you and what is your news? By God, I miss you so much. Yes, I miss my pious daughter. May God bless you and reward you for all that you have done for me. May God also reward your parents for their good upbringing of you, and make heaven their final destination. I yearn much for the beautiful days I spent with you, especially during travel. Indeed, you were the best companion. May God bless you. How is Sa'd doing? How far is he in studying the Qur'an and does he study other subjects? Make sure you and his father take good care of him, as he has great capabilities. At least teach him the basic principles of reading, writing, and mathematics and read to him the Prophet's biography and the stories of the Prophets. What is his latest funny news? And how is his sister Khawlah? I wish I could hear her talking. As I had indicated in my second letter, everyone misses you and hopes to see you. May God get us together soon. It is preferable

PART NINE: LETTERS TO FAMILY AND FRIENDS

to travel light by reducing what you carry as much as possible; only carry what is essential. We are well, praise be to God. The only thing we're lacking is getting together with you. Please forgive me if I made you mad – and perhaps for having done so frequently. If the security conditions permit, please extend my regards to the people with whom you are staying. I apologize for this brief letter, because the power keeps going on and off. Take care of yourself and give my greetings to Abu-Mu'adh, Sa'd, and Khawlah. Give them this message from my grandmother: "I miss you very much. May God unite us soon. Listen to and obey your mother and father and do not anger them." Do not forget us in your prayers, especially for martyrdom. Congratulations on the departure of the tyrants who have oppressed the nation for a long time and God willing the rest of them will also go. Peace and God's mercy and blessings be upon you.

(TN: End of Translation)

16. Letter to Hamza

Directions are given to Hamza to stay put and to travel to Qatar when it is safe.

Date: Unknown

From: Unknown

http://www.dni.gov/files/documents/ubl/english2/Letter%20to%20Hamza.pdf

In the Name of God, the Merciful, the Compassionate

Thanks be to God Almighty, and prayers and peace be upon our Prophet Muhammad, his family and followers. Amen.

To my dear son Hamza, may God protect you,

Peace and blessings of God be upon you. I hope my letter finds you, your family, and children in good health.

Anyway, I think that he should not leave the house unless it is absolutely necessary until you get released to your dear mother. I would like to break the good news to you that I have been working to get you to join us, along with Um-Usama and Hajja Um-Khaled in nine months.

Travel to Qatar, Muhammad is studying strategic sciences, sociology and psychology; write details no one but he is privy to, that way they make sure that the letter is in fact written by Hamza.

PART NINE: LETTERS TO FAMILY AND FRIENDS

> ### 17. Letter to Um Sa'ad from Aunt Um Khalid
>
> Aunt Um Khalid struggles with the death of Abu 'Abdallah and questions how martyrdom should be received.
>
> Date: Unknown
>
> From: Aunt Um Khalid
>
> http://www.dni.gov/files/documents/ubl/english/Letter%20to%20Um%20Saad%20from%20aunt%20Um%20Khalid.pdf

Full Translation Page 1

In the name of Allah the most gracious the most merciful

Thanks be to God, peace and prayers be upon the Prophet of Allah, his family, his companions and his followers

To my dear daughter Um Sa'ad – May God protect her

Peace, mercy and the blessings of Allah be upon you

I pray to the Almighty that this letter finds you all well, in good health, patient, with firmness and satisfied because he who is satisfied would be gratified as the Messenger of Allah, peace and prayers be upon him had said. Thanks be to God and the grace of Islam because the Muslim carries his paradise between his sides – we ask Allah to be generous and to make us amongst the martyrs.

My dear daughter,

Misfortune has enveloped us with Abu 'Abdallah and we were all sad; do we receive martyrdom and happiness in eternal paradise? Lucky is he, because he received what he wished for. In every letter, he would say to me, I pray for martyrdom my maternal aunt. Thanks be to God, he received it while he was fasting and would break his fast with his God. Miriam had seen that the tombs of the martyrs shall open, and he would be calling out their names from the sky to rise to it to include Abu 'Abdallah; what end is better than this end, we consider them as martyrs. Allah is the one to accept them as such; we ask Allah to join them.

My precious daughter:
We were very happy, so were the children, to learn about your pregnancy and perhaps you delivered – they were very happy with his (sic) brother Sa'ad, and 'Abdallah, 'A'ishah, and Usamah as they are divided into two teams; 'A'ishah wishes the newborn to be a daughter and 'Abdallah and Usamah wish for a boy. Their maternal aunt split them and said, pray to God for her to be safe, whether a girl or a boy.

We hope that God granted you an easy time – 'A'ishah wants to know whether it is a girl of a boy? I say, I would like to maintain communication between us and learn continuously about your news and also for you to write detailed news about you as soon as possible, until things would improve, and hopefully it would be soon, God willing. Especially following the revolutions, we would like to arrange for a meeting with you, God willing and gather all the children. Please give my regards to the respected mother and all the family and we remain at your service and are entirely ready. Sa'ad and the newborn are brothers to 'Abdallah and his sisters, as there is no difference between them all.

Were you able to communicate with the family of 'Abdallah, and did they receive the news of his martyrdom, may God have mercy on him. We did not inform the children of this news until we found the appropriate opportunity. At the time when I was writing this letter, the children were next to me and give you their regards. They will write to you later on, God willing.

Peace, mercy and the blessings of Allah be upon you.

The beloved,

Your maternal aunt Um Khalid

PART NINE: LETTERS TO FAMILY AND FRIENDS

18. Letter to Umm Khalid from Sarah

Sarah writes to her aunt, asking how her siblings are.

Date: Unknown

From: Sarah

http://www.dni.gov/files/documents/ubl/english/Letter%20to%20Umm%20Khalid%20from%20Sarah.pdf

Full translation

In the name of God, The Most Merciful, The Most Compassionate.

Thanks be to God, and peace upon the last Prophet.

Peace and blessings be upon you.

My dearest maternal aunt Umm Khalid, may God protect you, and may He award us heaven.

I pray to God this letter finds you well and in great health.

How are you? I hope all is well, God willing.

How are my sisters Maryam and Sumayah? I hope they are well. How are the heroes 'Abdallah and Usamah? How are the sweet roses 'A'ishah and Siham? I send them my regards, and I pray to God that He protect you and them from any harm. I am doing well, thank God.

Your daughter, Sarah

19. Letter to 'Abd-al-Rahman

This letter contains a personal note to Umm 'Abd-al-Rahman in which the sender promises to meet with her soon.

Date: Unknown

From: Unknown

http://www.dni.gov/files/documents/ubl/english2/Letter%20to%20Abd%20al%20Rahman.pdf

In the name of God the most merciful and gracious

Praises to God and prayers and peace upon our prophet Muhammad, and his family, and all of his companions

And following

Dear sister Umm 'Abd-al-Rahman,

God bless you

Peace be upon you and God mercy and praise

I am writing to you this letter and the happiness and joy are fulfilling us, and thank God for His generosity and kindness.

Dear sister, we had promised you in the previous letter that we would continue to make the efforts to meet with you, and praise to God who is overwhelming us with his generosity and kindness, and has granted us this wish, which the prophet had asked us to be patient and promised us that it is going to be solved one by one and after a long and strenuous discussion lasting more than one month between my son and his father, from one side and between the accompanying brothers with us. We were able to obtain a written promise and I want to assure you that this is the last and final appointment, no more and no less, God willing; so his father had signed an agreement with the brothers that we will be meeting with you after the 10th anniversary for the battle of New York and Washington and the American withdrawal from Afghanistan and this has made us overwhelmingly happy and joyful, who makes good deeds will be rewarded and God help me repay the favor back; and my son says he will compensate her for what she has missed and she is waiting for him, God reunite him with her and make them happy.

My sister (TN: end of text)

Selected Bibliography

Books

Alexander, M. *Kill or Capture: How a Special Operation Task Force Took Down a Notorious Al-Qaeda Terrorist.* New York: St. Martin's Press; 2011.

Alexander, Y, and Alexander, D. *The Islamic State: Combating the Caliphate Without Borders.* Lanham, MD: Lexington Books; 2015.

Alexander, Y, and Prosen, R. *NATO: From Regional to Global Security Provider.* Lanham, MD: Lexington Books; 2015.

Alexander, Y, and Swetnam, MS. *Al-Qa'ida: Ten Years After 9/11 and Beyond.* Arlington, VA: Potomac Institute Press; 2012.

---------------------------------------. *Usama bin Laden's al-Qaida: Profile of a Terrorist Network.* New York: Transnational Publishers; 2001.

Al-Zayyat, M, and Nimis, S. *The Road to Al-Qaeda: The Story of Bin Laden's Right-Hand Man.* London: Pluto Press; 2004.

Amoor, Louise de GM. *Risk and the War on Terror.* New York: Routledge; 2008.

Andress, C., and McConnell, M. *Victory Undone: The Defeat of al-Qaeda in Iraq and Its Resurrection as ISIS.* Washington, DC: Regnery Publishing; 2014.

Ardolino, B. *Fallujah Awakens: Marines, Sheikhs, and the Battle Against Al Qaeda.* Naval Institute; 2013.

Atwan, AB. *After Bin Laden: Al Qaeda, The Next Generation.* New York: The New Press; 2013.

-------------. *The Secret History of Al-Qaeda.* Berkeley, CA: University of California Press; 2008.

Avery, D. *Pathogens for War Biological Weapons, Canadian Life Scientists, and North American Biodefence.* Toronto: University of Toronto Press; 2013.

Barzilai, Y. *102 Days of War: How Osama bin Laden, al Qaeda, & the Taliban Survived 2001.* Dulles, Virginia; Potomac Books; 2013.

Beck, G. *It Is About Islam: Exposing the Truth about ISIS, Al Qaeda, Iran, and the Caliphate.* New York: Mercury Radio Arts; 2015.

Bergen, PL. *The Longest War: America and Al-Qaeda Since 9/11.* New York: The Free Press; 2011.

Selected Bibliography

Berntsen, G, and Pezzullo, R. *The Attack on Bin Laden and Al-Qaeda: A Personal Account by the CIA's Key Field Commander.* New York: Three Rivers Press; 2006.

Bin Laden, O; Bin Laden, N, and Sasson, J. *Growing up bin Laden: Osama's Wife and Son Take Us Inside Their Secret World.* New York: St. Martin's Press; 2009.

Binkey, B. *Al-Qaeda Strike Again.* Concord, MA: Infinity Publishing; 2008.

Blin, A, and Chalian, G. *History of Terrorism: From Antiquity to Al Qaeda.* Berkeley, CA: University of California Press; 2007.

Bodansky, Y. *Chechen Jihad: Al Qaeda's Training Ground and the Next Wave of Terror.* New York: harper Paperbacks; 2009.

Brantley, C. *Global Terror: An Overview of the Al-Qaeda Organization, Ideology and Leaders, Including Osama Bin Laden, Ayman Al-Zawahiri, Abu Musa.* UK: Lightning Source UK Ltd; 2011.

Bravin, J. *The Terror Courts: Rough Justice at Guantanamo Bay.* New Haven, CT: Yale University Press; 2013.

Burgat, F, and Hutchinson, P. *Islamism in the Shadow of Al-Qaeda.* Austin, TX: University of Texas Press; 2008.

Burke, J. Al-Qaeda: *The True Story of Radical Islam.* London, UK: Penguin; 2007.

Burleigh, M. *Sacred Causes: Religion and Politics from the European Dictators to Al Qaeda.* New York: Harper Perennial; 2007.

Byman, D. Al Qaeda, *The Islamic State, and the Global Jihadist Movement: What Everyone Needs to Know.* New York: Oxford University Press; 2015.

Celso, A. *Al-Qaeda's Post-9/11 Devolution: The Failed Jihadist Struggle Against the Near and Far Enemy.* New York: Bloomsbury; 2015.

Chivvis, CS, and Andrew, L. *North Africa's Menace: AQIM's Evolution and the U.S. Policy Response.* San Diego, CA: RAND Corporation; 2013.

Cleland, R, *Al Qaeda's New Strategy: Getting Back to Basics.* Victoria, Canada: Trafford Publishing; 2010.

Coolsaet, R, and Peeters, E. *Al-Qaeda: the Myth: The Root Causes of International Terrorism and How to Tackle Them.* Ghent, Belgium: Academia Press; 2005.

Cruikshank, P. *Al Qaeda (Critical Concepts in Political Science).* London, UK: Routledge Publishing; 2011.

Dahl, EJ. *Intelligence and Surprise Attack: Failure and Success from Pearl Harbor to 9/11 and Beyond*. Washington, DC: Georgetown University Press; 2013.

Datta, SK. *Inside ISI: The Story and involvement of the ISI in Afghan Jihad, Taliban, Al-Qaeda, 9/11, Osama Bin Laden, 26/11 and The Future of Al-Qaeda*. New Delhi: Vij Books India Pvt Ltd; 2015.

Davis, PK, and Jenkins, BM. *Deterrence and Influence in Counterterrorism: A Component in the War on AL Qaeda*. San Diego, CA: RAND Publishing; 2002.

Davis, PK, Eric, L, Zachary, H, Mustafa, O, and Yashodhara, R. *Understanding and Influencing Public Support for Insurgency and Terrorism*. Santa Monica, CA: RAND; 2012.

Fury, D. *Kill Bin Laden: A Delta Force Commander's Account of the Hunt for the World's Most Wanted Man*. New York: St. Martin's Griffin; 2009.

Gartenstein-Ross, D. *Why al Qaeda Is Winning: The War We're Fighting, and the War We Think We're Fighting*. New York: Wiley Publishing; 2011.

Gelzter, JA. *US Counter-Terrorism Strategy and Al-Qaeda: Signalling and the Terrorist World-View*. London, UK: Routledge; 2011.

Gentilini, F., and Angela, A. *Afghan Lessons: Culture, Diplomacy, and Counterinsurgency*. Washington, D.C.: Brookings Institution Press; 2013.

Gergers, FA. *The Rise And Fall of Al-Qaeda*. New York: Oxford University Press; 2014.

Goldman, J. *The War on Terror Encyclopedia: From the Rise of Al Qaeda to 9/11 and Beyond*. CA: ABC-CLIO, INC; 2014.

Gray, J. *Al Qaeda and What It Means to be Modern*. London: Faber and Faber; 2007.

Gunaratna, T., and Oreg, A. *The Global Jihad Movement*. Lanham, MD: Rowman & Littlefield Publishers; 2015.

Gutman, R. *How We Missed the Story: Osama Bin Laden, the Taliban, and the Hijacking of Afghanistan*. Washington, DC: United States Institute of Peace Press; 2013.

Hassan, HA. *Al-Qaeda: The Background of the Pursuit for Global Jihad*. Almqvist & Wiksell International; 2004.

Hellmich, C. *Al-Qaeda: From Global Network to Local Franchise – Rebels*. London: Zed Books; 2011.

Hesterman, JL. *Terrorist-Criminal Nexus: An Alliance of International Drug Cartels, Organized Crime, and Terror Groups*. Abingdon, Oxford: Taylor & Francis; 201

Hoffman, B., and Reinares, F. *The Evolution of the Global Terrorist Threat: From 9/11 to Osama bin Laden's Death*. New York: Columbia University Press; 2014.

Hoffman, T. *Al Qaeda Declares War: The African Embassy Bombings And America's Search For Justice*. NH: University Press of New England; 2014.

Holbrook, D. *The Al-Qaeda Doctrine: The Flaming and the Evolution of the Leadership's Public Discourse*. New York; Bloomsbury; 2014.

Hull, EJ. *High-Value Target: Countering Al Qaeda in Yemen*. VA: Potomac Books Inc; 2011.

Hutchinson, P, and Burgat, F. *Islamism in the Shadow of al-Qaeda*. Austin, TX: University of Texas Press; 2010.

Ibrahim, A. *Al-Qaeda in Syria and Iraq*. San Diego, CA: Didactic Press; 2015.

Ibrahim, A, and Venzke, B. *The Al-Qaeda Threat: An Analytical Guide to Al-Qaeda's Tactics & Targets*. Tempest Pub; 2003.

Ibrahim, R. The Al Qaeda Reader. New York: Broadway Books; 2007.

Jeffords, S., and Al-Sumait, FY. *Covering Bin Laden: Global Media and the World's Most Wanted Man*. Champaign, IL: University of Illinois Press; 2015.

Johnsen, GD. *The Last Refuge: Yemen, Al-Qaeda, and America's War in Arabia*. New York: W.W. Norton & Company; 2014.

Jenkins, B. *Countering Al Qaeda: An Appreciation of the Situation and Suggestions for Strategy*. San Diego, CA: RAND Publishing; 2002.

Jones, SG. *A Persistent Threat: The Evolution of al Qaeda and Other Salafi Jihadists* Santa Monica, CA: RAND Corporation; 2014.

Keegan, J. *Intelligence in War: Knowledge of the Enemy from Napoleon to Al-Qaeda*. Toronto, Canada: Key Porter Books; 2003.

Lambert, R. *Countering Al Qaeda in London*. London: C Hurst & Co Publishers; 2011.

Landau, E. *Osama bin Laden: The Life and Death of the 9/11 al-Qaeda Mastermind*. Minneapolis: Twenty-First Century Books; 2012.

Lankford, A. *Human Killing Machines: Systematic Indoctrination in Iran, Nazi Germany, Al Qaeda, and Abu Ghraib*. Lanham, MD: Lexington Books; 2010.

Levin, C. *The Iraq-Al Qaeda Relationship: An Alternative Analysis.* Scotts Valley, CA: Cosimo Reports; 2005.

Lia, B. *Architect of Global Jihad: The Life of Al-Qaeda Strategist Abu Mus'ab Al-Suri.* London: C Hurst & Publishers; 2009.

Mackey, C, and Miller, G. *The Interrogators: Task Force 500 and America's Secret War Against Al Qaeda.* New York: Little, Brown and Company; 2005.

Mardini, R. *The Battle for Yemen: Al-Qaeda and the Struggle for Stability.* Washington, DC: The Jamestown Foundation; 2011.

Marlin, RO. *What does Al Qaeda Want: Unedited Communiques.* Berkeley, CA: North Atlantic Books; 2005.

Mastors, EM. *Breaking al-Qaeda: Psychological and Operational Techniques.* Scotts Valley, CA: CreateSpace; 2010.

——————. *Breaking Al-Qaeda: Psychological and Operational Techniques, Second Edition.* FL: CRC Press; 2014.

Menelik, G. *Finances and Networks of Al-Qaeda Terrorists.* Munich, Germany: GRIN Verlag; 2009.

Miniter, R. *Mastermind: The Many Faces of the 9/11 Architect, Khalid Shaikh Mohammed.* New York: Sentinel HC; 2011

Mockaitis, TR. *Osama bin Laden: A Biography.* Westport, CT: Greenwood Publishing Group; 2010.

Moghadam, A. *The Globalization of Martyrdom: Al Qaeda, Salafi Jihad and the Diffusion of Suicide Attacks.* Baltimore, MD: Johns Hopkins University Press; 2011.

Mohamedou, M. *Understanding Al Qaeda: Changing War and Global Politics.* London: Pluto Press; 2011.

Morrel, M., and Harlow, B. *The Great War of Our Time: The CIA's Fight Against Terrorism From Al Qa'ida to ISIS.* New York: Hachette Book Group; 2015.

Mudd, P. *Takedown: Inside the Hunt for Al Qaeda.* Philadelphia: University of Pennsylvania Press; 2013.

Nance, MW. *The Terrorists of Iraq: Inside the Strategy and Tactics of the Iraq Insurgency 2003-2014, Second Edition.* Abingdon, Oxford; Taylor & Francis; 2014.

Naylor, DH. *Al Qaeda in Iraq.* Hauppauge, NY: Nova Science Publishers; 2009.

Neumann, PR. *Joining Al Qaeda: Jihadist Recruitment in Europe.* London: Routledge; 2009.

Norton, A. *On the Muslim Question*. Princeton: Princeton University Press; 2013.

Peters, G. *Seeds of Terror: How Heroin is Bankrolling the Taliban and Al Qaeda*. Oxford: Oneword Publications; 2011.

Petrou, M. *Is This Your First War?: Travels Through the Post-9/11 Islamic World*. Toronto: Dundurn Press; 2012.

Pope, H. *Dining with al-Qaeda Three Decades Exploring the Many Worlds of the Middle East*. New York: Thomas Dunne Books; 2010.

Post, JM. *The Mind of Terrorist: The Psychology of Terrorism from the IRA to al-Qaeda*. Basingstoke, UK: Palgrave Macmillan; 2009.

Rajan, JVG. *Al Qaeda's Global Crisis: The Islamic State, takfir, and the genocide of Muslims*. New York: Routledge; 2015.

Ressa, M. *Seeds of Terror: An Eyewitness Account of Al-Qaeda's Newest Center*. New York: Free Press; 2011.

Riedel, B. *The Search for Al Qaeda: Its Leadership, Ideology, and Future*. Washington, DC: Brookings Institution; 2010.

Rodriguez, JA., and Harlow, B. *Hard Measures: How Aggressive CIA Actions After 9/11 Saved American Lives*. New York: Threshold Editions; 2013.

Ryan, MWS. *Decoding Al-Qaeda's Strategy the Deep Battle Against America*. New York: Columbia University Press; 2013.

Sans, C. Al-Qaeda in Egypt. A Brief History of Islamic Jihad Within Mubarak's Egypt. UK: Lightning Source UK Ltd; 2011.

Scaglia, B. *Beyong Osama: The Al-Qaeda Organization and the Continued Rise of Militant Islam*. Webster's Digital Services; 2011.

Scahill, J. *Dirty War: The World Is a Battlefield*. New York: Nation Books; 2013.

Scheuer, M. *Osama Bin laden*. Oxford: Oxford University Press; 2011.

Shahzad, SS. *Inside Al-Qaeda and the Taliban Beyond 9/11*. London: Pluto Press; 2011.

Shultz, RH. *The Marines Take Anbar: The Four-Year Fight Against Al Qaeda*. Naval Institute Press; 2013.

Shapiro, JN. *The Terrorist's Dilemma Managing Violent Covert Organizations*. Princeton: Princeton University Press; 2013.

Silber, MD. *The Al Qaeda Factor: Plots Against The West*. Philadelphia, PA: University of Pennsylvania; 2011.

Silverman, ME. *Awakening Victory: How Iraqi Tribes and American Troops Reclaimed Al Anbar and defeated Al Qaeda In Iraq*. Havertown, PA: Casemate Publishers; 2011.

Small, T., and Hacker, J. *Path of Blood: The Story of Al Qaeda's War on the House of Saud*. New York: The Overlook Press; 2015.

Soufan, A. *The Black Banners: Inside the Hunt for Al Qaeda*. New York: W.W. Norton & Company; 2011.

Speckhard, A., and Shaikh, M. *Undercover Jihadi: Inside the Toronto 18 - Al Qaeda Inspired, Homegrown Terrorism in the West*. VA: Advances Press; 2014.

Springmann, MJ. *Visas For Al Qaeda: CIA Handouts that Rocked the World*. Washington, DC: Daena Publications LLC; 2014.

Staniland, P. *Networks of Rebellion: Explaining Insurgent Cohesion and Collapse*. Ithaca, NY: Cornell University Press; 2014.

Taylor, P. *Talking to Terrorists: Face to Face with the Enemy: A Personal Journey from the IRA to Al Qaeda*. New York: Harper Press; 2011.

Tucker, J. *War of Nerves: Chemical Warfare from World War I to Al-Qaeda*. New York: Anchor Books; 2007.

Uhl-Bien, M, and Marion, R. *Complexity Theory and Al Qaeda: Examining Complex Leadership*. Management Department Faculty Publications: University of Nebraska – Lincoln; 2003.

Van Linschoten, AS, and Kuehn, F. *An Enemy We Created: The Myth of the Taliban/Al-Qaeda Merger in Afghanistan, 1970-2010*. London: C Hurst & Co Publishers; 2011.

Williams, BG. *Predators: The CIA's Drone War on al Qaeda*. Dulles, Virginia: Potomac Books; 2013.

Articles

Agbiboa, DE. "Al-Shabab's Dangerous Affair with Al-Qaeda." *The Journal of Social, Political and Economic Studies*. 2013; 38(4): 425.

Al-Tamimi, AJ. "The Dawn of the Islamic State of Iraq and Ash-Sham." *Current Trends in Islamist Ideology*. 2014; 16: 5.

Aldrich, GH. "The Taliban, Al Qaeda, and the Determination of Illegal Combatants." *The American Journal of International Law*. 2002 Oct; 96(4): 891-898.

Beinart, P, and Katherine, T. "The Almanac of Al Qaeda." *Foreign Policy*. [Internet]. 2010 May/June [cited 2011 Aug 8]. Available from: http://www.foreignpolicy.com/articles/2010/04/26/the_almanac_of_al_qaeda.

Bell, JT. "Trying Al Qaeda: Bring Terrorists to Justice." *Perspectives on Terrorism.* 2010 Oct. 4; (4): 73-81.

Bell, K. "Usama bin Ladin's "Father Sheikh": Yunus Khalis and Return of al-Qa'ida's Leadership to Afghanistan." *Combatting Terrorism Center at West Point.* [Internet]. 2013 May [cited 2015 September 4] Available from: *http://worldaffairsjournal.org/content/osama-bin-ladens-father-sheikh-yunus-khalis-and-return-al-qaeda's-leadership-afghanistan.*

Bennett, M. "The Elusive Defeat of Al Qaeda." *Joint Force Quarterly: JFQ.* 2013; 71

Berger, CE. "Al Qaeda Reorganizes Itself for Syria." *Council on Foreign Relations.* [Internet]. 2014 April [cited 2015 September 2]. Available from: *http://www.cfr.org/terrorist-organizations-and-networks/al-qaeda-reorganizes-itself-syria/p32793.*

Berger, J.M. "The Islamic State vs. al Qaeda". *Foreign Policy.* [Internet]. 2014 September [cited 2015 September 3]. Available from: *http://foreignpolicy.com/2014/09/02/the-islamic-state-vs-al-qaeda/.*

Berman, I. "The Once and Future Threat: Al-Qaeda Is Hardly Dead." *World Affairs.* [Internet]. 2014 May/June [cited 2015 September 4]. Available from: *http://worldaffairsjournal.org/article/once-and-future-threat-al-qaeda-hardly-dead.*

Birke, S. "How Al-Qaeda Changed the Syrian War." *The New York Review of Books.* [Internet] 2013 December [cited 2015 September 4]. Available from: *http://www.nybooks.com/blogs/nyrblog/2013/dec/27/how-al-qaeda-changed-syrian-war/?insrc=hpss.*

Brachman, JM. "Stealing AL Qaeda's Playbook." *Studies in Conflict and Terrorism.* 2006 June; 29(4): 309-321.

Branchaud, C. "From Tripoli to Bamako, in the Wake of Al-Qaeda in the Islamic Maghreb." *Canadian Military Journal.* 2015; 15(2): 58.

Braniff, B, and Moghadam, A. "Towards Global Juhadism: Al-Qaeda's Strategic, Ideological and Structural Adaptations since 9/11." *Perspectives On Terrorism.* 2011 May; 5(2): 36-49.

Brannen, K. "Al Qaeda: Zawahiri Ordered Charlie Hebdo' Attack" *Foreign Policy.* [Internet]. 2015 January [cited 2015 September 3]. Available from: *http://foreignpolicy.com/2015/01/13/al_qaeda_zawahiri_ordered_charlie_hebdo_attack/.*

Buchanan, PJ. "Al-Qaeda in the Heart of Africa." *Washington Report on Middle East Affairs.* 2013; 32(2): 25.

Burke, J. "Al Qaeda is a Global Terrorist Organization." *Foreign Policy.* [Internet]. 2004 May [cited 2001 Aug 8]. Available from: *http://www.foreignpolicy.com/articles/2004/05/01/think_again_al_qaeda.*

Byman, D. "Al Qaeda is Alive in Africa." *Foreign Policy.* [Internet]. 2013 January [cited 2015 September 3]. Available from: *http://foreignpolicy.com/2013/01/17/al-qaeda-is-alive-in-africa/.*

------------. "Buddies or Burdens? Understanding the Al Qaeda Relationship with its Affiliate Organizations." *Security Studies.* 2014; 23(3): 431-470.

------------. "Can Al Qaeda in the Arabian Peninsular Survive the Death of Its Leader?" *Foreign Policy.* [Internet]. 2015 June [cited 2015 September 3]. Available from: *http://foreignpolicy.com/2015/06/16/yemen-al-qaeda-zawahiri-wuhayshi/.*

------------. "Review: Al-Qaeda as an Adversary: Do we Understand Our Enemy?" *World Politics.* 2003 Oct; 56(1): 139-163.

------------. "Why Drones Work, The Case for Washington's Weapon of Choice." *Foreign Affairs.* [Internet]. 2013 July/August [cited 2015 September 3]. Available from: *https://www.foreignaffairs.com/articles/somalia/2013-06-11/why-drones-work.*

Byman, D, and Williams, JR. "Al Qaeda Is Losing the battle for Jihadi Heart and Minds. *Foreign Policy.* [Internet]. 2015 August [cited 2015 September 4]. Available from *http://foreignpolicy.com/2015/08/19/al-qaeda-losing-battle-jihadi-hearts-minds-zawahiri-tape/.*

------------------------------. "Will al Qaeda Be the Great Winner of Yemen's Collapse?" *Foreign Policy.* [Internet]. 2015 April [cited 2015 September 3]. Available from: *http://foreignpolicy.com/2015/04/09/will-al-qaeda-be-the-great-winner-of-yemens-collapse/.*

Celso, AN. "Al Qaeda in Iraq's (AQI) Rebirth and the Syrian Jihad's Coming Failure." *Journal of Political Sciences & Public Affairs.* [Internet]. 2013 December [cited 2015 September 4]. Available from: *http://www.esciencecentral.org/journals/al-qaeda-in-iraqs-aqi-rebirth-and-the-syrian-jihads-coming-failure-2332-0761.1000e110.php?aid=32184.*

------------. "Al Qaeda's Post–Bin Laden Resurgence: The Paradox of Resilience and Failure." *Mediterranean Quarterly.* 2014; 25(2): 33-47.

------------. "Zarqawi's Legacy: Al Qaeda's ISIS 'Renegade.'" *Mediterranean Quarterly.* 2015; 26(2): 21-41.

Chilson, P. "Al Qaeda Country: Why Mali matters." *Foreign Policy.* [Internet]. 2013 January [cited 2015 September 3]. Available from: *http://foreignpolicy.com/2013/01/15/al-qaeda-country/.*

Cragin, RK. "Early History of al- Qa'ida." *The Historical Journal.* 2008 Dec; 51(4): 1047-1067.

Cronin, AK. "How al-Qaida Ends: The Decline and Demise of Terrorist Groups." *International Security.* 2006; 31(1): 7-48.

Cohen, HJ. "Al Qaeda in Africa: The Creeping Menace to Sub-Sahara's 500 Million Muslims." *American Foreign Policy Interests.* 2013; 35(2): 63.

David, H., Acharya, A., and Atwan, AB. "Ten Years After 9/11: Rethinking the Jihadist Threat After Bin Laden: Al-Qaeda, the Next Generation." *Perspectives on Terrorism.* 2013; 7(3).

Davidson, J. "Four Rules of War from Al-Qaeda." *Council on Foreign Relations.* [Internet]. 2014 August [cited 2015 September 2]. Available from: *http://www.cfr.org/terrorist-organizations-and-networks/four-rules-war-al-qaeda/p33416.*

Deazen, Y. "Al Qaeda in the Arabian Peninsula's Most Dangerous Man is Still Alive." *Foreign Policy.* [Internet]. 2015 June [cited 2015 September 4]. Available from: http://foreignpolicy.com/2015/06/16/al-qaeda-in-the-arabian-peninsulas-most-dangerous-man-is-still-alive/.

Dickey, C. "Women of Al Qaeda." *Harman Newsweek LLC.* [Internet]. 2005 [cited 2011 Aug 8]. Available from: *http://www.thedailybeast.com/newsweek/2010/01/12/divorce-jihadi-style.html.*

Donald, H. "Al-Qaeda and the Rise of ISIS." *Survival.* 2015; 57(2): 93-104.

Doran, M. "The Pragmatic Fanaticism of al Qaeda: An Anatomy of Extremism in Middle Eastern Politics." *Politic Science Quarterly.* 2002; 117(2): 177-190.

Fettweis, C. "Freedom Fighters and Zealots: Al Qaeda in Historical Perspective." *Political Science Quarterly.* 2009; 124(2): 269-296.

Gomes, JMdC. "A Financial Profile of the Terrorism of Al-Qaeda and its Affiliates." *Perspectives on Terrorism.* 2010 Oct; 4(4): 3-27.

Green, DR. "A New Strategy to Defeat Al-Qaeda in Yemen." Orbis. 2014; 58(4): 521.

Hashim, AS. "The Islamic State: From Al-Qaeda Affiliate to Caliphate." *Middle East Policy*. 2014; 21(4): 69-83.

Hellmich, C. "Al-Qaeda: Terrorists, Hypocrites, Fundamentalists? The View from Within." *Third World Quarterly*. 2005; 26(1): 39-54.

Hepworth, DP. "Analysis of Al-Qaeda Terrorist Attacks to Investigate Rational Action." *Perspectives on Terrorism*. 2013; 7(2).

Hersh, S. "Osama was planning US attack, grooming son to take over al Qaeda, show documents." *World Affairs*. [Internet]. 2015 May [cited 2015 September 4]. Available from: *http://worldaffairsjournal.org/content/osama-bin-laden-was-planning-attack-us-grooming-son-take-over-al-qaeda-show-declassified*.

Hobbs, JJ. "The Geographical Dimensions of Al-Qa'ida Rhetoric." *Geographical Review*. 2005 July; 95(3): 301-327.

Hoffman, B. "Al Qaeda's Uncertain Future. *Studies in Conflict and Terrorism*. 2013; 36(8): 635.

----------. "Terrorism in the West: Al Qaeda's Role in "Homegrown" Terror". " *Brown Journal of World Affairs*. [Internet]. 2007 April [cited 2011 Aug 8]; 13(2). Available from *http://www.bjwa.org/article.php?id=7g2aY29l77OM6LeiDWkwN3o0xvDb53Ysnfc7sCh*.

Hoffman, FG. "Al Qaeda's Demise - Or Evolution." *Proceedings Magazine*, US Naval Institute. 2008 Sept; 134(9): 19-22.

Holbrook, Donald. "Alienating the Grassroots: Looking Back at Al Qaeda's Communicative Approach Toward Muslim Audiences." *Studies in Conflict and Terrorism*. 2013; 36(11): 883.

Holtmann, Philipp. "Countering al-Qaeda's Single Narrative." *Perspectives on Terrorism*. 2013; 7(2).

Huckabey, JM. "Al Qaeda in Mali: The Defection Connections." *Orbis*. 2013; 57(3): 467.

Humud, CE. "Al Qaeda-Affiliated Groups: Middle East and Africa." Congressional Research Service. [Internet]. 2014 October [cited 2015 September 8]. Available from https://www.fas.org/sgp/crs/mideast/R43756.pdf

Jamal, A. "The Emergence of the Elite Arm of Al-Qaeda the Khorasan Group." *Special Warfare*. 2015; 28(1): 14.

IC Publications Ltd. *Evading the net: Al Qaeda triumvirate of terror.* 2010. Available from: *http://findarticles.com/p/articles/mi_m2742/is_417/ai_n56516356/?tag=mantle_skin;content*.

Javaid, U, and Nighatm, N. "An Insight into the Philosophical Dynamics of Al-Qaeda." *Journal of Political Studies*. 2013; 20(2): 201.

Jendruck, E. "Branching Out - Al-Qaeda Leader Announces New Affiliate for the Indian Subcontinent." *Jane's Terrorism & Security Monitor.* 2014; 14(9).

Johnson, PB. "Does Decapitation Work?: Accessing the effectiveness of leadership targeting in Counterinsurgency Campaign." *International Security.* 2012 Spring; 36(4): 47-79.

Jones, C. "Al-Qaeda's Innovative Improvisers: Learning in a Diffuse Transnational Network." *Review Literature and Arts of Americas.* 2006; 19(4): 555-569.

Jones, DT. "Al Qaeda's Grand Strategy." *American Diplomacy.* 2014.

Jordan, J. "Attacking the Leader, Missing the Mark: Why Terrorist Group Survive Decapitation Strikes." *International Security.* 2014; 38(4): 7-38.

Joscelyn, T. "Analysis: Al Qaeda attempts to undermine new Islamic State with old video of Osama bin Laden." *The Long War Journal.* [Internet]. 2014 July [cited September 4]. Available from: http://www.longwarjournal.org/archives/2014/07/osama_bin_laden_disc.php

--------------. "Osama bin Laden's Files: Al Qaeda;s deputy general manager in Yemen." *Long War Journal.* [Internet]. 2015 March [cited September 8]. Available from: *http://www.longwarjournal.org/archives/2015/03/osama-bin-ladens-files-al-qaedas-deputy-general-manager-in-yemen.php.*

Karmon, E. "Islamic State and al-Qaeda Competing for Hearts & Minds." Perspectives On *Terrorism.* 2015; 9(2).

Klein, A. "The End of Al Qaeda: Rethinking the Legal End of the War on Terror." *Columbia Law Review.* 2010 June; 110(5): 1865-1910.

Lebowitz, MJ. "The Value of Claiming Torture: An Analysis of Al Qaeda's Tactical Lawfare: Strategy and Efforts to Fight Back." *Case Western Reserve University Journal of International Law.* 2011; 43: 357-392

McCabe, TR. "The Strategic Failures of al Qaeda." *Parameters.* 2010 April; 40(1): 60-71.

McIntosh, C. "Ending the War with Al Qaeda." *Orbis.* 2014; 58(1): 104-118.

Mendelsohn, B. "Modern History and Politics-Decoding Al-Qaeda's Strategy: The Deep Battle Against America." *The Middle East Journal.* 2014; 68(2): 334.

──────────────. "Sovereignty Under Attack: The International Society Meets the Al Qaeda Network." *Review of International Studies.* 2005; 31: 45-68.

Moghadam, A. "How al Qaeda Innovates." *Security Studies.* 2013; 22(3): 466.

Mokhtari, F. "Dealing with Al Qaeda." *American Foreign Policy Interests.* 2010 March-April; 32(2): 75-82.

Naim, M. "Al Qaeda, the NGO." *Foreign Policy.* [Internet]. 2002 March [cited 2011 Aug 8]. Available from *http://www.foreignpolicy.com/articles/2002/03/01/al_qaeda_the_ngo*.

Orhan, M. "Al-Qaeda: Analysis of the Emergence, Radicalism, and Violence of a Jihadist Action Group in Turkey." *Turkish Studies.* 2010 June; 11(2): 143-161.

Ould Mohamedou, M-M. "The Militarization of Islamism: Al-Qa'ida and Its Transactional Challenge." *The Muslim World.* 2011; 101(2): 307-323.

Pham, PJ. "Foreign Influences and Shifting Horizons: The Ongoing Evolution of al Qaeda in the Islamic Maghreb." *Orbis.* 2011 Feb: 240-254.

Phillips, J. "ISIS vs. Al Qaeda: The good news and the bad news." *The Heritage Foundation.* [Internet]. 2015 January [cited September 8]. Available from: *http://www.heritage.org/research/commentary/2015/1/isis-vs-al-qaeda-the-good-news-and-the-bad-news*.

Postel, T. "The Young and the Normless: Al Aaeda's Ideological Recruitment of Western Extremists." *Connections: The Quarterly Journal.* 2013; 12(4): 99.

Price, E. "Literature on Al-Qaeda Since 2001." *Perspectives on Terrorism.* 2013; 7(1).

Ricks, TE. "Yemen movie: 'In the hands of al Qaeda'." *Foreign Policy.* [Internet]. 2013 February [cited 2015 September 4]. Available from: *http://foreignpolicy.com/2013/02/28/yemen-movie-in-the-hands-of-al-qaeda/*.

Riedel, B, and Saab, BY. "Al Qaeda's Third Front: Saudi Arabia." *The Washington Quarterly.* 2008; 31(2): 33-46.

Riedel, B. "Al Qaeda Strikes Back." *Foreign Affairs.* [Internet]. 2007 May/June [cited 2011 Aug 8]. Available from: *http://www.foreignaffairs.com/articles/62608/bruce-riedel/al-qaeda-strikes-back*.

Ronfeldt, D. "Al Qaeda and its Affiliates: A Global Tribe Waging Segmental War." *Information Strategy and Warfare: A Guide to Theory and Practice.* Routledge. 2007; p. 34-55.

Schanzer, J. "The Al Qaeda Reader." *Middle East Quarterly.* 2009 April; 16(2): 86-95.

Shavit, U. "Al Qaeda's Saudi Origins." *Middle East Quarterly.* 2006; 13(4); 3-13.

Silber, MD. "The Ever-Evolving Al-Qaeda." *Foreign Policy.* [Internet]. 2013 May [cited 2015 September 3]. Available from: *http://fpmigration.alley.ws/2013/05/16/the-ever-evolving-al-qaeda-threat/.*

Sinai, J. "Al qaeda." *Perspectives on Terrorism* 2013; 7(1).

Sinno, AH. "The Rise and Fall of Al-Qaeda." *Perspectives on Politics.* 2013; 11(2): 672.

Sohlman, E. "Al Qaeda in Yemen Pushed Back, but Terrorism Threat Remains Strong." *Current.* 2013; (550): 11.

Solomon, G., Solomon, A., and Solomon, H. "The Origins, Ideology and Development of Al-Qaeda in the Islamic Maghreb." *Africa Review.* 2015; 7(2): 149.

Steger, MB. "Religion and Ideology in the Global Age: Analyzing al Qaeda's Islamist Globalism." *New Political Science.* 2009 Dec; 31(4): 529-541.

Stenersen, A. "Blood Brothers or a Marriage of Convenience? The Ideological Relationship between al-Qaida and the Taliban." *International Studies Convention*, 2009 Feb 14-18.

Stuster, JD. "Al Qaeda-Trained Terrorists In New Zealand, Prime Minister Says." *Foreign Policy.* [Internet]. 2013 August [cited 2015 September 3]. Available from: *http://fpmigration.alley.ws/2013/08/12/al-qaeda-trained-terrorists-in-new-zealand-prime-minister-says.*

Thomas, TL. "Al Qaeda and the Internet: The Danger of "Cyberplanning"." *Foreign Military Studies Office* (Army) Fort Leavenworth; 2003: 112-123.

Tosini, D. "Al-Qaeda's Strategic Gamble: The Sociology of Suicide Bombings in Iraq." *Canadian Journal of Sociology.* 2010; 35(2): 271-308.

Ty, M. "Al Qaeda Core: A Short History." *Foreign Policy.* [Internet]. 2014, March [cited 2015 September 3]. Available from: *http://foreignpolicy.com/2014/03/17/al-qaeda-core-a-short-history/.*

Wedgwood, R. "Al Qaeda, Terrorism, and Military Commissions." *The American Journal of International Law.* 2002 April; 96(2): 328-337.

Zelin, AY. "The War between ISIS and al-Qaeda for Supreme of the Global Jihadist Movement." *The Washington Institute.* [Internet]. 2014 June [cited 2015 September 3]. Available from: *http://www.washingtoninstitute.org/uploads/Documents/pubs/ResearchNote_20_Zelin.pdf.*

Zenko, M. "Kill or Capture." *Foreign Policy.* [Internet]. 2015 April [cited 2015 April 20]. Available from: *https://foreignpolicy.com/2015/04/14/kill-capture-obama-drone-pakistan-cia-policy-special-operations/?utm_source=Sailthru&utm_medium=email&utm_term=%2AEditors%20Picks&utm_campaign=Russia_Direct_April_Promo4%2F14.*

Zhao, J. "Africa's New Bully: What Al Qaeda Movements Mean for Africa's Security." *Harvard International Review.* 2013; 34(4): 29.

Government Documents

A Transformation: Afghanistan Beyond 2014: Hearing Before Subcomm. On Near Eastern and South and Central Asian Affairs of the Senate Comm. on Foreign Relations, 113th Cong., 1st Sess. (April 30, 2014). Available from: *http://www.foreign.senate.gov/hearings/a-transformation-afghanistan-beyond-2014.*

Al Qaeda and the Global Reach of Terrorism: Hearing Before the US House of Representatives Committee on International Relations, 107th Cong., 1st Sess. (2001) 107-150 (testimony of Oliver B. Revell).

Al Qaeda in Afghanistan and Pakistan: An Enduring Threat: Hearing Before the Subcomm. on Terrorism, Nonproliferation, and Trade of the House Comm. on Foreign Affairs, 113th Cong., 1st Sess. (May 20, 2014). Available from: *https://foreignaffairs.house.gov/hearing/subcommittee-hearing-al-qaeda-afghanistan-and-pakistan-enduring-threat.*

Al Qaeda, the Taliban & Other Extremist Groups in Afghanistan and Pakistan: Hearing Before the Senate Comm. on Foreign Relations, 112th Cong., 1st Sess. (May 24, 2011). Available from: *http://www.foreign.senate.gov/hearings/al-qaeda-the-taliban-and-other-extremist-groups-in-afghanistan-and-pakistan.*

Selected Bibliography

Assessing U.S. Policy and Its Limits in Pakistan: Hearing Before the Senate Comm. on Foreign Relations, 112th Cong., 1st Sess. (May 5, 2011). Available from: *http://foreign.senate.gov/hearings/hearing/?id=8ec7ae3c-5056-a032-5292-4ec18865f8a0.*

Authorization For Use Of Military Force After Iraq And Afghanistan: Hearing Before the Senate Comm. on Foreign Relations, 113th Cong., 1st Sess. (May 21, 2014). Available from: *http://www.foreign.senate.gov/hearings/authorization-for-use-of-military-force-after-iraq-and-afghanistan-05-21-14.*

Bush, G; O'Neill, P, and Powell, C. *President Freezes Terrorists Assets,* Remarks by President. Available from: *http://georgewbush-whitehouse.archives.gov/news/releases/2001/09/20010924-4.html.*

Country Reports on Terrorism: 2006. U.S. Department of State. 2006 Apr 28. Available from: *http://www.state.gov/s/ct/rls/crt/2006/.*

Cummings, A. *IACP Committee on Terrorism at a COT conference:* 2008 May; Dublin, Ireland.

Evaluating Goals and Progress in Afghanistan and Pakistan: Hearing Before the Senate Comm. on Foreign Relations, 112th Cong., 1st Sess. (June 23, 2011). Available from*: http://www.foreign.senate.gov/hearings/evaluating-goals-and-progress-in-afghanistan-and-pakistan.*

Future of Al-Qaeda: Hearing Before the Subcomm. on Terrorism, Nonproliferation, and Trade of the House Comm. on Foreign Affairs, 112th Cong., 1st Sess. (May 24, 2011). Available from: *http://foreignaffairs.house.gov/hearing_notice.asp?id=1299.*

Global al-Qaeda: Affiliates, Objectives, and Future Challenges: Hearing Before the Subcomm on Terrorism, Nonproliferation, and Trade of the House Comm. on Foreign Affairs, 113th Cong., 1st Sess. (July 18, 2013). Available from: *https://foreignaffairs.house.gov/hearing/subcommittee-hearing-global-al-qaeda-affiliates-objectives-and-future-challenges.*

Implications of JCPOA for U.S. Policy in the Middle East: Hearing Before the Senate Comm. on Foreign Relations, 114th Cong., 1st Sess. (August 5, 2015). Available from: *http://www.foreign.senate.gov/hearings/implications-of-the-jcpoa-for-us-policy-in-the-middle-east.*

Is al-Qaeda Winning? Grading the Administration's Counterterrorism Policy: Hearing Before the Subcomm. on Terrorism, Nonproliferation, and Trade of the House Comm. on Foreign Affairs, 113th Cong., 1st Sess. (April 8, 2014). Available from: *https://foreignaffairs.house.gov/legislation?type=hearing&tid=All&tid_1=45&page=2.*

Juergensmeyer, M. *Global Rebellion: Religious Challenges to the Secular State, from Christian Militias to Al Qaeda.* Berkeley, CA: University of California Press; 2009 June 1. Sponsored by the U.S. Department of the Treasury. Available from: *http://www.treasury.gov/resource-center/terrorist-illicit-finance/Documents/guidelines_charities.pdf.*

Katzman, K. *Al Qaeda: Profile and Threat Assessment:* CRS Report for Congress; 2005.

Morris, MF. *Al-Qaeda as Insurgency.* USAWC Strategy Research Project. March 2005.

National Commission on Terrorist Attacks upon the US Cong. 2004; Testimony of John S. Pistole, Executive Assistant Director, Counterterrorism/Counterintelligence, FBI.

National Commission on Terrorist Attacks. *The 9/11 Commission Report: Final Report of the National Commission on Terrorist Attacks Upon the US.* Boston: W.W. Norton & Company; 2004.

Obama, BH. *Remarks on the Death of Al Qaida Terrorist Organization Leader Usama bin Laden:* Daily Compilation of Presidential Documents; 2011.

Poaching and Terrorism: A National Security Challenge: Hearing Before the Subcomm. on the Terrorism, Nonproliferation, and Trade of the House Comm. on Foreign Affairs, 114th Cong., 1st Sess. (April 22, 2015). Available from: *https://foreignaffairs.house.gov/hearing/subcommittee-hearing-poaching-and-terrorism-national-security-challenge.*

Regional Impact of U.S. Policy Towards Iraq and Syria: Hearing Before the Subcomm. on the Middle and North Africa of the House Comm. on Foreign Affairs, 114th Cong., 1st Sess. (April 30, 2015). Available from: *https://foreignaffairs.house.gov/hearing/subcommittee-hearing-regional-impact-us-policy-towards-iraq-and-syria.*

SELECTED BIBLIOGRAPHY

Shifting Sands: Political Transitions in the Middle East, Part 1: Hearing Before the Subcomm. on the Middle East and South Asia of the House Comm. on Foreign Affairs, 112th Cong., 1st Sess. (April 13, 2011). Available from: *http://foreignaffairs.house.gov/hearing_notice.asp?id=1262.*

Strategic Implications of Pakistan and the Region: Hearing Before the Senate Comm. on Foreign Relations, 112th Cong., 1st Sess. (May 17, 2011). Available from*: http://foreign.senate.gov/hearings/hearing/?id=5105c3eb-5056-a032-5263-30425149ff2c.*

Strengthening Enforcement and Border Security: The 9/11 Commission Staff Report on Terrorist Travel: Hearing Before US. Cong. Senate Judiciary Committee, Subcommittee on Immigration, Border Security, and Citizenship, and Subcommittee on Terrorism, Technology, and Homeland Security. 109th Cong., 1st Sess. S. Rept. 109-71. Available from: *http://frwebgate.access.gpo.gov/cgi-bin/getdoc.cgi?dbname=109_senate_hearings&docid=f:22470.pdf.*

Syria Spillover: The Growing Threat of Terrorism and Sectarianism in the Middle East: Hearing Before the Senate Comm. on Foreign Relation, 113th Cong., 1st Sess. (February 13, 2014). Available from *http://www.foreign.senate.gov/hearings/syria-spillover-the-growing-threat-of-terrorism-and-sectarianism-in-the-middle-east.*

Terrorist Financing: Better Strategic Planning Needed to Coordinate U.S. Efforts to Deliver Counter-Terrorism Financing Training and Technical Assistance Abroad. 2005. Sponsored by the U.S. Government Accountability Office. Available from: *http://www.gao.gov/new.items/d0619.pdf.*

The Glowing Crisis in Africa's Sahel Region: Hearing Before the Joint Subcomm of House Comm. on Foreign Affairs, 113th Cong., 1st Sess. (May 21, 2013). Available from: *https://foreignaffairs.house.gov/hearing/subcommittee-hearing-growing-crisis-africas-sahel-region.*

The Resurgence of al-Qaeda in Iraq: Hearing Before the Joint Subcomm of the House Comm. on Foreign Affairs, 113th Cong., 1st Sess. (December 12, 2013). Available from*: https://foreignaffairs.house.gov/hearing/joint-subcommittee-hearing-resurgence-al-qaeda-iraq.*

US Policy in Yemen: Hearing Before the Subcomm. on Near Eastern, South and Central Asian Affairs of the Senate Comm. on Foreign Relations, 112th Cong., 1st Sess. (July 19. 2011). Available from*: http://www.gpo.gov/fdsys/pkg/CHRG-112shrg73916/pdf/CHRG-112shrg73916.pdf.*

USA PATRIOT bill H.R. 3162, 107th Cong. (2001) (enacted).

US PATRIOT Improvement and Reauthorization Act of 2005: H.R. Res. 3199, 109th Cong. (enacted).

Databases/Websites

American Enterprise Institute. Terrorism. Available from: *https://www.aei.org/events/battling-al-qaeda-is-the-united-states-winning/.*

Bipartisan Policy Center. National Security. Available from: *http://bipartisanpolicy.org/topics/national-security/.*

Brookings Institution. Foreign Policy. Available from: *http://www.brookings.edu/foreign-policy.aspx.*

Brookings Institute. Subcommittee on Counterterrorist and Intelligence. Available from: *http://www.brookings.edu/research/testimony/2015/04/29-terrorism-in-africa-byman.*

Carnegie Middle East Center. Available from: *http://carnegie-mec.org/?lang=en.*

Center for a New American Security. Terrorism, Irregular Warfare and Crime. Available from: *http://www.cnas.org/node/3647.*

Center for Strategic & International Studies. Homeland Security and Counterterrorism Program. Available from*: http://csis.org/program/homeland-security-program.*

Chicago Project on Security and Terrorism. Available from: http://cpost.uchicago.edu.

Congressional Research Service [CRS] Reports. Homeland Security. Available from: *https://fas.org/sgp/crs/homesec/.*

Congressional Research Service [CRS] Terrorism. Available from: *http://www.fas.org/sgp/crs/terror/.*

Council on Foreign Relations. Al Qaeda in the Arabian Peninsula (AQAP). Available from: *http://www.cfr.org/yemen/al-qaeda-arabian-peninsula-aqap/p9369.*

Council on Foreign Relations. Al Qaeda in Islamic Maghreb (AQIM). Available from: *http://www.cfr.org/terrorist-organizations-and-networks/al-qaeda-islamic-maghreb-aqim/p12717*.

Council on Foreign Relations. Messages and Interview of Osama bin Laden. Available from: *http://www.cfr.org/terrorist-leaders/messages-interviews-osama-bin-laden/p25267*.

Council on Foreign Relations. Terrorism. Available from: *http://www.cfr.org/issue/terrorism/ri13*.

Counter Extremism Project. The Global Extremist Registry. Available from: *http://www.crisisgroup.org/en/publication-type/crisiswatch/crisiswatch-database.aspx?CountryIDs=%7B31850680-1559-4C86-BBA0-5BA3C87B8FEF%7D*.

Crisis Group. Crisis Watch Database. Available from: *http://www.crisisgroup.org/en/publication-type/crisiswatch/crisiswatch-database.aspx?CountryIDs=%7B31850680-1559-4C86-BBA0-5BA3C87B8FEF%7D*.

Foreign Policy Research Institute. Geopoliticus: The FPRI Blog. Available from: *http://www.fpri.org/geopoliticus/2015/04/one-year-later-isis-overtakes-al-qaeda-whats-next*.

Foundation for Defense of Democracies. Available from: *http://www.defenddemocracy.org*.

Global Research. 9/11 & "War on Terrorism". Available from: *http://www.globalresearch.ca/theme/9-11-war-on-terrorism*.

Hudson Institute. Homeland Security. Available from: *http://www.hudson.org/topics/25-homeland-security*.

Hudson Institute. International Security and Terrorism. Available from: *http://www.hudson.org/topics/32-terrorism-radical-ideologies*.

International Institute for Counter-Terrorism. Available from: *http://www.ict.org.il*.

Leiken, R. "Bearers of Global Jihad?: Immigration and National Security after 9/11". The Nixon Center. 2004 Mar. Available from: *http://www.mafhoum.com/press7/193S23.pdf*.

Levitt, M. "Navigating the U.S. Government's Terrorist Lists." The Washington Institute for Near East Policy. *Policy Watch*. 2001 Nov 30. Available from: *http://www.washingtoninstitute.org*.

Lieven, A. "How The Afghan Counterinsurgency Threatens Pakistan." *The Nation*. 2011 Jan. Available from: *http://www.thenation.com/article/157160/how-afghan-counterinsurgency-threatens-pakistan*.

Middle East Institute. Publications. Available from: *http://www.mei.edu/Publications.aspx.*

National Consortium for the Study of Terrorism and Responses to Terrorism. Available from: *http://www.start.umd.edu.*

National Counterterrorism Center. Available from: *http://www.nctc.gov/.*

National Counterterrorism Center. Worldwide Incidents Tracking System. Available from: *http://wits.nctc.gov/FederalDiscoverWITS/index.do?Rcv=Perpetrator&N=0.*

National Security Network. Terrorism & National Security. Available from: *http://www.nsnetwork.org/issues/terrorism.*

New America Foundation. Counterterrorism Strategy Initiative. Available from: *http://counterterrorism.newamerican.net/.*

Office of the Director of the National Intelligence. Bin Ladin's Bookshelf. Available from: *http://www.dni.gov/index.php/resources/bin-laden-bookshelf?start=1.*

Pew Research Center. Concerns about Islamic Extremism on the Rise in Middle East. Available from: *http://www.pewglobal.org/2014/07/01/concerns-about-islamic-extremism-on-the-rise-in-middle-east/pg-2014-07-01-islamic-extremism-03/.*

RAND Corporation. Al Qaeda. Available from: *http://www.rand.org/topics/al-qaida.html.*

RAND Corporation. Terrorism and Homeland Security. Available from: *http://www.rand.org/topics/terrorism-and-homeland-security.html.*

Rogan, H. "Jihadism Online – A study of how al-Qaida and radical Islamist groups use the Internet for terrorist purposes". *FFI Rapport* [Internet]. 2006 [cited 2011 Aug 8]. Available from: *http://rapporter.ffi.no/rapporter/2006/00915.pdf.*

Ron Paul Institute For Peace and Prosperity. Peace and Prosperity. Available from: *http://www.ronpaulinstitute.org/archives/peace-and-prosperity/.*

The Al-Qaida Sanctions Committee – 1267/1989. United Nations Security Council. Available from: *http://www.un.org/sc/committees/1267/aq_sanctions_list.shtm.*

The Heritage Foundation. Terrorism. Available from: *http://www.heritage.org/issues/terrorism.*

The Jamestown Foundation. Global Terrorism Analysis. Available from: *http://www.jamestown.org/programs/gta/.*

Selected Bibliography

The Long War Journal. Available from: *http://www.longwarjournal.org/.*
US Department of State Bureau of Diplomatic Security (OSAC). Available from: *http://www.osac.gov/Pages/Home.aspx.*

INDEX

A

Abassi Madani 304, 311
Abbas 175, 271, 392, 395
Abd-al-Ghaffar 114, 115
Abd-al-Jalil 107, 170
Abdallah vii, x, 68, 79, 84, 87, 90, 91, 94, 96, 99, 114, 115, 116, 118, 121, 126, 128, 130, 132, 134, 135, 136, 137, 138, 140, 162, 163, 165, 168, 174, 176, 179, 180, 181, 184, 185, 199, 234, 271, 297, 314, 320, 330, 376, 377, 378, 399, 406, 434, 436, 437, 438, 440, 441, 442, 443, 445, 446, 459, 460, 474, 480, 481, 482
Abdallah al-Halabi 136, 137, 138, 140, 437
Abdallah al-Sindi 180, 181
Abdallah Anas 91
Abdallah Bin Ghadyan 376, 377, 378
Abdallah Rajab 185
Abd-al-Latif x, 61, 90, 93, 173, 362, 442, 443, 447, 462
Abd-al-Malik 88, 281, 331
Abd-al-Muhaymin 114
Abd-al-Mun'im Riyad square 87, 330
Abd-al-Qayyum 176, 177
Abd-al-Rahman viii, x, 99, 103, 107, 115, 117, 128, 170, 174, 175, 189, 357, 412, 413, 434, 439, 442, 445, 462, 467, 468, 483
Abd-al-Rahman al-Kurdi 115
Abd-al-Razzaq 376, 377, 378
Abdullah Al-Sindi 188
Abu Ahl 395
Abu-al-Harith 133, 199
Abu-al-Hasan 155, 163
Abu-al-Layth viii, 68, 234
Abu-al-Miqdad 114
Abu-al-Samh 114

Abu-al-Zubayr 351
Abu Bakr al-Siddiq 121
Abu Basir 98, 108, 182
Abu Burhan 452
Abu Dawud 46
Abu Dujanah 115, 116, 125
Abu Ghazwan 205
Abu Ghurayb 387
Abu Hafs 91, 114, 115, 116, 125, 411
Abu Hafs al-Muritani 114, 115
Abu Hammam al-Ghurayb ix, 428
Abu Hammam al-Sa'idi 114
Abu Hazim 147, 150
Abu Hurayra 80
Abu Hurayrah al-Yafi'i 205
Abu Islam al-Busnah 114
Abu Jahl 336, 395
Abu Khalil 120, 124, 180
Abu Malik 115, 184, 185
Abu Malik al-Libi 184, 185
Abu Muhammad 58, 66, 80, 90, 91, 98, 99, 100, 108, 115, 120, 126, 147, 152, 153, 178, 185, 245, 246, 408, 410, 411
Abu Mus'ab 77, 373, 398, 399, 408, 489
Abu Mus'ab al-Zarqawi 398, 399
Abu-Salih Al Somali 212
Abu Sulayman x, 104, 107, 136, 442, 443
Abu Talha al-Almani 78
Abu Tarik al-Masri 115
Abu Yahya vii, viii, 62, 68, 103, 104, 106, 109, 118, 124, 126, 176, 180, 184, 249, 250, 408
Abu Yasir 273
Abu-Zir 233
Abu Ziyad al-Mawsili 114
Abu Zubaydah 273

INDEX

Abyan 98
Aden 401
Adnan 401
Afghanistan viii, ix, xiv, xvi, xvii, xviii, xix, xx, xxii, xxiii, xxiv, xxvi, xxvii, xxix, xxxiii, xlii, 55, 56, 66, 67, 69, 70, 71, 72, 73, 74, 77, 80, 86, 90, 91, 110, 112, 113, 134, 163, 164, 168, 171, 172, 173, 195, 196, 207, 240, 263, 275, 276, 279, 285, 286, 289, 290, 291, 292, 298, 299, 301, 305, 329, 338, 339, 341, 344, 347, 355, 358, 360, 388, 394, 396, 398, 403, 408, 409, 420, 432, 484, 487, 491, 492, 499, 500
Africa ix, xv, xix, 55, 77, 242, 350, 366, 367, 368, 422, 425, 486, 492, 493, 494, 495, 498, 499, 501, 502
Ahl al-Kinanah 86, 329
Ahmad 57, 60, 114, 124, 171, 174, 175, 204, 253, 313, 357, 361, 377, 382, 410, 413, 434
Ahmad Hasan 114
Ahmad Shawqi 313
Ahmad Walid Ahmad 174
Ahmad Zaydan 410, 413
Ahmad Zidan 60
A'isha 166, 167
A'ishah 130, 139, 430, 481, 482
Al-Anfal 394
Alawite 251, 256, 261, 262
A'lay Imarn 398
Al-Baqarah 394
Al-Bukhari 253, 271, 455
Al-Fajr 252
Algeria 49, 55, 65, 66, 87, 173, 174, 182, 194, 198, 206, 280, 301, 302, 304, 307, 309, 315, 330, 343, 408, 411, 412
Algerian Salafist group 208
Al-Hafiz 152
Ali Abdallah Salih 314
Ali Al-Hajj 311

Al-Jawfi 105
Al Jazeera xxx, 104, 171, 172, 200, 280, 361, 362, 409, 410, 413, 414
Al-Jihad 57, 148, 149
Al-Kata'ib 363
Allah xxvi, 54, 58, 62, 63, 64, 70, 76, 85, 87, 89, 94, 95, 114, 132, 133, 134, 136, 138, 139, 140, 142, 147, 148, 149, 150, 166, 167, 170, 173, 189, 190, 191, 192, 202, 208, 209, 236, 237, 238, 240, 241, 245, 246, 247, 248, 249, 272, 273, 275, 276, 277, 278, 290, 298, 300, 318, 320, 327, 328, 330, 332, 336, 337, 338, 364, 371, 381, 382, 383, 384, 385, 386, 387, 388, 389, 390, 391, 392, 393, 394, 395, 396, 397, 398, 399, 400, 401, 402, 403, 416, 417, 418, 420, 421, 422, 423, 425, 426, 427, 430, 432, 434, 435, 442, 443, 446, 453, 468, 469, 470, 473, 480, 481
Allawi 392, 393, 395, 398
Al-Ma'idah 392
Al-Qa'ida 1, 3, xi, xiii, xv, xx, xxv, xxxix, 170, 296, 314, 349, 366, 367, 368, 404, 485, 495, 497
Al Sa'ud 172, 286
Al-Shabaab 365, 367, 368, 371
Al-Tatar 263
Al-Tatarrus 95
Al-Zandani 311
America xiii, xiv, xxvi, xxvii, xxx, xxxvii, xli, 55, 56, 65, 66, 69, 70, 71, 72, 73, 80, 86, 92, 168, 284, 286, 287, 290, 307, 310, 314, 315, 329, 338, 360, 363, 366, 367, 369, 370, 386, 387, 392, 395, 396, 416, 485, 488, 489, 490, 496, 505, 508, 509
American people xxx, xxxii, 60, 70, 72, 73, 74, 75, 285, 289, 338, 341, 362

Amir 107, 179, 334, 475, 476
AMISOM 366, 369, 370
Amman 390
Anas al-Subay'i 60, 110, 117, 184
An-Nisa 381
An-Nur 390
Ansar al-Sunnah Army viii, 245
Ansar al-Sunnah group 374
Ans Bin Malik 264
Anwar 168, 358, 360
Arab ix, xviii, 65, 86, 99, 110, 112, 113, 114, 120, 134, 178, 182, 183, 193, 199, 255, 274, 293, 301, 302, 304, 308, 316, 318, 329, 333, 334, 392
Arabian Peninsula xix, 46, 50, 92, 121, 125, 168, 270, 271, 296, 494, 503
Arbil 343
Asia xv, xxi, 474, 502
Asiya 130
Asma 428, 437, 449, 450
Aswan Dam 309
Atiyatallah 118, 238, 244
Atiyyah 168, 169, 295
At-Tawba 396
Aws 400
Ayman al-Zawahiri xii, xv, 146, 396

B

Badr ix, 385, 398, 406, 432, 433
Baghdad xiv, 173, 382, 386, 396, 399
Bahrain xxix, 125
Bakarah Market 352
Bakr xv, 93, 104, 121, 137, 139, 140, 454
Balad 382
Balkans 293
Baluchistan 123, 126, 178, 179, 180, 185, 187, 188
Ba'qubah 382, 396
Bashir al-Madani 408, 409
Basir 80, 98, 108, 168, 169, 182, 296, 355, 358, 410
Bassam 114

Bayji 382
Bilal al-Habashi 393
Bin Ali 303, 313
Bin Kathir 396
Bin Taymiyyah 399
Blair xxviii, 387
Botswana 368
British xxviii, 288, 346, 412, 427
Burundi 367, 370
Bush xiv, xxvii, xxviii, xxx, xxxi, xli, 80, 270, 284, 285, 287, 289, 338, 339, 382, 383, 385, 387, 397, 399, 500, 510

C

Cairo 193, 280
Caliphate xv, xlii, 65, 66, 67, 196, 204, 302, 351, 386, 485, 495
Camp Kharan 374
Center for Monitoring and Reconnaissance 363
Chad 424
Chechnya 290, 398, 403
China 112
Chinese 365
Chirac 387
Christians 254, 271, 286, 369, 392, 426
Coalition Forces 285
Combating Terrorism Center xxxix, 416
Communism 278, 279
Condaleeza 387
Congress xli, 70, 73, 75, 284, 501, 510
Crusaders xix, xxix, 94, 95, 144, 145, 146, 271, 287, 384, 386, 388, 399, 401, 404

D

Dawigar 273
Dawud 46
Denmark xxxiv, 58, 344, 345, 349, 411
Department of Social Sciences 416
Djibouti 367

Doctor 148, 172, 173, 176, 208, 246
Duha 449, 450

E

Eastern Europe xx, 85, 278, 328
Egypt ix, xv, xvii, xviii, xxxv, xxxviii, 65, 66, 86, 87, 88, 147, 148, 149, 151, 153, 182, 189, 194, 206, 263, 278, 279, 280, 281, 286, 304, 305, 318, 319, 320, 321, 328, 329, 330, 331, 333, 335, 337, 401, 403, 472, 490
Emir 133, 136, 137, 295, 304, 307, 405
Emir Al Mu'minin 405
Emir of Kuwait 307
Emirs of al-Qa'ida 91
Ethiopia 238, 242, 243, 367
Euro 125, 342
Europe ix, xx, xxx, xxxiii, xxxvii, 85, 278, 279, 328, 342, 344, 346, 387, 489

F

Fallujah 382, 383, 384, 396, 485
Fatimah x, 437, 473, 475
Fatwa 376, 377
FBI 286, 501
Firas 273
Freedom Flotilla 99, 360
French xxxviii, 54, 55, 56, 87, 173, 174, 199, 261, 312, 313, 318, 322, 330, 357, 408, 409
French revolution 87, 322, 330

G

Gabriel 373, 398
Gaza xxxv, xxxvi, 49, 205, 262, 263, 312
General Assembly 383
Germany 183, 342, 343, 344, 488, 489
Global Jihad Movement 487
Great Britain 110
Greater Middle East Project 387
Guantanamo 290, 486

Guinea 367

H

Hadith 46, 190, 289, 396, 398, 456
Hafiz Sultan 154
Hajjah Um Hamzah 211
Hakimullah viii, 100, 101, 102, 249
Hamas xxx, 207
Hamid 101, 395, 437, 449
Hamid Karzai 395
Hammadah 475, 476
Hamzah viii, x, 61, 103, 104, 121, 122, 123, 125, 178, 179, 180, 181, 185, 186, 187, 188, 198, 211, 282, 294, 362, 399, 415, 436, 437, 438, 440, 449, 453, 458, 460, 469, 472, 473
Hamzah al-Jawfi 104, 294
Hamzah Bin al-Husayn 399
Harakat al-Mujahidin 101
Haram 395
Harun 63, 114
Harun al-Kurdi 114
Hasan Nasrallah 261
Hassan Bin Talal 399
Hassan Bin-Thabit 288
Haykal 280
Hejaz 137
Hijri 91, 137, 146, 418, 458, 461
Hindu 85, 86, 279, 328, 329
Hindu Kush 85, 86, 279, 328, 329
Hittin 385
Hizballah 260, 261, 263, 264, 266, 268
Horn of Africa 242
House of Representatives 395, 499
Hud 393, 430
Hudhud 233
Husni Mubarak 286, 395
Hussayn 474

I

Ibn-al-Haqiq 288
Ibrahim 123, 130, 131, 175, 209, 469, 474, 488
Iftar 460

IGAD 367
Iman 161, 162, 449, 473
India 119, 286, 403, 487
Indonesia 112, 285, 353
Iran xv, xlii, 61, 80, 81, 82, 83, 84, 91, 103, 110, 112, 113, 115, 121, 124, 126, 183, 184, 185, 262, 263, 294, 307, 347, 390, 437, 485, 488
Iranian revolution 87, 321, 330
Iraq viii, ix, xiv, xv, xxviii, xxxi, xxxii, xxxiii, xxxiv, xlii, 57, 58, 71, 72, 73, 74, 80, 90, 91, 92, 163, 164, 168, 198, 199, 207, 240, 245, 248, 263, 285, 287, 290, 307, 324, 338, 339, 343, 348, 355, 356, 372, 374, 375, 381, 382, 383, 385, 386, 387, 388, 390, 394, 395, 396, 397, 398, 399, 400, 410, 411, 412, 485, 488, 489, 490, 491, 493, 498, 500, 501, 502
Isa Bin-Maryam 294
Ishaq Bin Abdullah 264
Islam 2, ix, xiv, xxvii, xxxii, xxxiv, 49, 50, 66, 67, 70, 88, 108, 114, 117, 124, 145, 148, 155, 156, 157, 159, 160, 161, 162, 163, 209, 242, 243, 244, 247, 254, 263, 264, 270, 271, 281, 283, 285, 286, 287, 288, 295, 299, 312, 314, 320, 327, 331, 333, 335, 344, 355, 357, 372, 379, 381, 382, 387, 394, 395, 399, 400, 401, 436, 452, 457, 464, 480, 485, 486, 490
Islamabad xx, 101
Islamic Arab World 86, 329
Islamic Emirate viii, 92, 110, 112, 113, 207, 272, 275, 276, 286
Islamic Emirate of Afghanistan viii, 110, 113, 275, 276, 286
Islamic Maghreb 55, 62, 63, 77, 91, 203, 204, 350, 355, 408, 409, 492, 497, 498, 504
Islamic Movement for Reform 416

Islamic State xv, xxxiv, xlii, 91, 117, 204, 207, 299, 374, 485, 486, 490, 491, 492, 495, 496
Islamic State of Iraq xv, xxxiv, 91, 491
Isma'il al-Qusaimi 133
Israel xxxvii, 75, 76, 116, 241, 286

J

Ja'far 209
Jalbib al-Ruqi 133
Jama 57, 148, 149, 185, 355
Jeddah xvi, 167, 172, 423
Jews xix, xxxv, 56, 70, 112, 143, 145, 172, 262, 263, 264, 265, 266, 270, 271, 286, 297, 303, 313, 340, 344, 349, 388, 409
Jihad viii, ix, xix, xxviii, xxix, xxxii, xxxvi, xxxviii, xliv, 57, 66, 67, 91, 92, 105, 106, 109, 110, 114, 115, 144, 148, 149, 161, 163, 164, 168, 184, 185, 194, 195, 196, 232, 235, 238, 242, 244, 245, 248, 254, 255, 270, 271, 286, 287, 288, 290, 291, 292, 295, 301, 339, 371, 372, 373, 374, 375, 377, 382, 383, 384, 385, 387, 388, 389, 390, 391, 392, 395, 396, 397, 398, 400, 401, 403, 405, 411, 416, 418, 421, 426, 442, 486, 487, 489, 490, 493, 504
Jordan 65, 194, 280, 308, 390, 396, 496
Jumadi al-Thani 443
Jurisprudence 109

K

Ka'b 233, 288, 389, 400
Ka'bah 395
Ka'b Bin-al-Ashraf 288
Ka'b Bin Malik 389
Kabul 107, 272, 289
Kaldars 93
Kampala ix, 363, 364, 365, 367, 369, 371

Karachi 113, 172, 181, 187, 188
Karzai 289, 392, 395
Kashmir 286, 290
Kenya 76, 365, 367, 370
Khadijah vii, 130, 131, 444, 460, 469, 473, 474
Khalid vii, x, xx, xxiii, 58, 61, 80, 82, 95, 105, 117, 128, 129, 166, 167, 180, 181, 187, 188, 273, 292, 437, 441, 444, 446, 447, 454, 459, 462, 463, 466, 467, 468, 470, 472, 480, 481, 482, 489
Khalid al-Habib 292
Khalid Habib x, 466
Khalifah Haqqani 181
Khamenei 80
Khan ix, 99, 120, 123, 406
Khawlah 477, 478
Khazraj 400
Khisat al-Dar 428
Khomeini 307
Khowst 107, 272
Khubab 114
Khurasan 135, 293
Khyber 179, 385
King xvi, 45, 88, 270, 331
King Fahd 270
Kirkuk 382
Kissinger 387
Korea 80, 344
Krinkov 99
Kurdish 382, 392
Kurds 121, 256
Kuwait xxi, xxix, 303, 304, 307, 316, 390, 396

L

Ladin xxxix, 51, 124, 308, 338, 451, 473, 492, 505
Lahore 100, 113, 123
Lebanon xviii, 65, 80, 194, 255, 256, 260, 261, 262, 263, 264, 266, 267, 296, 297
Levantine region 251, 255

Liberation Square 333
Libya xxxviii, 65, 77, 103, 115, 176, 178, 182, 183, 184, 185, 186, 193, 194, 235, 343
London 173, 426, 485, 486, 487, 488, 489, 490, 491, 508

M

Maghreb 54, 55, 62, 63, 77, 90, 91, 203, 204, 350, 355, 408, 409, 492, 497, 498, 504
Mahmud vii, viii, 52, 53, 54, 62, 65, 77, 78, 90, 91, 96, 105, 109, 118, 127, 128, 152, 153, 154, 155, 165, 169, 173, 178, 186, 188, 193, 203, 236, 237, 249, 250, 350, 392, 395, 437, 460, 467
Ma'rib 324
Maryam 294, 438, 473, 474, 482
Mas'ud 120, 152, 172, 346
Mauritania 77, 171, 173, 174, 307
Mecca xvi, xvii, 134, 171, 172, 173, 247, 283
Middle East xv, xvii, xxix, 69, 387, 490, 492, 495, 496, 498, 500, 502, 503, 504, 505, 509
Miriam 481
Mogadishu 241, 364, 371
Morocco 65, 110, 112, 194, 270, 280, 285, 337, 343, 403
Mosque 174, 396
Mosul 382, 396
Ms'udis 181
Mu'awiyah al-Balushi 123
Mubarak 65, 194, 286, 318, 319, 395, 490
Muhajir Ibrahim 209
Muhammad viii, x, xv, 46, 49, 51, 53, 54, 55, 56, 57, 58, 61, 62, 64, 66, 68, 69, 80, 81, 90, 91, 98, 99, 100, 108, 110, 112, 114, 115, 120, 123, 126, 132, 146, 147, 151, 152, 153, 155, 166, 170, 172, 174, 175, 178, 185,

187, 195, 201, 210, 234, 238, 245, 246, 247, 269, 270, 272, 278, 280, 290, 295, 298, 301, 318, 334, 337, 338, 344, 350, 351, 357, 360, 361, 362, 372, 373, 375, 381, 391, 395, 397, 400, 401, 403, 408, 410, 411, 416, 421, 428, 434, 436, 437, 440, 441, 449, 451, 453, 460, 462, 468, 470, 471, 473, 479, 483
Muhammad al-Fatih 401
Muhammad Aslam viii, 210
Muhammad Bin Abdullah 187
Muhammad Bin Muslim 400
Muhammad Iqbal 175
Muharram 48, 167, 461
Mujahidin viii, 57, 58, 65, 66, 77, 90, 91, 92, 93, 101, 104, 110, 132, 153, 159, 161, 164, 179, 195, 198, 199, 204, 205, 206, 207, 212, 238, 239, 240, 243, 245, 246, 247, 248, 263, 271, 275, 288, 302, 308, 312, 338, 339, 356, 357, 359, 362, 364, 369, 374, 375, 381, 382, 388, 389, 391, 392, 396, 398, 399, 400, 401, 403, 426, 453, 454
Munir 104, 105, 118, 119, 180
Musannad Ahmad Bin Hanbal 377
Museveni 352, 364, 365, 371
Musharraf 286
Muslim ix, xv, xvii, xix, xxvi, xxviii, xxx, xxxii, xxxv, xxxviii, 45, 46, 49, 65, 66, 67, 75, 85, 86, 94, 95, 99, 111, 120, 145, 164, 171, 194, 195, 206, 247, 255, 264, 279, 280, 282, 283, 286, 305, 306, 309, 312, 322, 324, 326, 328, 329, 334, 355, 357, 368, 375, 377, 381, 382, 383, 386, 387, 392, 393, 394, 395, 399, 400, 418, 422, 423, 425, 454, 480, 490, 495, 497
Mustafa Abu al-Yazid 120, 295, 434
Mustapha Hamdan 266

N

Nairobi 404, 405
Najd 306
Najm al-Khayr 295
National Assembly 395
National Guard 397
Nation of Islam 452
NATO xxxiii, xxxvii, 80, 206, 366, 485, 509
New York xiii, xiv, xvii, xviii, xxx, xxxix, xli, xlii, xliii, xliv, 73, 82, 84, 288, 289, 483, 485, 486, 487, 488, 489, 490, 491, 492, 508
Nixon 71, 504
Nuristan 105

O

Obama xiv, xv, xxi, xxxvii, xlii, xliii, 80, 119, 338, 339, 363, 366, 501
Omar Farouk 73
Omar Khaleel 124
Organization 74, 75, 234, 235, 296, 417, 486, 490, 493, 501
Oslo 395

P

Pakistan ix, xii, xiv, xv, xvi, xvii, xviii, xx, xxi, xxii, xxiii, xxiv, xxviii, xxix, xxxii, xxxviii, xliv, 58, 71, 73, 76, 77, 80, 96, 100, 101, 103, 105, 110, 112, 113, 118, 119, 120, 125, 161, 171, 172, 179, 181, 274, 286, 291, 292, 294, 338, 348, 355, 360, 362, 403, 411, 419, 422, 423, 426, 427, 432, 499, 500, 502, 504
Palestine xxxiv, xxxv, xxxvi, 71, 73, 90, 91, 262, 290, 336, 340, 344, 388, 390, 394, 395, 396, 397, 398, 403
Panama 385

INDEX

Pashtun 60
Pentagon xiv, xix, xxxi, 75, 350, 360
Pervez Musharraf 286
Peshawar xvi, xvii, xxi, 67, 103, 128, 129, 178, 179, 187, 188, 190, 196, 294
Petraeus 339
Pindi 101
Pivotal Points 56
President xiv, xv, xxi, xxiii, xxviii, xxx, xxxi, xxxii, xxxvii, xl, 71, 87, 206, 284, 320, 321, 330, 350, 352, 365, 377, 378, 382, 500, 510
Prophet Sulayman 233
Psychology 490
Punjabi 101, 123

Q

Qahtan 401
Qandahar 147, 148, 273
Qatar 61, 103, 316, 343, 362, 479
Qattal al-Najdi 133
Qur'an 46, 47, 51, 141, 143, 170, 171, 172, 238, 275, 276, 277, 379, 380, 386, 391, 396, 418, 421, 422, 442, 477
Quraysh 283, 288, 395

R

Rabi'ah 165, 401
Rabi' Awal 468, 470
Ramadan ix, 94, 95, 111, 113, 131, 404, 407, 415, 421, 438, 439
Red Mudar 401
Riyadh xviii, 270, 390, 396, 403
Romans 312, 391, 400
Russians 288, 293, 339, 340

S

Sa'ad x, 114, 167, 204, 449, 451, 452, 480, 481
Sa'ad Ibn Usama 449
Sa'd 81, 122, 200, 253, 416, 459, 460, 461, 464, 473, 477, 478

Sa'd al-Faqih 416
Saddam xiv, xxxi, 382
Sa'duf 107
Sa'dun 91, 460
Safiyah 131, 437, 474
Safwan 294
Sahib Sharif 92
Sahih al-Bukhari al-Ahkam 377
Sahih Muslim al-Imarah 377
Saladin 312
Salafi 173, 195, 235, 314, 315, 488, 489
Salah 114, 115, 272, 312, 401, 475
Salah al-Din 401
Salah al-Yamani 114
Salih Abdullah Al-Qar'awi 251
Salman al-Farisi 401
Samarra 382, 396
Sana 280, 320
Sanaa 87, 324, 330
Sarah x, 482
Saudi Arabia xv, xvi, xvii, xviii, xix, xxix, xxxi, 45, 46, 110, 112, 125, 137, 294, 307, 308, 314, 315, 343, 390, 497
Sayyaf 107
Secretary of State xxii, 65, 80
Security Council xxi, 383, 505
September 11 xix, xli, 71, 73
Sh'aban 53
Shabwah 324
Shah 87, 101, 119, 321, 330
Shahbur 87, 321, 330
Shakir-Allah 114
Shari'a 66, 79, 156, 157, 158, 189, 195, 206, 255, 282, 299, 354, 355, 373, 418
Shari'ah 48, 49, 50, 91, 92, 145, 171, 286, 324, 394, 396, 421, 427
Sharif 92, 101
Sharm ash-Shaykh conference 286
Sharon xl, 396

Shaykh vii, viii, xxxv, xxxvi, xxxvii, 49, 52, 53, 54, 55, 56, 57, 58, 60, 62, 65, 66, 68, 77, 78, 79, 80, 87, 90, 91, 94, 96, 98, 99, 100, 102, 103, 104, 105, 106, 107, 108, 110, 111, 114, 115, 116, 120, 128, 136, 137, 138, 139, 140, 151, 153, 155, 156, 157, 158, 162, 169, 170, 171, 172, 173, 174, 175, 176, 178, 183, 193, 195, 197, 202, 203, 232, 233, 234, 235, 237, 246, 249, 250, 273, 274, 275, 276, 280, 286, 295, 320, 330, 337, 350, 356, 357, 358, 360, 361, 362, 373, 374, 399, 408, 409, 410, 411, 413, 414, 434, 435, 437, 460, 464, 467
Shaykh Abu al-Walid al-Masri 115
Shaykh Abu Husayn 202
Shaykh Abu Khabbab 115
Shaykh Abu Layth 91
Shaykh Abu Muhammad 58, 80, 90, 91, 99, 178, 408, 410, 411
Shaykh Abu Yahya vii, viii, 62, 68, 104, 106, 176, 249
Shaykh Ahmad al-Sanusi Ahmad 175
Shaykh Fawwaz al-Qa'idi 175
Shaykh Ibrahim Walid Ibn 175
Shaykh Ikramallah 175
Shaykh Mahmud vii, viii, 52, 53, 54, 62, 77, 78, 90, 91, 128, 153, 169, 193, 249, 350, 437, 460, 467
Shaykh Mansur al-Da'jani 175
Shaykh Muhammad al-Amin al-Hirrari 175
Shaykh Muhammad al-Islambuli 110, 114
Shaykh Muhammad al-Mandili 175
Shaykh Muhammad al-Ruqibah 175
Shaykh Muhammad Qutb 280, 337
Shaykh Muhammad Walid al-Mukhtar Walid Al 174
Shaykh Muhammad Walid Sidi Habib 175
Shaykh Musa 114, 174
Shaykh Musa Sukkar Bu-Qas 174
Shaykh of Islam 399
Shaykh Sa'id 60, 99, 105, 120, 174, 360, 413, 434, 435
Shaykh Salih 114
Shaykh Sami al-Jihani 175
Shaykh Sid Ahmad Walid al-Imam 175
Shaykh Sidi Muhammad al-Ansari 175
Shaykh Sulayman Abu-Ghayth 114
Shaykh Walid Dayfallah 174
Shaykh Yahya Bin Fahd al-Makki 175
Shaykh Younis 77
Shaykh Yunis 106, 183, 357
Sheikh Mahmud 188
Sheikhs 348, 485
Shia 90, 92
Shi'ites 254, 255, 256, 258, 264, 265, 266, 267, 268
Shu'ayl al-Lahyani 175
Shuja 101
Shura 66, 87, 181, 195, 198, 330, 354, 405
Shura Council 87, 330
Siham 166, 167, 438, 460, 469, 482
Sinai 286, 498
Sociology 498
Somalia viii, xviii, xxxvi, 69, 71, 90, 91, 98, 182, 183, 206, 238, 239, 240, 241, 242, 244, 312, 348, 350, 351, 352, 353, 354, 356, 364, 365, 366, 367, 368, 369, 370, 411, 412, 424
South Africa 366, 368
Soviet Union 85, 278, 279, 328
State of the Union 284
Sudan xviii, xix, 206, 307, 354, 424, 451
Sulayman Abu-Ghayth 114
Sumayah 482
Sunnah viii, 63, 236, 237, 245, 246, 247, 251, 252, 254, 256, 258, 259, 261, 263, 264, 271, 355, 374, 386, 391
Supreme Paradise 459, 460

Surah 142, 143, 144, 145, 164, 275, 276, 277, 391, 401
Surah al-Baqarah 401
Surat al-Anfal 70
Surat al-Tawbah 70
Surat Hud 430
Syria viii, xv, xvii, 66, 81, 182, 183, 194, 206, 251, 252, 253, 254, 255, 256, 258, 261, 262, 263, 267, 390, 401, 488, 492, 501, 502

T

Tabuk 389, 391, 430, 431, 455
Tahrik Taliban 292
Taliban viii, xiv, xvii, xxii, xxiv, xxxiii, 54, 56, 96, 100, 101, 181, 199, 200, 249, 289, 292, 355, 356, 404, 405, 485, 487, 490, 491, 498, 499
Tariq Bin Ziyad 401
Tarmadhi 46
The Permanent Committee for Scientific Research and the Issuing of Fatwas 377, 378
The Prince 232, 237
The Prophet 389, 392, 428
Tikrit 382
Tripoli 256, 492
Tunisia xxxviii, 86, 189, 278, 279, 301, 302, 308, 310, 313, 322, 328, 329, 333, 337, 472
Tunisian 65, 86, 183, 279, 304, 306, 308, 313, 329
Turkey 99, 103, 119, 348, 360, 390, 396, 497, 509
Turkistanis 293
Turkmen 392
Turks 119, 293

U

Uganda ix, 350, 352, 363, 364, 365, 366, 367, 370, 371
Umar 73, 106, 107, 110, 112, 124, 125, 132, 135, 147, 150, 162, 205, 254, 295, 311, 339, 428

Umar al-Faruq 73, 339
Um Hamzah x, 121, 122, 181, 211, 436, 437, 449
Um Khalid x, 437, 480, 481
Umma 242, 333, 335
Ummah ix, xxxviii, 75, 79, 85, 86, 89, 136, 209, 321, 326, 328, 329, 332, 422, 445, 446
Umm Hamzah 460
Umm-Ibrahim 131
Umm-Khalid x, 459
Umm-Mu'adh x, 477
Umran 164, 240, 275, 276, 397
Um Sa'ad x, 480
Um Safiyah 437
UNIFIL 297
United Nations 273, 289, 369, 383, 426, 505
United States 2, ix, xi, xiv, xv, xix, xxii, xxiv, xxviii, xxix, xxx, xxxii, xxxiii, xxxvii, xxxix, 70, 105, 118, 241, 243, 338, 339, 341, 364, 379, 416, 432, 487, 509
United States Military Academy 416
Urwah al-Libi 184
Usama 1, 2, 3, vii, xi, xii, xiii, xv, xvi, xviii, xix, xx, xxiv, xxv, xxvi, xxvii, xxviii, xxix, xxx, xxxi, xxxii, xxxiii, xxxiv, xxxv, xxxvi, xxxvii, xxxviii, xxxix, xl, xli, xliii, 45, 51, 65, 85, 90, 105, 153, 171, 172, 240, 295, 338, 442, 449, 450, 451, 452, 474, 479, 485, 492, 501, 509
Usama Bin Muhammad Bin Ladin 51, 338
Usamah 100, 120, 124, 132, 166, 167, 373, 374, 434, 438, 453, 457, 458, 460, 481, 482
Usamah Bin Laden 373
USS Cole xix
Uthman vii, x, 69, 90, 107, 114, 125, 138, 203, 436, 437, 464, 465
Uzbeks 293

V

Vietnam 71, 72
Vietnam War 71

W

Wafa 81, 437, 473
Waqqas 253, 273
War on Terror xli, 285, 485, 487, 496
Washington xxxi, xli, xlii, xliii, 73, 82, 84, 288, 289, 483, 485, 487, 489, 490, 491, 492, 493, 497, 499, 504, 508
Waziristan 67, 101, 104, 105, 119, 134, 135, 174, 179, 180, 196, 355, 357, 426, 435
Weapons of Mass Destruction 287
Western xvii, xviii, xxxii, 66, 78, 86, 195, 279, 328, 329, 365, 386, 419, 421, 427, 496, 497
White House xxvii, xxxiii, 70, 75, 134, 368, 370, 383, 396

Y

Yahya vii, viii, 62, 68, 103, 104, 106, 109, 118, 124, 126, 155, 156, 157, 159, 160, 162, 169, 175, 176, 180, 184, 197, 198, 234, 249, 250, 356, 360, 362, 408, 413
Yarmuk 385
Yasir 91, 152, 273, 334
Yemen ix, xvi, xviii, xix, 56, 65, 66, 94, 96, 98, 110, 112, 161, 162, 168, 169, 182, 193, 194, 198, 205, 206, 280, 307, 308, 313, 314, 315, 323, 324, 325, 328, 355, 401, 411, 412, 424, 488, 489, 493, 494, 496, 497, 498, 503
Yemeni Islah Party 87, 330
Yuri Museveni 365
Yusuf 63, 232

Z

Zaynab 474
Zionist xxxvi, 94, 95, 144, 282, 287, 288, 290, 310, 382, 386, 388, 401, 404

Selected Bibliography

About the Authors

YONAH ALEXANDER
Director, Inter-University Center for Terrorism Studies
Director, International Center for Terrorism Studies
Potomac Institute for Policy Studies
and
Co-Director, Inter-University Center for Legal Studies
The International Law Institute

Professor Yonah Alexander is a Senior Fellow, Member of the Board of Regents, and Director of the International Center for Terrorism Studies of the Potomac Institute for Policy Studies, Arlington, VA, US. Concurrently, he is Director of the Inter-University Center for Terrorism Studies and Co-Director of the Inter-University Center for Legal Studies, a consortia of universities and think tanks throughout the world. Professor Alexander previously directed the Terrorism Studies Program at George Washington University, Washington, DC, US, and the Institute for Studies in International Terrorism at the State University of New York (US).

He was awarded a PhD from Columbia University (NY), MA by the University of Chicago (IL), and received his baccalaureate degree from Roosevelt University of Chicago (IL). With over 40 years experience devoted to the field of terrorism studies, Professor Alexander has held academic appointments at The George Washington University, American University, the Columbus School of Law at Catholic University of America, Tel Aviv University, The City University of New York, and The State University of New York, and has lectured at numerous institutions and universities throughout the world, and is a member of the International Institute of Strategic Studies, London, UK.

Dr. Alexander is Founder and Editor-in-Chief of the international academic journals *Terrorism; Minorities and Group Rights*; and *Political Communication and Persuasion*. Since 2010, he has served as Editor-in-Chief of the *Partnership for Peace Review*, a journal

ABOUT THE AUTHORS

published under the auspices of NATO. Professor Alexander is also the founder and Editor-in-Chief of *Terrorism: An Electronic Journal and Knowledge Base*.

He has published over 100 books including *Terrorists in Our Midst: Combating Foreign Affinity Terrorism in America*; *Terrorism on the High Seas: From Piracy to Strategic Challenge*; *Evolution of U.S. Counterterrorism Policy* (three volumes); *Turkey: Terrorism, Civil Rights, and the European Union*; *The New Iranian Leadership: Terrorism, Nuclear Ambition, and the Middle East Conflict*; and *Counterterrorism Strategies: Success and Failures of Six Nations*. Translated into more than two dozen languages, Professor Alexander's personal papers and collection on terrorism are housed at the Hoover Institution Library and Archives at Stanford University, Palo Alto, CA (US).

MICHAEL S. SWETNAM
CEO and Chairman
Potomac Institute for Policy Studies

Michael Swetnam was one of the principal founders of the Potomac Institute for Policy Studies in 1994. Since its inception, he has served as Chairman of the Board and currently serves as the Institute's Chief Executive Officer. His authored and edited publications include: *Cyber Terrorism and Information Warfare (vols 1-4)*; *Usama bin Laden's al-Qaida: Profile of a Terrorist Network*, (with Yonah Alexander); *ETA: Profile of a Terrorist Group* (with Yonah Alexander and Herbert M. Levine); and *Best Available Science: Its Evolution, Taxonomy, and Application*, co-authored with A. Alan Moghissi, Betty R. Love and Sorin R. Straja.

Mr. Swetnam is currently a member of the Technical Advisory Group to the United States Senate Select Committee on Intelligence. In this capacity, he provides expert advice to the US Senate on research and development (R&D) investment strategy for the US Intelligence Community (IC). He has also served on the Defense Science Board (DSB) Task Force on Counterterrorism, and the Task Force on Intelligence Support to the War on Terrorism.

From 1990 to 1992, Mr. Swetnam served as a Special Consultant to President Bush's Foreign Intelligence Advisory Board (PFIAB) and provided expertise on Intelligence Community issues inclusive of budget, community architecture, and major programs. He was also involved in authoring the Board's assessment of Intelligence Community support to Operations Desert Storm and Shield.

Prior to forming the Potomac Institute for Policy Studies, Mr. Swetnam worked in private industry as a Vice President of Engineering at the Pacific-Sierra Research Corporation, Director of Information Processing Systems at GTE, and Manager of Strategic Planning for GTE Government Systems.

Previously, he worked for the Director of Central Intelligence as a Program Monitor on the Intelligence Community Staff (1986-1990), was responsible for the development and presentation to Congress of the budget of the National Security Agency, and helped develop, monitor and present the DOE Intelligence Budget to Congress. Mr. Swetnam was assigned as the IC Staff Representative to intergovernmental groups responsible for developing the INF and START treaties, and assisted in presenting these treaties for Congressional ratification. His collateral duties included serving as the host to the DCI's Nuclear Intelligence Panel, and Co-Chairman of the Science and Technology Requirements' Analysis Working Group.

Mr. Swetnam served in the US Navy for 24 years as an active duty and reserve officer, Special Duty Cryptology. He has served in several public and community positions and serves on the Board of Directors of Space and Defense Systems Inc., Dragon Hawk Entertainment Inc., and the Governing Board of The Potomac Institute of New Zealand.

Made in the USA
Columbia, SC
23 July 2021